P9-BZO-211

The Longman Handbook
of the Modern World

Also by Chris Cook and John Stevenson

The Longman Handbook of Modern British History, 1714–1995, 3rd edn
The Longman Handbook of Modern European History, 1763–1997, 3rd edn
The Longman Companion to Britain since 1945
Britain in the Depression: Society and Politics, 1929–39, 2nd edn
British Historical Facts: 1688–1760
British Historical Facts: 1760–1830

Other books by Chris Cook

Post-war Britain: a Political History (*with Alan Sked*)
The Age of Alignment: Electoral Politics in Britain 1922–1929
A Short History of the Liberal Party, 1900–1997
By-elections in British Politics (*ed. with John Ramsden*)
The Politics of Reappraisal 1918–1939 (*ed. with Gillian Peele*)
The Decade of Disillusion (*ed. with David McKie*)
Crisis and Controversy: Essays in Honour of A.J.P. Taylor (*ed. with Alan Sked*)
Trade Unions in British Politics, 2nd edn (*ed. with Ben Pimlott*)
The Dictionary of Historical Terms
The Facts on File World Political Almanac
The Longman Guide to Sources in Contemporary British History (*2 vols with David Waller* et al.)
The Longman Handbook of Modern American History, 1763–1996 (*with David Waller*)
What Happened Where (*with Diccon Bewes*)

Other books by John Stevenson

Popular Disturbances in England, 1700–1870, 2nd edn
British Society, 1914–1945
Order and Disorder in Early Modern England (*with A.J. Fletcher*)
The Working Class and Politics in Britain and America, 1929–1945 (*ed. with S. Salter*)
Third Party Politics since 1945

The Longman Handbook of the Modern World

International History and Politics since 1945

Chris Cook
John Stevenson

LONGMAN
London and New York

Addison Wesley Longman Limited
Edinburgh Gate,
Harlow, Essex CM20 2JE, United Kingdom
and Associated Companies throughout the world.

*Published in the United States of America by Addison Wesley Longman,
New York.*

© Chris Cook and John Stevenson 1998

The right of Chris Cook and John Stevenson to be identified as authors of
this Work has been asserted by them in accordance with the Copyright,
Designs and Patents Act 1988.

All rights reserved; no part of this publication may be reproduced, stored in
any retrieval system, or transmitted in any form or by any means, electronic,
mechanical, photocopying, recording, or otherwise without either the prior
written permission of the Publishers or a licence permitting restricted
copying in the United Kingdom issued by the Copyright Licensing Agency
Ltd, 90 Tottenham Court Road, London W1P 9HE.

First published 1998

ISBN 0–582–30413–X PPR
ISBN 0–582–30412–1 CSD

Visit Addison Wesley Longman on the world wide web at
http://www.awl-he.com

British Library Cataloguing in Publication Data

A catalogue entry for this title is available from the British Library

Library of Congress Cataloging-in-Publication Data

Cook, Chris, 1945–
    Longman handbook of the modern world : international history and
politics since 1945 / Chris Cook, John Stevenson.
        p. cm.
    Includes index.
    ISBN 0–582–30412–1. — ISBN 0–582–30413–X (pbk.)
    1. History, Modern—1945- —Handbooks, manuals, etc. 2. World
politics—1945- —Handbooks, manuals, etc. I. Stevenson, John,
1946- . II. Title.
D840.C66   1998
909.82′5—dc21   98–19337
                                                                        CIP

Set by 35 in 9½/12pt New Baskerville
Produced by Addison Wesley Longman Singapore (Pte) Ltd
Printed in Singapore

Contents

List of maps

Preface and acknowledgements

This handbook attempts to provide a convenient reference work for both teachers and students of modern world history. It covers the period from 1945 to the present day – an era of enormous and continuing change.

It is a much condensed work, bringing together chronological, statistical and tabular information which is not to be found elsewhere within the confines of a single volume. The handbook covers not only political and diplomatic events but also the broader fields of social and economic history. It includes biographies of important individuals, a glossary of commonly used historical terms, and a topic bibliography. The extensive glossary included in this volume embraces not just historical terms but a variety of current political terms with which historians need to be familiar. No book of this type can be entirely comprehensive, nor is it intended to substitute for textbooks and more detailed reading, but we have attempted to include those facts and figures which we believe are most useful for understanding courses in modern world history.

It is hoped that the volume has included essential material on all the major themes of modern world history. The authors would, however, welcome constructive ideas and suggestions for future editions of this book. For secretarial help, we are indebted as ever to the long labours of Linda Hollingworth and Anne Borg.

Chris Cook
John Stevenson
1 May 1998

SECTION ONE

Political history

Europe

The Coming of the Cold War, 1942–49

1942 May 26   Twenty-year Anglo–Soviet treaty signed, but without any territorial agreement for post-war Europe.

June–Aug.   Stalin steps up demands for opening of 'second front' to relieve pressure on Russia.

July   British suspension of convoys to Russia because of losses causes Stalin to accuse allies of lack of genuine support.

1943 Jan. 14–24   Churchill and Roosevelt agree to insist on the 'unconditional surrender' of Germany. The decision to mount an invasion of Italy, agreed by the Allied commanders, led to bitter recriminations from Stalin, who saw it as bad faith on the part of the Western powers.

Aug.   Stalin objects to not being consulted about the surrender of Italy and demands a say in the Italian settlement.

Oct.   Three-power Foreign Ministers' conference in Moscow agrees upon an advisory council for Italy and makes broad plans for a world security organization.

Nov. 28– Dec. 1   Meeting of 'Big Three' (Churchill, Roosevelt, and Stalin) at Tehran, the first conference attended by Stalin. As well as discussing arrangements for the Allied landings in Europe and a renewed Soviet offensive against Germany, the main lines of a territorial settlement in Eastern Europe were agreed, including the Polish frontiers. No agreement was reached about the future of Germany, although there was discussion of its dismemberment.

1944 Aug. 21– Oct. 9   Dumbarton Oaks Conference draws up broad framework of the United Nations.

Sept. 11–17   Churchill and Roosevelt meet at Quebec and move towards acceptance of Morgenthau Plan for the

	destruction of German industry and the conversion of Germany into a pastoralized state.
Oct. 9–10	Churchill and Stalin meet in Moscow and decide on 'spheres of influence'. Romania and Bulgaria are ceded predominantly to Russian influence, Greece to Britain, and Yugoslavia and Hungary equally between Russia and Great Britain.
Dec. 3	Attempted Communist insurrection in Athens.

1945	Jan. 11	Communists in Greece seek truce.
	Feb. 4–11	Meeting at Yalta between Churchill, Roosevelt and Stalin decides upon four occupation zones in Germany, the prosecution of war criminals, and prepares Allied Control Commission to run Germany on the basis of 'complete disarmament, demilitarization and dismemberment'. Removals of national wealth from Germany were to be permitted within two years of the end of the war and reparations were tentatively agreed. Agreement reached that the Provisional Government already functioning in Poland, i.e. the communist Lublin-based group, with the addition of other groups including the London Poles, be the Government. A three-power commission based in Moscow would supervise the setting up of the new regime. The Provisional Government was pledged to hold free and unfettered elections as soon as possible. Declaration on Liberated Europe signed by the three powers to allow European states to 'create democratic conditions of their own choice'.
	Feb. 12	Greek communists granted amnesty and lay down arms.
	April	Members of non-communist delegation to the three-power commission in Moscow arrested. Russians conclude a treaty of alliance with the Lublin administration in Poland.
	July 5	Great Britain and United States recognize Provisional Government of National Unity in Poland.
	July 17–Aug. 1	Stalin, Truman, Churchill (after 25th, Attlee) meet at Potsdam and finalize four-power agreement on administration of Germany and the territorial adjustments in Eastern Europe. The Oder–Neisse line is to mark the new boundary between Germany and Poland. Although Germany is to be divided into

zones, it is to be treated as a single economic unit. Germans living in Poland, Hungary and Czechoslovakia are to be sent to Germany.

Oct. 28   Provisional Czech National Assembly meets, representing communist and non-communist parties.

Nov.   Tito elected President of Yugoslavia.

1946   Mar. 6   Churchill makes 'Iron Curtain' speech at Fulton, Missouri: 'From Stettin in the Baltic to Trieste in the Adriatic, an Iron Curtain has descended upon the Continent'.

May 26   At Czech elections, communists win 38% of the vote and set up a single party 'National Front' government.

May   Fighting breaks out in northern Greece, marking renewal of civil war between monarchist forces, assisted by Britain, and communist guerrillas, backed by Albania, Bulgaria and Yugoslavia.

1947   Feb. 21   The British inform the Americans that they cannot afford to keep troops in Greece because of their domestic economic difficulties and intend to withdraw them by the end of March.

Feb. 27   Dean Acheson privately expounds the 'Truman Doctrine' of economic and military aid to nations in danger of communist take-over.

Mar. 12   In message to Congress, President Truman outlines the Truman Doctrine 'to support free peoples who are resisting attempted subjugation by armed minorities or by outside pressures', effectively committing the United States to intervene against communist or communist-backed movements in Europe and elsewhere.

Apr. 22   Truman Doctrine passed by Congress.

Apr. 24   Council of Foreign Ministers in Moscow ends without formal peace treaties for Germany and Austria.

May 22   US Congress passes Bill for $250 million of aid for Greece and Turkey.

June 5   George Marshall, American Secretary of State, calls for a European recovery programme supported by American aid.

June 12–15   Non-communist nations of Europe set up Committee of European Economic Co-operation to draft European Recovery Programme.

1947	Aug.	First American aid arrives in Greece, followed by military 'advisers' to assist in the Civil War against the communists.
1948	Feb. 25	Czech President Beneš accepts a communist-dominated government.
	Mar. 10	Czech Foreign Minister, Jan Masaryk, found dead in suspicious circumstances.
	Mar. 14–31	Congress passes the Foreign Assistance Act, the Marshall Plan. $5,300 million of 'Marshall Aid' is initially allocated for European recovery.
	Mar. 17	Belgium, France, Luxembourg, the Netherlands and Great Britain sign a treaty setting up the Brussels Treaty Organization for mutual military assistance.
	Mar. 20	Russian representative walks out of Allied Control Commission, over plans for unified German currency.
	Mar. 30	Russians impose restrictions on traffic between Western zones and Berlin.
	April	Paris Treaty sets up Organization for European Economic Co-operation to receive Marshall Aid.
	May 30	No opposition parties are allowed to stand at Czech elections and electors called on to vote for a single list of National Front candidates.
	June 7	Beneš resigns as President of Czechoslovakia; succeeded by Gottwald.
	June 24	Russians impose a complete blockade of traffic into Berlin. Berlin airlift begins (25th).
	June	Yugoslavia expelled from Comintern, effectively putting it outside direct Soviet control.
	Sept. 5	Head of Polish Communist Party, Gomulka, forced to resign.
	Nov. 30	Russians set up municipal government for East Berlin.
1949	Jan. 25	Comecon, Communist economic co-operation organization, set up.
	Apr. 4	Creation of NATO, North Atlantic Treaty Organization. North Atlantic Treaty signed by members of Brussels Treaty organization, plus Canada, Denmark, Iceland, Italy, Norway, Portugal, and the United States. It pledges mutual military assistance to its members and sets up military headquarters.

May 4	Representatives of four occupation powers in Germany come to an agreement for ending of Berlin blockade.
May 12	Berlin blockade lifted.
Sept. 21	Federal Republic of Germany comes into existence (West Germany).
Sept. 30	Occupation Statute comes into force which reduces the responsibilities of the three occupying powers in what is now the Federal German Republic. Berlin airlift ends.
Oct. 7	German Democratic Republic (East Germany) comes into existence.

Eastern Europe since 1949

1949	Jan. 25	Comecon, Communist economic co-operation organization, set up.
	Apr. 4	Creation of NATO for containment of Soviet aggression against the west.
	May 4	Soviet Union agrees to end the Berlin blockade.
	May 15	Communists take power in Hungary on the basis of a single-list election for the 'People's Front', replacing the Communist-dominated coalition which had been elected in 1947.
	June	Purge of Albanian Communist Party.
	Aug. 29	Soviet Union tests its first atomic bomb.
	Oct. 7	German Democratic Republic (East Germany) comes into existence.
	Oct. 16	Greek communists cease fighting.
	Nov.	Russian Marshal takes command of Polish army.
	Dec.	Beginning of purge of Bulgarian Communist Party.
1950	May 28	Pro-Stalinist Hoxha confirmed in power in single-list elections in Albania.
	May–June	Last non-communist expelled from Hungarian government.
	July	Romanian Communist Party admits to expulsion of almost 200,000 members in past two years.
	July 6	Agreement proclaiming the Oder–Neisse line the permanent frontier between Germany and Poland concluded between German Democratic Republic and Poland.
1951	Jan. 27	Protocol on delineation of Oder–Neisse frontier signed between German Democratic Republic and Poland.

1952	Jan. 2	East German government rejects a UN request to supervise free national elections.
	Aug. 14	Rakosi appointed premier of Hungary.
1953	Jan. 13	Jewish doctors arrested in Soviet Union as 'Doctors' Plot' is accused of planning to assassinate top party leaders and military personnel. Fears that Stalin is about to launch a new purge are widespread.
	Jan. 14	Tito is elected Yugoslav President, pledged to 'non-alignment'.
	Mar. 5	Death of Stalin. Khrushchev confirmed as First Secretary of the Party (Sept.).
	June	Widespread risings in East Germany suppressed.
	July 4	Moderate Imre Nagy takes over premiership in Hungary, though Rakosi retains control of police.
	July 10	Beria, Soviet secret police chief, arrested for spying and later executed (Dec.).
	Aug. 14	Soviet Union explodes hydrogen bomb.
1954	Jan.	Over 300,000 East German refugees registered in West Germany in past twelve months. Tito re-elected President of Yugoslavia.
	Feb. 18	Four Power talks fail to make headway on future of Germany and Austria.
1955	Apr. 18	Hungarian Premier, Nagy, dismissed for 'deviation'.
	May 9	West Germany admitted to NATO.
	May 14	Warsaw Pact formed.
	June 2	Khrushchev and Tito sign a declaration normalizing relations.
	July 3	Geneva meeting of East–West Heads of Government fails to achieve any decisive breakthroughs.
	Sept. 13	Soviet Union establishes diplomatic relations with West Germany.
1956	Jan. 15	New five-year plan announced in Soviet Union.
	Feb.	At Twentieth Party Congress, Khrushchev attacks abuses of the Stalin era in 'Secret Speech', marking beginning of era of de-Stalinization.
	June	In Hungary, hard-liner Rakosi replaced as First Secretary by Gerö.
		Suppression of workers' riots in Poznan, Poland. Gomulka becomes First Secretary of Polish United Workers' Party.

	Oct.–Nov.	Hungarian uprising. General strike and street demonstrations depose existing leadership, seize major buildings and appoint Nagy premier. Soviet troops withdraw from Budapest but return after 4 November to crush the rising. Nagy deposed and Kadar appointed. Several thousand killed and thousands flee as refugees.
1958	Feb.	Khrushchev replaces Bulganin as Prime Minister.
1961	Apr.	First manned Soviet space flight. Arrests of dissident writers.
	July	Anti-clerical legislation in Russia, restricting role of the clergy in parish councils.
	Aug.	Berlin Wall constructed to prevent flight from East to West Berlin.
	Oct.	Twenty-second Party Congress; new Party programme and further 'de-Stalinization', including the removal of Stalin's body from Red Square mausoleum.
1962	Oct.	Cuban missile crisis after Soviet Union attempts to set up ballistic missile bases in Cuba. Imposition of naval 'quarantine' by the United States forces the Soviet Union to back down in the face of the threat of nuclear war. A major diplomatic triumph for the will and resolve of President John F. Kennedy.
	Nov.	Publication of Solzhenitsyn's *A Day in the Life of Ivan Denisovitch* marks first public recognition of the conditions in Soviet labour camps.
1963	Mar.	Khrushchev warns Writers' Union of 'bourgeois influences'.
	Aug. 5	Partial Test Ban Treaty signed in Moscow, banning nuclear weapon tests in the atmosphere, outer space, and under water (in force from October).
1964	Oct.	Brezhnev replaces Khrushchev as First Secretary.
1965	Mar.	Central Committee of the Soviet Union makes a number of agricultural reforms.
	Sept.	Central Committee approves further set of economic reforms.
1966	Feb.	Trial of leading 'dissidents', Sinyavsky and Daniel, who are sentenced to periods of imprisonment.

1967	June	Arab–Israeli Six-Day War leads to acute tension between United States and Soviet Union.
1968	Jan.	Soviet dissidents Ginsburg and Galanskov tried and imprisoned. Dubček becomes First Secretary of Czechoslovak Communist Party and process of liberalization begins – 'Socialism with a human face' – including decentralization of economic planning and more open contacts with the West.
	July 1	Non-proliferation treaty signed in London, Moscow and Washington.
	Aug.	The Soviet Union and other Warsaw Pact forces invade Czechoslovakia and end the 'Prague Spring'. The Czech leaders are forced to agree in Moscow to the re-imposition of censorship, return to centralized planning, and the abandonment of closer links with the West. Husak takes over Party Secretaryship from Dubček (Jan. 1969).
1969	Mar.	Dubček demoted and sent as ambassador to Turkey; he is eventually expelled from the Party and given menial work.
	Oct.	Czechoslovakia repudiates its condemnation of the Warsaw Pact invasion and consents to the stationing of Russian troops.
1970	Dec.	Widespread rioting in Poland over food prices and economic conditions; Gierek replaces Gomulka as First Secretary of Polish United Workers' Party.
1971	Feb.	Mass Jewish demonstration at Supreme Soviet building. Jewish emigration to Israel increases.
1972	Jan.	Seizure of documents and leading intellectuals in Ukraine.
	May 26	President Nixon visits Moscow. Strategic Arms Limitation Treaty (SALT I) signed between United States and Soviet Union on limitation of anti-ballistic missile systems (in force from October) and interim agreement on limitation of strategic offensive arms.
	May	Disturbances in Lithuania.
1973	Apr.	Andropov and Gromyko join Politburo.
1974	Feb.	Solzhenitsyn deported from Soviet Union.

1975	Aug.	Helsinki agreement on European Security and Co-operation provides for 'Human Rights'.
	Oct.	Soviet physicist and dissident Andre Sakharov awarded Nobel Peace Prize.
1976	June	Strikes and sabotage in Poland in opposition to attempted price rises which were temporarily withdrawn, although unrest is severely put down.
1977	Jan.	Dissident civil rights group 'Charter 77' formed in Prague.
	June	Brezhnev replaces Podgorny as President of the Soviet Union.
1978	July	Trial of Scharansky.
1979	June	Visit of Polish Pope John Paul II to Poland helps to arouse strong national feeling.
	Dec.	Soviet invasion of Afghanistan. The United States imposes a grain embargo on Russia. Large commemorative services held in Poland for those killed in the disturbances of 1970.
1980	Jan.	Sakharov sentenced to internal exile in Gorky.
	Mar.–Apr.	Dissident groups in Poland advocate boycott of official parliamentary elections on 23 March, and mass commemorative service for Polish officers killed at Katyn in April 1940 leads to arrests.
	July	Olympic Games in Moscow boycotted by the United States.
	July–Sept.	Widespread strikes among Polish workers at Gdansk (Danzig) and elsewhere as a result of rise in meat prices. In August, Gdansk workers publish demands calling for free trade unions. Soviet Union begins jamming of Western broadcasts. Resignation of Babinch as Prime Minister (24 Aug.) and of Gierek as First Secretary of the Polish United Workers' Party (6 Sept.); replaced by Pinkowski and Kania. Gierek's departure followed by the signing of the Gdansk agreement with Lech Walesa, the leader of the Gdansk 'inter-factory committee'. This recognized the new Solidarity unions, granted a wage agreement and promised a 40-hour week, permitted the broadcast of church services on Sunday, relaxed the censorship

laws, promised to re-examine the new meat scales, and review the case of imprisoned dissidents. National Confederation of Independent Trade Unions, 'Solidarity', formed under leadership of Lech Walesa (8 Sept.) attracts an estimated 10 million members. 'Rural Solidarity' claims an estimated half a million farmers.

Dec.   Death of Russian leader Kosygin.

1981 Jan.   Walesa visits Pope in Rome.

Feb.   General Jaruzelski replaces Pinkowski as Prime Minister of Poland.

Dec.   After visiting Moscow, General Jaruzelski declares martial law in Poland. The leading members of Solidarity are arrested and the organization banned.

1982 Nov.   Death of Brezhnev. Andropov becomes First Secretary of the Communist Party of the Soviet Union.

1984 Feb.   Death of Andropov. Chernenko becomes First Secretary of the Communist Party of the Soviet Union.

1985 Mar.   Death of Chernenko. Gorbachev becomes First Secretary of the Communist Party of the Soviet Union. Announces programme of *glasnost* and *perestroika*.

July   Gorbachev replaces four members of Politburo with his own supporters; veteran Foreign Minister, Gromyko, moved to Presidency and replaced by Gorbachev supporter Shevardnadze.

1986 Jan.   Gorbachev continues process of removing the personnel of the Brezhnev era from central and regional government.

Sept.   Solidarity announce intention of working within the existing system.

1987 June   Karoly Grosz, an economic liberal, becomes Prime Minister in Hungary.

July   Protests by Crimean Tartars in Moscow permitted to take place.

Aug.   Protests in the Baltic States demanding greater autonomy and an end to 'Russification'.

Nov.   Polish government hold referendum for programme of radical reform; Solidarity calls for boycott and the proposals are rejected. Radical Boris Yeltsin dismissed as head of Moscow Party for outspoken criticisms of conservatives.

Dec.   President Reagan and General Secretary Gorbachev sign Intermediate Nuclear Forces Treaty in Washington; a major breakthrough in East–West arms negotiations.

Dec. 17   Gustav Husak resigns party leadership in Czechoslovakia; succeeded by another conservative, Milos Jakes.

1988 Jan.   Gorbachev calls for acceleration of drive to democratization; calls special party Congress in the summer. Major reform of Soviet Constitution sets up a Supreme Soviet consisting of two chambers to meet in almost continuous session, the members selected by a Congress of People's Deputies representing national areas, social organizations and constituencies. Hungarian government announces end of price controls.

Feb.   Serious ethnic riots in Nagorno-Karabakh region of Azerbaijan.

Mar.–Aug.   Wave of strikes and unrest in Poland; Solidarity demands talks with government.

May   Russian agreement to withdraw all troops from Afghanistan by February 1989.
In Hungary, Kadar relegated to post of Party President; Grosz becomes Party Secretary and Prime Minister; purge of conservatives in Central Committee and Politburo.

Dec.   Polish government accepts 'round table' talks with Solidarity.
Gorbachev announces unilateral force reductions of 500,000 troops and 10,000 tanks.

1989 Jan.   Law on Association in Hungary allows political parties to be formed; new draft constitution (Mar.) drops reference to leading role for Communist Party.

Feb. 6   Solidarity and Polish government open talks on future of Poland.

Mar.–Apr.   Solidarity accepts terms for participation in elections; government agrees to admit opposition to the lower house of parliament (*sejm*), a freely elected Senate, and create office of President. Solidarity legalized.

June   First free parliamentary elections in Poland since Second World War; Solidarity obtains landslide victory

	in seats it is allowed to contest. Hungarian government recognizes Imre Nagy, leader of 1956 rising, and permits his reburial with full honours.
July	General Jaruzelski elected President of Poland by one-vote margin. General Kiszcak appointed Prime Minister but fails to form a government and resigns; Solidarity activist Tadeusz Mazowiecki becomes Prime Minister heading first non-communist government.
Sept.	Hungary opens border with Austria allowing flight of thousands of East Germans to the West.
Oct.	Erich Honecker replaced as President by Egon Krenz in East Germany (18th) following flight of East Germans to the West and mass demonstrations in East German cities organized by New Forum opposition group. Krenz meets opposition group (26th); travel restrictions discussed.
Nov.	East German Council of Ministers resigns *en masse* following huge demonstrations in East Berlin and other cities. New Forum opposition legalized and Politburo resigns (7th–8th). Berlin Wall opened and travel restrictions lifted on East German citizens (9th). Reformer, Hans Modrow, becomes President (13th). President Todor Zhivkov of Bulgaria resigns (10th). Entire Czech Politburo resigns (24th) following mass demonstrations in Prague by Civic Forum opposition group.
Dec.	Malta summit between President Bush and President Gorbachev; declare the Cold War 'at an end' (4th). Resignation of Czech Prime Minister, Adamec, forced by further mass demonstrations and General Strike. Communist monopoly of power ended and joint interim government formed with members of Civic Forum (7th–9th). Resignation of Egon Krenz as Communist leader in East Germany (8th). Preparations for free elections begin. Thousands reported killed in anti-Ceauçescu demonstrations in Romanian city of Timisoara (19th). Bulgaria declares it will hold free elections (19th). Brandenburg Gate opened between East and West Berlin as symbolic act of reconciliation between the two Germanies (22nd). Mass demonstrations in Bucharest and other Romanian cities. After initial attempts to disperse them, the

army joins the crowds and Ceauçescu and his wife flee (22nd). Heavy fighting between pro-Ceauçescu forces and the army leaves several hundred killed and wounded in Bucharest and other Romanian cities; Ceauçescu and his wife arrested and executed by Military Tribunal (25th). Free elections announced for April 1990; Ion Iliescu becomes President (26th). Václav Havel, former dissident and political prisoner, unanimously elected President of Czechoslovakia (29th); Alexander Dubček earlier elected Chairman (Speaker) of Czech Parliament (28th).

1990	Jan.	Czechoslovakia calls for abolition of Comecon.
	Feb.	First steps to German reunification with establishment of commission on single currency (13th). Victory of *Sajudis* (Lithuanian nationalist movement) in general election. First Soviet troop withdrawals from Czechoslovakia (26th).
	Mar.	Lithuanian declaration of independence (11th); Gorbachev pronounces declaration 'illegal and invalid' (13th); Soviet troops seize Lithuanian Party headquarters (27th); Estonia pledges restoration of independence (30th).
	Apr.	Oil supplies to Lithuania cut by Moscow (18th).
	May	'Consultation with the people' promised by Gorbachev on future of the economy (23rd), followed by panic buying in shops; renewed violence in Armenia; Yeltsin successfully challenges for Presidency of Russian Federation.
	July	Economic union of East and West Germany.
	Sept. 12	Treaty signed following 'Two plus Four' talks agreeing to ending of special powers by the war-time Allies over Germany and for reunification with full sovereignty of East and West Germany.
	Oct. 3	Reunification of Germany.
	Dec. 2	First all-German polls elect Kohl's CDU/CSU government; ex-Communist PDS reduced to 17 seats.
	Dec. 9	Lech Walesa elected Polish President.
	Dec. 20	Resignation of Soviet Foreign Minister, Schevardnadze, because of 'reactionary elements'.
	Dec.	Widespread anti-communist riots in Albania after first legal opposition party formed.
1991	Jan. 13	Soviet special forces kill 14 Lithuanian demonstrators in Vilnius.

1991	Jan. 20	Special forces assault key buildings in Latvian capital, Riga.
	Mar.	Huge majorities in Latvia and Estonia for independence.
	Apr.	Soviet Georgia declares independence. Miners' strikes in the Soviet coalfields.
	May	First serious casualties in fighting between Serbs and Croats in Yugoslavia.
	June 25	Croatia declares independence from Yugoslavia. Widespread fighting begins as Yugoslav army seizes Slovenia border posts; fighting between Croatian militias and Serbian irregulars and Federal army.
	Aug.	Gorbachev prepares new all-Union treaty to preserve the Soviet Union. Attempted hard-line coup in Moscow while Gorbachev on holiday in Crimea. Russian Premier Boris Yeltsin defies coup and prepares to defend Russian parliament building with aid of loyal troops and populace. Coup collapses in face of popular resistance and declarations of independence by Republics. The leading plotters are arrested. Gorbachev returns to Moscow. Under pressure from Yeltsin, adopts sweeping reforms. Baltic States become independent states of Latvia, Estonia and Lithuania; Communist Party of Soviet Union dissolved, ending 74-year rule; Gorbachev resigns as General Secretary, retaining office of Executive President of rapidly dissolving Soviet Union. Negotiates an association with 10 Republics for a looser union with a common foreign and defence policy.
	Sept.	Armenia becomes 12th Soviet Republic to declare independence.
	Oct.	First completely free election in Poland produces inconclusive result, proliferation of parties and turnout below 50 per cent.
	Nov. 4	Formation of independent National Guard in Ukraine.
	Nov. 18	European Community imposes sanctions on Yugoslavia.
	Dec. 1	Ukraine votes overwhelmingly for independence.
	Dec. 8	Leaders of Belarus, Russian Federation and Ukraine declare that the Soviet Union is dead: in Declaration of Minsk they proclaim new 'Commonwealth of Independent States' (CIS) with headquarters at Minsk in Belarus.

Dec. 10	Ukrainian Parliament ratifies new Commonwealth.
Dec. 12	Russian Parliament votes 188 to six to approve new Commonwealth.
Dec. 13	Five Central Asian Republics, meeting at Ashkhabad, vote to join new Commonwealth as founding members.
Dec. 22	Leaders of 11 former Soviet Republics sign Treaty of Alma Ata, establishing new Commonwealth of Independent States. Georgia does not join.
Dec. 25	Resignation of Gorbachev as President of now defunct Soviet Union.
Dec. 30	Minsk Summit of Commonwealth of Independent States agrees future of strategic nuclear forces.
1992 Jan.	European Union (EU) recognizes Croatia and Slovenia.
Feb.	UN Security Council agrees to send a 14,000-strong force to Bosnia (21st). Bosnia-Herzegovina declares independence; Bosnian Serbs proclaim separate state.
Apr. 3	The leader of the Albanian Democratic Party, Sali Berisha, elected President by People's Assembly.
Apr. 6	Bosnia recognized as independent by EU and US; Serbs begin campaign of 'ethnic cleansing' in north and east Bosnia, expelling Muslim population to create a pure Serb corridor linking Serb areas of western Bosnia with Serbia. Serbian forces begin artillery bombardment of Sarajevo.
May	'Cleansing' of Muslims and Croats from Brcko begins and systematic killing at Luka and elsewhere, resulting in some 3,000 dead. UN trade embargo placed on Serbia.
June	Yegor Gaidar becomes Premier of Russia.
	Vote of no confidence in Polish government of Prime Minister Jan Olszewski.
	Czechoslovakian general elections held, dominated by issue of dissolution of the state. Klaus becomes Czech Premier, Merciar Premier of Slovakia; talks on split proceed in earnest.
July	Airlift of relief supplies into Sarajevo begins. Slovak National Council approves declaration of sovereignty; resignation of Václav Havel as Federal President.
Aug.	Existence of Serb-run concentration camps disclosed. President Franjo Tudjman and Croatian Democratic Union win victory in first Croatian elections. London

Conference sets up Geneva peace talks for former Yugoslavia.

Agreement reached on split of Czechoslovakia into two independent states on 1st Jan. 1993.

Sept. 15   Federal Republic of Yugoslavia excluded from UN General Assembly.

Lithuania signs agreement with Russia for withdrawal of former Soviet troops.

Oct.   In Georgia, Chairman of State Council, Eduard Shevardnadze, elected parliamentary Speaker and *de facto* head of state.

President Iliescu wins further four-year term in Romania.

Nov.   Lithuanian ex-communist Democratic Labour Party defeats nationalist Sajudis Party in first post-Soviet parliamentary elections.

Czechoslovak Federal Parliament approves split into Czech and Slovak states.

UN Security Council enforces naval blockade on Serbia and Montenegro.

Dec.   Ex-Communist President Milan Kučan and ruling Liberal Democrat Party win elections in Slovenia; UN peace-keeping forces deployed in Macedonia to prevent spread of unrest.

Russian Congress blocks President Yeltsin's plans for a referendum on the powers of the President; also removes Yegor Gaidar as Premier and replaces him with Viktor Chernomyrdin (14th).

Slobodan Milošević wins Presidential elections in Serbia (21st).

1993 Jan.   Formal separation of Czech and Slovak states; Havel appointed President of Czech Republic.

Geneva peace conference on Bosnia opens; Bosnian Serbs provisionally agree to end the war, but fighting continues.

Feb.   UN Security Council votes to create war crimes tribunal for Yugoslavia. Bosnian town of Cerska falls to Serbs.

Mar.   President Yeltsin announces rule by decree and plan to hold a national referendum on 25 April (21st). Move to impeach the President by Congress defeated (28th).

Apr.	Athens peace talks on former Yugoslavia open (1st). Serbs reject UN peace plan (3rd); Bosnian Serbs also reject UN peace plan (25th). Former Yugoslav Republic of Macedonia admitted to UN. Russian referendum gives vote of confidence to President Yeltsin and his socio-economic policy.
May 6	UN Security Council declares Sarajevo and other Muslim enclaves UN-monitored safe areas. War crimes tribunal for former Yugoslavia established at The Hague.
June	Provisional agreement at Geneva on three-way partition of Bosnia-Herzegovina into Muslim, Serb and Croat areas.
July	Guntis Ulmanis of the Farmers' Union elected President of Latvia.
Aug.	Last Russian troops leave Lithuania.
Sept. 21	President Yeltsin suspends parliament and calls for elections.
Oct. 3–4	Suppression of rising against President Yeltsin's suspension of Parliament.
Oct. 26	Coalition government formed under Polish Peasant Party leader Waldemar Pawlak.

1994 Jan.	Reformers Gaidar and Fedorov leave Yeltsin government.
Feb. 9	Serb mortar attack on Sarajevo market, killing over 60 people, leads to UN ultimatum on removal of Serb artillery from 20 km exclusion zone. NATO fighters shoot down Serbian aircraft (28th).
Apr.	UN safe area of Goradze comes under Serb attack; NATO aircaft bomb Serb positions; Serbs retaliate by taking UN observers hostage.
May 29	Former communists, now Hungarian Socialist Party, come to power after two rounds of voting.
July	Contact Group of diplomats from Russia, the United States, France, Britain and Germany propose division of Bosnia, but rejected by Serbs. New constitution adopted in Moldova, establishing a presidential parliamentary republic.
Aug.	Serbian government imposes sanctions on the Bosnian Serbs.
Nov.	US announces unilateral suspension of international arms embargo following renewal of fighting in Bosnia.

1994 Dec. 1   Russia gives ultimatum to breakaway Chechen Republic to disband army and free all prisoners; failure to reach agreement leads to major military assault on Chechen Republic (27th). (See p. 279 for the Chechen conflict.)

Former communists win outright majority in Bulgaria. Four-month truce agreed in Bosnia.

1995 Mar. 1   In Poland former communist Jozef Oleksy elected Prime Minister following resignation of Waldemar Pawlak.

May   Croatian forces open fighting against Serbs. NATO planes attack Serb positions and Bosnian Serbs again take UN hostages.

June   Russia and Ukraine finally settle dispute over Black Sea fleet.

Western nations send 'rapid reaction' force to Bosnia.

July   Serb forces overrun UN safe areas of Srebrenica and Zepa; by the end of the month photographic evidence of mass graves leads to the indictment of Bosnian Serb leader Radovan Karadzic and military chief Ratko Mladic for crimes against humanity.

Aug.   Further Serb mortar attacks on Sarajevo lead to NATO air strikes against Bosnian Serbs.

Oct. 12   New cease-fire comes into effect in Bosnia.

Nov. 1   Yugoslav peace talks open in Dayton, Ohio. Peace plan agreed (21st).

Nov. 3   President Yeltsin forced to relinquish control of four key ministries after second heart attack.

Polish President Lech Walesa defeated by former communist Aleksander Kwàsniewski in Presidential election.

Shevardnadze begins new term as President of Georgia.

Dec. 14   Yugoslav peace agreement signed in Paris.

Dec. 26   Yeltsin resumes powers.

1996 Jan. 5   Resignation of Liberal Russian Foreign Minister, Andrei Kozyrev.

Resignation of Polish Prime Minister Oleksy over allegations of once spying for Russia.

Feb. 15   President Yeltsin announces intention of seeking a second term in office.

Feb. 29   Siege of Sarajevo officially ends.

Apr.	Presidents of Belarus and Russia sign a treaty providing for political, economic and military integration.
May	Ruling Albanian Democratic Party claims to have won 100 of 140 seats in flawed general election.
June	Ruling Civic Democratic Party wins Czech elections.
July 4	Yeltsin wins Presidential election in second-round run-off.
	Ukraine Premier survives an assassination attempt.
Sept.	First elections in Bosnia.
Nov.	Constitutional referendum in Belarus gives greater powers to President.
Dec.	Romanian general election won by reform candidate.
	Persistent street demonstrations in Serbia against government's refusal to accept opposition successes in municipal elections.

1997	Jan.	Serbian government concedes opposition victories.
		Massive street demonstrations in Bulgaria against socialist (ex-communist) government.
	July	Serious rioting in major towns of Albania.
		Hungary, Poland and Czech Republic invited to join NATO.
	Sept.	Coalition of new Solidarity win Polish elections.
	Oct.	Yeltsin promises major drive against corruption.
	Nov. 16	Hungarian referendum votes to join NATO.

1998	Mar.	Yeltsin dismisses Chernomyrdin and entire ministry.
		Kiriyenko eventually approved by Duma (24 Apr.).
	Apr.	Crisis in Kosovo intensifies as Serbs deploy military.

Western Europe since 1945

1945	June 5	Allied Control Commission set up in Germany.
	July	Churchill voted out as Prime Minister in Britain; Labour Party under Attlee takes power.
	Dec.	De Gasperi becomes Prime Minister of Italy as head of Christian Democrat Party.

1946	Jan.	De Gaulle resigns as President of French Provisional Government after his draft constitution is rejected; he tries to rally right-wing opinion in his non-party, *Rassemblement du Peuple Français (RPF)*.
	Mar.	Churchill makes 'Iron Curtain' speech at Fulton, Missouri.

1946 May   King Victor Emmanuel II of Italy abdicates; a refer-
                 endum votes Italy a Republic.
      July   Bread rationing introduced in Britain; more severe
                 rationing than the war because of economic crisis.
      Oct.   Fourth Republic established in France.
      Dec.   Britain and the United States agree economic mer-
                 ger of their zones in Germany.

1947 Mar.   Anglo-French Treaty of Alliance.
      June   General Marshall proposes economic aid to rebuild
                 Europe; Paris Conference (July) meets to discuss
                 the 'Marshall Plan'.

1948 Apr.   Organization for European Economic Co-operation
                 (OEEC) set up to receive $17,000 million of
                 Marshall Aid from the United States. Member states
                 are: Austria, Belgium, Denmark, France, West Ger-
                 many, Greece, Iceland, Ireland, Italy, Luxembourg,
                 the Netherlands, Norway, Portugal, Spain, Sweden,
                 Switzerland, Turkey and the United Kingdom. Cus-
                 toms Union set up between Belgium, the Nether-
                 lands and Luxembourg – 'Benelux'.

1949 May 23   German Federal Republic comes into existence on
                 basis of constitution drafted the previous year with
                 Konrad Adenauer as first Federal Chancellor.
                 Council of Europe set up for 'political co-opera-
                 tion', consisting of the OEEC states apart from Spain
                 and Portugal. Strasbourg becomes head-quarters for
                 a Consultative Assembly.
      Aug. 24   North Atlantic Treaty Organization (NATO) formed
                 including United States, Canada, United Kingdom,
                 Norway, Denmark, Holland, Belgium, France, Italy,
                 Greece and Turkey.

1950   Britain rejects idea of joining a European coal and
                 steel community.

1951 Apr. 18   Paris Treaty between Benelux countries (Belgium,
                 Netherlands and Luxembourg), France, Italy and
                 West Germany – 'the Six' – sets up a 'Common
                 Market' in coal and steel. A European Commission
                 is set up as the supreme authority.

	Oct.	Fall of Labour Government in Britain; Churchill returns to office. De Gaulle retires from politics.
1952	Oct.	Britain explodes an atomic bomb in Monte Bello islands, off N.W. Australia.
1953		European Court of Human Rights set up in Strasbourg.
1954		Western European Union proposed by the British as a substitute for a single European army.
	May	Defeat for French forces at Dien Bien Phu (see p. 246).
	Aug.	Death of De Gasperi, Christian Democrat Prime Minister of Italy, 1945–53.
1955	Jan.	West Germany joins NATO.
	Apr. 5	Resignation of Churchill as British Prime Minister. Anthony Eden takes over. Messina Conference of 'the Six' discusses a full customs union. Britain expresses preference for a larger free trade area of the OEEC countries.
1956	Oct.–Nov.	Anglo–French intervention at Suez (see pp. 252–3).
1957	Jan. 9	Fall of Eden as a consequence of Suez Crisis; Harold Macmillan takes over (10th) as Prime Minister.
	Mar. 25	Rome Treaties between 'the Six' set up the European Economic Community (EEC) and Euratom.
1958	May	Rioting by French settlers in Algeria leads to French army taking over (13th); de Gaulle voted into power in France after period of chronic political instability (29th) and given power to produce a new constitution.
	Oct. 9–28	Death of Pope Pius XII; election of John XXIII.
	Dec. 21	De Gaulle elected President of Fifth French Republic.
1959	Nov.	European Free Trade Association (EFTA) set up as a counterweight to the EEC, comprising Austria, Denmark, Norway, Portugal, Sweden, Switzerland and the United Kingdom.

1960	Feb.	France explodes her first atomic device.
1961	Apr. 21	French army revolt begins in Algeria against de Gaulle's plans for Algerian independence.
	Aug. 10	United Kingdom, Ireland and Denmark apply for membership of EEC; also Norway (1962).
	Aug. 17–18	Berlin Wall erected to halt flood of refugees to West.
1962		EEC agrees Common Agricultural Policy to come into operation in 1964; a system of high guaranteed prices to be paid for out of a common fund; beginning of period of agricultural prosperity in rural Europe and huge food surpluses.
	Dec.	Britain arranges with the United States to adopt Polaris missile system as its nuclear deterrent.
1963	Jan.	De Gaulle vetoes British entry into EEC; Irish, Danish and Norwegian applications suspended.
	June 3–21	Death of John XXIII; election of Pope Paul VI.
	Aug. 5	France refuses to sign Test Ban Treaty, signalling intention to build up *force de frappe.*
	Oct.	Adenauer retires as Chancellor of Germany; succeeded by Dr Ludwig Erhard.
1964	Oct.	Labour, under Harold Wilson, returns to power in Britain after 13 years of Conservative rule.
1966	Mar.	France withdraws from Military Committee of NATO.
		Labour government re-elected in Britain.
	Nov. 30	Dr Kurt-Georg Kiesinger becomes Chancellor of Germany.
1967	Nov. 27	Further British, Irish, Danish and Norwegian application to join EEC vetoed by de Gaulle.
1968	May	Violent student unrest in Paris and mass strikes against de Gaulle's government.
	Sept.	Dr Salazar of Portugal, Western Europe's longest surviving dictator, succeeded by Dr Marcello Caetano.
1969	Apr. 28	De Gaulle resigns as President after unfavourable vote in referendum on the constitution; Gaullist Georges Pompidou becomes President.

	Aug.	First British troops sent to Northern Ireland (see p. 264).
	Oct.	German Social Democrats take power under Willy Brandt; begins policy of *Ostpolitik*, seeking friendly relations with Eastern Europe, and encourages enlargement of EEC.
1970	Mar.	Heads of East and West Germany meet for first time.
	June 18	Defeat of Labour government in Britain, Edward Heath, a committed European, leads Conservative government.
	Nov. 9	Death of de Gaulle.
1971	Oct. 28	British Parliament votes in favour of application to join the Common Market.
1972	Mar. 24	Britain imposes direct rule in Northern Ireland.
	Apr.	Defection from German coalition leads to early election in November.
	Sept. 5	Arab terrorists kill Israeli athletes at Munich Olympics.
	Nov.	Brandt's government returned to power with SPD as largest party in Bundestag.
1973	Jan	Britain, Denmark and Ireland join EEC; Norway does not, following unfavourable referendum vote.
	May	Britain in dispute with Iceland over fishing rights – 'Cod War'.
	June 22	West and East Germany join the United Nations.
	Dec.	Conservative Prime Minister Heath declares state of emergency as a result of miners' strike.
1974	Feb. 28	Heath defeated in general election; Labour government in Britain under Wilson.
	Apr. 2	Death of Georges Pompidou; Giscard d'Estaing becomes President (May).
	Apr. 25	Military junta deposes Portuguese government, ending dictatorship and colonial wars.
	May	Willy Brandt resigns following security scandal; Helmut Schmidt takes over as Chancellor.
	Sept. 30	General Spinola resigns and replaced by Costa Gomes in Portugal.
	Oct. 10	Labour Party in Britain obtains small majority at general election.

1975	Jan.	British government announces referendum on EEC membership.
	Feb. 28	German opposition leader, Peter Lorenz, kidnapped by terrorists.
	Apr. 25	Portugal holds first free elections for 50 years.
	June	Britain votes by two to one in referendum to remain in EEC. Greece, Spain and Portugal apply for membership.
	Nov. 20	Death of Franco; King Juan Carlos I succeeds to the throne (27th).
	Dec.	Terrorist attacks by Indonesian immigrants in the Netherlands.
1976	Apr. 5	James Callaghan becomes Prime Minister of Britain following resignation of Harold Wilson.
	Sept. 19	Social Democratic Party in Sweden defeated for first time in 44 years.
1977	June 15	First general election in Spain for 40 years. Señor Suarez's Democratic Centre Party wins power.
	Sept. 5	German terrorists kill Dr Hans-Martin Schleyer, head of West German Employers' Federation.
1978	Mar. 16	Aldo Moro, former Prime Minister of Italy, kidnapped in Rome by Italian terrorists; found dead (9 May).
	Aug. 6–26	Death of Pope Paul VI; election of John Paul I.
	Sept. 28–Oct. 16	Death of Pope John Paul I; election of John Paul II, former Cardinal Karol Wojtyla, first non-Italian Pope for 400 years.
	Dec. 27	First democratic government in Spain.
	Dec.–Apr.	'Winter of Discontent' in Britain with widespread strikes against Labour government's wage policy.
1979	May 3	Conservatives under Margaret Thatcher take power following general election in Britain. European Monetary System (EMS) introduced with common European Currency Unit (ECU) linking the exchange rates of the individual countries.
	June	First direct elections to the European Parliament.
1980	Apr. 30–May 5	Iranian embassy in London seized by terrorists. Stormed by British specialist anti-terrorist forces, the SAS.

Aug. 2	Terrorist bomb explodes at Bologna railway station killing 76 people.
Oct. 5	German coalition of SPD and Free Democrats retains power in elections.
Dec. 4	Prime Minister of Portugal, Dr F. Sá Carneiro, killed in air crash.

1981	Jan. 1	Greece becomes member of EEC.
	Feb. 23	Attempted coup in Spain led by Lt.-Col. Trejero Molina; leaders arrested.
	Mar. 26	Social Democratic Party formed in Britain by breakaway of four senior figures from Labour Party.
	May 10	François Mitterrand, leader of the Socialists, becomes President of France in place of Giscard d'Estaing.
	May 13	Pope John Paul II shot and injured by Turkish terrorist.
	July	Rioting in several inner city areas of Britain.
	Nov.	Sensational by-election successes of British SDP/ Liberal Alliance leads to predictions of Alliance victory if an election called.

1982	Apr.	Britain sends Task Force to recapture Falkland Islands from Argentina (see p. 273).
	May 30	Spain joins NATO.
	June 15	Argentine forces on Falklands surrender.
	Sept. 19	Social Democrats return to power in Sweden.
	Oct.	Felipe González leads socialists to victory in Spanish elections.
		Helmut Kohl of Christian Democrats becomes Chancellor of Germany following break-up of governing coalition.

1983	Mar.	Crisis economic package in France and Cabinet re-shuffle.
	Mar. 6	Helmut Kohl wins a substantial electoral victory; Green Party passes 5% threshhold for seats in the Bundestag.
	June 9	Mrs Thatcher returned for second term of office in Britain. Labour Party and Alliance split the opposition vote.

1984	Mar. 9	Beginning of 12-month miners' strike in Britain.
	Apr. 20	Britain confirms intention to leave Hong Kong in 1997 when the lease from China expires.

1984	July 19	French communists withdraw support from Mitterrand.
	Sept. 4	Erich Honecker, East German leader, cancels trip to West Germany because of Soviet opposition.
	Oct.	IRA bomb explosion at Grand Hotel, Brighton, narrowly misses killing Mrs Thatcher.
1985	Nov.	Anglo–Irish agreement signed between Mrs Thatcher and Dr Fitzgerald, the Irish Premier, giving Irish government a consultative role in Northern Irish affairs.
	Dec.	Single European Act agreed at Luxembourg Summit.
1986	Jan. 1	Spain and Portugal join the Common Market.
	Jan.	Two Cabinet ministers resign in Britain over 'Westland Affair'.
	Mar. 12	Referendum in Spain favours continued membership of NATO.
	Mar.	General election in France gives socialists largest number of seats, but neo-Gaullist Jacques Chirac forms government; beginning of period of 'cohabitation' between Socialist President Mitterrand and Conservative Chirac.
	June 22	González and Socialists returned to power in Spanish elections.
1987	Jan. 25	Helmut Kohl's government confirmed in office at elections.
	June 11	Mrs Thatcher wins an unprecedented third term as Prime Minister of Britain.
1988	Apr.–May	Mitterrand defeats Chirac in French Presidential elections.
	June 5–12	Mitterrand calls elections for National Assembly but fails to achieve the expected overall majority.
	Sept. 20	Mrs Thatcher's 'Bruges Speech' attacks EEC attempts to introduce socialism by the back door.
1989	June–July	Victory of Polish Solidarity movement in elections (June) and formation of first non-communist government in Poland signals beginning of breakdown of East European Communist regimes.

	Sept.	Hungary opens borders with Austria, allowing flight of thousands of East Germans to the West.
	Nov.	Collapse of East German regime; opening of Berlin Wall (9 Nov.); freedom of travel to the West granted. Chancellor Kohl calls for united Germany. Reformer, Hans Modrow, becomes East German leader.
	Dec.	First Four-Power Conference since 1971 to discuss future of Berlin and East Europe. Cold War declared at an end at Malta Summit. Brandenburg Gate opened and Kohl visits East Germany to wide acclaim. Preparations for free elections in East Germany.
1990	Jan.	East German elections brought forward to March.
	Feb.	East German proposal for their neutrality rejected by West Germany. West German Cabinet agrees to currency union between East and West Germany.
	Mar.	Pro-unification Alliance for Germany wins East German elections and prepares for economic union in July and all-German elections in December.
	July	Economic unification of East and West Germany on the basis of the West German currency. West German–Soviet agreement that a united Germany will have full sovereignty, including the right to join NATO. The Soviet Union agrees to withdraw its troops from East Germany within three to four years.
	Oct. 3	Political unification of East and West Germany.
	Nov.	Mrs Thatcher replaced as Conservative leader by John Major following leadership contest.
	Dec.	First all-German elections since 1932 result in victory for Chancellor Kohl's Conservative coalition.
1991	Jan.	Italian Communist Party changes name to 'Democratic Party of the Left' (PDS) and adopts sweeping changes in policy.
	Jan.–Feb.	British and French forces participate in Gulf War against Iraq.
	Mar.	British government abandons poll tax.
	Apr.	German Chancellor Kohl suffers humiliating defeat in Rhineland Palatinate local elections.
	May	Resignation of French Premier Rocard; Edith Cresson becomes France's first woman Prime Minister.

1991	July–Oct.	European Community makes failed attempts to obtain cease-fire agreements in Yugoslavian conflict.
	Oct.	Luxembourg draft plan on European and Monetary Union of European Community fails to win agreement.
	Dec.	Maastricht Summit on economic and political union. Britain wins opt-out clause on monetary union and Social Charter. (For ratification of Maastricht, see p. 37.)
1992	Apr.	Pierre Bérégovoy appointed Prime Minister in France (2nd); President Francesco Cossiga resigns in Italy. John Major leads Conservatives to fourth election victory in Britain (9th).
	May	France's President Mitterrand and Germany's Chancellor Helmut Kohl announce creation of a Franco–German 'Eurocorps'.
	June	Socialist Unity Party leader Giuliano Amato becomes Italian Prime Minister, leading Italy's 51st administration since the war.
	Aug.	Demonstrations and acts of violence against foreign workers in Germany lead to call for restrictions on asylum provisions.
	Sept.	Constitutional changes in Belgium devolve more power to regions.
	Nov. 23	Neo-Nazi fire-bombing in Möln kills three Turkish women.
1993	Jan.	Social Democrat coalition government takes office in Denmark.
	Feb.	Belgium takes first steps towards a federal state.
	Apr.	Italian referendum approves modification of proportional representation system for elections to Senate; Carlo Ciampi forms new government after resignation of Amato.
	June	Spanish Workers' Socialist Party win general election with reduced majority.
	Aug.	Italian Senate and Chamber of Deputies approve of electoral reform for the Chamber.
	Nov.	General Strike in Belgium against economic austerity package.
1994	Mar. 28	Right-wing and nationalist Freedom Alliance coalition wins overwhelming victory in elections to reformed parliament in Italy.

Apr.	Silvio Berlusconi appointed Italian Prime Minister.
June	Resignation of French Socialist Party leader, Michel Rocard, after defeat in European elections.
Aug.	Labour Party leader Wim Kok leads coalition government in Holland. IRA announce a cease-fire in Northern Ireland.
Oct. 16	Chancellor Helmut Kohl's ruling Christian Democrat coalition remains in power following general election.
Nov. 16	Fall of Irish government led by Albert Reynolds.
Dec. 22	Resignation of Prime Minister Berlusconi after Northern League abandons coalition government.

1995	Jan. 13	Former Italian Treasury Minister, Lamberto Dini, appointed new Prime Minister.
	Apr. 23	Lionel Jospin, the French socialist candidate, wins most votes in first round of Presidential elections.
	May 7	Jacques Chirac wins French Presidential election.
	Oct. 12	Socialist Party takes power in Portugal as minority government, ending 10 years of Social Democratic rule.
	Nov. 15	French Prime Minister, Alain Juppé, introduces reforms to cut health and social security expenditure.

1996	Jan. 8	Death of former President François Mitterrand. Resignation of Greek Prime Minister, Andreas Papandreou, due to ill-health; replaced by Costas Simitis.
	Mar. 3	In Spain, Conservative Popular Party, led by José Maria Aznar, defeats ruling Socialists in general election.
	Apr.	Olive Tree Alliance wins Italian general election (21st); former Italian Prime Minister, Bettino Craxi, fined £15 million and sentenced to eight years' imprisonment for corruption.
	May	Strikes in Germany against austerity measures.
	July	Following end of conscription, announced in May, France announces the disbandment of a quarter of regiments to create a purely professional army by 2002.
	Sept. 22	Greek PASOK party retains majority in election following death of leader Andreas Papandreou (23 June).

1997 Apr. 21   Snap elections called in France for June. They re-
                 sult in victory for Socialists under Jospin.
      May 1   British Labour Party under Tony Blair wins a land-
                 slide election victory.

1998 Apr. 10   Peace deal brokered by British and Irish govern-
                ments in Northern Ireland.

The Road to European Union

1946 Sept. 19 Winston Churchill, in a speech at Zurich, urges
                Franco–German reconciliation with 'a kind of
                United States of Europe'.

1947 June 5   General Marshall proposes US aid to stimulate re-
                covery in Europe.
      Oct. 29   Creation of Benelux – economic union of Belgium,
                Luxembourg and the Netherlands.

1948 Apr. 16   Convention for European Economic Co-operation
                signed – the birth of OEEC.

1949 May 5   Statute of the Council of Europe signed. (See
                p. 213.)

1950 May 9   Robert Schuman makes his historic proposal to
                place French and German coal and steel under a
                common authority.

1951 Apr. 18   Treaty setting up the European Coal and Steel
                Community (ECSC) is signed in Paris by Belgium,
                France, Federal Republic of Germany, Luxembourg,
                Italy and the Netherlands.

1953 Feb. 10   ECSC common market for coal, iron ore, and scrap
                is opened.
      May 1   ECSC common market for steel is opened.

1955 June 1–3 Messina Conference: the Foreign Ministers of the
                ECSC's six member states propose further steps
                towards full integration in Europe.

1957 Mar. 25   Signing of the Rome treaties setting up the
                European Economic Community (EEC) and the
                European Atomic Energy Community (Euratom).

The Treaty of Rome was signed by Belgium, France, Federal Republic of Germany, Luxembourg, Italy and the Netherlands.

1958	Jan. 1	Rome treaties come into force: the EEC and Euratom are established.
	Mar. 19–21	First session of the European Parliament – Robert Schuman elected President.

1959   Jan. 1   First tariff reductions and quota enlargements in the EEC. Establishment of common market for nuclear materials.

Nov. 20   European Free Trade Association (EFTA) convention signed between Austria, Denmark, Norway, Portugal, Sweden, Switzerland and the United Kingdom.

1961   July 9   Greece signs association agreement with EEC (comes into force 1 Nov. 1962).

Aug. 1   Republic of Ireland applies for membership of EEC.

Aug. 10   UK and Denmark request negotiations aiming at membership of EEC.

Nov. 8   Negotiations with the United Kingdom open in Brussels.

Dec. 15   The three neutral countries (outside the NATO alliance) – Austria, Sweden and Switzerland – apply for association with EEC.

1962   Apr. 30   Norway requests negotiations for membership of EEC.

1963   Jan. 14   President de Gaulle declares that the United Kingdom is not ready for membership of EEC.

Jan. 29   UK negotiations with the EEC broken off.

July 1   Yaoundé Convention is signed, associating 18 independent states in Africa and Madagascar with the EEC for five years from 1 June 1964.

Sept. 12   Turkey signs association agreement with EEC (comes into force 1 Dec. 1964).

1964   Dec. 15   Council of Ministers adopts the Mansholt Plan for common prices for grains.

1965   Mar. 31   European Commission proposes that, as from 1 July 1967, all EEC countries' import duties and levies be

		paid into Community budget and that powers of European Parliament be increased.
	Apr. 8	Six sign treaty merging the Community Executives.
	May 31	European Commission publishes first memorandum proposing lines of Community policy for regional development.
	July 1	Council fails to reach agreement by agreed deadline on financing common farm policy; French boycott of Community institutions begins seven-month-long crisis.
	July 26	Council meets and conducts business without French representative present.
1966	Jan. 17	Six Foreign Ministers meet in Luxembourg without Commission present and agree to resume full Community activity.
	Nov. 10	UK Prime Minister Harold Wilson announces plans for 'a high-level approach' to the Six with intention of entering EEC.
1967	May 11	United Kingdom lodges formal application for membership of the European Economic Community.
1968	May 16	Second de Gaulle veto on British application.
1969	Apr. 25	General de Gaulle resigns as President of France.
	Dec. 2	At a Summit Conference at The Hague the Community formally agrees to open membership negotiations with the United Kingdom, Norway, Denmark and the Republic of Ireland on their applications of 1967.
1970	June 29	Talks begin in Luxembourg between the Six and the United Kingdom, Norway, Denmark and the Republic of Ireland.
1971	June 23	The Council of Ministers of the Community announces that agreement has been reached with the United Kingdom for the basis of the accession of the UK to the Communities.
	July 11–13	At a ministerial-level negotiating session, agreement is reached on major outstanding issues: the transitional period for the UK, Commonwealth Sugar, Capital Movements, and the common agricultural policy.

	Oct. 28	Vote in the House of Commons on the motion 'That this House approves Her Majesty's Government's decision of principle to join the European Communities on the basis of the arrangements which have been negotiated'. The voting figures in the House of Commons were 356 for, 244 against, majority of 112; in the House of Lords 451 for, 58 against, majority of 393.
1972	Jan. 22	Treaty of Accession was signed in Brussels between the European Communities (France, Belgium, Germany, Italy, Luxembourg and the Netherlands) on the one side and the United Kingdom, Denmark, Norway and the Republic of Ireland on the other.
	July 22	EEC signs free trade agreements with Austria, Iceland, Portugal, Sweden and Switzerland.
	Sept. 26	Rejection by Norway of full membership of EEC following a referendum.
	Dec. 31	The United Kingdom and Denmark withdraw from EFTA.
1973	Jan. 1	The United Kingdom, Republic of Ireland and Denmark join the EEC.
1974		Agreement that heads of government should meet three times a year under the title of the European Council.
1975		UK confirms membership of the EEC by referendum (see p. 26). Greece applies for membership.
	June	European Regional Development Fund set up.
1977		Portugal and Spain apply for membership of the EEC. Roy Jenkins appointed President of the Commission.
1979	May	European Monetary System introduced with a common European Currency Unit (ECU) linking the exchange rates of individual countries.
	June	First direct elections held to the European Parliament, when 410 members (MEPs) are elected.
1980		'Crocodile Group' established by MEPs wishing to see radical reform of the Community.

1981 Jan.   Greece becomes tenth member of the EEC: entry
                    to be phased over five years.

1983 June   Agreement at Stuttgart Summit on principle of
                    budgetary reform and reform of Common Agri-
                    cultural Policy (CAP); Common Fisheries Policy
                    established.

1984 June   Fontainebleau Summit agrees principles of budget-
                    ary discipline and UK budget rebate.

1985   Spain and Portugal sign accession treaty to join the
                    EC from 1 Jan. 1986. At summit meeting in Luxem-
                    bourg heads of state draw up main principles of a
                    'single Europe' defining 1992 as date for comple-
                    tion of frontierless internal market within the EC
                    with open frontiers, harmonization of regulations,
                    and free movement of labour and capital. These
                    principles were contained in the Single European
                    Act which also extended majority voting in the
                    Council of Ministers.

1986 Feb.   Single European Act signed by member states and
                    ratified by their parliaments. European flag adopted.

1988 Feb.   Delors reforms of the European budget agreed,
                    putting controls on farm spending and expanding
                    structural funds. Committee set up under Delors
                    to prepare plans for European Monetary Union
                    (EMU).
      Sept.   Mrs Thatcher makes Bruges speech attacking
                    attempts to create a European 'superstate'.

1989 Apr.   Agreement reached that first stage of EMU would
                    begin on 1 July 1990 with all 12 members begin-
                    ning to adhere to the EMS. Austria applies to join
                    EEC.
      June   Third direct elections to European Parliament.
                    Madrid Summit receives Delors Plan for three-stage
                    plan for European Monetary Union.

1990 Oct.   Britain joins EMS.
      Dec.   Inter-government Conference on EMU plans fur-
                    ther development of EMU.

1991	Oct.	Luxembourg plan for inter-government conference at Maastricht turned down.
	Dec.	Maastricht Summit gives Britain opt-out clauses over monetary union and Social Charter.
1992	June	Danes reject Maastricht in referendum. Mitterrand announces French referendum for 20 September. Irish ratify Maastricht Treaty. Britain and Italy forced out of ERM, following huge speculation. France, Holland, the United Kingdom, Spain, Germany and the Netherlands vote to ratify Maastricht Treaty.
	Nov.	Norway applies for EC membership.
1993	Jan.	Irish punt devalued. Spanish and Portuguese currencies follow. Single market comes into force. Austria agrees to seek EC membership.
	May	Danes finally approve Maastricht Treaty.
	Aug.	ERM bands widened to 15%, virtually destroying the existing system.
	Nov.	Maastricht Treaty on European Union takes effect. European Community (EC) now becomes European Union (EU).
1994	Feb.	EU agrees basis for discussing membership applications of Finland, Austria, Norway and Sweden.
	Mar.	The United Kingdom opposes dilution of veto rules consequent on EU enlargement.
	Apr.	Hungary and Poland apply for EU membership.
	May	European Parliament votes to approve accession treaties of Austria, Finland, Norway and Sweden.
	July	Jacques Santer of Luxembourg chosen to succeed Jacques Delors as President of European Commission. Austrian, Finnish and Swedish referenda approve EU membership. Norway votes against.
1995	July	Schengen Group, seven out of 15 EU states, remove all border controls.
	Nov.	Czech Republic, Latvia and Estonia apply for EU membership. EU Summit in Madrid confirms timetable for a single currency by 1999, to be named the 'euro'. Italy rejoins ERM.
1996	Mar.	British beef banned after UK government announces link between BSE ('mad cow' disease) and Creutzfeld-Jakob Disease in humans.

1996 Dec.   Plans for 'euro' currency and timetable for single
                        currency confirmed at Dublin Summit.

1997 Jan.   John Major effectively rules out the United King-
                        dom joining single currency in 1999 (now 'extremely
                        unlikely').
      May   Labour victory in British general election followed
                        by outline acceptance of 'Social Charter'.
      June   Amsterdam Treaty signed. European Union accepts
                        principle of negotiated entry for Cyprus, Slovenia,
                        Estonia, Hungary, Poland and the Czech Republic.

1998 May   EU summit agrees on 11 countries to become first
                        members of the single currency. All of EU mem-
                        bers join (except Denmark, Greece, Sweden and
                        United Kingdom).

Middle East

The Middle East since 1942

1942   British victory at El Alamein and pursuit of German and Italian forces across Libya into Tunisia (Oct.–May).

1943   Axis armies in Tunis surrender (May).
Independent Lebanese state established.

1944   Free French concede Syrian independence.

1945   Formation of the Arab League by Egypt and five other Arab states in March (see p. 211).
Fighting in Syria over delay in implementing French withdrawal.

1946   Syria becomes fully independent of the French.
Abdullah Ibn Hussein becomes King of Jordan.

1948   State of Israel established.

1948–49 Arab–Israeli War (see pp. 246–7).
Jordan seizes West Bank and part of Jerusalem; Egypt takes Gaza.

1949   Britain recognizes Mohammed Idris al-Senussi as Emir of Libya.

1950   Jordan annexes the West Bank of Palestine.

1951   Military government in Syria.
Idris becomes King of Libya as an independent state.
Iran nationalizes oil-fields and refineries, including giant Abadan complex.

1952   Anti-British riots in Egypt.

1953   Overthrow of the Egyptian monarchy; Egypt becomes a Republic and one-party state; disbanding of the Wafd and other groupings.

1954   Civilian rule returns to Syria.

1956   Gamal Abdel Nasser elected President of Egypt; nationalization of the Suez Canal and Suez invasion by Anglo–French and Israeli forces (see pp. 252–3).

1958   Anti-Western insurrection in Lebanon put down with assistance of US marines.
Military coup in Iraq, which is declared a Republic.

1961   Syria joins Egypt to form United Arab Republic (UAR).
Break-up of United Arab Republic.
Kuwait becomes an independent state; Iraq's claim to the territory resisted with the aid of British troops.

1963   *Coup d'état* brings radical Ba'ath Party to power in Syria as a socialist military government.

1964   Palestine Liberation Organization (PLO) founded by Yasser Arafat in Jordan.

1967   Six-Day War between Israel and Arab states (see p. 262).

1968   Coup in Iraq led by Saddam Hussein and Ba'ath Party.

1969   King Idris of Libya overthrown by military coup; Revolutionary Command Council led by Qadhafi proclaims a Republic, institutes Koranic law, a welfare system, and economic development programme. Colonel Nimeiri seizes power in the Sudan.

1970   Death of Nasser; Anwar Sadat becomes President of Egypt.
Palestine Liberation Organization moves headquarters to Beirut.
General Assad seizes power in Syria.

1973   Qadhafi takes control of foreign-held oil interests in Libya.
'Yom Kippur' War (see p. 266).
Arab oil boycott against the West.

1975   Outbreak of fighting in Beirut.

1976   Syrian troops enter Lebanon.

1977   President Sadat visits Israel in major gesture of reconciliation.
Short war between Egypt and Libya.

1979   Overthrow of the Shah's regime in Iran. Ayatollah Khomeini returns from exile in France to Iran and becomes head of government. Beginning of institution of Islamic fundamentalist regime in Iran and elimination of opponents.
Soviet Union invades Afghanistan and installs Babrak Karmal as head of new government; beginning of Mujaheddin resistance, partly influenced by Islamic fundamentalism.
Saddam Hussein becomes President of Iraq and begins purge of rivals and of Iraqi Shi'ite community.
Riots by Iranian fundamentalists in Mecca.

1980   Iran revives claim to Shatt-al-Arab waterway; Iraq bombs Iranian targets and launches land assault on Iran beginning Iran–Iraq War (see p. 272).

1981   President Sadat assassinated by Islamic fundamentalists. Islamic Commission fails to end Iran–Iraq War.

1982   Temporary cease-fire by Iraq fails to end the war (June).
Israeli troops invade Lebanon (see p. 267); PLO evacuated from Lebanon.

1983   Major Iranian offensive recaptures much of territory seized by Iraq.

1984   Iran–Iraq War escalates into attacks on Iran's Kharg Island oil installations by Iraqis and Iranian attacks on foreign ships entering the Persian Gulf *en route* to Iraq and Kuwait.

1987   'Intifada' begins among Palestinians on West Bank and in Gaza (see p. 275).
United States and Britain step up naval activity in the Persian Gulf; Iranian mine-layer seized.
Iraqi warplane accidentally hits American frigate.
Rioting by Iranian pilgrims in Mecca put down.

1988   American warship in Persian Gulf mistakenly shoots down civilian Iranian airliner (July).
UN-sponsored peace accord with Afghanistan, USSR, United States and Pakistan for removal of Russian troops from May 1988 to be completed by February 1989. Mujaheddin denounce cease-fire.
PLO declare Palestinian independence and renounce terrorism.

1989   Final removal of Russian troops from Afghanistan completed
            but fighting continues between Mujaheddin and Marxist Kabul
            government under Najibullah.
            Death of Ayatollah Khomeini; elections lead to his replace-
            ment as head of government by Hashami Rafsanjani.

1990   For the first time in Syria, independent candidates are allowed
            to run in the parliamentary elections, and they win 84 places
            in the 250-representative People's Assembly. The absolute
            majority (134 seats) is again gained by the Ba'ath Party (May).
            Northern and Southern Yemen are united as Yemen Republic
            (22 May).
            Iraqi troops suddenly attack and invade Kuwait (2 Aug.).
            Saddam Hussein later claims Kuwait as the 19th province of
            Iraq (28 Aug.). The UN Security Council endorses sanctions
            against Iraq (6 Aug.). The United States decides to send troops
            to the area (7 Aug.). Next day, Britain and other countries
            (among them several Arab states) join the US in its decision.
            Resolution 678 of the UN Security Council presents an ultima-
            tum to Iraq for it to withdraw its troops from Kuwait by 15
            January 1991 and – at the same time – authorizes the member
            states co-operating with Kuwait to use force against the aggres-
            sor if the ultimatum is not met (28 Nov.).

1991   The allied forces led by the United States begin their military
            action 'Desert Storm' against Iraq (17 Jan.). After the liber-
            ation of Kuwait and Iraq's total military defeat, military action
            ends with a cease-fire (28 Feb.). The truce concluding the war
            commences on 11 April.
            At the general elections in Egypt the governing National Demo-
            cratic Party wins 348 out of the 444 seats (Nov.).
            In Syria, Assad is again re-elected for seven years as the Pres-
            ident of the Republic.

1992   In Iran the moderate forces close to President Rafsanjani win
            the general election.
            The UN Security Council orders economic sanctions against
            Libya since Libya has declined to hand over to the United
            States and Britain the two Libyan men who are charged with
            having bombed PanAm Flight 103 in December 1988 (Apr.).
            In Saudi Arabia a 60-member Consultative Assembly is set up
            but the King still possesses absolute power.

1993   US forces launch bomb and rocket attacks on Iraq in response
            to Iraqi non-compliance with UN requirements (June).

Rafsanjani wins Iranian Presidential elections (June).
Palestine–Israeli agreement (Sept.).
UN Security Council restricts sanctions on Libya (Nov.).

1994   Outbreak of civil war in Yemen between northern and southern
        forces after failure to evolve a system of devolved government;
        northern forces capture Aden (July).
        Israel and Jordan sign peace treaty (26 Oct.) (see p. 46).

1995   Israel and PLO sign agreement on Palestinian self-rule in the
        West Bank (Sept.).
        Yitzhak Rabin, Israeli Premier, shot dead by a Jewish national-
        ist at peace rally (4 Nov.).

1996   Iraq and United Nations agree to the sale of Iraqi oil up to $4
        billion to pay for food and medicines.

1997   Libya agrees that two Libyans should be put on trial for bomb-
        ing of PanAm Flight 103, but disputes location of that trial.
        Iran and Syria end two decades of enmity (Nov.).

1998   Renewed crisis over UN inspection teams in Iraq defused by
        visit of Kofi Annan (Feb.).

Arab–Israeli conflict since 1948

1949   Armistice agreements are signed between Israel and Egypt,
        Lebanon, Jordan and Syria which set Israel's borders until 1967
        (Feb.–July). Israel admitted to United Nations. Ben Gurion
        elected Prime Minister.

1953   USSR breaks off relations with Israel.

1954   Israeli agents are caught and hanged in Cairo. Increasing
        fedayeen (Arab commando) attacks on Israel.

1955   Ben Gurion again becomes Prime Minister (Nov.).

1956   Nasser announces nationalization of Suez Canal Company
        (July). Israel invades Egypt (Oct.). British and French attack
        the Canal Zone but soon withdraw under super-power pres-
        sure (Nov.). United Nations Expeditionary Forces (UNEF) take
        over Canal Zone.

1957   Israel withdraws from Sinai and Gaza. UNEF stationed there.

1958–59   Al-Fatah founded.

1962   Adolf Eichmann, the Austrian Nazi war criminal, executed in
          Israel (May).

1964   Palestine Liberation Organization (PLO) formed under
          Nasserite auspices.

1967   Nasser closes Gulf of Aqaba to Israeli shipping (May). Six-Day
          War gives Israel a total victory over Egypt, Syria and Jordan
          (June, 5–10). UN Security Council Resolution 242 calls for a
          complete peace in Middle East (see p. 262).

1968–69   Re-organization of PLO with Yasser Arafat as chairman.

1969   Golda Meir becomes Prime Minister of Israel.

1970   Sadat succeeds Nasser in Egypt.

1972   Israeli athletes kidnapped at Munich Olympics by al-Fatah.

1973   Yom Kippur War (see p. 266). Egypt and Syria launch a sur-
          prise attack on Israel (Oct. 6–25).
          Arab–Israeli cease-fire agreement is signed (Nov.).

1976   Menachem Begin, former leader of Irgun, forms a government.

1977   Sadat visits Jerusalem (Nov.).

1978   Israel invades southern Lebanon (Mar.). Camp David summit
          in the United States between Carter, Begin and Sadat (Sept.).
          Arab summit in Baghdad denounces the Camp David Accords
          (Nov.).

1979   Egypt and Israel sign peace treaty which ends the state of
          war which had existed between the two countries since 1948
          (Mar. 26). Israel agrees phased withdrawal from Sinai.

1981   Israel annexes the Golan Heights (Dec.).

1982   Israel invades southern Lebanon as far as Beirut (June). PLO
          evacuate Beirut (Aug.). Massacre of Palestinians in refugee
          camps in Chatila and Sabra with Israeli complicity, causes out-
          cry in Israel. Begin agrees to full and independent inquiry and
          sets up Kahan commission (Sept.).

1983   Kahan commission report precipitates government crisis (Feb.).
        Begin resigns and is succeeded by Shamir (Sept.).

1985   Israel completes the withdrawal from Lebanon. Arafat and
        King Hussein reach accord on common approach to negotia-
        tions, but hijackings frustrate peace process.

1986   King Hussein repudiates PLO as partner in Middle East and
        closes PLO offices in Jordan.

1987   Arafat unites Palestinian movement at meeting of Palestinian
        National Council in Algiers (Apr.).
        Beginning of *intifada*, widespread unrest among Palestinians
        in occupied West Bank and Gaza Strip (Dec.).

1988   Jordan renounces role of representing Palestinians at future
        peace negotiations (June); PLO decares Palestinian independ-
        ence (Nov.) and acceptance of Security Council Resolutions
        242 and 338 recognizing Israeli independence.
        Arafat renounces terrorism at General Assembly of UN in
        Geneva.

1990   During disturbances in Jerusalem, Israeli forces shoot into
        crowd, killing 21 Palestinians and injuring 150 (Oct. 8).

1991   In the course of the Gulf War (see p. 277), Iraq launches 21
        Scud missiles at Israel.
        Washington and Moscow announce they will act as joint chairs
        of Middle East peace talks in Madrid (July); Madrid peace
        talks inconclusive.

1992   Likud victory in Israeli elections in July suggests promise of
        movement over the peace talks amidst extensive bilateral nego-
        tiations between the super-powers and the principal figures
        concerned.

1993   Israel and the PLO sign 'Declaration of Principles' in Wash-
        ington, following secret talks in Norway ('Oslo Accord').
        Israel recognizes the PLO and Arafat acknowledges Israel's
        right to exist in peace and security. The Declaration provides
        for Palestinian self-rule in the Gaza Strip and part of West
        Bank; Israel to retain sovereignty over Jewish settlements as
        interim stage (Sept. 13).

1994   Israel and Jordan sign peace treaty; Israeli–Jordanian border demarcated and Jordan agrees to non-return of Palestinian refugees in return for US aid (Oct. 26).

1995   Israel and PLO sign agreement in Washington for interim Palestinian self-rule in the West Bank under the Palestinian authority; withdrawal of Israeli troops from some West Bank towns, joint control of others, but Israelis retain control of 128 Jewish settlements (Sept. 28).

1996   Suicide bombings (Feb.) kill 57 Israelis; Israel retaliates by closing the West Bank and Gaza Strip and launching raids into south Lebanon (Apr.). Election of Likud's Benjamin Netanyahu as Israeli Premier (May). Renewed violence following opening of tunnel under Mosque in Jerusalem; over 50 Palestinians and some 18 Israelis killed (Sept.). Israeli Cabinet approves further settlement (Dec.).

1997   In spite of continuing violence, Arafat and Netanyahu agree to resume talks on remaining Oslo agenda (Feb.).

1998   Tony Blair visits Israel and organises new conference on Middle East peace in London (Apr.).

Africa

The Making of Modern Africa

1945 *Buganda*   Rioting in Buganda (later part of Uganda).
     Algeria   Nationalist demonstration at Setif in Algeria leads to rioting which is suppressed by French authorities – the 'Setif massacre'.
     Nigeria   Nigerian strike.
     Africa   Egypt, Liberia, Ethiopia and South Africa join the United Nations as founder members. Fifth Pan-African Congress held in Manchester. Arab League founded in Cairo.

1946 *Gold Coast*   Gold Coast Constitution published and becomes first British colony to have an African majority on legislative council (Mar.); Nkrumah attends Fabian Conference at Clacton, England (Apr.).
     Nigeria   Tour of Nigeria by NCNC leaders.
     Algeria   *Mouvement pour le Triomphe des Libertés Démocratiques* founded by Nessali Hadj in Algeria.
     Fr. Colonies   French abolish forced labour in the colonies; by Loi Lamine-Gueye French citizenship extended to all inhabitants of overseas territories. *Fonds d'Investissement pour le Développement Economique et Social* (FIDES) set up by France for development of the colonies.
     Gen. Africa   *Rassemblement Démocratique Africain* (RDA) founded by Bamako Congress.

1947 *Nigeria*   New Constitution for Nigeria with African majority on the legislature.
     Madagascar   Nationalist insurrection in Madagascar.
     Gold Coast   United Gold Coast Convention founded by Dr J.B. Danquah; Kwame Nkrumah appointed Secretary.
     Tanganyika   Groundnut scheme begun in Tanganyika.

1948	*Gold Coast*	Boycott of European goods in Gold Coast and riots in Accra (Feb.); Watson Report (June).
	Cameroon	*Union des Populations du Cameroun* (UPC) formed.
	Egypt	Egyptian war with Israel begins.
	South Africa	Smuts defeated by Malan in South African election. National Party begins implementation of apartheid policy.
	Tunisia	Bourguiba returns to Tunis.
	Senegal	*Bloc Démocratique Sénégalais* founded.
	Zanzibar	General Strike in Zanzibar.
1949	*Gold Coast*	Convention People's Party (CPP) founded in Gold Coast by Nkrumah (June); British Cabinet accepts Coussey report on Gold Coast (Oct.).
	Rhodesia/ Nyasaland	Victoria Falls Conference in favour of federation of Rhodesia and Nyasaland; African opposition to proposed federation.
	Buganda	Riots in Buganda.
	Nigeria	Industrial disturbances and shootings at Enugu colliery and riots in southern Nigeria.
	Somalia	United Nations decide that Britain should return Somalia to Italy as a United Nations' trust territory for ten years.
	Ivory Coast	Widespread disturbances in Ivory Coast.
1950	*Gold Coast*	'Positive Action' policy in Gold Coast.
	South Africa	Apartheid laws passed in South Africa.
	S.W. Africa	International Court rules that South West Africa should remain under United Nations' trusteeship.
	Congo	*Association des Bakongas* (Abako) formed in Belgian Congo.
	Nigeria	Action Group formed in Nigeria.
	Sierra Leone	Sierra Leone People's Party (SLPP) founded by Milton Margai.
1951	*Gold Coast*	Gold Coast constitution becomes operative (Jan.); CPP wins general election in Gold Coast; Nkrumah becomes 'leader of government business' (Feb.).
	Nigeria	Macpherson constitution enacted in Nigeria.
	Sierra Leone	Elections in Sierra Leone; Milton Margai in office.
	Libya	Libya becomes an independent kingdom.

1952	*Gold Coast*	Kwame Nkrumah becomes Prime Minister of the Gold Coast.
	Egypt	Army coup in Egypt; committee of 'Free Officers' forces King Farouk to abdicate; General Neguib takes power.
	Ethiopia	Eritrea federated with Ethiopia.
	Kenya	Following increased violence in Kikuyu areas, 'Mau Mau' Emergency proclaimed.
	South Africa	All non-whites compelled to carry passes in South Africa; non-white political organizations launch 'passive resistance' campaign against apartheid; leaders arrested.
1953	*South Africa*	Emergency powers introduced by the South African government against passive resistance; new racial laws introduced.
	Sudan	Anglo–Egyptian agreement on the Sudan.
	Egypt	Egypt becomes a republic; Party of National Liberation under Neguib becomes Egypt's sole political party.
	Kenya	Jomo Kenyatta and five others convicted of managing 'Mau Mau' in Kenya.
	Gold Coast	Nkrumah announces 'Motion of Destiny'.
	Nigeria	Nigerian Constitutional Conference held in London.
	Morocco	French deport Mohamed V from Morocco.
	Rhodesia/ Nyasaland	Central African Federation of Rhodesia and Nyasaland created.
	Tanganyika	Julius Nyerere elected President of Tanganyika African Association.
1954	*Egypt*	Colonel Nasser seizes power in Egypt.
	Nigeria	Nigerian Constitutional Conference in Lagos (Jan.). Federal system of government formalized by Lyttleton Constitution (Oct.).
	Gold Coast	CPP wins elections in Gold Coast and Britain promises independence.
	Tanganyika	Tanganyika African National Union (TANU) formed with Julius Nyerere as President.
	Egypt	Anglo–Egyptian agreement on the evacuation of Suez Canal Zone.
	Algeria	Beginning of Algerian War of Independence (see p. 251).

1955	*Africa*	Bandung Conference in Indonesia (see pp. 382–3).
	Morocco	Moroccan Army of Liberation attacks French posts in West Algeria (Aug.); King Mohamed V restored to throne by French (Nov.).
	Sudan	Beginning of armed rebellion in South Sudan.
1956	*Sudan*	Sudan becomes an independent Republic.
	Algeria	Violent settler demonstrations in Algiers.
	Fr. Colonies	Deferre introduces *loi cadre* providing for local autonomy in Black African territories.
	Morocco/ Tunisia	France recognizes independence of Morocco and Tunisia.
	Egypt	Nasser nationalizes the Suez Canal (July); Egypt–Israel War and British and French landings at Suez (Nov.).
	Cameroon	Civil war in Cameroon.
	Algeria/Nigeria	Oil discovered in Algeria and Nigeria.
	Northern Rhodesia	State of emergency declared in Northern Rhodesia after miners' strike in the copper-belt.
	Port. Guinea/ Cape Verde	African Party for the Independence of Guinea and Cape Verde (PAIGC) founded.
	Angola	Popular Movement for the Liberation of Angola (MPLA) founded.
1957	*Gold Coast/ Ghana*	Gold Coast becomes independent as Ghana.
	Nigeria	Second London Conference on Nigerian constitution; eastern and western regions of Nigeria become self-governing.
	Fr. West Africa	Houphouet-Boigny President of Grand Council of French West Africa.
	Sierra Leone	SLPP wins general election in Sierra Leone.
	Tunisia	Bey of Tunis deposed; Tunisia becomes a republic.
	Africa	Afro–Asian Solidarity Conference in Cairo.
1958	*Tunisia*	French military raids into Tunisia.
	Togo	Togo becomes independent.
	Nyasaland	Dr Hastings Banda returns to Nyasaland.
	Fr. Colonies	General de Gaulle advocates a federation with internal autonomy for French overseas territories as the French Community; at Brazzaville he announces independence for French Africa.

	Algeria	Algerian provisional government set up in Cairo.
	Guinea	Guinea becomes independent with Sekou Touré as President; all other French African territories remain within French Community.
	Sudan	Military coup led by General Abboud overthrows Sudanese government.
1959	*Nyasaland*	State of emergency declared in Nyasaland; Dr Banda imprisoned.
	Libya	Oil discovered in Libya.
	Nigeria	Northern Region of Nigeria becomes self-governing.
	Africa	Saniquellie meeting of Presidents Nkrumah, Tubman and Toure to plan union of free African states.
	Congo	Riots in Belgian Congo.
	Fr. Colonies	Senegal and Sudan demand independence and bring about the end of the French Community.
1960	*Africa*	Harold Macmillan's 'wind of change' speech in Cape Town.
		French atomic device exploded in the Sahara.
	South Africa	Demonstration on 21 March at Sharpeville fired on by South African police; 67 Africans killed.
	Congo	Belgian Congo becomes independent; *Force publique* mutinies; United Nations troops sent into Congo.
	Tanganyika	TANU wins election in Tanganyika and Julius Nyerere becomes Chief Minister.
	Nigeria	Nigeria becomes an independent state within the Commonwealth.
	Namibia	SWAPO (South West African People's Organization) founded.
1961	*Algeria*	Armed forces announce that they have taken over control of Algeria; OAS terrorism begins. Algerian peace talks begin in Evian, France.
	Congo	Lumumba, the Premier, murdered in Katanga.
	Angola	Rebellion begins in Angola against the Portuguese.
	Sierra Leone	Sierra Leone becomes an independent state within the Commonwealth.
	South Africa	South Africa becomes a republic and leaves the Commonwealth.

1961	*Tanganyika*	Tanganyika becomes an independent state within the Commonwealth.
	Rhodesia	Rhodesia Front party formed.
1962	*Rwanda/ Burundi*	Rwanda and Burundi become independent.
	Ghana	Plots against President Nkrumah's life in Ghana.
	Uganda	Uganda becomes an independent state within the Commonwealth.
	Algeria	Algerian independence agreed to at end of Evian peace talks.
	N. Rhodesia	First African government formed in Northern Rhodesia.
	Mozambique	Frelimo headquarters set up in Dar es Salaam, Tanganyika.
1963	*Congo*	End of Katanga secession in Congo.
	Togo	President Olympio killed in Togo coup.
	Africa	Organization of African Unity (OAU) formed in Addis Ababa by 30 heads of state.
	Rhodesia/ Nyasaland	End of the Federation of Rhodesia and Nyasaland.
	Kenya	Jomo Kenyatta becomes Prime Minister of Kenya.
	Zanzibar	Zanzibar becomes an independent state within the Commonwealth.
	Tunisia	French evacuate the naval base at Bizerta, Tunisia.
	Kenya	Kenya becomes an independent state within the Commonwealth.
1964	*Rwanda*	Massacre of Tutsi in Rwanda.
	Zanzibar	Revolution in Zanzibar; Sultan overthrown and Karume becomes President.
	East Africa	Army mutinies in Kenya, Tanganyika and Uganda; British troops called in to help restore order.
	Tanganyika	Union of Tanganyika and Zanzibar as Tanzania.
	South Africa	Rivonia trial in South Africa; Nelson Mandela, nationalist leader, sentenced to life imprisonment.
	Congo	Tshombe becomes President of Congo; revolts in Congo provinces; Belgian paratroops land at Stanleyville and elsewhere to rescue Europeans.
	Malawi/ Zambia	Malawi and Zambia become independent states within the Commonwealth.
	Mozambique	Frelimo begins armed struggle against Portuguese in Mozambique.

1965	*Fr. Colonies*	Organisation Commune Africaine et Malagache (OCAM) formed at conference of French-speaking heads of state at Nouakchott.
	Tanzania	Zhou Enlai (Chou En-lai), the Chinese Premier, visits Tanzania; one-party state adopted in Tanzania.
	S. Rhodesia	Rhodesia Front party wins general election in Southern Rhodesia; Ian Smith declares Rhodesia's 'unilateral declaration of independence' (UDI); UN Security Council embargo placed on Rhodesia.
	Congo	General Mobutu takes over complete power in Congo.
1966	*Africa*	Commonwealth Conference in Lagos.
	Nigeria	First military coup in Nigeria led by Ibo officers; a counter-coup follows six months later.
	Ghana	President Nkrumah deposed by military and police coup in Ghana.
	Uganda	Milton Obote seizes the Kabaka's palace in Kampala and makes Uganda into a centralized state.
	Botswana	Botswana becomes an independent state within the Commonwealth.
	Congo	Union Minière du Haut-Katanga taken over by Congo government.
1967	*Tanzania*	Arusha Declaration issued in Tanzania.
	Sierra Leone	Two army coups in Sierra Leone.
	Egypt	Arab–Israeli Six-Day War; Israelis occupy Sinai and defeat Egypt.
	Congo	Uprising in eastern and northern Congo ended by foreign mercenaries employed by Gen. Mobutu's central government.
	E. Africa	East African Community established by Kenya, Tanzania and Uganda.
	Nigeria	Secession of Eastern Region as independent state of Biafra; beginning of civil war in Nigeria (see p. 262).
1968	*Malawi*	Malawi establishes diplomatic relations with South Africa.
	Rhodesia	Start of guerrilla war in Rhodesia.
	Nigeria	Tanzania, Ivory Coast and two other African states recognize Biafran independence.

1968	*Eq. Guinea*	Equatorial Guinea becomes independent of Spain.
	Mali	Military coup in Mali.
	Swaziland	Swaziland becomes an independent state within the Commonwealth.

1969	*Libya*	King Idris deposed by a military coup in Libya; Colonel Qadhafi comes to power.
	Ghana	General election in Ghana returns Dr Busia as Prime Minister. Ghana expels thousands of aliens.
	Kenya	Serious political disturbances in western Kenya.

1970	*Nigeria*	End of Nigerian civil war.
	Libya	British withdrawal from military bases in Libya.
	Uganda	President Obote's 'Common Man's Charter' introduced in Uganda.
	Tanzania	Chinese offer aid to Tanzania to build railway from Dar es Salaam to Zambian copper-belt.
	Egypt	Aswan High Dam in Egypt comes into operation.

1971	*Uganda*	General Amin leads military coup which overthrows President Obote of Uganda.
	South Africa	Central African Republic recognizes South Africa and receives economic aid from it.
	Congo/Zaïre	Congo renamed Zaïre.
	South Africa	Declaration of Mogadishu issued by eastern and central African states stating their intention to continue the armed struggle to liberate South Africa.
	S. Rhodesia	African National Council (ANC) formed in Rhodesia by Bishop Muzorewa.

1972	*Zaïre*	'African authenticity' campaign launched by President Mobutu in Zaïre.
	Ghana	Army coup in Ghana; General Acheampong overthrows Busia government.
	S. Rhodesia	Pearce Commission in Rhodesia reports an overwhelming 'no' by African population to settlement proposals.
	Uganda	President Amin begins to expel Asians from Uganda.
	Sudan	Agreement in Sudan on 'southern problem'; regional autonomy granted to the south.

	Burundi	Hutu rising in Burundi suppressed with great loss of life.
	Madagascar	Military coup in Madagascar.
1973	*S. Rhodesia/ Zambia*	Zambia–Rhodesia border closed by President Kaunda.
	South Africa	Serious strikes by black workers in South Africa.
	S. Rhodesia	Prime Minister Smith of Rhodesia begins talks with African nationalists in an attempt to find some form of internal settlement.
	Egypt	Israel–Egypt War; Egyptian troops retake part of Sinai.
	Africa	Oil crisis brings great increase in prices for African states.
	Ethiopia	Widespread drought in Ethiopia.
1974	*Ethiopia*	Emperor Haile Selassie overthrown by a military coup; Dergue established to rule the country.
	Portuguese Colonies	Coup in Lisbon by army officers disillusioned with the African wars brings down the Caetano regime and begins the process of decolonization in the Portuguese empire in Africa.
	Guinea-Bissau	Guinea-Bissau becomes independent.
1975	*Africa*	Lomé Agreement signed between EEC and 37 African states.
	West Africa	Economic Community of West African States (Ecowas) Treaty signed by 15 states.
	Portuguese Colonies	Portugal's withdrawal from Africa; independence for Cape Verde Islands, São Tomé and Principé, Mozambique (June) and Angola (Nov.). Civil war in Angola.
	Zambia/ Tanzania	Tanzam railway officially opened between Zambia and Tanzania.
	S. Rhodesia	Four 'front-line' presidents at Quilemane pledge support for the Zimbabwe National Liberation Army.
	Nigeria	General Murtala Mohamed, President of Nigeria, assassinated in Lagos.
	Angola	South African troops invade Angola in support of UNITA forces.
1976	*South Africa*	Soweto riots and boycotts. Over 700 dead by 1977.
	Spanish Morocco	Spain withdraws from Western Sahara; territory partitioned between Morocco and Mauritania.

	Proclamation of Sahara Arab Democratic Republic, which through its armed Polisario Front wages a guerrilla war against both occupying states.
South Africa	South Africa declares Transkei independent.
Ethiopia	'Palace coup' in Addis Ababa.

1977	Djibouti	Djibouti became an independent state; final withdrawal of France from African territory.
	Zaïre	Invasion of Shaba province, Zaïre, by Katangese rebels.
	Ethiopia	Somali-supported forces invade Ogaden; serious fighting in the region. Cuban aid to Ethiopia in the war.
	Central African Rep.	Central African Empire proclaimed by Bokassa.
	Ethiopia	Widespread purge in Ethiopia by the Dergue.
	Nigeria	Constituent Assembly meets in Nigeria in preparation for a return to civilian government.

1978	Tunisia	Serious strikes in Tunisia.
	S. Rhodesia	Internal agreement in Rhodesia; transitional government formed.
	Ethiopia/ Somalia	Somali forces defeated by Ethiopia in Ogaden War; Ethiopia steps up its attacks on Eritrean nationalist forces.
	Guinea	Reconciliation of Guinea with France.
	Uganda	Uganda invasion of Kagera salient in north-west Tanzania.
	South Africa	'Muldergate' scandal in South Africa.
	Ghana	Gen. Acheampong deposed in Ghana.

1979	Tanzania/ Uganda	Tanzania supports Ugandan Liberation Front in invasion of Uganda; President Amin overthrown.
	Central African Rep.	Emperor Bokassa overthrown and Central African Republic re-established.
	Eq. Guinea	President Macias Nguema of Equatorial Guinea overthrown.
	Ghana	Junior officers coup in Ghana led by Flt-Lt. Rawlings; three former heads of state executed.
	Ghana/Nigeria	Elections in Ghana and Nigeria return both countries to civilian rule.
	S. Rhodesia/ Zimbabwe	Lancaster House talks in London on a settlement for Zimbabwe; the country reverts to British rule for a transitional period.

1980	*Zimbabwe*	Elections in Zimbabwe result in an overwhelming victory for Robert Mugabe's ZANU-PF party. Mugabe becomes Prime Minister of an independent Zimbabwe.
	Liberia	Military coup in Liberia by junior army officers.
	Uganda	Military-backed coup in Uganda deposes President Binaisa; Dr Obote winner in first Ugandan elections for 18 years.
	Tunisia/Libya	Tension between Tunisia and Libya after clashes at Gafsa.
	Chad	Unrest in Chad leaves 700 dead.
1981	*Zimbabwe*	Serious clashes between ZANLA and ZIPRA guerrilla forces.
	Egypt	President Sadat of Egypt assassinated in Cairo; Vice-President Hosni Mubarrak becomes President.
	Gambia	Coup in Gambia fails when British SAS free hostages held by rebels.
1982	*Uganda*	Further coup fails in Uganda.
	South Africa	Dr Treurnicht launches ultra-right-wing Conservative Party in South Africa.
	Kenya	Army coup in Kenya foiled.
	Lesotho	South African raid on Lesotho.
	Upper Volta	Army coup in Upper Volta.
1983	*Chad*	French troops sent to Chad to resist Libyan invasion.
	Ethiopia	Serious drought and famine in Ethiopia, affecting between two and four million people; world-wide mobilization of aid.
1984	*Nigeria*	Major-General Buhari takes power in Nigeria.
	Mozambique/ South Africa	Mozambique government signs peace accord with South Africa.
	Nigeria	Serious religious riots in Yola, northern Nigeria.
	Chad	French and Libyan forces agree to evacuate Chad.
	South Africa	P.W. Botha returned to power as President of South Africa; new tri-racial parliament opened.
1985	*Uganda*	President Obote overthrown by army coup in Uganda. Major-General Okello sworn in as country's new leader.

1985   *Nigeria*   Further coup in Nigeria.

        South Africa   Emergency legislation in South Africa; hundreds
                           detained and many killed following serious
                           violence and school boycotts. Press reporting re-
                           stricted. Botha promises reform but at own pace.

        Sudan   Sudanese army seizes power deposing President
                           Nimeiri.

        South Africa/   South African troops withdraw from southern
        Namibia   Angola; an independent government to be set
                           up in Namibia.

1986   *Uganda*   Yoweri Museveni backed by the National Re-
                           sistance Army overthrows President Okello in
                           Uganda.

        South Africa   South African backed coup in Lesotho; South Af-
                           rican raids into Zambia, Zimbabwe and Botswana.
                           Widespread boycotts and violence lead to state of
                           emergency; hundreds killed by government forces
                           and in communal violence; over 8,000 detained.
                           US applies trade sanctions and disinvestment by
                           US companies begins.

        Mozambique   President Machel of Mozambique killed in plane
                           crash; succeeded by Joachim Chissano.

        Libya   US air attack on Libya for complicity with
                           terrorism.

1987   *Tunisia*   President Habib Bourguiba overthrown in
                           Tunisia.

1988   *South Africa*   Nelson Mandela moved into hospital accom-
                           modation.
                           'Free Nelson Mandela' campaign intensifies.

1989   *Sudan*   Coup in Sudan.

        Namibia   Agreement on future independence of Namibia;
                           UN peace-keeping force supervises departure of
                           SWAPO guerrillas and South African forces.

        South Africa   Botha suffers stroke. De Klerk President follow-
                           ing narrow victory in general election. Several
                           killed during boycott and demonstrations dur-
                           ing elections.

1990   *South Africa*   30-year ban on ANC lifted; final release from
                           Victor Verster prison, Cape Town, of Nelson

Mandela (11 Feb.). Preliminary talks on future of South Africa between de Klerk and ANC delegation (May).

Namibia Namibia achieves independence (20 Mar.), becoming 50th member of Commonwealth and 160th member of United Nations.

Nigeria Coup attempt by junior officers failed (Apr.).

Liberia Civil war in Liberia. The rebels seize and murder President Doe (Sept.).

Tanzania After holding the position of head of state (1985), Ali Hassan Mwinyi takes leadership of the Tanzanian Revolutionary Party over from Nyerere.

Rwanda Tutsi guerrillas from neighbouring Uganda break into the country in order to overthrow the Hutu majority government in power (Oct.).

Chad The rebels, led by General Idriss Deby, overthrow President Hissène Habré who has been in power since 1982 (Dec.).

1991 *Somalia* President Mohamed Siad Barra, who came to power in October 1969 with a military coup, is forced to flee from the country because of an armed uprising (Jan.). Northern Somalian separatists proclaim the Republic of Somaliland (its border identical to the former British Somalia) (May).

Angola The last Cuban soldier leaves the territory of the country. In Lisbon, a 'final' cease-fire agreement is signed by the leader of MPLA, José E. dos Santos, and the leader of UNITA, Jonas Savimbi (May).

Ethiopia President Mengistu resigns and flees from the country. The dissident armed forces seize the capital (May); Meles Zenawi, the leader of the Ethiopian People's Revolutionary Democratic Front, forms a provisional government (June). An agreement is reached between the Eritrean People's Liberation Front and the new Ethiopian government that a plebiscite will be held in two years on the issue of the independence of Eritrea (July).

Africa In the Nigerian town of Abuja, heads of state of the Organization of African Unity sign a treaty for creating an African Economic Community by 2025 (June).

1991 *Zaïre*   President Mobutu allows a multi-party system and, as a result of the rebellions, he appoints the leader of the opposition, Etienne Tshisekedi, as Prime Minister (Oct.).

     Zambia   At the multi-party elections held for the first time after 18 years, the opposition Movement for a Multi-party Democracy wins against the United National Independence Party, led by President Kaunda. The new President is Frederick Chiluba (Nov.).

     Nigeria   Disturbances and bloody religious clashes between Christians and Muslims (Nov.).

1992 *Algeria*   After the first round of the multi-party parliamentary elections, the fundamentalist Front of Islam Salvation achieves a landslide victory (Dec. 1991); the election process is suspended (12 Jan.). A five-member Supreme State Council takes powers of head of state over from the resigned President Chadli Bendjedid. The head of this state council is Mohammed Budiaf (15 Jan.). After a ban on the FIS (Mar.), civil war threatens the country. Budiaf is assassinated (29 June). The new state council chairman is Ali Khafi.

     Tanzania   The Executive Committee of the Tanzanian Revolutionary Party accepts a resolution to introduce a multi-party system (Jan.).

     Libya   The UN Security Council orders economic sanctions against Libya after it rejected the extradition of Libyan terrorists (Apr.).

     Sierra Leone A military coup overthrows President Joseph Momoh, who has been in power since 1985. The new head of state is the President of the National Provisional Governing Council, Captain Valentine Strasser (May).

     Angola   The parliamentary and presidential elections are won by the MPLA and former President dos Santos (Sept.). UNITA declares the outcome fraudulent and fighting flares up once again.

     Madagascar The third unsuccessful coup attempt within three years takes place against the political regime of President Didier Ratsiraka (July).

     Mozambique In Rome an agreement on the discontinuation of the 15-year-long civil war is signed by President

Chissano and the leader of the Mozambique National Resistance Movement (RENAMO), Alfonso Dhlakama (Oct.).

Ghana   The first Presidential elections since 1979 are won by the President-in-Office, Rawlings (Nov.).

Africa   An international conference is held to provide support for starving African children (Nov.).

Somalia   Under the auspices of the UN, a large-scale humanitarian and military aid-action (Operation 'New Hope') is organized in order to revitalize the country devastated by civil war and famine (Aug.). The landing of 28,000 US troops begins (Dec.).

Kenya   The first multi-party parliamentary and Presidential elections held in 26 years are won by the governing party KANU and President Daniel Arap Moi (Dec.).

1993 *Zaïre*   Military rebellion breaks out in the capital (Jan.). President Mobutu appoints Faustin Birindwa as Prime Minister (Mar.).

Madagascar The Presidential election is won by the opposition's candidate, Albert Zafy (Mar.).

Niger   The first free Presidential election is won by the opposition Social Democrats' candidate, Mahamane Ousmane (Mar.).

Eritrea   On the basis of 95% of the votes of its population (Apr.), Eritrea separates from Ethiopia and becomes an independent republic (May). Its first President is the leader of the EPLF, Isajas Afeverki.

Somalia   Troops arrive from 20 member states of the UN, replacing the American soldiers (May). The clashes with armed gangs who control a great part of the country become more and more serious.

Malawi   At a plebiscite, the population votes for the introduction of a multi-party system (June).

Egypt   Mubarrak is elected as President for the third time (June). Terrorist attacks by Islamic extremists become more and more frequent, resulting in a dramatic decrease in the tourist industry.

Nigeria   The military leadership denounces the results of the Presidential election (June), yet President Babangida still renounces power to a civilian

	government (Aug.). Ernest Shonekan is soon replaced by General Sani Abacha, who dissolves all the democratically elected institutions and establishes the Provisional Governing Council (Nov).
Liberia	In Benin the representatives of the provisional government and various armed groups sign a peace treaty ordering an end to the war and announcing multi-party elections (July).
Rwanda	A peace treaty is signed ordering the end of civil war (Aug.). In order to ensure that the treaty is observed, UN forces arrive in the country (Nov.).
Togo	In an election boycotted by the opposition, General Eyadéma, who has been in power since 1967, is elected.
Burundi	During an unsuccessful coup attempt by Tutsi officers, President Melchior Ndadaye, who has been in power since June as a result of the first multi-party elections in the country's history, is assassinated (21 Oct.).
South Africa	At the CODESA negotiations an agreement is reached on the draft of an apartheid-free constitution, thus ending the rule of the white minority.
1994 *Algeria*	Failure of conference on transition to democracy (Jan.) when boycotted by all major parties leads to escalating terrorism and civil war.
Ghana	In widespread ethnic disorder, over 1,000 killed (Feb.).
Kenya	Death of Mr Odinga, leader of Kenyan opposition (Jan.); economic reforms launched to encourage foreign investment.
Zimbabwe	New opposition party formed (Jan.); exposure of corruption stemming from compulsory land purchase in 1992 by government officials (Mar.–May).
Mozambique	All-party defence force set up as part of process of reconciliation (Aug.). Multi-party elections lead to narrow victory for Frelimo under President Chissano (Oct.).
Angola	Renewed cease-fire agreement (Nov.).
Zambia	President Chiluba forced to restructure his Cabinet following accusations of corruption (Feb.); further resignations follow Western pressure (July).

	Ethiopia	New constitution adopted providing for a federal government of nine states.
1995	*Kenya*	Stock exchange opened to foreign investment (Jan.); arrest of opposition MPs (Jan.); Moi's government accused by Roman Catholic bishops of inept handling of economy (Apr.). Riots in Kibera district of Nairobi (Oct.); continuing Western pressure on Moi to reform his government and human rights record.
	Ethiopia	Ethiopian People's Revolutionary Democratic Front wins overwhelming victory in May elections; Republic of Ethiopia proclaimed (Aug.).
	Somalia	Final UN forces leave Somalia (Mar.).
	Algeria	Further attempts at reconciliation fail to halt cycle of terrorism and repression between Islamic forces and Algerian government.
	Nigeria	General Abacha postpones Constitutional Conference preparing the way for civilian rule and arrests opponents (Mar.); death sentences on 14 passed (July). Deadline for new elections set for 1 October 1998 but followed by execution of writer Ken Saro-Wiwa and eight other Ogoni activists amidst world-wide protests (Nov.).
	Ghana	Violent protests against economic reforms (May).
	Zimbabwe	Mugabe's ZANU-PF wins elections on low turnout (May); arrest of Rev. Sithole, accused of plotting against Mugabe.
	Mozambique	Reports of serious famine in central and southern Mozambique (Sept.); Mozambique admitted to the Commonwealth (Dec.).
	Angola	Meeting of President dos Santos and UNITA leader Jonas Savimbi (May) agrees to bring Savimbi into government as one of two joint Vice-Presidents in return for demobilizing UNITA forces. Demobilization halted (Dec.) after fresh clashes between UNITA and government forces.
	Zambia	President Chiluba continues process of dismissing corrupt ministers. Former President Kaunda arrested following his return to politics; then threatened with deportation. Closure of Lusaka University following student protests (Nov.), but President Chiluba swept to election victory after opposition boycotts election.

1996	*Zimbabwe*	President Mugabe wins Presidential elections but other candidates withdraw to reduce elections to a formality (Mar.). Government proposes further land reform (June). National strike of public sector workers forces large pay increases to be phased over three years (Aug.).
	Somalia	Factional fighting resumes (Apr.), with hundreds of casualties, including President Aidid who is shot while leading an attack (died 1 Aug.). Peace talks in November fail to prevent further fighting and over 300 casualties.
	Nigeria	United Liberation Front claims responsibility for death of General Abacha's eldest son in plane crash (Jan.). New opposition organization, the United Democratic Front of Nigeria, formed (1 Apr.); Abacha purges army and air force (Mar.–May) and on 4 June gunmen kill wife of Chief Abiola, winner of quashed 1993 elections. Following demonstrations, government closes Ibadan University; Abacha government also puts down Muslim demonstrations in the north with heavy casualties (Sept.).
	Ghana	President Rawlings wins sweeping victory in Presidential elections over John Kufor of the People's National Convention Party; in the National Assembly elections Rawlings's National Democratic Congress wins 130 of the 200 seats (Dec.).
	Kenya	President Moi responds to Western criticism of human rights violations by establishing a standing committee to investigate human rights violations (May).
	Zaïre	Zaïre government accuses Rwanda of organizing anti-Mobutu guerrillas; fighting breaks out in eastern Zaïre forcing Hutu refugees in Zaïre to flee. As Hutu refugees stream back to Rwanda, the anti-Mobutu alliance advances deeper into Zaïre led by Laurent Kabila. President Mobutu returns to Kinshasa (17 Dec.) from France where he was undergoing surgery.
	Mozambique	IMF loan of $110 million to underpin economic recovery.
	Angola	Demobilization of UNITA forces proceeds, but Savimbi rejects his place in the government,

forestalling attempts to set up a government of national unity (Sept.).

1997	*Zaïre*	President Mobutu returns to France (8 Jan.). Rebel forces enter Kinshasa and overthrow Mobutu regime (Apr.).
	Nigeria	Further arrests and trials of opposition groups; 12 dissidents charged with treason (Mar.).
1998	*Nigeria*	Mass boycott of elections (Apr.). Death of General Abacha (June).
	Algeria	EU concern over human rights abuses.

The Development of South Africa

1941   Afrikaner Party formed.

1942   Draft Constitution for South African Republic published; coup attempt discovered and suspects interned.

1943   United Party wins general election.
ANC Youth League founded; formation of Non-European Unity Movement.

1945   Native (Urban Areas) Consolidation Act.

1946   Asiatic Land Tenure and Indian Representation Act; passive resistance by Indians begins.
African mineworkers strike.
Adjournment of the Native Representative Council.

1948   National Party under Malan and Afrikaner Party defeat Smuts.
National Party begins implementation of apartheid policy.
Apartheid introduced on surburban railways in the Cape Peninsula.

1949   Prohibition on Mixed Marriages Act.
Rioting between Zulus and Indians in Durban.
ANC adopts Programme of Action.

1950   Apartheid laws passed including Immorality Act, Population Registration Act, Group Areas Act, Suppression of Communism Act. Communist Party dissolves itself.
Stay-away campaign in Transvaal, 18 people killed by police.

1951   Bantu Authorities Act; Separate Representation of Voters Act removes 'Coloureds' from common voters' roll.

1952   Separate Representation of Voters Act ruled invalid. Passive resistance campaign against apartheid; arrest of campaign leaders and riots in various cities.

1953   Emergency powers introduced by South African government against passive resistance movement, including Criminal Law Amendment Act and Public Safety Act.
Reservation of Separate Amenities Act, Bantu Education Act, and Native Labour Act introduced. Strikes by African workers illegal. National Party retains majority in general election.
Liberal Party formed.

1954   Malan retires, Strijdom becomes Prime Minister.
Federation of South African Women established.

1955   Formation of South African Congress of Trade Unions.
Congress of the People Act. Cape Town adopts the 'Freedom Charter'.

1956   Parliament validates removal of 'coloured' voters from common roll.
ANC accepts Freedom Charter.
Mass women's anti-Pass Law demonstration in Pretoria.

1957   Amendments to Native Laws permit government to forbid African–White contacts. Stay-away protests and bus boycotts.

1958   National Party wins 103 of 163 parliamentary seats.
Death of Strijdom; Verwoerd succeeds as Prime Minister.

1959   Apartheid introduced into higher education.
Formation of Pan-Africanist Congress (PAC).
Progressive Party formed when eleven United Party members resign.
ANC decides on anti-Pass Law campaign.

1960   African representation in Parliament abolished; riots in Durban.
Harold Macmillan makes 'Wind of Change' speech in Cape Town.
Demonstration at Sharpeville fired on by police; 67 killed.
Police announce suspension of Pass Laws (21 Mar.).

ANC announces general strike; state of emergency proclaimed; ANC and PAC banned; strike broken by detention of thousands of people; Pass Laws reimposed.
Attempted assassination of Verwoerd.
Majority of voters vote in favour of a Republic.

1961   South Africa becomes a Republic and leaves Commonwealth (31 May); renewed state of emergency leads to thousands of detentions.
Verwoerd appoints Vorster Minister of Justice and Police.
Sabotage campaign begun by National Liberation Committee.
National Party wins general election.

1962   Sabotage Act makes sabotage a capital offence; house arrests introduced and banning powers extended.
United Nations votes for economic and diplomatic sanctions against South Africa.

1963   90-day detention without trial introduced.
Arrest of leaders of sabotage movement at Rivonia, Johannesburg.
Transkei given self-government after first elections for Transkei Legislative Assembly.

1964   Rivonia trial in South Africa; Nelson Mandela sentenced to life imprisonment. Several sabotage trials; members of African Resistance Movement gaoled.

1965   Members of underground Communist Party gaoled; period of detention without trial extended to 180 days.

1966   National Party wins general election.
Verwoerd assassinated; Vorster becomes Prime Minister.

1967   Terrorism Act provides for indefinite detention without trial; Planning Act controls influx of black population into urban areas.

1968   Progressive Party drops black members and becomes all-white party. Liberal Party dissolves itself.
'Coloured' Representatives in Parliament abolished.

1969   Bureau of State Security (BOSS) established.

1970   Bantu Homelands Citizenship Act offers Africans citizenship only of homelands.

1971   Declaration of Mogadishu issued by eastern and central African states, stating their intention to continue the armed struggle to liberate South Africa.
President Banda of Malawi makes state visit to South Africa; Ivory Coast delegation also visits South Africa.

1972   Black People's Convention formed; Africans in 'white areas' brought under Bantu Affairs Administration Boards.

1973   Strikes in Durban.

1974   National Party wins general election.

1975   South African troops cross into Angola in support of UNITA forces; clashes with Cuban troops sent to support Angolan independence.

1976   South African troops withdraw to Namibian border following clashes with Cuban forces. Troops withdrawn into Namibia.
Uprising in Soweto black township; spreads to Cape Town.
Widespread boycotts, rioting, detentions and shootings. Over 700 deaths.
Transkei declared 'independent' state by South Africa.

1977   Steve Biko dies while under arrest.
Mandatory arms embargo imposed on South Africa by UN Security Council.
National Party wins 145 seats to Progressive Party's 16 at general election.
Bophuthatswana declared 'independent' by South Africa.

1978   Eventual independence for Namibia accepted.
'Muldergate' scandal erupts discrediting government; Vorster retires as Prime Minister and is succeeded by P.W. Botha.

1979   Vorster resigns from position as State President following further 'Muldergate' revelations.
African trade unions recognized.
Talks between ANC and Chief Buthelezi, the Zulu leader, in London.

1980   Zimbabwe gains independence and elections result in over-whelming victory for Robert Mugabe's ZANU-PF party.
School boycotts in the Cape; 45 people shot in disturbances.
Sabotage destroys South Africa's major oil from coal plant.

1981   School boycott ends.
Major cross-border raids by South African forces into Angola and Mozambique.
Negotiations with Western powers over future of Namibia.

1982   Dr Treurnicht and 16 rebel members of National Party form ultra-right-wing Conservative Party.
Constitutional proposals set up 'Coloured' and Indian participation in central and local government.

1983   Referendum supports political rights for 'Coloureds' and Indians but not Africans.
Banning orders tightened on Mrs Winnie Mandela.

1984   P.W. Botha returned to power as President of South Africa; new tri-racial Parliament opened.
Peace accord with Mozambique to end cross-border raids.

1985   Government announces end to ban on mixed marriages.
Hundreds detained under emergency laws in South Africa; many deaths in rioting and school boycotts.
Botha pledges reform programme but at own pace.
Severe restrictions put on press.
South African troops withdraw from southern Angola in preparation for independence of Namibia.

1986   South African coup in Lesotho; South African raids into Zambia, Zimbabwe and Botswana.
Serious rioting in Alexandra township.
Bishop Desmond Tutu of Johannesburg calls for international sanctions against South Africa.
Strike by over million black workers in Johannesburg.
Crossroads squatters' camp broken up.
Indefinite State of Emergency declared; over 8,000 black activists, trade unionists and church leaders arrested.
Commonwealth 'Eminent Persons' Group predicts 'bloodbath' if reform delayed. US votes for sanctions against South Africa and disinvestment by US companies begins.

1987   National Party wins election, gaining 123 of 166 seats, but Conservative Party with 22 displaces Liberals as official Opposition.

1988   Nelson Mandela moved into hospital accommodation; campaign to free him from custody gathers pace.

1989   P.K. Botha suffers stroke; F.W. de Klerk becomes President following elections in which both Conservatives and Liberals make gains. Serious disturbances and mass boycotts of elections lead to several deaths.

1990   30-year ban on ANC lifted. Nelson Mandela released from Victor Verster prison, Cape Town (Feb). Triumphant return to Soweto. First talks of de Klerk with ANC delegation on future of South Africa.
The South African Communist Party is re-established (July).
The ANC makes an agreement with the government that it will cease armed rebellion against the government in exchange for the rehabilitation of those ANC members banished for political reasons and for the dissolution of the state of emergency (Aug.). The apartheid law which forbids the simultaneous appearance of black and white people in public places is abolished (Oct.). Clashes between ethnic-based black political organizations competing with one another become more and more frequent. In 1990 alone, approximately 3,000 people die in these clashes.

1991   Parliament abolishes the laws on race segregation according to place of residence, as well as the laws restricting the possession of land (June). Parliament abolishes the law on the classification of the population according to race. With this measure, apartheid ceases to exist (June). Mandela is elected as the President of the ANC (July). The Republic of South Africa joins as a member of the Anti-Nuclear Proliferation Treaty (July).
General amnesties are offered to those who were banished because of apartheid (Aug.). This measure involves 40,000 persons.
National round-table negotiations begin on plans for the future constitution (Conference for a Democratic South Africa, CODESA) (Dec.).

1992   The European Community withdraws the last of the sanctions against South Africa (Jan.).
At a plebiscite, 68.7% of the white population votes for the continuation of de Klerk's reforms (Mar.).

Five white members of Parliament leave their own party and join the ANC (Apr.).

In Boipatong town, armed members of the Zulu tribe kill 39 black people (women among them). As a result of this massacre, various serious disturbances break out in the town (June).

1993   A Polish immigrant kills Chris Hani, the Chief Secretary of the Communist Party and the former leader of the armed wing of the ANC (13 Apr.). After the murder, bloody clashes break out in several cities of the country.

The General Assembly of the UN cancels the sanctions against South Africa (Oct.).

F.W. de Klerk and Nelson Mandela share the Nobel Peace Prize (Oct.).

At the CODESA negotiations the new anti-apartheid draft of the Constitution, which discontinues the rule of the white minority, is signed (18 Nov.). (An agreement is reached on the eradication of Bantustans (homelands); from 1 January 1994 their inhabitants again receive South African citizenship.) The Constitution becomes applicable after the general election on 27 April 1994. However, it is rejected by both the Zulu Inkatha Freedom Party and the white far-right Afrikaner Resistance Movement (AWB).

President Clinton signs the bill abolishing American sanctions against South Africa (23 Nov.).

A provisional governing council is formed in which there are both white and black representatives (7 Dec.). The task of the council is to govern the country until the elections.

The white majority Parliament endorses the new Constitution elaborated at the CODESA negotiations, thus creating equal rights for whites and blacks for the first time in the history of the country (22 Dec.).

1994   At the parliamentary elections, the ANC almost achieves an absolute majority; the runner-up is the National Party (Apr.). The new President of the country is Nelson Mandela, and one of its new deputy Presidents is F.W. de Klerk.

Wave of strikes and continuing clashes between ANC and Inkatha supporters (July). Land Rights Act attempts redress of grievances of those who had lost land (Nov.).

1995   Death of Joe Slovo (Jan.). 'Fresh start' announced by Mandela and de Klerk following bitter disputes with ANC over indemnities from prosecution for police and government members. Murder

charges laid against former Defence Minister, Gen. Malan, and 10 other officers.
Draft of new Constitution presented (22 Nov.).

1996   Trial of Malan and 15 co-defendants on charges of murder and conspiracy against ANC supporters ends in acquittal (Mar.–Oct.). New Constitution approved (7 May). De Klerk announces withdrawal of National Party from government at end of June to normalize politics. Thabo Mbeki designated successor to Mandela. New Constitution signed (10 Dec.).

1997   F.W. de Klerk announces his retirement from active politics (Sept.)

1998   P.W. Botha refuses to attend hearing of Truth and Reconciliation Committee and is threatened with prosecution.

Asia

China since 1949

1949   Chinese People's Republic proclaimed (1 Oct.). A People's Political Consultative Conference passes Organic Laws and a Common Programme setting up a multi-national, communist state with Chairman of the Republic as head of state. Mao Zedong first Chairman (Oct.). Chinese Nationalist forces take refuge on Formosa (Taiwan) and garrison islands of Quemoy, Matsu and Tachen.

1950   Outbreak of Korean War (June). Chinese troops intervene to repulse United Nations counter-offensive into North Korea (Oct.); 250,000 Chinese troops cross the Yalu River and force retreat of UN forces. Chinese invasion of Tibet (Oct.). Agrarian Law dispossesses landlords and gives land to peasants who are grouped together into collectives.

1951   UN condemns Chinese aggression in Korea (Feb.); further Chinese offensives held by UN troops (Feb.–May). Tibet signs agreement giving China control of Tibet's affairs (May); Chinese troops enter Lhasa (Sept.).

1953   Cease-fire in Korea (July). First Five Year Plan nationalizes most of industry.

1954   Permanent constitution established; guarantees dominant place of the Communist Party.

1955   US Navy evacuates 42,000 Nationalist troops and civilians from Tachen Islands following artillery bombardment.

1956   Mao encourages criticism of regime – 'a hundred flowers' to bloom.

1958   Shelling of Quemoy leads to US military build-up. Mao Zedong inaugurates Second Five Year Plan and 'Great Leap Forward' to increase industrial production by 100% and agricultural output by 35%. Collective farms to be grouped in communes and industrial production based on them.

1959   Great Leap Forward yields disappointing results following huge dislocation of production; major famine in parts of China. Uprising in Tibet put down and Dalai Lama forced to flee to India (Mar.).

1960   Quarrel with Russia over 'revisionism' leads to withdrawal of Russian advisers and technical support.

1962   Chinese war with India in Himalayas (see p. 257).

1964   China explodes first atomic bomb.

1966   Beginning of Cultural Revolution, attempt to introduce Maoist principles in all aspects of life. Red Guards inaugurate attacks on all hierarchic and traditional features of society. Intellectuals and others forced to undergo 'self-criticism'.

1967–68   Schools and educational institutions closed by Red Guards.

1969   Chairman of Republic, Liu Shaoqi disgraced. Border clash with Soviet Union (see p. 263).

1971   Lin Biao, deputy Prime Minister, disgraced and reportedly killed in air crash. Later reports suggest that he was executed.

1973   Deng Xiaoping, disgraced in Cultural Revolution, becomes Deputy Prime Minister.

1975   New constitution replaces single head of state with a collective, the Standing Committee of the National Peoples' Congress.

1976   Death of Mao Zedong (Sept.); Hua Guofeng becomes Chairman and Prime Minister. Begins action against 'Gang of Four' and Mao's widow, Jiang Qing.

1977   Deng Xiaoping reinstated. Jiang Qing expelled from Party and sentenced to death, but sentence commuted to life imprisonment. More pragmatic economic policy adopted.

1978   New constitution moderates constitution of 1975. China opens diplomatic relations with the United States.

1979   Chinese invasion of Vietnam (see p. 272). Demonstrations for greater freedom in Beijing. Cultural Revolution denounced as a disaster.

1980   Zhao Ziyang becomes Prime Minister, succeeding Hua Guofeng.

1981   Hu Yaobang succeeds Hua Guofeng as Chairman of Party until post abolished in 1982.

1982   New constitution approved for Communist Party abolishing posts of Chairman and Vice-Chairman. New constitution for China as a whole approved, increasing powers of Prime Minister.

1983   National People's Congress elects Li Xiannian to revived post of President; Deng Xiaoping chosen as Chairman of new State Military Commission. 'Rectification' campaign against corrupt officials.

1984   Modernization drive reverses emphasis on collective agriculture; relaxation of central quotas and price controls; factories given greater autonomy. Agreement reached with Britain on future of Hong Kong (Sept.).

1985   Five Year Plan announces slow down in pace of economic reform; fewer cities open to foreign investment and party control reasserted.

1986   Campaign for greater democracy suggested by leadership; student demonstrations in Shanghai and Beijing (Dec.).

1987   Backlash against reform; Hu Yaobang forced to resign and succeeded by Zhao Ziyang. Agreement with Portugal on return in 1999 of Macao to China. Thirteenth Party Congress (Oct.) leads to retirement of eight senior politicians and promotion of younger technocrats. Li Peng becomes Prime Minister in place of Zhao Ziyang who is confirmed as General Secretary.

1988   Demand for greater speed in reform by Zhao Ziyang (Mar.), but inflation and industrial unrest lead to freeze on price reforms for two years (Sept.).

1989   Death of Hu Yaobang (Apr.) leads to student demands for his rehabilitation; sit-ins and demonstrations in several cities.

100,000 students march through Beijing (27 Apr.). Students occupy Tiananmen Square (4 May). Hunger strike among students (13 May); million-strong pro-democracy march through Beijing (17 May); Li Peng announces martial law (20 May). Chinese troops disperse students in Tiananmen Square, causing over a 1,000 deaths, and similar protests quelled in other Chinese cities (4 June). Chinese government arrests thousands of pro-democracy supporters in spite of world outrage at events of 4 June.

1990   The state of emergency is lifted (Jan.). After Deng Xiaoping's resignation, Jiang Zemin becomes President of the Central State Military Committee (Apr.).

1991   The state of war and the cold war confrontation between Taiwan and China end (May).

1992   China joins the Anti-Nuclear Proliferation Treaty (Mar.). China and South Korea establish full diplomatic relations with one another (Aug.).

1993   At the National People's Assembly, Deng Xiaoping's political line – a mix between economic reforms and political conservatism – is dominant. The constitution is modified; one of its clauses claims that 'the Chinese state is working on creating a Socialist market economy' but the clauses referring to the leading role of the Communist Party and the dictatorship of the proletariat are not altered. Jiang Zemin is elected as the President of the country; thus the leadership of the Party, the state, and the army is concentrated in his hands (Mar.). In Beijing, a Chinese–Indian Treaty is signed (Sept.).

1994   Premier Li Peng institutes price controls on basic commodities (Mar.). Quarrel between the United States and China over human rights leads to defiant China suppressing dissidents (Apr.). Nonetheless, US grants China 'most favoured nation' status (May). New labour law introduced guaranteeing eight-hour day and minimum wage but ending guarantee of a job for life.

1995   Jiang Zemin secures position amidst growing rumours of Deng's ill-health. Jiang Zemin welcomes talks with Taiwan (Oct.) while carrying out military manoeuvres against Taiwan.

China announces new Five Year Plan doubling national output by the year 2000 (Sept.). Further appointments made strengthening Jiang Zemin's position.

1996   China threatens missile attacks on Taiwan (Jan.), then makes missile tests in March and deploys troops opposite island of Quemoy, though later gives a private assurance (Mar.) that will take no direct action. Deng confined to hospital (May). Meeting of Communist Party leaders in July and August confirms Jiang's position, confirmed at Party Central Committee's meeting in October.
China accuses Dalai Lama (June) of acting as a 'puppet of international forces'.

1997   Death of Deng Xiaoping (19 Feb.). Jiang Zemin assumes authority. China assumes sovereignty over Hong Kong (July).

Japan since 1945

1945   Atomic bombing of Hiroshima and Nagasaki. Japan accepts the terms of surrender (Aug.). Authority passes to General MacArthur as Supreme Commander of the Allied Powers (SCAP).

1946   Emperor Hirohito makes the 'Human Being Declaration' (Jan.). New Japanese constitution is promulgated (Nov.); women obtain the vote. War crimes trials begin.

1947   Japanese women obtain rights to property and divorce.

1948   Tojo, Hirota and five others are executed for war crimes (Dec.).

1950   The 'Red Purge' – dismissal of suspected communist sympathizers from office – begins (Feb.). The Japanese create the National Police Reserve (Oct.).

1951   Japanese peace treaty with Allies is signed in San Francisco. Japan signs the Mutual Security Agreement with the United States (Sept.).

1952   The occupation of Japan ends.

1955   Liberals and Democrats in Japan merge to form the Liberal Democratic Party.

1956   Japan is admitted to the United Nations.

1960   Demonstrations occur when the Mutual Security Agreement with the United States is ratified (May). Prime Minister Ikeda announces the 'Income Doubling Plan' (Sept.).

1964   Olympic Games held in Tokyo (Oct.).

1967   Demonstrations against Japan's support for the US's involvement in the Vietnam War (Oct.).

1968   Students occupy Tokyo University Campus (June–Jan. 1969).

1970   Mutual Security Agreement with the United States renewed (June). Mishima Yukio attempts a coup and then commits suicide (Nov.).

1971   The United States agrees to return Okinawa to Japan (June).

1976   Investigation into 'Lockheed affair' begins (Apr.).

1978   Treaty of Peace and Friendship between China and Japan signed (Aug.).

1980   Prime Minister Masayoshi Ohira dies (23 June). Zenko Suzuki forms government (July).

1982   Nakasone forms government (Nov.).

1983   Ex-Prime Minister Tanaka found guilty on charges arising from the Lockheed affair.

1986   Nakasone wins outright victory in general election after period of dependence on minority parties (July).

1987   Takeshita chosen to succeed Nakasone (Oct.).

1989   Death of Emperor Hirohito (7 Jan.); succeeded by Crown Prince Akihito. Takeshita forced to resign over 'Recruit' scandal (Apr.). Foreign Secretary Uno succeeds, but forced to resign over sexual allegations (July). Toshiki Kaifu becomes Prime Minister (9 Aug.).

1990   The LDP once more wins an absolute majority at the parliamentary elections (Feb.). At his official accession to the throne,

Emperor Akihito announces the commencement of the Heisei, the 'age of peace' (Nov.).

1991   Negotiations commence on the possibility of repossessing the Kuril Islands which were seized by the Soviet Union during the last days of the Second World War (Mar.). Kiichi Miyazawa succeeds Kaifu as the leader of the LDP and the government (Nov.).

1993   The opposition's vote of no-confidence overthrows the Miyazawa government (June). More than 40 MPs leave the LDP and create a new opposition group. At the unscheduled early elections, the LDP remains the strongest party but loses its majority in parliament (July). The opposition creates a seven-party coalition government (for the first time since 1955), headed by Hosokawa (Aug.). In his speech to the parliament, Hosokawa apologizes to the peoples of Asia for Japan's deeds during the Second World War.

1994   Reform programme accepted in upper house (Jan.). Resignation of Hosokawa following corruption allegations (Apr.); short-lived Hata administration succeeded by first socialist premier, Murayama (29 June). Electoral reform package passed (Nov.) replacing multi-member constituencies with single-member constituencies. New opposition party Shinshinto (New Frontier Party) formed (Dec.).

1995   Government wins no-confidence debate amidst concern about how to deal with anniversary of end of war in Europe (June).

1996   Murayama resigns (5 Jan.); succeeded by Hashimoto, restoring LDP rule. Joint Japanese–American declaration emphasizes Japan's role in regional security (Apr.).
In October elections LDP under Hashimoto take 239 out of 500 Diet seats, forming minority government.

1997   Growing financial turmoil in South-East Asia casts doubts on Japanese banking system (Nov.).

The Indian sub-continent since 1942

1942   Sir Stafford Cripps sent from Britain with proposals to rally Indian opinion at time of Japanese advances in South-East Asia. British promise independence at the end of the war and a new constitution. British offer Muslims and princely states the prospect of staying out of the projected India union and forming separate unions. Both Congress and Muslim League reject offer. Congress begins 'Quit India' movement and most of its leaders arrested, meanwhile Jinnah consolidates his position as head of the Muslim League.

1945   New Labour government in Britain announces that it seeks 'an early realization of self-government in India'.
In Indian elections, Muslim League strengthens its hold on Muslim areas.

1946   British offer full independence to India. Negotiations between British Cabinet Mission and Indian leaders fail to agree a plan acceptable to both Congress and Muslim League.
Muslim League declares 'direct action' to achieve Pakistan.
'Direct Action Day' (16 Aug.) provokes massive communal rioting in Calcutta leaving over 4,000 dead; spreads to Bengal, Dacca and Bihar.
Lord Wavell succeeds in drawing Congress and League representatives into an interim government but fails to bring Congress and the League into a Constituent Assembly to create a constitution for a united India.

1947   British government declares (Feb.) it will transfer power not later than June 1948 to responsible Indian hands; announces that Lord Mountbatten to replace Lord Wavell as Viceroy. Serious communal rioting in the Punjab and elsewhere in anticipation of partition (Mar.).
Mountbatten becomes Viceroy (Mar.) and advances the date for the transfer of power from June 1948 to 15 August 1947. British government announces plan for the partition of India and the creation of two separate dominions of India and Pakistan; the plan is accepted by Congress, the Muslim League and the Sikhs (June).
India and Pakistan become independent states (15 Aug.); Nehru and Liaquat Ali Khan lead their respective Cabinets. Rioting and massacres accompany the partition process in which up to 250,000 people die.
Mass exodus of refugees across new borders between India and Pakistan in the west, smaller flow and less violence in the east between India and East Pakistan.
Hindu ruler of Kashmir 'accedes' his largely Muslim state to India.

Sikh Punjab is scene of some of most serious violence; two million Sikhs flee across border into India where they begin demand for greater autonomy or independence for Sikh Punjab.

1948   Assassination of Mahatma Gandhi in Delhi (30 Jan.) Ceylon becomes independent dominion (Feb.). Mohammed Ali Jinnah dies.
UN truce line established in Kashmir leaving one-third of the state in Pakistan hands and two-thirds in Indian.
Pakistan demands implementation of UN-sponsored plebiscite on future of Kashmir.
India sets up Atomic Energy Commission.

1950   Constitution of Indian Union promulgated. India becomes a Republic within British Commonwealth.

1951   Liaquat Ali Khan assassinated.

1951–52   First national general election in India confirms Congress Party dominance.

1954   Indo-Chinese Treaty.

1955   Bulganin and Khrushchev visit India.

1956   States Reorganization Act in India.
New constitution declares Pakistan an Islamic state.
India begins Second Five Year Plan and builds several steel plants.

1958   Ayub Khan becomes President of Pakistan.

1959   Tibetan uprising; Dalai Lama flees to India.
Treaty of India and Pakistan over Indus waters.

1960   Union of Kashmir with India.

1962   Indian and Chinese forces fight in the Himalayas; cease-fire agreed (see p. 257).

1964   Death of Nehru; Lal Bahadur Shastri Prime Minister.

1965   Indo–Pakistan War (see p. 259).
Tamil riots against Hindi language; English confirmed as official language of India.

1966   Death of Shastri; Mrs Indira Gandhi becomes Prime Minister. Indian government redraws boundary of the Punjab state to give it a majority of Sikhs, and attempts to appease Sikh separatist agitation.

1969   Yahya Khan President of Pakistan.

1971   Revolt in East Pakistan, which secedes from Pakistan to form state of Bangladesh (Mar.). Revolt crushed (May), but guerrilla war continues.
Growing clashes with India and state of emergency in Pakistan (Nov.). War with India (Dec.) and Indian invasion of East Pakistan; Pakistan accepts cease-fire and recognizes new state of Bangladesh (see p. 265).
Adjustment of border between India and Pakistan in Kashmir agreed at Simla Conference.
Zulfikar Ali Bhutto becomes President of Pakistan.
State of emergency declared in Ceylon following disclosure of plot to overthrow government by ultra-left JVP. Over 1,000 killed and 4,000 arrested.

1972   Pakistan leaves the Commonwealth.
Ceylon adopts new constitution and becomes Republic of Sri Lanka.

1973   Bhutto becomes Prime Minister of Pakistan under new constitution.

1975   State of emergency declared in India because of growing strikes and unrest; opposition leaders arrested.
Sheikh Mujibur Rahman, ruler of Bangladesh, is deposed and killed in military coup; Khandakar Mushtaque Ahmed is sworn in as President.

1977   Morarji Desai leads Janata Party to victory over Mrs Gandhi in general election – first defeat of Congress Party since independence.
Bhutto overthrown after allegations of ballot-rigging; constitution suspended.
Serious rioting in Tamil areas of Sri Lanka. Constitution amended to strengthen President.

1978   General Zia ul-Haq becomes President of Pakistan.

1979   Ex-Prime Minister Bhutto executed.

1980   Indira Gandhi wins election victory for Congress Party and returns to power.

1981   State of emergency declared in Sri Lanka because of attacks by Tamil Liberation Tigers.

1983   General Ershad assumes Presidency of Bangladesh.
Serious violence between Sinhalese and Tamils in Sri Lanka.
Emergency rule invoked in Punjab to suppress Sikh terrorism.

1984   Indian troops storm Golden Temple in Amritsar, centre of Sikh separatists (June). Indira Gandhi assassinated by Sikh members of her bodyguard and her son, Rajiv Gandhi, becomes Prime Minister; Hindu attacks on Sikhs kill an estimated 2,000 people. Talks between Tamils and President Jayawardene of Sri Lanka break down; conflict escalates in Tamil areas.
Fighting between Indian and Pakistan troops on the Sianchin Glacier in Kashmir (see p. 274).
General Zia confirmed as President by referendum.

1985   Further heavy fighting in Kashmir.
President Zia confirmed in office for five-year period.

1986   Tamils kill Sinhalese in further terror raids in Sri Lanka.
Ms Benazir Bhutto returns to Pakistan and demands end to martial law and free elections.

1987   Emergency rule imposed in Punjab.
Rajiv Gandhi and President Jayawardene sign an accord (July) offering more autonomy to Tamil areas; Indian peace-keeping force invited into Sri Lanka to supervise. Attacks on Indian army lead to assault on Tamil strongholds in Jaffna peninsula.

1988   President Zia of Pakistan killed in air crash (Aug.); Benazir Bhutto wins largest number of seats in general election (Nov.) and becomes Prime Minister.

1989   Amid continuing violence in Sri Lanka the Indian forces agree to withdraw.
Pakistan rejoins the Commonwealth.

1990   The withdrawal of Indian forces from Sri Lanka is completed (Mar.). In Pakistan, President Khan dismisses Benazir Bhutto, who is charged with abuse of power (Sept.). The parliamentary

84   POLITICAL HISTORY

elections are won by the Islamic Democratic Association (Oct.);
Mian Nawaz Sharif becomes the new Prime Minister (Nov.).
Chandra Sekhar is the new Prime Minister of India (Nov.).

1991   The Pakistani parliament endorses laws reinforcing Islamic
jurisdiction (May). Rajiv Gandhi is assassinated in a bomb attack
(29 May). After the election victory of the Indian National
Congress, the new President of the party, Narasimha Rao, forms
a government (June).

1992   Hindu extremists destroy the Babri mosque in Ayodhya (Dec.);
in the religious clashes that spread across the country some
1,200 people are killed.

1993   In Sri Lanka, fanatics of the LTTE murder President Premadasa
(1 May). His successor is the former Prime Minister, Dingiri
Banda Wijetunge. In bomb attacks in Bombay and Calcutta
more than 200 people are killed (Mar.). Concluding the year-
long power struggle, President Khan and Prime Minister Sharif
– under pressure from the chief-of-staff – resign (July). After
the election victory of her party, Ms Bhutto forms a government (Oct.); her candidate, the former minister of foreign
affairs, Faruk Ahmed Leghari, is elected as the President of
the country.
Indian security forces close in on the Hazratbal mosque in
Srinagari (Kashmir) (Oct.). The armed Kashmir separatists,
who have seized the building earlier, peacefully surrender in
November.

1994   Strikes and demonstrations in New Delhi against India's accession to the Uruguay Round of the General Agreement on Tariff
and Trade (Apr.). Rao government loses support in state elections (Dec.).
Benazir Bhutto acquitted of corruption charges which had
caused her downfall in August 1990 (Feb.). Opposition parties
withdraw from National Assembly (Aug.).
In Sri Lanka, following elections (Aug.), Chandrika Bandaranaike Kumaratunga is appointed Prime Minister. She wins Presidential elections (Oct.) and appoints her mother, Mrs Sirimavo
Bandaranaike, Premier (Nov.).

1995   Rao government wins vote of censure over Kashmir (Apr.).
Chief Minister of Punjab killed by Sikh separatists (May).
Religious and factional clashes in Pakistan lead to over 1,000
deaths by July; breakdown of negotiations between Benazir

Bhutto and opposition over political violence (Aug.). Army officers arrested for plotting Islamic fundamentalist coup.

Breakdown of cease-fire with Tamil Tigers (Apr.) leads to continuing clashes. President Kumaratunga offers plan for Tamil autonomy (Aug.), but rejected. Sri Lankan government forces surround Jaffna, the Tamil stronghold.

1996   In India, £11 million corruption scandal prompts resignation of three ministers and early general election (Jan.). Congress Party heavily defeated in elections (Apr.–May) which sees rise of Hindu nationalist Bharatiya Janata Party (BJP) and National Front–Left Front (NF–LF). Short-lived BJP government under Atal Behari Vajpayee followed by NF–LF administration led by H.D. Deve Gowda (June). After persistent bribery allegations, Rao resigned leadership of Congress Party (Sept.).

Imran Khan founds new party (Apr.) in Pakistan (the Justice Movement) amidst continuing violence. Benazir Bhutto dismissed from office by President Leghari following murder of her brother (leader of a breakaway faction) and renewed charges of corruption.

Sri Lankan army seals off Jaffna peninsula (Apr.) but Tamil bomb attacks continue in Colombo and elsewhere (July).

1997   Congress Party removes support from government and Gowda stands down as leader; replaced by Inder Kumer Gujral (Apr.). In Pakistan, the military form a ten-member security council giving armed forces a formal advisory role in government (Jan.). In elections in February the Pakistan Muslim League won a decisive victory under Nawaz Sharif over Bhutto's Pakistan People's Party (Feb.). Benazir Bhutto faced with new charges of corruption (Sept.).

1998   BJP government formed in India after inconclusive election. India and Pakistan explode nuclear devices.

Indo-China and Vietnam, 1945–75

1945   Japanese disarm French forces and an 'independent' Vietnam with Bao Dai as Emperor is proclaimed (Mar.).

Japan surrenders (15 Aug.); demonstrations in Hanoi spread throughout the country.

Communist-dominated Viet Minh seize power; Ho Chi-minh declares Vietnam independent and founds Democratic Republic of Vietnam (2 Sept.).

1945   French troops return to Vietnam and clash with Communist forces; Chinese occupy Vietnam north of 16th Parallel (Sept.).

1946   Franco–Chinese accord allows French to re-occupy northern half of Vietnam (Feb.).
France recognizes the Democratic Republic of Vietnam as a free state within the French Union (6 Mar.).
Breakdown of March accord. French bombard Haiphong and Ho Chi-minh calls for resistance to the French; beginning of Indo-Chinese War with surprise attack on French bases (Dec.).

1948   French create 'State of Vietnam' with Bao Dai as head of state (June).

1949   Laos recognized as an independent state linked to France (July).
Cambodia recognized as an independent state linked to France (Nov.).

1950   Communist China and the Soviet Union recognize the Democratic Republic of Vietnam led by Ho Chi-minh (Jan.). United States announces military and economic aid for the French in Vietnam, Laos and Indo-China (May).

1951   Communist offensive takes most of northern Vietnam.

1954   Battle of Dien Bien Phu (Mar.–May) ends in French defeat.
Ngo Dinh Diem appointed Premier in South Vietnam by Bao Dai (July).
Geneva Agreements on Vietnam, partitioning Vietnam along 17th Parallel (July).
Peace agreement signed in Geneva providing for a referendum in 1956 to decide government of a united Vietnam is not signed by the United States or South Vietnam (Aug.).
South-East Asia Treaty Organization (SEATO) set up in Manila to combat communist expansion (8 Sept.).
Viet Minh assume formal control of North Vietnam (Oct.).

1955   United States begins direct aid to government of South Vietnam (Jan.); US instructors requested (May).
Cambodia becomes an independent state (Sept.).
Diem deposes Bao Dai and proclaims the 'Republic of Vietnam' (Oct.).

1956   Prince Sihanouk renounces SEATO protection for Cambodia (Feb.).
Communists share power in Laos (Aug.).

1957   Communist Pathet Lao attempt to seize power in Laos (May).

1958   Communist guerrillas involved in attacks in South Vietnam.

1959   Communist Party Central Committee sanctions greater reliance on military activity; Communist underground activity increases; Diem government steps up repressive measures.
Communist Pathet Lao seek to gain control over northern Laos.

1960   Communist National Liberation Front of South Vietnam formed (Dec.). US advisers number 900.

1961   Pro-Western government formed in Laos; North Vietnam and Soviet Union send aid to communist insurgents.
President Kennedy decides to increase military aid and advisers in South Vietnam (Nov.); US personnel reach over 3,000 by end of year.

1962   'Strategic hamlet' programme begun in South Vietnam (Feb.)
Australian 'Military Aid Forces' arrive in Vietnam (Aug.); American forces reach 11,000 (Dec.).

1963   Buddhist riots in Hué against government repression; seven monks commit suicide by fire as part of protests; martial law introduced (May–Aug.).
American-backed coup overthrows Diem (1–2 Nov.); General Duong Van Minh takes over (6 Nov.).
President Kennedy assassinated; Lyndon Johnson takes over (22 Nov.).

1964   Military coup led by Major-General Nguyen Khanh replaces Minh government (Jan.).
US destroyers attacked in Gulf of Tonkin (2–4 Aug.); US aircraft retaliate against targets in North Vietnam (4 Aug.); US Congress passes Gulf of Tonkin resolution authorizing use of US forces in South-East Asia 'to prevent further aggression' (7 Aug.).
Number of US forces in South Vietnam reaches 23,000 by end of year.

1965   Sustained aerial bombardment of North Vietnam begins, 'Operation Rolling Thunder' (Mar.).
US marines arrive at Da Nang (Mar.); the United States announces that its troops will now be used routinely in combat (June).

1965   Period of political turmoil ends with Air Vice-Marshal Nguyen Cao Ky as head of South Vietnamese government (June). US military strength reaches 181,000 by end of year; widespread anti-war demonstrations in the United States.

1966   Air attacks on North Vietnam resume after 37-day pause (31 Jan.).
B-52 bombers first used (Apr.).
Buddhist and student protests against the war in Hué, Da Nang and Saigon, put down by South Vietnamese troops (Mar.–June).
American strength reaches 385,000 by end of year.

1967   'Operation Cedar Falls' against Communist-held 'Iron Triangle' north of Saigon (Jan.).
'Operation Junction City', biggest land offensive of the war along Cambodian border (Feb.).
General Nguyen Van Thieu elected President; Ky Vice-President (Sept.).

1968   Communist 'Tet' offensive against major cities of South Vietnam (30–31 Jan.); intense fighting in Hué and Saigon. 'My Lai Massacre' (Mar.).
President Johnson announces withdrawal from presidential race and will seek negotiations (31 Mar.).
Paris Peace Conference opens (31 May).
Bombing of North Vietnam halted (31 Oct.).
President Nixon elected and promises gradual troop withdrawal (Nov.).

1969   American troops in Vietnam reach peak of 541,500 (31 Jan.). US raids against North Vietnam resume (5 June); Nixon announces first withdrawal of 25,000 combat troops (8 June). Death of Ho Chi-minh (3 Sept.).
Laotian government requests US aid to resist Communist pressure (Oct.).
Widespread anti-war demonstrations in the United States (Nov.–Dec.); 250,000 march in Washington (15 Nov.).

1970   US backed Lon Nol ousts President Sihanouk in Cambodia (Mar.); Khmer Republic set up. American and South Vietnamese forces invade Cambodia (Mar.–Apr.).
Anti-war demonstrations in American universities; six students shot at Kent State (4 May).

US ground troops withdraw from Cambodia (June).
US forces in Vietnam 335,800 (Dec.).

1971   South Vietnamese forces invade Laos to attack Ho Chi-minh
        Trail (Feb.–Mar.).
        Nixon announces withdrawal of 100,000 US troops by end of
        year (7 Apr.); 500,000 anti-war demonstrators march in Wash-
        ington (24 Apr.).
        Australia and New Zealand announce withdrawal of troops from
        South Vietnam (Aug.).
        Nguyen Van Thieu confirmed as President in one-man 'elec-
        tion' (3 Oct.).

1972   Nixon announces reduction of US forces to 69,000 by 1 May
        (13 Jan.).
        North Vietnamese forces invade South Vietnam (30 Mar.); re-
        newed bombing of North authorized (Apr.); mining of ports
        ordered (May).
        Last American ground combat troops leave Vietnam (Aug.).
        Peace negotiator Henry Kissinger reports substantial agreement
        on 9-point plan with North Vietnam (26 Oct.); US suspends
        talks (13 Dec.); bombing of North Vietnam resumed (18 Dec.);
        bombing halted after North Vietnamese agree a truce (30 Dec.).

1973   Kissinger and Le Duc Tho sign peace agreement ending the
        war (27 Jan.).
        Cease-fire in Laos concluded (21 Feb.).
        Last US military personnel leave Vietnam (29 Mar.).

1974   War in South Vietnam resumes (Jan.).
        Communist insurgents advance on capital of Cambodia (July).
        President Nixon resigns (Aug.); US Congress puts ceiling on
        military aid to South Vietnam.

1975   North Vietnamese forces launch offensive; the north and cen-
        tral highlands fall to communists and South Vietnamese forces
        forced into headlong retreat (Mar.).
        Cambodian capital, Phnom Penh, falls to communist insurgents
        (17 Apr.).
        President Thieu resigns and flees to Taiwan (21 Apr.); North
        Vietnamese troops enter Saigon (29 Apr.) and unconditional
        surrender announced by President Van Minh (30 Apr.).
        Pathet Lao consolidate communist take-over of Laos; Laos be-
        comes a communist state (3 Dec.).

South-East Asia since 1945

1945   *Indonesia*   Unilateral declaration of independence by Republic of Indonesia (17 Aug.); Sukarno becomes President (18 Nov.).

        Vietnam   Ho Chi-minh seizes power and declares Vietnam independent.

1946   *Thailand*   King Ananda Mahidol shot dead; succeeded by Bhumibol Adulyadej (June).

        Philippines   Philippines gain independence from United States.

        Indonesia   Linggadjati agreement between Dutch and Indonesian Republic, agreeing Republic's control of Java, Madura and Sumatra as part of a federal United States of Indonesia in a Netherlands-Indonesian Union (17 Nov.).

        Vietnam   Outbreak of Indo-Chinese War between French and Vietminh (see p. 246).

        Malaya   Malayan Union established (Apr.); Sarawak and North Borneo ceded to Britain (May–July).

1947   *Indonesia*   Formal signature of Linggadjati agreement (Mar.), but breakdown leads to 'police action' by Dutch (July).

        Philippines   Untied States signs 99-year lease for air and naval bases (Mar.).

1948   *Vietnam*   French create 'state of Vietnam' (June).

        Burma   Burma becomes independent (Jan.).

        Malaysia   Malayan Union becomes Federation of Malaya (Feb.); beginning of Communist insurgency (May).

        Indonesia   Dutch and Indonesian truce agreement (Jan.), but communist rebellion leads to renewed fighting (Nov.–Dec.).

1949   *Laos*   Laos recognized as independent state (July).

        Cambodia   Cambodia recognized as independent state (Nov.).

        Indonesia   Peace Conference at the Hague opens (Aug.); transfer of sovereignty to United States of Indonesia agreed (Nov.) and formal independence granted (Dec.).

1954   *Vietnam*   Defeat of French forces at Dien Bien Phu (May); Vietnam partitioned (July).

1955	*Cambodia*	Cambodia becomes fully independent state (Sept.).
1957	*Malaysia*	Malay states become independent as Federation of Malaya (Aug.).
	Indonesia	Sukarno introduces authoritarian rule as 'guided democracy'.
1958	*Indonesia*	Revolt in Sumatra and Sulawesi.
1960	*Malaysia*	Official end to 'emergency' (July).
1962	*Vietnam*	Major build-up of US forces in Vietnam begins.
	Burma	Military coup led by General Ne Win (Mar.); Revolutionary Council set up and publishes programme, 'Burmese Way to Socialism'. Burma Socialist Programme Party set up and all others abolished (July).
1963	*Malaysia &* *Indonesia*	Federation of Malaysia established (Sept.); beginning of 'confrontation' with Indonesia (see p. 257).
	Vietnam	Diem regime overthrown (Nov.).
1964	*Vietnam*	Gulf of Tonkin incident and Tonkin Resolution (Aug.).
1965	*Philippines*	Ferdinand E. Marcos elected President (Nov.).
	Indonesia	Following abortive coup, Communist Party banned and thousands of members killed.
	Cambodia	Sihanouk breaks relations with United States (May).
	Singapore	Singapore becomes independent from Malaysia (Aug.).
1966	*Indonesia*	General Suharto assumes emergency powers (Mar.).
	Malaysia	Agreement signed ending 'confrontation' with Indonesia (June).
1967	*Indonesia*	President Sukarno hands over power to Suharto (Feb.).
1968	*Vietnam*	'Tet' offensive by Communists (Jan.).
	Indonesia	General Suharto elected President (Mar.) and introduces 'New Order'.
1969	*Philippines*	Marcos becomes first President to be re-elected.
	Vietnam	American troops in Vietnam peak at 542,000 (Jan.); gradual withdrawal begins after pledges by President Nixon.

1970   *Cambodia*   US-backed General Lon Nol ousts President Sihanouk (Mar.); US and South Vietnamese forces cross into Cambodia (Apr.).

1972   *Philippines*   Marcos declares martial law and arrests Benigno Aquino along with several hundred of opposition (Sept.).

        Burma   Ne Win and 20 army commanders retire and become civilian members of government.

        Vietnam   Beginning of peace talks on Vietnam (Oct.).

1973   *Burma*   New Constitution agreed by referendum (Dec.).

        Vietnam   Americans sign peace agreement with North Vietnam (Jan.); last US military personnel leave (Mar.).

        Laos   Cease-fire in Laos (Feb.).

        Thailand   Civilian rule returns to Thailand after resignation of military rulers following death of 400 student protesters (Oct.).

1974   *Burma*   Military rule formally ended and Revolutionary Council dissolved; Ne Win becomes first President of Burma as a one-party Socialist Republic (Mar.).

1975   *Cambodia*   Phnom Penh falls to Communist Khmer Rouge (Apr.).

        Vietnam   Fall of Saigon to North Vietnamese forces and end of Vietnamese War (Apr.).

1976   *Cambodia*   Democratic Kampuchea established under Pol Pot, who inaugurates programme of revolutionary upheaval and terror (Jan.).

        Burma   Attempted coup by young officers fails (July).

        Thailand   Army seizes power after violent clashes between police and students (Oct.).

1979   *Cambodia*   Vietnamese invasion of Cambodia deposes Pol Pot and installs Heng Samrin as head of People's Republic of Kampuchea. Khmer Rouge and Pol Pot take up guerrilla war.

        Vietnam   Chinese troops launch invasion of Vietnam; withdraw after bitter fighting (Feb.–Mar.).

1980   *Philippines*   Opposition leader Benigno Aquino allowed to leave for United States (May).

	Thailand	General Prem Tinsulanonda sets up civilian-military government.
1981	*Philippines*	Martial law lifted (Jan.).
	Burma	General San Yu becomes new President.
	Thailand	Unsuccessful coup attempt in Bangkok (Apr.).
1982	*Cambodia*	Forces opposed to Heng Samrin regime form a coalition at Kuala Lumpur, including Khmer Rouge, Prince Sihanouk and Son Sann (June).
1983	*Philippines*	Benigno Aquino assassinated at Manila airport on his return from the United States (21 Aug.).
1984	*Indonesia*	Muslim riots in Jakarta suppressed by troops (Sept.).
	Cambodia	Vietnamese launch major offensive on guerrilla bases on Thai border; UN calls on Vietnam to withdraw from Cambodia/Kampuchea (Oct.).
	Thailand	Attempted coup in Thailand against Prem Tinsulandonda fails (Sept.).
1986	*Philippines*	Corazón Aquino, widow of Benigno Aquino, elected President of Philippines; President Marcos goes into exile (Feb.); coup attempts in July and November suppressed.
1987	*Philippines*	New Constitution approved (Feb.); coup suppressed (Aug.).
	Cambodia	Talks between Prince Sihanouk and Vietnamese Prime Minister Hun Sen in Paris on Cambodian settlement.
	Indonesia	Official Golkar Party wins landslide victory in general election (Apr.).
1988	*Burma*	Student demonstrations against Ne Win's government suppressed by the army (Mar.–July); Ne Win resigns as Party Chairman and San Yu as President (July). Brigadier-General Sein Lwin becomes President and Party Chairman and imposes martial law but resigns after riots (Aug.). General Saw Maung takes power but declares commitment to elections; BSPP becomes National Unity Party.

1988   *Cambodia*   Vietnam announces it will remove all troops by December 1990 (May); Jakarta talks on peace settlement (June); resumed in Beijing (Aug.) and Jakarta (Feb. 1989) fail to reach earlier date for withdrawal.

1989   *Burma*   Military government announces elections will take place in May 1990 (Feb.).

     Cambodia   Vietnamese forces begin withdrawal (Sept.).

1990   *Vietnam*   Indicating an improvement in Chinese–Vietnamese relations, the Friendship Pass on the border of the two countries, which has been closed, is reopened (Sept.).

     Burma   The elections are won by the opposition National League for Democracy led by Aung San Suu Kyi, but the soldiers do not hand over power. The name of the country is changed to the Union of Myanmar (Dec.).

1991   *Thailand*   A new military coup takes place (Feb.).

     Laos   The new Constitution of the country reinforces the leading role of the Laotian People's Revolutionary Party and hands over power to the head of state. After Souphanouvong's resignation, Kaysone Phomvihane, the former Chief Secretary of the LPRP and former Prime Minister, is elected as the President of the People's Republic (Aug.).

     Vietnam   At the Beijing Summit between the leaders of the two countries, Chinese–Vietnamese relations are normalized (Sept.).

     Myanmar   The Nobel Peace Prize is awarded to the opposition politician, Aung San Suu Kyi, who is being held under house arrest (Oct.).

     Cambodia   In Paris, the treaty concluding the Cambodian civil war is signed. Until the general elections, the country is governed by the Supreme National Council, which comprises the representatives of four formerly opposing camps, and whose President is Prince Norodom Sihanouk (Oct.).

1992   *Vietnam*   The endorsed new Constitution still contains reference to the leading role of the Communist Party but restricts its power; the collective governing body is replaced by a President; the Prime Minister gains greater power (Apr.).

Myanmar	General Sau Maung, who has been in power since September 1988, resigns (May). Several imprisoned politicians are set free.
Philippines	Former Defence Minister, General Fidel Ramos, who is supported by Mrs Aquino, is elected as the President of the country (May). Since the Senate rejected the extension of the leasing contract with the United States in September 1991, the last member of the US army leaves the military base in Subic Bay, thus concluding the approximately 100-year-long US military presence in the Philippines (Nov.).
Thailand	After the elections resulting in the victory of the leftist opposition, Chuan Leekpai forms a coalition government (Sept.).
1993 *Indonesia*	Suharto is elected as President for another five years (Mar.).
Cambodia	After the parliamentary elections in May, won by Prince Sihanouk's party FUNCINPEC which defeated the governing Cambodian People's Party (until 1991 called the Cambodian People's Revolutionary Party), a new provisional government is formed, co-presided over by Prince Norodom Ranariddh (Sihanouk's son) and Hun Sen (June). In accordance with the new Constitution, Cambodia becomes a constitutional monarchy; its monarch is Norodom Sihanouk (Sept.).
Vietnam	As the first step in the complete cancellation of the sanctions against Vietnam, the United States significantly reduces the trade embargo against Vietnam, which has existed for 19 years (Sept.).
1994 *Vietnam*	US trade embargo lifted (Feb.); agreement on Australian aid to Vietnam (Apr.).
Cambodia	Meeting in North Korea between Khmer Rouge leaders and Government (May), but cease-fire proposals rejected by Khmer Rouge leader, Khiev Samphan.
Myanmar	House arrest of Aung San Suu Kyi extended into 1995 by the military junta on the grounds that her release would 'create unrest' (Feb.).
Indonesia	Widespread industrial unrest (Feb.–Mar.). Renewed riots in East Timor (July and Nov.).

1995	*Vietnam*	Announcement by President Clinton of establishment of full diplomatic relations with the United States (July). Talks with China lead to reopening of railway links, resolution of border dispute, and economic co-operation (July).
	Cambodia	Major Khmer Rouge offensive forces 40,000 refugees to flee (Feb.–Mar.). Khmer Rouge guerrillas forced into Thailand, provoking clashes with Thai troops.
	Karen	Government troops capture main bases of Karen separatists (Jan.–Feb.). Release of Aung San Suu Kyi from house arrest (July); appointed General Secretary of National League for Democracy. Military junta drafts new Constitution (Nov.); NLD refuses to participate.
	Indonesia	Further ethnic clashes in Dili, East Timor (Jan. and Sept.).
1996	*Vietnam*	Government launches campaign against 'social evils' of prostitution, drug abuse, gambling and pornography (Feb.). Deputy Premier Phan Van Khai announces 9.5% increase in GDP.
	Cambodia	King Sihanouk's half-brother found guilty in absence of plotting assassination of Hun Sen (Feb.). Major government offensive against Khmer Rouge (Jan.); China offers aid to Cambodian government (Apr.). Major defection of 3,000 Khmer Rouge under Ieng Sary who join Government forces.
	Myanmar	Military rulers disrupt NLD conference and arrest and imprison leaders (May–Aug.); also crack down on weekly addresses made by Aung San Suu Kyi, arresting 500 (Sept.). Calls for trade sanctions against Myanmar by Aung San Suu Kyi, and EU withdraws special trading rights amidst widespread student protests.
	Indonesia	Serious rioting in Irian Jaya between immigrants and local population (Mar.). Government refuse to recognize new political party, the Indonesian United Democratic Party, and to oust the leader of the Indonesian Democratic Party, leading to serious rioting in Jakarta (July). National Commission on Human Rights condemns armed forces for human rights abuses in the July riots (Oct.).

Bishop Carlos Belo of East Timor and resistance leader José Ramos-Horta awarded Nobel Peace Prize (Oct.). Suharto government bans outdoor rallies and proceeds with trials of opposition groups (Oct.–Nov.).

1997   *Cambodia*   Pol Pot taken prisoner by Khmer Rouge General Ta Mok. Show trial follows and Pol Pot sentenced to life imprisonment.

Indonesia   Elections in Indonesia.

1998   *Indonesia*   Huge fall in value of Indonesian currency caused by general collapse of confidence in 'Tiger' economies and their banking systems. Suharto re-elected President. Anti-Suharto riots sweep Indonesia following shooting of six students. Violence in Jakarta leaves 500 dead (May). Suharto resigns. Replaced by Habibie.

Cambodia   Death of Pol Pot, former leader of Khmer Rouge (15 Apr.).

Australasia

Australia and New Zealand since 1945

1945   Death of Australian Premier Curtin (July); Finance Minister Joseph Chifley succeeds. Cessation of hostilities with Japan (15 Aug.); comprehensive social security system introduced.

1946   Commonwealth government of Australia given powers in respect of social services.

1948   Australia introduces 40-hour week. Rocket range at Woomera begun.

1949   Seven-week coal strike in Australia heightens fears of communist influence; Labour government of Chifley defeated and Liberals under Menzies assume office.
Snowy Mountain hydro-electric scheme commenced.
New Zealand referendum approves compulsory military training; Labour government of Peter Fraser defeated and National government takes office in New Zealand.

1950   Menzies introduces bill to ban Communist Party, later modified. Australian and New Zealand forces sent to Korea.

1951   The United States, Australia and New Zealand sign ANZUS treaty for mutual military security in the Pacific.
State of emergency in New Zealand following dock strike.

1952   United Kingdom atomic bomb test at Monte Bello Islands, off Australia; uranium discovered.

1953   Australian Atomic Energy Commission set up.

1954   Australia and New Zealand sign Manila Pact for collective defence against aggression in South-East Asia and South-West Pacific.

1956   Australia and United Kingdom agree on trade pact to replace Ottawa Agreement of 1932.

1957   Preferential treatment given to New Zealand dairy produce entering United Kingdom; New Zealand National government defeated by Labour.

1959   Australian New Immigration Act opens way to non-English-speaking immigrants.
Australia signs Antarctic Treaty.

1960   Social service benefits extended to Aborigines in Australia. Labour defeated in New Zealand elections and replaced by National government under Keith Holyoake.

1961   Menzies government returned in Australia; huge iron ore deposits discovered.

1962   Australian Aborigines given vote.
New Zealand trade pact with Japan.

1963   Huge bauxite deposits discovered in Australia; Australia adopts decimal currency. Liberal-Country Party returned, eighth Menzies government.

1966   Menzies retires from office in Australia (Jan.).
Australian troops sent to Vietnam.

1967   Australian Prime Minister, Harold Holt, drowned; John McEwen sworn in as acting Premier (Dec.).

1968   John Gorton becomes Prime Minister of Australia (Jan.).

1972   New Zealand Labour Party under Norman Kirk wins landslide victory (25 Nov.).
Australian Labour Party wins election under Gough Whitlam.

1974   Death of Norman Kirk, New Zealand Prime Minister; succeeded by Wallace Rowling.
Whitlam returned in Australia with reduced majority.

1975   Papua New Guinea becomes independent of Australian control. Constitutional crisis in Australia following blocking of Labour budget in Senate; Governor-General dismisses Labour Prime Minister Whitlam and caretaker Liberal government formed (11 Nov.). Malcolm Fraser leads Liberal-Country Party to election victory (Dec.).

1975   Robert Muldoon of National Party defeats Labour in New Zealand election.

1978   Death of Robert Menzies (June).

1983   Australian Labour Party under Bob Hawke returns to power (Mar.).

1984   Labour Party under David Lange defeats Muldoon in New Zealand (July). Hawke retains office in Australian election (Dec.).

1985   Crisis in ANZUS Pact because Lange government declares the country a nuclear-free zone, refusing port facilities to US destroyer. Hawke refuses facilities for US ships monitoring missile tests (Feb.). New Zealand protests against French atomic tests at Mururoa Atoll. French secret service agents sink Greenpeace ship *Rainbow Warrior* in Auckland Harbour. Two French saboteurs arrested. South Pacific Forum declares South Pacific a nuclear-free zone.

1986   Australia Act makes Australia fully independent of United Kingdom (Mar.); Queen remains sovereign.
United States announces suspension of security obligations to New Zealand (Aug.).

1987   United States withdraws concessions to New Zealand on military equipment (Feb.); Labour wins general election (Aug.).
Labour under Hawke confirmed in office in Australian general election (July).

1988   Australia celebrates Bicentenary of first settlement.

1989   David Lange resigns as New Zealand Premier (July).

1990   New Zealand celebrated 150th anniversary of Treaty of Waitangi (original treaty between the Europeans and Maoris).
Labour, under Hawke, wins narrow fourth election victory (Mar.).
The elections in New Zealand are won by the National Party; the new Prime Minister is Jim Bolger.

1991   Due to the deteriorating economic situation, Hawke resigns. His successor as head of the Labour Party and the government is Paul Keating (Dec.).

1993   Labour Party led by Keating again wins the elections (Mar.).
        In the elections in New Zealand, the governing National Party
        gains a one-person victory in the new parliament (Nov.).
        The new Australian Land Law accepted by parliament recog-
        nizes the Aborigines' priority in possessing land over the rights
        of the white settlers (Dec.).

1994   Following the setting up of a Ministry of Maori Development in
        1991, proposals for a compensation fund with a limit of NZ$1
        billion are outlined (Dec.).

1995   Maori protesters over compensation fund disrupt Waitangi Day
        celebrations (Feb.). Queen makes formal apology to Maoris as
        head of state (Nov.). French atomic tests at Mururoa Atoll lead
        to trade boycotts by Australia and New Zealand (Sept.–Oct.).

1996   John Howard wins landslide victory in Australian general elec-
        tion as head of Liberal-National Coalition (Mar.). Gun controls
        introduced by Federal and State governments following mas-
        sacre of tourists at Port Arthur, Tasmania, in April.
        Jim Bolger calls election in New Zealand under new system of
        proportional representation, resulting in a hung parliament.
        Bolger remains as Prime Minister with the leader of the New
        Zealand First Party as Treasurer and Deputy Prime Minister
        (Oct.).

1997   Mrs Shipley, leader of the Labour Party, replaces Bolger as Prime
        Minister (Nov.) in New Zealand.

1998   Constitutional Convention meets; Australia to vote in referen-
        dum over the republic issue. Constitutional deadlock over the
        Wik bill.

Latin America and the Caribbean

Latin America and the Caribbean, 1945–59

1945   *Peru*   José Luís Bustamante, leader of the National Demo-
                        cratic Front, is elected President (June) but APRA
                        emerges as the dominant force in Congress and
                        Bustamente is forced to accept APRA Cabinet mem-
                        bers (to the chagrin of military and right-wing forces).

        Colombia   López resigns the Presidency (July) and Alberto Lleras
                        Camargo finishes his term of office as the party pol-
                        itical structure cracks under intense social pressure.

        Venezuela   Revolt led by elements within the military co-operat-
                        ing with a revamped centrist political force formed in
                        1941 (Acción Democrática) removes dictatorship of
                        Medina Angarita (Oct.). New junta appoints Rómulo
                        Betancourt, the leader of AD, as Provisional President
                        until February 1948.

        Brazil   Getulio Vargas, President since 1930, is removed in a
                        bloodless coup which dismantles the 'Estado Novo'
                        corporate state and installs the head of the Supreme
                        Court as provisional President (Oct.). Vargas remains
                        prominent in Brazilian politics. General Enrico Gaspar
                        Dutra of the Social Democratic Party (PSD) defeats
                        the candidate of the National Democratic Union
                        (UDN) in a Presidential contest restricted to the two
                        traditional elite parties (Dec.).

1946   *Argentina*   Juan D. Perón is elected President (Feb.). In general
                        election his movement gains a majority in the Legis-
                        lature, defeating an alliance of political groupings
                        termed the Democratic Union. Perón is President
                        (June 1946–Sept. 1955).

        Colombia   Split Liberal Party vote between the 'official' candid-
                        ate Gabriel Turbay and the 'populist' Jorge Elicier
                        Gaitan allows the Conservative Party candidate, Mariano
                        Ospina Pérez, to 'steal' the Presidency (May), ruling
                        until August 1950 as acrimony and bitterness pen-
                        etrate the political system.

Bolivia	The government of the National Revolutionary Movement (MNR) is deposed in a rebellion (July); Victor Paz Estenssoro escapes into exile.
Chile	Gabriel González Videla is elected President by Congress (Sept.). Chilean politics hampered by the close balance of conflicting forces throughout the post-war period. Videla owes his election to a coalition of the Radical, Liberal and Communist parties in Congress.
Mexico	Miguel Alemán assumes the Presidency (Dec.) until 1952, a compromise candidate agreed upon by President Camacho, Lombardo Toledano and Lazaro Cárdenas. Alemán's former position of Governor of the populous state of Veracruz aided his nomination, which was a defeat for the Callista faction within the Revolutionary Party.

1947 *Venezuela* — Acción Democrática gains a majority in Congressional elections (Dec.) and the party's Presidential candidate Rómulo Gallego is victorious; assumes office in February 1948.

1948 *Argentina* — The Peronist Party (PP) wins a majority in congressional elections, consolidating Juan Perón's government (Feb.).

Colombia — Popular Liberal politician, Jorge Elicier Gaitan, is assassinated in Bogotá (Apr.) unleashing mass violence which devastates the capital – the *Bogotazo* – and ushers in a period of bitter civil conflict known as *La Violencia* (between Conservative and Liberal party supporters) which is severely complicated by rural social pressures and agrarian disputes. Estimates of number of people killed (1948–57) are as high as 200,000.

Peru — President Bustamente is deposed in a coup led by General Manuel A. Odria (Oct.), who rules as head of military junta until June 1950, when he seeks Presidency.

Venezuela — Army coup ousts the Acción Democrática government (Nov.). President Gallego and party leader Rómulo Betancourt exiled; Communist Party outlawed.

1949 *Bolivia* — Mamerto Urriolagoitia assumes the Presidency (May); despite MNR rebellion in August 1949, rules until May 1951.

1949   *Colombia*   Political acrimony causes the Liberal Party candidate to withdraw and the right-wing Conservative Laureano Gómez is elected unopposed (Nov.) as the nation's political situation worsens.

1950   *Peru*   General Odria assumes the Presidency in an uncontested election (July) enabling him to continue autocratic rule until July 1956.

    Brazil   Getulio Vargas returns to the centre of the political stage when, as the candidate of the re-vamped populist Brazilian Labour Party (PTB), he is elected President (Oct.), defeating Eduardo Gómez, the candidate of the traditionalist National Democratic Union (UDN). Vargas assumed the Presidency in January 1951, ruling Brazil until his suicide in 1954.

    Guatemala   Jacabo Arbenz of Partido Acción Revolucionario (PAR) is elected President in a contest in which suffrage is extended to all adult males and all adult literate females (Nov.). PAR also obtains majority in Congress, raising hopes for continued reform.

1951   *Bolivia*   Victor Paz Estenssoro, the MNR candidate, wins a large plurality while in exile (May). President Urriolagoitia hands over power to military rather than acknowledge an MNR victory. General Hugo Ballivian Rojas assumes Presidency and annuls election result.

    Argentina   Juan Perón is re-elected President (Nov.) and PP maintains its majority in Congress.

1952   *Bolivia*   Social revolution led by the tin miners' union and labour confederation (COB) ousts the government (Apr.); installs Hernán Siles Zuazo as MNR interim President. Victor Paz Estenssoro assumes office until 1956, when the MNR retains the Presidency. Paz Estenssoro and Siles Zuazo remain prominent politicians in Bolivia but move substantially to the right. Bolivian political system remains unstable, oscillating between ineffective civilian government and harsh military rule.

    Chile   General Carlos Ibáñez is elected President by vote in Congress as no candidate obtained majority (Sept.). Salvador Allende polls well for the Frente del Pueblo. Ibáñez forms an unstable coalition Cabinet, forced

| | to endlessly re-shuffle it as Chile confronted economic difficulties. |

Mexico   Adolfo Ruíz Cortines emerges as the most innocuous of the three pre-candidates as bureaucratic control of the Revolutionary Party (PRI) assumes greater importance than any 'Callista', 'Cardenista', or left/right polemic (Dec.). Ruíz Cortines introduces female suffrage on election and rules until 1958.

Venezuela Colonel Marcos Pérez Jiménez terminates a period of military chaos in government since the coup of 1950 by declaring himself President (Dec.). Imposes hardline dictatorship until 1958.

1953 Colombia General Rojas Pinilla leads a bloodless coup which removes the Conservative Party government (June). Liberal Party boycotted elections and both national political parties involved in bitter conflict.
Rojas Pinilla attempts to legitimize regime (1953–57) electorally in 1954.

1954 Argentina Peronism continues to dominate Argentinian politics in general election (Apr.).

Paraguay   General Alfredo Stroessner assumes Presidency (May), confirmed by July contest, in which he runs unopposed as Colorado Party candidate. Stroessner installs one of harshest and most durable dictatorships in Latin America, intact until 1989 when factionalism within the Colorado Party prompted a coup forcing Stroessner into exile in Brazil.

Guatemala CIA-sponsored invasion of exile forces from Honduras led by Colonel Carlos Castillo Arnes ousts the mildly reformist government of Jacobo Arbenz amidst allegations of communist influence in his government (June). In 1953 the Arbenz government had introduced a land reform programme which the United Fruit Company saw as a threat to its influence in Guatemala.

Brazil   Twenty-seven generals support a 'Manifesto to the Nation' demanding that the ageing President Getulio Vargas resign (Aug.). Investigation of attempted assassination of a government critic (Carlos Lacerda) had revealed a web of corruption in the Presidential entourage; Getulio Vargas committed suicide rather than resign.

1955 *Argentina*   Leading sectors of army and navy combined with some air force units to oust President Perón (Sept.). Five-man junta assumes dictatorial political power, led by General Pedro Eugenio Aramburu, President until May 1958. Bitter rivalry between the military elite and the Peronist movement continues to dominate Argentinian political life.

      Brazil   Juscelino Kubitschek, candidate of the Social Democratic Party (PSD) is elected President (Oct.), defeating the former *tenente* Juárez Tavora who stood for the National Democratic Union (UDN). João 'Jango' Goulart, a populist figure within the Brazilian Labour Party (PTB), is elected Vice-President. Marshal Henrique Teixera Lott leads a constitutionalist coup to prevent a UDN Senate manoeuvre to block Kubitschek's inauguration as President (Nov.). Kubitschek and Goulart assume power in January 1956. Kubitschek initiates 'development project' approach in his economic policy. Brasilia, the new capital, built during his Presidential term, which ended in 1961.

1956 *Chile*   Left-wing parties form an electoral alliance, the Frente de Acción Popular (FRAP), in an attempt to remove the impasse in Presidential contests (May).

      Peru   Voters turn to a former President, Manuel Prado to ease out the regime of General Odria (June). In Congress APRA offers Prado its support in return for political concessions.

      Nicaragua   Assassination of President Anastasio 'Tacho' Somoza García (Sept.) fails to remove the Somoza dictatorship; his eldest son Luís Somoza Debayle, assumes Presidency.

1957 *Colombia*   General Rojas Pinilla attempts to amend the Constitutional provision of no re-selection for President and is ousted by a junta led by War Minister, General Gabriel Paris (May).
Plebiscite held to legitimize the 'National Front' system of bi-partisan government. Scheme did bring an end to the main phase of social conflict (*La Violencia*) but tended to reinforce the oligarchic nature of the Colombian party system. Agreement guaranteed both parties equal representation in the Legislature, while

the Presidential terms were to be held alternately by
the two parties until 1970.

Haiti   François 'Papa Doc' Duvalier is elected to the Presidency amid accusations of fraud in a hectic contest
(Sept.). Bans political parties and installs his repressive dictatorship (Nov.).

1958   *Venezuela*   General strike called by a civilian political alliance
against the Jiménez regime (Jan.). Spontaneous riots
prompt military rebels to oust Jiménez and install a
provisional government.

Argentina   Return to civilian politics; Arturo Frondizi of the Radical Civic Union (UCRI) elected President with the
aid of Peronist votes (Feb.). The UCRI has majority
in Congress when Frondizi assumes the Presidency
(May).

Chile   Jorge Alessandri Rodríguez (independent supported
by Radical Party and the right) narrowly defeats both
the Christian Democrat, Eduardo Frei (PDC) and
Salvador Allende, the candidate of the left coalition
(FRAP). Alessandri is elected by Congressional vote
(Sept.).

Mexico   Performance of Adolfo López Mateos as Labour Secretary to President Cortines gains him Presidential
nomination and he rules until 1964. Quickly realizes
the increase in importance of the middle classes in
Mexican society that had accompanied economic
growth and also makes skilful use of the 'Cuba card'
in Mexican–US relations.

Venezuela   Rómulo Betancourt (AD) defeats Junta's candidate in
Presidential election (Dec.), ushering in era of domination of Venezuelan politics by Acción Democrática
(until 1968). Factionalism and division within AD
ranks as much as corruption scandals weakened the
party's hold over national politics, although AD remains an important force.

Cuba   Batista flees Cuba as Santiago and Santa Clara fall to
Castro's guerrillas on 31 December.

1959   *Cuba*   Official anniversary of Cuban Revolution, when Fidel
Castro names Manuel Urrutia Lleo as President and
José Miro Cardona as Prime Minister; new govern-
ment formed in Havana (Jan.).

The Cuban Revolution

1952	Mar.	President Prio Socarras ousted by General Fulgencia Batista. The scheduled June 1952 election is cancelled. Congress is dissolved, political parties banned, as Batista consolidates dictatorial power.
1953	July 26	Fidel Castro Ruíz is prominent in rebel force which unsuccessfully attacks Moncada barracks in Santiago. Most rebels are killed or imprisoned. Fidel Castro makes famous 'History Will Absolve Me' speech at his trial. In subsequent imprisonment on 'Isle of Pines', a revolutionary group coalesces.
1954	Nov.	Batista is re-elected in a contest boycotted by most political groupings amid allegations of fraud and government repression.
1955	May	An amnesty bill frees some political prisoners including Fidel Castro and members of the 'July 26th Movement'.
1956	Dec.	Fidel Castro and 82 men sail from Mexico to Cuba aboard the yacht *Granma*. Only 12 men survive the initial skirmishes with Batista's forces and retreat to the Sierra Maestra, whence a growing rural guerrilla resistance to Batista unfolds.
1958	Dec. 31	Santiago and Santa Clara fall to Castro's guerrillas. Batista flees (1 Jan.). Castro marches on Havana.
1959	Jan.	Castro names Manuel Urrutia Lleo as President and José Miro Cardona as Prime Minister.
	Feb.	Miro Cardona and Cabinet resign and Castro becomes Premier.
		First Soviet–Cuban trade agreement signed in Havana, pledging the Soviet Union to import one million tons of Cuban sugar annually for five years. Soviet importance as a sugar market and as source of economic aid becomes crucial to the Cuban economy.
	May	Agrarian Reform Law passed, authorizing confiscation of estates of over 1,000 acres (30 *cabellerias*). Estates were either divided among landless peasants

and sharecroppers, or formed the basis of State Farms in the Cash Crop Sector.

July   Castro provokes Urrutia into resigning and Osvaldo Dorticos Torrado becomes President, with Castro centrally placed as Premier.

Nov.   Ernesto 'Che' Guevara is made head of the National Bank.

1960 Mar. State Central Planning Board (JUCEPLAN) is established.

Apr.   Interests of the United Fruit Company are expropriated.

           200 Cuban troops fight with the National Revolutionary Committee in the Congo against the forces of Moise Tshombe in a gesture of solidarity.

May   Cuba re-establishes diplomatic relations with USSR.

June–July Oil refineries in Cuba are nationalized.

July   Law passed instigating the State takeover of US-owned economic activity in retaliation for the US abolition of Cuba's share in the sugar quota.

Aug.   CIA approach John Roselli to persuade him to organize an attempt to poison Fidel Castro.

Sept.   Local political organization and participation developed by formation of nation-wide structure of 'Committees for the Defence of the Revolution'.

Oct.   Nationalization of all sugar mills and sugar-cane land. Major foreign banks nationalized.

           US embargo on all imports to Cuba.

Nov.   President Kennedy informed of CIA training of exile 'Brigade 2506' in Guatemala.

1961 Jan. US severs diplomatic relations with Cuba.

           Fidel Castro declares 1961 'the Year of Education' as mass literacy drive is undertaken.

Apr.   CIA-backed attempt to build an invasion beachhead in east Cuba. Cuban airfields bombed (15th) but Castro's small air force isolates the 1,500 men of 'Brigade 2506' that reached the shore, in the 'Bay of Pigs' fiasco (16th–17th) (see p. 256).

           Castro for the first time asks the people to defend 'a socialist revolution'. In December 1962 the 1,200 prisoners are allowed to travel to the United States.

July   Integrated Revolutionary Organization (ORI) is formed combining the '26th July Movement', the

		PSP (the old Communist Party) and student revolutionary directorate.
	Nov.	The Partido Socialista Popular (PSP), the old Communist Party, is formally dissolved.
	Dec.	Fidel Castro, in a speech on Popular University TV, declares himself a Marxist-Leninist, further disturbing the Kennedy administration in Washington.
1962	Feb.	Cuba suspended from the Inter-American System due to US pressure.
		A national campaign of polio vaccination is initiated.
	Mar.	Anibal Escalante and other 'old guard' communists purged from the government and the ORI.
		President Kennedy makes his 'We will build a wall around Cuba' speech in Costa Rica.
	Apr.	CIA agent William Hunter provides poison pills and money to Cuban contacts who undertake to poison Fidel Castro. Mission not attempted.
	July	US embassy property in Havana is expropriated.
	July–Aug.	Raul Castro, Cuban Minister of the Armed Forces, and later Ernesto 'Che' Guevara visit Moscow.
	Sept.	Moscow statement confirms Cuba's request for arms and USSR's agreement to dispatch weapons and technical experts. Kennedy asks Congress for authority to call up 150,000 reservists.
	Oct.	The Cuban Missile Crisis:
	Oct. 16–17	US reconnaisance planes photograph Soviet intermediate-range missiles being installed in Cuba.
	Oct. 22	Kennedy denounces the 'deliberately provocative and unjustified change in the status quo'.
		NATO Supreme Allied Commander in Europe alerted.
	Oct. 23	A Soviet broadcast denounces US blockade of Cuba. UN Security Council meets and US calls for dismantling and withdrawal of missiles.
	Oct. 24	US blockade effective. U Thant (UN Secretary General) petitions both sides.
	Oct. 26	Letter from Khrushchev to Kennedy offering to withdraw the missiles under UN supervision if US blockade of Cuba is lifted and guarantee is given that Cuba will not be invaded.
	Oct. 27	Second letter from Khrushchev linking initial offer to conditional withdrawal of US missiles from Turkey. Kennedy replies on basis of first proposal.

	Oct. 28	Firm undertakings given on removal of missiles under UN supervision. In November Castro's 'Five Points' to guarantee Cuban territory are debated.
1963	Jan.	A diving-suit treated with poison fungi is prepared by the CIA as a 'present' for Castro, but attempted delivery of the suit is cancelled.
	Feb.	ORI replaced by more formalized structure, the United Party of the Socialist Revolution (PURS).
	Sept.	Symbolic attack by US planes on Las Villas province.
	Oct.	Second Agrarian Reform confiscates all holdings in excess of 67 hectares. Agricultural small-holdings in private hands remain and constitute 40% of agricultural land.
	Nov.	Conscription is introduced.
		Desmond Fitzgerald, head of CIA special affairs, offers a Cuban agent poisoning gadgetry to attempt to assassinate Castro. The agent rejects the equipment as too amateurish.
1964	Jan.	Fidel Castro visits Moscow.
	Feb.	The US sacks Cuban workers at its controversial Guantanamo military base on the island.
1965	Mar.	Cuba donates sugar supplies to Vietnam.
	Sept.	Students are mobilized to help in the coffee harvest.
	Oct.	Castro announces that the Cuban Communist Party (PCC), is to replace the PURS.
1966	Jan.	First Tri-Continental Conference held in Havana. Revolutionaries from Africa, the Americas and Asia meet to discuss strategy and forms of solidarity.
	Feb.	Fidel Castro attacks China's economic policy towards Cuba and accuses Chinese authorities of attempting to subvert the Cuban armed forces by distributing propaganda.
		Soviet–Cuban trade agreement increases trade volume by 22% and guarantees larger Soviet aid credits.
		Camilo Torres Restrepo (Colombian priest and revolutionary) is killed by the military in Santander, Colombia. Camilo Torres was a national hero who had joined and fought with the Cuban-inspired National Liberation Army (ELN). Announcement of his death causes student riots in Bogotá.

1967	Oct.	'Che' Guevara shot by Bolivian rangers at Hiquera, Bolivia, after being captured and wounded: a demoralizing blow to insurgency in Latin America based upon the Cuban-style rural *foco* theory. Political groups on the left increasingly looked to the 'specific local conditions' in which they operated, and the Cuban revolutionary road became a secondary inspiration rather than a definitive model for the whole continent.
1968	May	Cuba refuses to sign the UN nuclear non-proliferation treaty. Change in economic policy precipitates the nationalization of over 50,000 small private businesses. The PCC is purged of a 'USSR micro-faction'.
1969	July	Soviet naval task force visits Havana to join tenth anniversary celebrations on symbolic 26th.
1970	Sept.	Soviet government assures the United States that it has no intention of building a strategic submarine base in Cuba, accusing Nixon administration of developing 'war psychosis'. Economic problems continue; record sugar *zafra* but numerous economic dislocations caused by the concentration on drive for a 10 million ton harvest.
	Nov.	Salvador Allende's Popular Unity government renews diplomatic relations between Chile and Cuba.
1971	Oct.	The Cuban air force is strengthened by delivery of Mig-21 jets.
	Nov.	Castro visits Allende in Chile in a display of solidarity; later journeys to Peru and Ecuador.
1972	May	Cuba is re-elected as administrative member on UN Development Council. Castro undertakes a two-month diplomatic tour to Africa, Eastern Europe and the Soviet Union.
	July	Cuba joins COMECON. Peru's nationalist military government renews diplomatic relations with Cuba.
1973	Feb.	Cuba and US sign a five-year anti-hijacking pact to apply to aircraft and vessels. Similar agreement reached with Mexico in June.

	Mar.	Completion of child health programme gives Cuba lowest child mortality in Latin America.
	May	Cuba and Argentina renew diplomatic relations.
	July	The US joins 5 Latin American countries in voting to lift OAS commercial sanctions against Cuba.
	Aug.	United States eases some economic sanctions. Foreign subsidiary companies of US corporations allowed to sell goods to Cuba under licence.
		Judicial reform restructures Cuba's legal system, establishes new People's Supreme Court.
	Sept.	All Chilean assets in Cuba frozen, following military coup that ousts Allende.
	Oct.	In an incident in the Panama Canal zone the United States detains a Cuban merchant vessel.

| 1974 | Jan. | Soviet leader Brezhnev visits Cuba. |
| | Oct. | Committee established to supervise drafting of new Constitution. |

1975	Jan.	Cuba and West Germany renew diplomatic relations.
	Mar.–May	First commitment of military advisers to help MPLA forces in Angola.
	July	Castro offers evidence of attempts on his life to US Senate Committee on Intelligence investigating CIA 'dirty tricks' – eight such schemes between 1960 and 1965 alone.
	Nov.	A crack Cuban battalion is sent to Angola following increased South African intervention since August in the Angolan conflict.
	Dec.	First Congress of the Cuban Communist Party approves the new Constitution, instituted in 1976. Major provisions include directly elected municipal assemblies and indirectly elected provincial authorities and a National Assembly. Within the National Assembly the Council of State is the executive branch with the Chairman head of the government and Commander-in-Chief of the Armed Forces. Fidel Castro holds these positions.
		Several troop-ships arrive in Angola as the Cuban commitment to the MPLA cause is deepened.

| 1976 | Feb. | Annual Soviet–Cuban trade treaty includes five-year commitment to double volume of trade. Soviet Union accounts for 50% of Cuba's total international trade. |

1976	Apr.	Terrorist campaign against Cuban interests. Fishing vessels attacked and bomb explosions at the embassy in Lisbon and at the UN.
	Oct.	Cuban electorate vote for 170 municipal assemblies, 14 provincial assemblies and a new National Assembly.
		Fidel Castro declares the hi-jacking agreement with the United States void from April 1977 following the bombing of a civilian Cuban jet by anti-Castro terrorists. The Venezuelan government indicts four people for the bombing.
	Dec.	The National Assembly of People's Power is inaugurated.
1977	Mar.	Fidel Castro's African tour is a diplomatic offensive in part to explain Cuban involvement in Angola. US government lifts ban on travel to Cuba.
	Apr.	US–Cuban fishing treaty signed defining national fishing zones.
	May	The United States and Cuba exchange diplomats and set up 'interest' offices in Havana and Washington. The Republican Party opposes the move.
1978	Apr.	New USSR–Cuba protocol strengthens trading agreements.
	Sept.	Scientific and technical agreement is signed with Spain.
1979	Apr.	High turnout for Municipal Assembly elections. Cuba establishes diplomatic relations with the government of Maurice Bishop in Grenada and offers aid.
	July	Cuba establishes diplomatic relations with the new Sandinista government in Nicaragua and offers aid.
	Sept.	Havana is host to the the Sixth Conference of Non-Aligned Countries.
1980	Apr.	Over 100,000 émigrés leave Cuba for the United States from the port of Mariel.
	May	Liberalization of agricultural trading markets in an effort to stimulate output of staple foodstuffs.
	Dec.	Second Congress of the Cuban Communist Party.
1981	Jan.	Cuba condemns the worsening human rights situation in El Salvador.

	Feb.	Cuba denounces South African incursions into Mozambique.
	Aug.	Cuba reaffirms commitment to aid MPLA government in Angola in resisting South African military pressure. Besides military aid, Cuba has undertaken numerous social and health projects in Angola.
1982	May	Cuba condemns British policy in the Falklands/ Malvinas dispute with Argentina.
1983	Mar.	A Paris agreement reschedules Cuba's foreign debt.
	Oct.	In the US invasion of Grenada, 24 Cubans are killed in fighting with US troops.
1984	Apr.	High turnout in the election for a National Assembly of People's Power.
		US–Cuban discussions on migration levels. Agreement that 3,000 criminals included in the Mariel evacuation will be returned to Cuba.
1985	Nov.	The Cuban government acts as an intermediary between the Colombian government and the M-19 guerrillas during the siege of the Colombian Supreme Court.
	Dec.	Third Congress of the Cuban Communist Party discusses mistakes in economic policy.
1986	May	Cuba forced to propose a postponement of debts due in 1986.
	Dec.	Castro unveils the 'rectification' campaign to reaffirm revolutionary ideals, reduce corruption and bureaucratic inefficiency and improve economic performance. In a desire to return to 'moral incentives', the campaign echoed the concept of the 'new man' outlined by 'Che' Guevara in the 1960s. 'Rectification' campaign uses methods which conflict with the *perestroika* championed by Gorbachev; Castro's commitment leads to cooling of Soviet–Cuban relations in 1988–89.
1987	Jan.	Political prisoners go on hunger-strike at Combinado del Este prison.
	July	Paris Club debts fall due, eventually forcing Cuba to reschedule a total of $850 million in 1988.

1988	Jan.	Cuba dispatches elite troops and officers to Angola in response to the South African offensive of October 1987, committing an estimated 45,000 troops in the conflict.
	Feb.	Cuban and Angolan forces successfully defend Cuito Cuanavale in a crucial battle.
	May	Cuban and Angolan troops advance to Luena on the Namibian border in a successful counter-attack.
	June	Cuban Mig-23s provide crucial air support in heavy fighting which sees South African casualties rise, prompting cease-fire negotiations.
	Aug.	Cease-fire agreement in Angola includes provision for the withdrawal of Cuban troops.
	Sept.	UN Human Rights Commission is invited to inspect Cuban prisons.
1989	Jan.	Thirtieth Anniversary of the Revolution.
		First Cuban troops to be withdrawn from Angola as part of cease-fire agreement arrive home.
	Apr.	Gorbachev pays four-day visit to Cuba. Outlines Soviet desire to reduce the economic subsidies to Cuba and implies need for *perestroika*-type reforms. Castro emphasizes dangers of excessive reform.
	June	Following an investigation in April, and earlier US tip-offs, General Arnaldo Ochoa Sánchez (a hero of the Angolan campaign) is arrested with fellow officers and Ministry of Interior officials for their co-operation with the Medellín drug cartel.
	July	Following their court-martial General Arnaldo Ochoa and three other officers are executed by firing squad. Ten leading officials of the Ministry of the Interior are given long gaol sentences and the Ministry is purged.
	Aug.	Construction minister is sacked in a shake-up in the housing sector.
		Two Soviet publications are banned, including *Moscow News*, a leading advocate of *perestroika*.
		Soviet economic pressure upon Cuba increases.
		Oil shortages reveal a suspension of the 30-year Soviet practice of exporting crude oil at a low price to Havana.
1990	Sept. 18	'A peace-time state of emergency' is introduced. Consequently, economic restrictions introduced

because of the lack of food are increased (e.g. the system of vouchers becomes widespread) and the fight against the domestic opposition groups is intensified.

1991	May 25	The last Cuban soldier leaves the territory of Angola.
	June 25	Charged with planning an assassination attempt against Fidel Castro, two doctors are sentenced to 12 and 10 year prison terms.
	Sept.	Unprecedented in the history of the Castro system, an opposition organization, the Cuban Democratic Concord, is created by eight opposition groups.
	Oct. 10–14	At the Fourth Congress of the Cuban Communist Party, the possibility of introducing a multi-party system and of liberalizing the economy is rejected.
1992	July	References to the Soviet Union and the Socialist world community are deleted from the Cuban Constitution but the entry referring to the leading role of the Communist Party remains. The reformed Constitution offers greater powers to the head of state (he becomes the commander of all armed forces and gains the right to order a 'state of emergency' in all, or parts of, the country), and prescribes direct parliamentary elections in place of the previous representative-delegate system.
1993	Feb. 24	At the first direct and secret provincial and parliamentary elections ever held in the Castro system – with a 97.7% turn-out – the official candidates are elected as deputies with large majorities.
	July 3	On board the passenger boat *Yuri Gagarin*, the last Russian soldier leaves the territory of Cuba.
	Aug.	As a result of the extensive lack of food, trade isolation and the plummeting level of agricultural production (sugar production fell 40% in 1993), the leaders of the country decide on the careful liberalization of economic life.
1998	Mar.	Visit by the Pope to Cuba.

Latin America and the Caribbean since 1960

1960	*Argentina*	President Frondizi's UCRI loses majority (Mar.). Peronist Party barred from participation.

1960   *Brazil*   Janio Quadros is elected President with UDN sup-
                        port (Oct.), defeating the candidate of the PSD,
                        Marshall Teixera Lott. Populist leader João 'Jango'
                        Goulart is re-elected Vice-President. Increasing
                        inflation and foreign debt produced by President
                        Kubitschek's ambitious development projects ham-
                        per campaign of PSD candidate. Quadros assumed
                        the Presidency in January 1961 faced by a hostile
                        opposition majority in Congress.

1961   *Haiti*   'Papa Doc' Duvalier is re-elected (Apr.). Consolid-
                        ates his regime by dissolving legislature and instal-
                        ling rubber-stamp assembly.

        Dominican   Dictator Rafael Trujillo assassinated (May). Trujillo
        Rep.   had dominated political life since 1931. Although
                        he at times assumed the Presidency, he allowed his
                        brother and Joaquín Balaguer to hold the highest
                        office for 'cosmetic' reasons. The Trujillo 'dynasty'
                        rallied briefly under his son General Rafael 'Ramfo'
                        Trujillo, but by December 1961 the family was ex-
                        pelled from the island.

        Brazil   President Quadros resigns in protest at Congres-
                        sional opposition to his agrarian and tax reforms.
                        Congress passes a constitutional amendment to es-
                        tablish a parliamentary system and much reduced
                        powers for the Presidency (Sept.). This comprom-
                        ise allows João Goulart to assume the Presidency,
                        but military opposition to his rule increases.

1962   *Argentina*   President Frondizi alienates the military hierarchy
                        by permitting Peronist participation in Congres-
                        sional elections (Mar.). Peronists win a majority
                        but Frondizi is pressurized by the military to nullify
                        election results in provinces where Peronism is
                        successful. The military removes President Frondizi
                        and installs the Leader of the Senate as an interim
                        President.

        Jamaica   The Jamaican Labour Party, headed by its founder
                        Sir Alexander Bustamente, wins 26 of the 45 seats
                        available in the election (Apr.), which followed
                        Jamaica's withdrawal from the Federation of the
                        West Indies (Sept. 1961).

        Peru   Military junta led by General Ricardo Pérez Godoy
                        seizes power to block APRA's political ambitions,

and annuls June election (in which APRA leader successful). General Godoy ousted by officers in favour of an electoral contest in March 1963.

Argentina   Arturo Illia (UCRP) is elected President.

Jamaica   Becomes independent within the British Commonwealth (Aug.). Constitution guarantees opposition some representation in Upper House.

Trinidad   Trinidad and Tobago become independent within the British Commonwealth (Aug.). Eric Williams, who formed the People's National Party (PNP) in 1956, dominates both the PNP and politics in Trinidad until his death (Mar. 1981).

Chile   Three right-wing organizations form an electoral alliance, the Frente Democrático (FD), to counter growing left-wing organization before the 1964 Presidential election.

Mexico   Gustavo Díaz Ordaz assumes Presidency. The organization of the Olympic Games in 1968 by the Díaz Ordaz administration provided an opportunity for protest by dissident groups, notably the student movement.

Dominican Rep.   Juan Bosch of the Democratic Revolutionary Party (PRD) is elected President and assumes office in February 1963.

1963   *Brazil*   The electorate votes to restore a full Presidential system and grant President Goulart extensive executive powers (Jan.), sowing the seeds of military alienation that lead to the coup of 1964.

Peru   In a return to civilian politics Fernando Belaunde Terry, candidate of new moderate force in Peruvian politics (Acción Popular), is elected (June).

Dominican Rep.   Democratically elected government of Juan Bosch is removed by Colonel Elias Wessen y Wessen; Bosch exiled (Sept.). Military factions develop around 'constitutionalist' and 'loyalist' positions.

1964   *Brazil*   President João Goulart removed in a coup (Apr.) ushering in a long period of dictatorship. Marshal Humberto Castelo Branco is approved by Congress; the first of a series of military nominees as President. Congress approves a constitutional amendment extending his term to March 1967.

1964	*Haiti*	'Papa Doc' Duvalier installs himself as President for Life (Apr.).
	Chile	Eduardo Frei, the Christian Democrat candidate is elected President (Sept.), defeating the candidate of the left-wing coalition (FRAP) Salvador Allende.
1965	*Dominican Rep.*	United States supports coup leader Colonel Wessen y Wessen in the conflict between military factions following the removal of Juan Bosch's civilian government. Lyndon Johnson sends the marines to the Dominican Republic to guarantee US interests. Joaquín Balaguer, the trusted lieutenant of the dictator Trujillo, assumes the Presidency in 1966 and dominates the political system.
1966	*Guyana*	British Guiana gains independence within the Commonwealth as the state of Guyana (May).
	Argentina	President Illia is deposed as the military re-enter politics (June). A hard-line junta led by Juan Carlos Ongania seizes power.
	Brazil	Congress approves Marshal Costa e Silva as sucessor to Castelo Branco as military President in 1967.
1967	*Nicaragua*	Major-General Anastasio 'Tachito' Somoza Debayle assumes the Presidency on the death of his brother (Feb.). 'Tachito's' corrupt dictatorship provokes increasing popular opposition to the Somoza 'dynasty'.
	Peru	General Juan Velasco Alvardo leads a military coup which ousts the ineffectual Belaunde administration (Oct.). General Velasco introduces nationalist measures in the export sector and attempts to tackle Peru's structural socio-economic problems, particularly the land reform issue (1968–86).
	Brazil	Military President Costa e Silva suspends Congress indefinitely, initiating government by decree.
	Guyana	Forbes Burnham, leader of the People's National Congress Party (PNC) wins the election that establishes his stranglehold on Guyanese politics (Dec.).
1969	*Argentina*	Military suppression of the *Cordobazo* – a mass insurrection in the city of Cordoba – prompts resignation of five ministers (May) and greatly weakens the Ongania regime.

	Brazil	Military high command choses General Emilio Garrastazu Medici as President following Costa e Silva's incapacity by a stroke. Medici assumes power in October.
1970	*Guyana*	Guyana becomes a 'co-operative' republic within the Commonwealth. In March the National Assembly elects Raymond Chang of the ruling PNC as President.
	Argentina	Military President Juan Carlos Ongania is removed by a junta dissatisfied by his loss of political control. The terrorist murder of a former military President, Pedro Aramburu, in May 1970, sealed Ongania's fate.
	Mexico	Luís Echevarria Alvárez, candidate of the ruling Institutional Revolutionary Party (PRI), is elected President (July). PRI wins all 60 seats in the Senate and gains a majority in Congress. Luís Echevarria Alvárez had been the hard-line Minister of the Interior during the social protests of 1968.
	Chile	Salvador Allende, the candidate of the Left Coalition (Popular Unity) wins a plurality in a polarized contest (Sept.). Allende assumes Presidency in November.
1971	*Haiti*	'Papa Doc' Duvalier dies and his son Jean-Claude 'Baby Doc' Duvalier succeeds him as President for Life (Apr.). The Duvaliers' repressive apparatus remains intact.
1972	*El Salvador*	Liberal Coalition led by José Napoleon Duarte and Guillermo Ungo win a rare free election, but are opposed by right-wing military elements which force both Duarte and Ungo into exile.
1973	*Chile*	The Popular Unity government is ousted by a military coup (Sept.). Salvador Allende dies defending the Presidential palace; thousands of Popular Unity supporters are killed or imprisoned as the military junta led by General Augusto Pinochet installs a repressive dictatorship.
1976	*Argentina*	Chaotic Peronist government is removed by a military coup. A series of military dictatorships rule

Argentina until October 1983. The original junta led by General Videla dissolved Congress and used state-of-siege legislation to justify mass arrests, torture and political murder. Over 15,000 people 'disappear' during military rule. General Videla succeeded briefly by Genera Viola in 1981 before General Galtieri assumes power.

Chile   Orlando Leterlier, former Cabinet minister and diplomat in the Allende government is assassinated in Washington DC by members of the Chilean Secret Services (Sept.).

1979   *Grenada*   The New Jewel Movement led by Maurice Bishop ousts the repressive regime of Sir Eric Gairy (Mar.).

Brazil   General João Baptista Figuerado assumes the Presidency, last in a line of military Presidents. His '*abertura*' (opening) policy unleashes popular pressures for democratic elections.

Nicaragua   Popular resistance led by the Sandinista National Liberation Army (FSLN) forces Anastasio 'Tachito' Somoza out of power (June), ending the family's 'dynastic' control of Nicaragua politics since the 1920s. In the conflict against the Somoza regime 40,000 people died and a further 750,000 were made homeless.

El Salvador   A young officers' coup ousts the repressive regime of General Romero and forms a reformist military-civilian junta, joined by Guillermo Ungo who returns from exile.

1980   *El Salvador*   Civilian members of the junta resign, ushering in '*Romerismo sin Romero*' as the regime's emphasis moves from reform to repression. State of siege is declared, leading to civil war. The murder of Archbishop Romero, a prominent human rights activist, symbolizes the extent of official violence. Subsequently over 70,000 people are killed, mainly at the hands of the security forces and the right-wing death squads.

Peru   The Maoist-influenced guerrilla group *Sendero Luminoso* ('Shining Path') begins its insurgency in the Andean province of Ayacucho. By 1989 *Sendero Luminoso* threatens Lima by isolating the capital from its hinterland.

	Chile	A referendum held under state-of-emergency provisions (Sept.), with all political parties banned and no use of electoral registers, adopts a new constitution which appoints Pinochet as President for a renewable eight-year term.
	Jamaica	Edward Seaga's right-wing Jamaican Labour Party (JLP) wins a violent electoral campaign (Oct.) against Michael Manley's People's National Party (PNP).
1982	*Honduras*	Roberto Suoza Cordova, a conservative civilian politician, is elected to the Presidency (Jan.) but real power is still firmly held by the armed forces, who have dominated Honduran politics for over 25 years.
	Honduras/ Nicaragua	First in a series of joint US/Honduran military exercises began with simulated air and amphibious landings in the Cabo Gracias a Dios area, near Nicaragua (Feb.). These manoeuvres expand annually, exerting considerable pressure upon the Sandinista government.
	Guatemala	General Lucas García, who seized power in July 1978, becomes the most brutal of a series of military dictators since 1954. 20,000 people died at the hands of the security forces and the death squads during his rule. García ousted by a young officers' coup (Mar.). General Efrain Rios Montt, a born-again Christian, assumed the Presidency but the continued massacre of civilians by government paramilitary groups removed grounds for any guarded optimism. The suspension of US arms shipments to Guatemala is lifted.
	El Salvador	Roberto D'Aubuisson's far-right ARENA party gains a majority in the Constituency Assembly, but moderate Alvaro Magana is appointed President due to US pressure (Apr.).
	Argentina	Argentina forces invade the Falkland Islands. Britain declares a naval exclusion zone around the islands. British navy sinks the Argentinian cruiser *Belgrano* (May) on orders from the War Cabinet. General Galtieri rejects Peruvian peace plan. British force despatched from the Ascension Islands undertakes landings at San Carlos and wins the Battle of Goose Green. British win the Battle of

| | Port Stanley, prompting the surrender of Argentinian forces on the islands (see p. 273). |
| *Colombia* | Belisario Betancur assumes the Presidency (Aug.) and attempts to draw dissident guerrilla forces into a political truce. |

1983	*Guatemala*	Defence Minister, General Mejia, ousts General Rios Montt from the Presidency in a near bloodless coup (Aug.), continuing Guatemalan political process of coup and counter-coup within a narrow political caste.
	Argentina	Leader of the Radical Party, Raul Alfonsín, is elected in return to civilian rule. President Alfonsín enjoys a 'honeymoon' period but his government's popularity is worn away by failure to solve the aftermath of the 'Malvinas' (Falklands) fiasco, the undertaking of adequate judicial procedures against military personnel responsible for the 'disappearances' during military rule and Argentina's deep-rooted economic problems.
	Grenada	Maurice Bishop is ousted in October (and later murdered) by a hard-line faction led by Deputy Prime Minister Bernard Coard and General Hudson Austin which provides an opportunity for US intervention. US naval task force (backed by a small contingent from the conservative Organization of Eastern Caribbean States) successfully invades Grenada (Oct.) after three days of bitter fighting.

1984	*Nicaragua*	CIA initiates the mining of Nicaraguan ports (Feb.). The Sandinista government takes its case to the World Court.
	Colombia	Assassination of Minister of Justice Lara Bonilla (Apr.) prompts President Betancur to attempt a clampdown on the drugs mafia.
	El Salvador	In a bitter run-off election, the Christian Democrat, José Napoleon Duarte is elected President. The US administration guarantees his government unprecedented levels of economic aid. President Duarte holds first exploratory talks (Oct.) with guerrilla political leaders (the FDR-FMLN).
	Nicaragua	The Sandinistas win 65% of the votes in national elections. Daniel Ortega is elected President (Nov.).

Chile   President Pinochet re-introduces state-of-siege provisions (Nov.).

1985 *Brazil*   Tancredo Neves, the candidate of the opposition alliance dominated by Brazilian Democratic Movement (PMBD), defeats the government candidate Paulo Maluf in a contest for the Presidency (Jan.).

   Nicaragua US administration initiates a three-year trade embargo against the Sandinista government (Apr.). In 1988 President Reagan attempts to tighten the economic noose around Nicaragua.

   Peru   Alan García (APRA candidate) wins Presidential election (Apr.). He fails to improve Peru's dire economic situation or ease the civil conflict.

   Brazil   Smooth transition to civilian rule is prevented by death of Tancredo Neves. Vice-President Sarney is sworn in as President amid much confusion (Apr.). José Sarney is the leader of the Liberal Front (PFL), a small conservative faction of the victorious opposition alliance.

   Chile   The Democratic Alliance is formed (Aug.), unifying parties across the political spectrum opposed to General Pinochet's intransigent rule. Unsuccessful assassination attempt on General Pinochet by the increasingly active Manuel Rodríguez Patriotic Front (FPMR) associated with the illegal Communist Party (Sept.). Pinochet regime tightens existing press censorship, arrests trade union and socialist leaders, increases mass army raids on working-class *poblaciones* in Santiago.

   Guatemala The Christian Democratic Party's candidate, Venecio Cerezo, is an easy victor in the Presidential election. Military leadership remains the power source in the Guatemalan political system.

1986 *Honduras* José Azcona, dissident Liberal Party candidate, assumes the Presidency after his narrow November victory. The military leadership remain the real fulcrum of power.

   Haiti   Mounting popular unrest forces 'Baby Doc' Duvalier into exile (Feb.). Popular celebrations cut short as the transitional military government, fronted by General Henri Namphy, is not over-rigorous in its dismantling of the dictatorship.

1986   *Peru*   President García's administration is tainted by indirect complicity with the military's massacre of over 300 *Sendero Luminoso* prisoners while subduing prison protests (Apr.).

El Salvador   President Duarte's government fails to halt growing economic dislocation despite massive aid from the Reagan administration. Economic austerity measures prompt greater unity of peasant and trade union groups, which organize May protests against the government.

Colombia   Virgilio Barco, the successful Liberal Party candidate, assumes the Presidency (Aug.). Efforts to open up the political system hampered by informal political power of drug interests, especially the 'Medellin Cartel'. The six major guerrilla groups form the Simón Bolívar Guerrilla Co-ordinating Board as a reaction to increasing right-wing death squad activity.

Brazil   The initial success of the anti-inflationary package – the Cruzado plan – benefits the government alliance electorally: the Brazilian Democratic Movement (PMBD) sweeps to power in Congressional State elections (Nov.).

Chile   Meeting between Christian Democratic and moderate conservative leaders with two junta members is first formal contact between government and opposition for 13 years.

Argentina   President Alfonsín rushes a 'final point' Bill through Congress designed to prevent further prosecution of military personnel after February 1987.

1987   *Brazil*   As foreign exchange reserves fall below \$4 billion, Brazil forced to suspend interest payments on its foreign debt (Feb.).

Haiti   New constitution approved by the populace (Apr.) but military rule casts shadow over forthcoming elections.

El Salvador   An FDR-FMLN peace plan is rejected by Duarte (May) and talks are suspended.

Nicaragua   Investigations into the Iran–Contra scandal prompt Congress to suspend aid to the Contras.

Panama   Colonel Roberto Díaz, a retired deputy military commander, accuses General Manuel Antonio Noriega of murder and corruption. Noriega had dominated

Panamanian politics since 1983 but since July 1987 has come under increased US pressure to resign.

Central America   'Guatemalan Pact' or Arias initiative is signed by Presidents of Central American countries. Hope of progress in solving the conflicts which envelop El Salvador and Nicaragua and enmesh Honduras and Guatemala.

Argentina   The Congressional elections (Sept.) are a triumph for the Peronist movement, taking 42% of the vote as against 37% for the government.

Colombia   Jaime Pardo, the leader of Union Patriotica (UP) and its former Presidential candidate, is shot dead by unidentified gunmen (Oct.). Over 500 UP members are killed by right-wing death squads in 1986–87.

1988   *Argentina*   Colonel Aldo Rico, freed by a military court to house arrest, leads a second unsuccessful insurrection against President Alfonsín.

Haiti   In an electoral contest without a secret ballot or voting lists and boycotted by the four main opposition candidates, Leslie Mainigat is briefly elected President (Jan.). Following his first dispute with the military, Mainigat is removed by General Henri Namphy, who reimposes rule by military junta.

Panama   General Noriega is indicted (in absentia) in Miami on drugs offences. President Delvalle attempts to remove Noriega as defence chief but the National Assembly ousts Delvalle and installs the anti-US nationalist Manuel Solis Palma as President (Feb.).

Mexico   The lacklustre candidate of the ruling Institutional Revolutionary Party (PRI), Carlos Salinas, is belatedly declared the winner in the controversial Presidential election demonstrating the party's bureaucratic control of Mexican politics (July).

Chile   Opposition alliance of 16 political parties forms the basis of successful 'No' vote against the Pinochet regime (Oct.).

Brazil   The murder of 'Chico' Mendes (Dec.), prominent ecologist and peasant leader, demonstrates the intransigence of the rural elite in the north to environmental pressures for conservation of the forest resources of Amazonia.

1989   *Paraguay*   General Andrés Rodríguez ousts General Stroessner's 34 year dictatorship in Paraguay. General Alfredo

Stroessner is sent into exile in Brazil. General Rodríguez receives over 70% of the votes in an unreliable Presidential election termed fraudulent by the opposition (May).

1989 *Jamaica*   Michael Manley's People's National Party (PNP) defeats the JLP incumbent Edward Seaga in a general election (Feb.). The PNP wins 44 of the 60 parliamentary seats.

El Salvador   The right-wing ARENA party wins both the Presidential and legislative elections. Cristiani is elected President (but hard-liner Roberto D'Aubuisson controls the party by his domination of its executive committee); as he assumes power in June the activity of death squad organizations is again on the increase.

Nicaragua   US administration claims that the Sandinista army's pursuit of Contra forces into Honduras constituted an invasion and dispatches 3,000 US troops for joint manoeuvres with Honduran forces. Later in the month, Contra/Sandinista talks produce the fragile Sapoa truce.

Argentina   Carlos Menem, the Peronist candidate, defeats Eduardo Angeloz of the Radical party in the Presidential election, and initiates severe programme of economic austerity in an attempt to combat inflation and the worsening foreign debt.

Chile   The supporters of the military government have agreed upon Hernán Buchi as Presidential candidate to face an opposition candidate, the Christian Democrat, Patricio Aylwin. Patricio Aylwin is backed by the 16-party opposition alliance and goes on to win the December election.

Colombia   Murder of the leading Presidential candidate, Liberal Senator Luís Carlos Galán, by the drugs barons steels the government of Virgilio Barco to declare war on the 'Drugs Mafia' (Aug.). The narcotics interests answer the challenge by bombing the offices of the Liberal and Conservative parties.

Nicaragua   The five Central American Presidents agree to the closure of 'Contra' bases in Honduras within three months (Aug.). US administration decreases funds to Contras.

	Panama	US forces invade Panama (Dec.). Major US operation to overthrow the Noriega regime and seize Noriega himself. US airborne troops seize Panama City and key towns. Noriega evades capture, seeking refuge in Vatican mission. Guillermo Endara installed as President of Panama. Noriega subsequently surrenders and is flown to the United States to face trial.
1990	*Nicaragua*	Sandinistas defeated in general election; Mrs Violetta Chamorro becomes President.
	Haiti	General Prosper Avril, who achieved power via a coup in September 1988, resigns and leaves the country (Mar.). Until the general elections, Mrs Ertha Pascal-Trouillot, a member of the Supreme Court, becomes the provisional President of Haiti.
	Colombia	The Presidential elections which follow the bloody election campaign, in which, among others, three Presidential candidates were killed, and in which the M-19 guerrilla organization also participated as a political movement, are won by the candidate of the Liberal Party, César Gaviria Trujillo (May).
	Peru	In opposition to the world-famous writer, Mario Vargas Llosa (the candidate of the political right), an agricultural expert of Japanese origin, Alberto Fujimori, wins (June). Instead of a shock-therapy approach, Fujimori, who rejects the classical system of party rotations, promises gradual reforms and the injection of foreign capital into the Peruvian economy, which has been devastated by the enormous rate of inflation.
	Brazil	At the parliamentary elections, the right-wing political parties supporting the President's PRN gain an absolute majority in Congress (Oct.).
	Argentina	A rebellion led by Colonel Mohamed Ali Seineldin breaks out in the army. The coup attempt is suppressed in two days by forces loyal to the government (Dec.).
1991	*Chile*	The report by the Committee of Truth and Reconciliation (Rettig Committee) reveals the horrors of the Pinochet dictatorship (Mar.). The commander of the army, General Pinochet, obstructs the prosecution of those found liable.

1991	*El Salvador*	The military leader of the FMLN, Joaquín Villalobos, declares that the organization is not Marxist any longer and that its objective is to create a pluralist democracy in El Salvador.
	Haiti	General Raoul Cedras overthrows Jean-Bertrand Aristide, the first democratically elected President of the country (Sept.). Aristide has only been in office since February.
	Paraguay	At the parliamentary elections, the governing Colorado Party gains more than 60% of the votes (Dec.). The new parliament starts work on a new constitution which forbids the election of a President for two consecutive terms.
1992	*Guatemala*	After the election campaign spoiled by political murders, in the second round of voting the leader of the Solidarity Action Movement (MAS), the neoliberal Jorge Serrano Elias, is elected as President of the country (Jan.).
	El Salvador	The civil war which has been going on for 10 years concludes with a cease-fire agreement (Jan.). The FMLN turns into a political party (May) and by the end of the year the last guerrilla surrenders his weapons. The United States cancels three-quarters of the half billion US dollar El Salvador state debt.
	Venezuela	In February and November, unsuccessful military coups are attempted against Carlos Andrés Pérez of the Democratic Action Party (AD) who took office in 1989 (and was already President between 1974 and 1979).
	Peru	Pointing to the consistent application of economic reform, the increasing fight against terrorism, and the corruption of the deputies, Fujimori carries out a Presidential coup with the aid of the armed forces. He suspends the constitution, dissolves the parliament, and introduces a state of emergency and censorship (Apr.). In an attempt to overthrow him, unsuccessful coup attempts are launched in November 1992 and May 1993.
	Panama	Because of drug-smuggling and other charges, a court in Florida sentences General Noriega, the former dictator of Panama, to 40 years in prison (July).

Honduras/El Salvador	The decree of the Hague International Court finally concludes the so-called football war which broke out between the two countries in 1969 (Oct.).
Colombia	For a more efficient struggle against the guerrillas and the drug barons, a state of emergency is introduced in the whole of the country (Nov.).
Mexico	President Salinas de Gortari, with the President of the United States and the Canadian Prime Minister, signs the NAFTA Treaty in Washington (Dec.). The Senate ratifies the treaty in November 1993.
Brazil	President Collor de Mello, whose liberal economic policies were initially successful but ultimately failed, is forced to resign on corruption charges. His successor is the former Vice-President, Itamar Franco (Dec.).

1993	*Jamaica*	At the parliamentary elections, the People's National Party, headed by James Percival Patterson, who took over the position of Prime Minister in April 1992 from Manley who had to leave due to health reasons, wins ahead of the Jamaican Labor Party (Mar.).
	Paraguay	Building entrepreneur Juan Carlos Wasmosy, of the Colorado Party (founded by Stroessner), wins the first democratic Presidential elections of the country, ahead of Guillermo Caballero Vargas, the candidate of the opposition electoral union, National Collaboration (May).
	Venezuela	Accused of the embezzlement of public funds and of corruption, criminal proceedings are launched against President Pérez, who is suspended (May), then finally removed from office (Sept.). The Presidential elections are won by Rafael Caldera, who held this office from 1969 to 1974, and now heads the electoral union called Convergence (Dec.). In this way the period of party rotations between the AD and the COPEI (Christian Social Party) comes to an end.
	Guatemala	Pointing to the need to bring order and governability of the country, and to the need to reduce corruption and the drug trade, President Serrano dissolves the parliament and the Supreme Court, suspends constitutional rights, and introduces absolute Presidential powers (May). After an initial period

of support, the army turns against him and forces Serrano to resign, claiming that the events were tantamount to a coup. The parliament elects lawyer Ramiro de León Carpio, human-rights activist, as the new President of the government – instead of the Vice-President who supports Serrano (June).

Bolivia   The candidate of the largest opposition party, the National Revolutionary Movement (MNR), Gonzalo Sánchez de Lozada, wins the Presidential elections (Aug.).

Haiti   As a consequence of the international sanctions, the Haiti leadership agrees on the return of former President Aristide to his office (July), but the agreement is never observed and terrorist activities commence again. In response, the UN orders an embargo against Haiti and a naval blockade is set up around the island (Oct.).

Peru   A plebiscite accepts the new constitution of the country. The new constitution allows the re-election of the President and the death penalty for terrorists (Oct.).

Honduras   The candidate of the opposition Liberal Party, Carlos Roberto Reina, wins the Presidential elections (Nov.).

Curaçao   As a result of a plebiscite, the population of the Caribbean island rejects independence and expresses their wish to remain a part of the Antilles (Nov.).

Colombia   Pablo Escobar, the head of the Medellín drug Mafia, is killed in a shoot-out with the police (2 Dec.).

Chile   As a result of the economic boom, the candidate of the governing centre-left coalition, the Christian Democrat Eduardo Frei, wins the Presidential elections (Dec.). He takes office in March 1994.

1994   *Argentina*   President Menem's PJ party remained the largest party in the elections but lost its overall majority. Menem launches major anti-poverty campaign, while introducing free market reforms (May). Demonstrations and general strike (July–Aug.).

Brazil   Cardoso wins another four-year term as President (Oct.).

El Salvador   Presidential and legislature elections lead to victory of ARENA candidate Calderon over the Left candidate Rubín Zamora. Split occurs in the former Liberation Front group.

Guatemala   Agreement reached to end civil war and negotiate peace treaty by end of the year (Jan.). Elections held (Aug.), leading to coalition government, but talks collapse with the Marxist guerrilla movement in November.

Mexico   Uprising in southern Chiapas region by armed Indian groups (Zapatistas) against the effects of North American Free Trade Agreement and demanding social reform; cease-fire agreed (Jan.). Ernesto Zedillo elected President (Aug.); forced to devalue *peso* after further unrest in Chiapas.

1995   *Argentina*   Following huge fall in inflation rate, President Menem wins an easy victory in the Presidential and Congressional elections (May). Serious rioting in Córdoba (June) following austerity measures. Menem calls for emergency powers to deal with the economy (Nov.).

Brazil   Cardoso forced to set aside ambitious plans for tackling poverty as a result of general economic crisis, forcing devaluation of the *real* in March. Large-scale privatization plan introduced but faced by strikes and demonstrations.

El Salvador   Demobilized FMLN soldiers besiege government and take hostages in protest at being betrayed over promises of jobs, housing and credit. New centre-left Democratic Party makes pact with Calderón government (Apr.).

Guatemala   New schedule for peace talks set up (Feb.), leading to first participation in elections of left-wing candidates for 40 years. Alvaro Arzu of the Conservative Party wins largest share of vote (Nov.).

Mexico   President Zedillo introduces austerity campaign but fails to secure foreign loans to shore up the currency (Jan.) Signs reform pact with other main parties (Feb.) and then attempts to overwhelm the Zapatistas by military force, but has to accept a stalemate and peace talks (Feb.–Mar.). Accord on future negotiations agreed (Sept.).

Peru   President Fujimori wins a second term in office (Apr.).

1996	*Argentina*	Budget cut of $200 million forced on Menem government by IMF (Jan.); Menem takes further powers to cut government spending (Feb.). Tax rises by new Finance Minister met by strikes and protests (Aug.–Sept.).
	Brazil	Decree allows Indian land to be opened up (Jan.) – met by protests and land occupations by landless families. Further cuts in government spending launched (June).
	El Salvador	Protests against dismissals of 15,000 public service workers.
	Guatemala	President Arzu and Guatemalan Revolutionary Unity (URNG) meet for peace talks in Mexico City (Feb.). Peace accord reached over a wide range of issues (May) and signed (29 Dec.), ending 36 years of civil war.
	Mexico	Peace talks between government and EXLN resumed (Jan.). Pact on electoral reform signed with other main parties (Aug.). Government mounts attack on new revolutionary group, the People's Revolutionary Army (ERP) operating in southern state of Guerrero (Aug.–Sept.).
	Peru	Arrest of leader of 'Shining Path' guerrilla movement (Jan.). Tupac Amaru terrorists seize 430 hostages at Japanese embassy in Peru (Dec.).
1997	*Peru*	Peruvian security forces storm Japanese embassy killing all terrorists and freeing hostages.

North America

United States since 1945

1945   Apr. 12   Roosevelt dies. Harry Truman sworn in as successor.

        July 16   Atomic bomb exploded near Alamogordo, New Mexico.

1946   Apr. 11   McMahon Act declares government monopoly over all US atomic energy activities.

        July 4   United States grants Philippines independence.

1947   June 23   Taft–Hartley Act outlawing trade union closed shop and allowing government to impose 'cooling-off' period before strike passed by Congress despite Presidential veto.

        July 26   Defense Department formed to co-ordinate military organization.

1948   Nov. 2   Truman defeats Republican candidate Thomas Dewey in Presidential election.

1949   Oct. 14   Eleven Communist Party leaders jailed for advocating overthrow of government.

        Oct. 26   Minimum Wage Bill raises minimum wage from 40¢ to 75¢ an hour.

1950   Jan. 21   Alger Hiss, a former State Department official, jailed for perjury after denying membership of a Communist spy organization.

        Jan. 31   Truman orders work to proceed on development of hydrogen bomb.

        Aug. 1   Guam becomes a US territory.

        Aug. 28   Truman takes control of railways to avert a strike. Returned to private owners 23 May 1952.

        Dec. 11   Supreme Court rules that 5th Amendment to the Constitution protects an individual from being forced to incriminate him or herself.

1951	Jan. 3	22nd Amendment to the Constitution limits Presidents to two terms in office.
1952	Apr. 8	Truman takes control of steel-works to avert strike; action ruled unconstitutional by Supreme Court.
	July 25	Puerto Rico becomes a self-governing US common-wealth territory.
	Nov. 1	First hydrogen bomb exploded at Eniwetok Atoll, Marshall Islands.
	Nov. 4	Republican Dwight Eisenhower defeats Democrat Adlai Stevenson in Presidential election.
1953	Jan. 20	Eisenhower inaugurated as 34th President.
	Apr. 20	US Communist Party ordered to register with Justice Department as an organization controlled by the USSR.
	June 19	Julius and Ethel Rosenberg executed as spies for pass-ing atomic secrets to the USSR.
1954	Apr. 22	Senate hearings into Sen. Joseph McCarthy's claims of communist subversion in army begin. They continue until 17 June.
	May 17	Supreme Court outlaws racial segregation in schools.
	May 24	Supreme Court declares Communist Party member-ship valid grounds for deportation of aliens.
	Dec. 2	Senate vote of censure against McCarthy effectively ends his witch-hunt campaign.
1955	Dec. 1	Black bus boycott led by Revd Martin Luther King begins in Montgomery, Alabama, in protest against racial discrimination.
	Dec. 5	American Federation of Labor and Committee for Industrial Organization merge under leadership of George Meany.
1956	Nov. 6	Eisenhower defeats Stevenson in Presidential election.
	Nov. 13	Supreme Court outlaws racial segregation on buses.
1957	Sept. 24	Eisenhower despatches 1,000 paratroops to protect black high school students asserting their rights to non-segregated education in Little Rock, Arkansas.
1959	Jan. 3	Alaska becomes 49th state.
	Aug. 21	Hawaii becomes 50th state.

| 1960 | Nov. 9 | Democrat John Kennedy narrowly defeats Republican Richard Nixon in Presidential election. |

1961	Jan. 20	Kennedy inaugurated as 35th President.
	Oct. 6	Kennedy declares that a 'prudent family' should possess a fall-out shelter to protect itself in event of nuclear war.
	Dec. 5	Kennedy announces 5 out of 7 Army recruits are rejected on physical grounds and calls for public to take up exercise and become 'athletes' rather than 'spectators'.

| 1962 | Jan. 12 | State Department announces that Communist Party members will be denied passports. |
| | Nov. 20 | Kennedy signs order prohibiting racial discrimination in housing built with federal funds. |

1963	June 17	Supreme Court rules religious ceremonies not essential in schools.
	Aug. 28	Martin Luther King leads 200,000 strong civil rights 'freedom march' in Washington.
	Nov. 22	Kennedy assassinated in Dallas, Texas, by Lee Harvey Oswald. Lyndon Johnson sworn in as 36th President.

1964	July 2	Civil Rights Act bans racial discrimination in services provision and by trade unions and businesses carrying on inter-state commerce.
	Aug. 30	Johnson signs anti-poverty Economic Opportunity Policy providing almost $1 billion for community action programmes.
	Sept. 27	Warren Commission appointed to investigate Kennedy assassination declares there was no conspiracy and that Oswald acted alone.
	Nov. 3	Johnson defeats Republican Barry Goldwater in Presidential election.

1965	July 30	Congress passes Medicare programme providing Federal medical insurance for over-65s.
	Aug. 6	Government takes powers under Voting Rights Act to compel local authorities to register black voters and to remove obstacles to their voting.
	Aug. 11	Black riots begin in Watts, Los Angeles, and continue until 16 August; 35 die.

1965	Oct. 17	Demonstrations throughout the United States against involvement in Vietnam.
	Oct. 19	House Committee on Un-American Activities begins investigation into Ku Klux Klan.
	Nov. 27	25,000 demonstrate in Washington against Vietnam War.
1966	July 1	Medicare comes into operation.
	Nov. 8	Republican Edward Brooke becomes first black ever elected to Senate.
1967	July 23	Black riots in Detroit. Troops deployed as disturbances continue until 30 July; 40 die and over 2,000 injured.
	Oct. 20	Major anti-Vietnam War demonstration in Washington.
1968	Feb. 29	National Advisory Committee on Civil Disorders (Kerner Commission) report condemns white racism in the United States and calls for aid to black communities.
	Mar. 31	Johnson announces he will not run for second term as President.
	Apr. 4	Martin Luther King assassinated in Memphis, Tennessee. Riots in over 100 cities follow.
	May 2	Black 'Poor People's March' on Washington begins. Culminates in 3,000 strong camp at 'Resurrection city'.
	June 5	Sen. Robert Kennedy shot in Los Angeles while campaigning for Democratic Presidential nomination. Dies on 6 June.
	Aug. 26	Anti-Vietnam War demonstrations at Democratic convention in Chicago quelled by police and troops. Disturbances continue until 30 August.
	Nov. 8	Republican Richard Nixon defeats Democrat Hubert Humphrey in Presidential election.
1969	Jan. 20	Nixon inaugurated as 37th President.
	Oct. 15	Mass demonstrations against Vietnam War throughout the United States.
1970	May 4	National Guard kills four anti-war students demonstrating at Kent State University, Ohio.
1971	Apr. 20	Supreme Court upholds bussing as a means of achieving racial balance in schools.
	May 2	Beginning of three-day anti-Vietnam War protest in Washington. Over 13,000 arrests.

June 3	Publication of leaked 'Pentagon Papers' disclosing hidden background to Vietnam War. Supreme Court refuses to prevent publication, 30 June.
July 5	26th Amendment to Constitution reduces voting age to 18.
Aug. 11	Law enforcing educational desegregation in 11 Southern states comes into effect.
Aug. 15	Nixon introduces anti-inflation wages and prices freeze; suspends convertibility of dollar into gold.

1972	May 15	Alabama Governor George Wallace, in the past an uncompromising segregationist, is wounded and crippled in assassination attempt.
	June 17	Five men arrested burgling the Democratic National Committee offices at Watergate building, Washington. On 22 June Nixon denies White House involvement.
	Nov. 7	Nixon wins landslide victory over Democrat George McGovern in Presidential election.

1973	Jan. 8–30	Watergate burglary trial. Two of the seven convicted had been 'Committee to Re-elect the President' officials, and one a White House consultant.
	Feb. 7	Senate forms a committee to investigate the Watergate affair.
	Feb. 27	Indians protesting against government treatment mount Siege of Wounded Knee. Two Indians die before it ends on 8 May.
	Apr. 30	White House advisers H.R. Haldeman and John Ehrlichman and staff member John Dean resign over participation in Watergate cover-up.
	May 11	'Pentagon Papers' case against Daniel Elsberg dismissed because government used burglary to obtain evidence.
	July 16	Revelation that Nixon has taped his White House conversations since 1970, eventually showing his active involvement in Watergate cover-up.
	Oct. 10	Vice-President Spiro Agnew forced to resign after disclosure of income tax evasion.
	Oct. 23	Nixon ordered to surrender White House tapes to Senate Watergate investigation under threat of impeachment.
	Nov. 7	Congress votes to limit Presidential powers to wage war.
	Dec. 6	Gerald Ford sworn in as Vice-President.

1974 Jan. 1   Three former Cabinet members and Nixon's two lead-
                  ing White House aides are convicted for their part in
                  covering up Watergate events.

      July 24   Supreme Court orders Nixon to release his tape-
                  recorded conversations.

      Aug. 9   Nixon resigns under threat of impeachment proceed-
                  ings for involvement in Watergate. Ford sworn in as
                  38th President.

      Sept. 8   Ford grants Nixon full pardon.

      Sept. 16   Ford announces amnesty for Vietnam War draft
                  evaders and deserters.

1976 Apr. 26   Senate Committee on Central Intelligence Agency
                  demands stronger control over and greater account-
                  ability of intelligence services following concern over
                  activities.

      Nov. 1   Democrat Jimmy Carter defeats Ford in Presidential
                  election.

1977 Jan. 20   Carter inaugurated as 39th President.

1978 June 6   Proposition 13 in California state referendum limits
                  local taxes, triggering a campaign nationally to reduce
                  federal and state taxation.

1979 Feb. 12   Carter appeals for voluntary conservation to limit
                  effects of growing energy crisis.

      Mar. 28   Serious atomic reactor accident at Three Mile Island,
                  Pennsylvania, provokes loss of public confidence in
                  nuclear power.

      June 13 $100 million awarded to Sioux Indians as compensa-
                  tion for land taken from them in 1877.

      Oct. 23   Congress grants Carter powers to introduce petrol
                  rationing because of world oil crisis.

1980 Nov. 4   Republican Ronald Reagan gains landslide Presiden-
                  tial election victory over Carter.

1981 Jan. 20   Reagan inaugurated as 40th President.

      Mar. 30   Reagan wounded in assassination attempt in Wash-
                  ington.

      Aug. 13   Reagan's New Economic Programme projects 25%
                  income tax reductions in 1981–84.

1982	June	Resignation of Alexander Haig as Secretary of State.
1983	Oct. 23	241 US Marine members of peace-keeping force killed by suicide bombers in Beirut.
	Oct. 25	US troops invade Grenada.
1984	June 6	Former Vice-President Walter Mondale wins Democratic nomination.
	July 12	Geraldine Ferraro first woman Vice-Presidential candidate.
	Nov. 6	Landslide re-election victory for Ronald Reagan.
1985	Jan. 20	Reagan inaugurated to 2nd term as President.
	May 1	US bans all trade with Nicaragua.
	Nov. 19–21	Reagan and Gorbachev summit in Geneva.
1986	Nov. 13	Reagan admits US arms sales to Iran, opening what becomes known as the Iran–Contra scandal.
	Nov. 25	Further revelations about arms sales to Iran force resignation of National Security Adviser Adm. John Poindexter and Marine Col. Oliver North.
	Dec. 2	Reagan appoints special prosecutor to investigate Iran–Contra scandal. As investigation develops details emerge of plan for proceeds of arms sales to Iran to be diverted to aiding Contra forces in Nicaragua.
1987	Mar. 3	Reagan says arms for Iran had been intended to help in release of hostages held in Middle East.
	July 15	Adm. Poindexter says Reagan unaware of plan to divert Iran arms sales proceeds to aid Contras.
	Aug. 12	Reagan accepts responsibility for Iran–Contra affair but denies knowledge of diversion of funds.
	Oct. 19	'Black Monday': massive slump in share prices on Wall Street.
1988	Mar. 16	Poindexter and North indicted on Iran–Contra charges.
	Nov. 8	George Bush defeats Democrat Michael Dukakis in Presidential election.
1989	Jan. 20	Bush is sworn in as the 41st President. The Vice-President is Dan Quayle.
	Sept.	In his address, Bush asks Congress for $8 billion to bolster the fight against drugs.

1989 Nov. 7   Democrats have striking success in mid-term elections.
                Douglas Wilder (Democrat) is elected Governor of
                Virginia, the nation's first black Governor since the
                Reconstruction Era.
                First elected black mayor of New York City (David
                Dinkins).
      Nov. 18   Pennsylvania becomes first state to restrict abortions
                (Supreme Court gave states this right in July).
      Nov. 19   Increase in minimum wage from $3.35 an hour to
                $4.25 by 1991.
      Dec. 20   US troops invade Panama. Noriega regime over-
                thrown; Noriega seeks asylum in Vatican nuncio's
                mission.

1990 Aug. 7   US forces embark for Saudi Arabia to repel Iraqis
                from Kuwait (Operation Desert Shield) (see p. 277).
      Nov. 15   President Bush signs Bill designed to reduce federal
                budget deficits by $500 billion over five years. Upper
                personal income tax rate to rise from 28% to 31%.

1991 Jan.–Feb. Defeat of Iraqi forces and liberation of Kuwait
                (Operation Desert Storm) in '100-hour war'.
      July 9   President Bush cancels the sanctions set up against
                the Republic of South Africa in 1986.
      July 10   Defense Base Closure and Realignment Commission
                proposals to reduce military bases accepted (start of
                post-Cold War run-down).

1992 Apr.–May Rioting and arson in South-Central Los Angeles fol-
                lowing acquittal of those police accused of beating
                Rodney King. Death toll estimated at 52.
      May   27th Amendment concerning Congressional pay rises
                finally becomes part of Constitution when Michigan
                becomes 38th state to approve.
      July 15   Governor Bill Clinton of Arkansas is nominated as
                candidate for Presidential election (Senator Al Gore
                of Tennessee is nominated for Vice-President on 16
                July). The populist H. Ross Perot, a Texan billionaire,
                temporarily withdraws from the Presidential race (17
                July).
      Nov. 3   Bill Clinton is elected 42nd President, defeating
                Bush. Independent candidate H. Ross Perot polls 19%
                of vote. Record number of women elected to the
                Senate. Carol Moseley Braun of Illinois becomes the
                first black woman to serve in the Senate.

	Nov. 24	The last American soldier leaves the military base in Subic Bay, thus ending the US military presence (since 1898) in the Philippines.

Nov. 24   The last American soldier leaves the military base in Subic Bay, thus ending the US military presence (since 1898) in the Philippines.

Dec. 9   UN military force, led by US troops, arrives in Somalia.

Dec. 17   United States, Canada and Mexico sign the NAFTA Treaty.

1993   Jan. 20   Inauguration of Bill Clinton as 42nd President.

Jan. 22   Executive order of Clinton overturns restrictions on abortion imposed under Presidents Reagan and Bush.

Jan. 25   Hillary Clinton appointed to head Task Force on National Health Care Reform.

Feb. 26   Bombing of World Trade Center, New York City, kills six people.

Feb. 28   Four federal agents killed in botched raid on Branch Davidian site in Waco, Texas. Beginning of 51-day siege, and storming of compound.

Mar. 12   Janet Reno becomes first woman Attorney-General of the United States.

Apr. 19   FBI agents launch final assault on the Branch Davidian ranch at Waco, Texas; 80 die.

May 13   Formal abandonment of Strategic Defense Initiative ('Star Wars') programme.

June 26   US rocket attack on Iraq in retaliation for earlier attempt on the life of George Bush.

July 19   Clinton appears to remove ban on gays and lesbians serving in armed forces.

July 20   Death of Vincent Foster, Deputy White House counsellor and close friend of Bill Clinton.

July 26   Disaster areas now proclaimed in nine states after worst Mississippi floods in living memory – 'The Great Flood of 1993'.

Aug. 6   Tax-raising budget breaks election pledges.

Sept. 29   Health-care reform package unveiled – the 1993 American Health Security Act.

Nov. 4   Democrat David Dinkins narrowly defeated as Mayor of New York.

Nov. 24   Following successful passage through the House of Representatives, the Senate also endorses the Brady Bill which creates a compulsory five-day waiting period for the purchase of fire-arms.

1994   Jan. 1   North American Free Trade Agreement (NAFTA) comes into force (endorsed earlier, on 18 November 1993, by Congress).

1994	Feb. 3	The 19-year old economic embargo against Vietnam is lifted.
	Mar. 25	Last US troops leave Somalia.
	May 30	Dan Rostenkowski, Chairman of House Ways and Means Committee, is indicted on fraud and corruption charges.
	June 15	Four-day tour of North Korea by ex-President Jimmy Carter. Threat of US sanctions avoided.
	Aug. 18	State of emergency in Florida in anticipation of influx of Cuban refugees. President Clinton ends 30-year policy of right to asylum for Cuban refugees (19th).
	July	Special counsel, Kenneth Starr, is appointed to probe Whitewater allegations.
	Sept. 26	US sanctions lifted against Haiti (US troops had earlier landed in a mission to restore democracy (19th)).
	Nov. 9	Sweeping Republican gains in mid-term elections. Republicans gain control of the Senate and (the first time for 40 years) the House of Representatives. Triumph of Newt Gingrich and the 'Contract with America'.
	Dec. 11	Miami Summit pledges the creation of a Free Trade Area of the Americas to end trade barriers by 2005.
1995	Jan. 4	Senator Bob Dole (Kansas) becomes Majority Leader. Newt Gingrich becomes first Republican Speaker since 1954.
	Mar. 2	Republican amendments to balance budget rejected by Senate.
	Mar. 7	Gerry Adams, Sinn Fein leader, received at White House.
	Apr. 19	Oklahoma bombing by right-wing anti-government militia leaves 168 dead. Arrest of Timothy James McVeigh.
	May 2	Agreement signed with Cuba regulating immigration policies.
	July 11	Establishment of full diplomatic links with Vietnam.
	Aug. 17	Special prosecutor indicts business associates of Clintons over Whitewater affair.
	Sept. 5	Ross Perot announces formation of the Reform Party.
	Oct. 26	Senate legal affairs committee resumes investigation into the Whitewater affair.
	Nov. 14	Government 'shut-down' after Budget deadlock between President and Congress.
	Nov. 21	Dayton Peace Accords signed. United States commits 20,000 troops to Bosnia.

1996	Jan. 7	Longest-ever government shut-down ended by compromise Budget proposals.
	Feb. 21	In primary elections, Republican Pat Buchanan wins New Hampshire, followed by victory for millionaire Steve Forbes in Arizona, 27 February.
	Mar. 6	Senator Bob Dole wins vital primaries, effectively securing Republican Party Presidential nomination.
	Mar. 20	US navy task force sent to Taiwan in stand-off with China.
	July	Explosion aboard TWA flight 800 over Long Island. Over 220 dead. Bomb blast at Centennial Olympic Games at Atlanta. Two die; over 100 injured.
	Aug.	Welfare Reform Bill signed by Clinton. End of the 60-year-old 'safety-net' for those in poverty.
	Aug. 29	Resignation of Dick Morris, top presidential adviser, in sex scandal, overshadows Chicago Democratic Convention.
	Sept. 3	Missile strike launched to punish Iraqi action over Kurds.
	Oct. 14	Dow Jones passes 6,000 mark.
	Nov.	Presidential election results in comfortable victory for incumbent Bill Clinton (with 49% of the vote and 379 electoral votes). Bob Dole (Republican) took 42% of the vote and 159 electoral votes. Ross Perot's Reform Party polled only 9% of the vote. Turn-out dropped to its lowest in post-war history (at 49.1%).
1998	Apr.	Second Clinton administration survives repeated allegations of sexual misconduct.

United States and the world from 1945

1945	May 8	VE Day. End of war in Europe.
	June 26	50 nations sign United Nations Charter in San Francisco.
	July 17–Aug. 2	Potsdam Conference between Truman, Stalin and Churchill (later Attlee) reaches decision on division of Germany and demand for Japan's unconditional surrender.
	Aug. 6	Atomic bomb dropped on Hiroshima.
	Aug. 9	Atomic bomb dropped on Nagasaki.
	Aug. 14	VJ Day. Japan acknowledges defeat.
	Sept. 2	Japan formally surrenders on USS *Missouri* in Tokyo.

1946   Aug. 1   Atomic Energy Act restricts exchange of nuclear information with other nations.

        Oct. 16   UN General Assembly opens in New York.

1947   Mar. 12   Truman signs Greek-Turkish Aid Bill promising the two states $400 million aid to resist Soviet aggression and internal communist subversion. Becomes known as the 'Truman Doctrine'.

        June 7   Secretary of State George Marshall proposes Marshall Plan to assist European economic recovery.

1948   Apr. 3   Marshall's European Recovery Programme enacted. By 1952 Europe receives $17,000 million in aid.

        June 24   Berlin airlift begins. United States and Britain fly in 2 million tons of supplies to counter Soviet rail and road blockade. Ends following negotiations, 12 May 1949.

1949   Apr. 4   United States signs North Atlantic Treaty in Washington with 11 other states to create NATO alliance.

1950   May 25   United States, Britain and France conclude Tripartite Agreement to reduce Middle East tension by guaranteeing existing borders and limiting arms sales.

        July 1   US troops arrive as part of United Nations force to assist South Korea, invaded by North Korea on 25 June.

        Sept. 26   US troops recapture South Korean capital Seoul.

        Oct. 7   US troops cross 38th Parallel into North Korea and advance to Manchurian border on Yalu River by 20 November.

        Nov. 29   US troops forced to retreat in Korea by heavy Chinese attack.

        Dec. 19   US Gen. Dwight Eisenhower appointed Supreme Commander of NATO forces in Europe.

1951   Jan. 4   Seoul abandoned by US forces.

        Mar. 14   Seoul recaptured by US troops.

        Apr. 11   Gen. Douglas MacArthur dismissed by Truman from command in Korea and all military offices for defying policy by advocating attack on Communist China.

	Oct. 10	Truman signs Mutual Security Act authorizing over $7 billion expenditure overseas on economic, military and technical aid.
1952	Nov. 1	United States explodes first hydrogen device at Eniwetok Atoll, Marshall Islands.
1953	July 27	Armistice signed at Panmunjon ends fighting in Korea. 54,000 US servicemen died in war.
1954	Jan. 12	Secretary of State John Foster Dulles announces doctrine of 'massive retaliation' warning USSR that aggression will be met with nuclear attack.
	Mar. 8	US mutual defence agreement with Japan allows gradual re-arming of Japan.
	Sept. 8	Manila Treaty creates South-East Asia Treaty Organization (SEATO) of US and seven other states for military and economic co-operation (see p. 223).
	Dec. 2	United States signs Mutual Security Pact with Taiwan guaranteeing protection from Chinese attack. In effect until 1978.
1955	Feb. 12	Eisenhower despatches troops to South Vietnam as military advisers.
	Mar. 16	Eisenhower announces that atomic weapons would be used in event of war. US reported to have 4,000 bombs stockpiled.
	July 18–23	United States attends summit meeting with Britain, France and USSR. Independence of East and West Germany recognized; Eisenhower proposes 'open skies' aerial photography plan as move towards disarmament.
1955	Aug. 15	United States signs Austrian State Treaty with Britain, France and USSR restoring Austrian independence within 1937 borders.
1957	Jan. 5	Eisenhower Doctrine proposes military and economic aid to Middle East states threatened internally or externally by communism. Congress votes $200 million.
1958	July 15	US troops intervene in Lebanon Civil War under Eisenhower Doctrine following appeal from Lebanon President. Withdraw 25 October.

1958	Aug. 23	US military preparations provoked by fears that Chinese shelling of offshore Nationalist island of Quemoy is a prelude to invasion of Taiwan.
1959	Sept. 15–27	Eisenhower meets Soviet leader Nikita Khrushchev at Camp David and both agree on need for 'peaceful co-existence'.
	Dec. 1	United States signs Antarctica Treaty with 11 other states guaranteeing the area's neutrality.
1960	Jan. 19	United States and Japan sign mutual defence pact. Comes into effect 23 June.
	May 1	American U-2 spy plane shot down over USSR and pilot captured.
	May 9	United States announces suspension of U-2 flights.
	May 16	Summit conference with USSR in Paris terminated when Eisenhower refuses to apologize to Khrushchev over U-2 incident.
	July 11	American RB-47 reconnaissance bomber shot down over Soviet Union.
1961	Jan. 3	United States breaks off diplomatic relations with Cuba over nationalization of American property without compensation.
	Mar. 1	Kennedy sets up Peace Corps as part of overseas aid programme.
	Apr. 17	1,600-strong invasion of Cuba at Bay of Pigs by CIA-trained Cuban exiles with Kennedy's backing. Crushed by 20 April.
	June 3–4	Kennedy and Khrushchev discuss German unification at unsuccessful summit conference in Vienna.
	Dec. 11	United States despatches helicopters and crews to assist South Vietnam; 3,500 US troops in area.
1962	May 12	US troops deployed in Thailand to counter communist threat. They withdraw by 27 July.
	June 16	Defense Secretary Robert McNamara announces 'flexible response' to replace 'massive retaliation' strategy.
	June 27	Kennedy promises Taiwan military assistance in event of Chinese attack.
	Oct. 22–28	Cuban missile crisis. Kennedy announces aerial photography reveals Soviet missile sites in Cuba. Places Cuba under naval and air blockade to pre-

vent delivery of missiles. Khrushchev removes missiles in return for US promise not to invade Cuba.

Dec. 18   Nassau Agreement between Kennedy and British Prime Minister Macmillan to provide Britain with Polaris nuclear missiles for submarines.

1963 Apr. 5   Hot-line connected between White House and Kremlin.

June 25   Kennedy announces on European tour that US 'will risk its cities to defend yours'.

Aug. 5   Nuclear weapons tests in atmosphere, space and underwater banned by treaty between United States, Britain and USSR.

Oct. 7   White House announces aid to Vietnam will continue and that war could be won by end of 1965.

1964 Aug. 5   First US bombing of North Vietnam.

Aug. 7   Congress grants Johnson sweeping military powers under Gulf of Tonkin Resolution, following alleged North Vietnamese attacks on US destroyers, 2–4 August.

1965 Feb. 7   United States begins heavy sustained bombing of North Vietnam.

Feb. 18   Defense Secretary McNamara announces deterrent strategy of 'mutually assured destruction'.

Mar. 8   US combat troops land in Vietnam bringing numbers involved to 74,000.

Apr. 28   400 US marines land in Dominican Republic to prevent left-wing take-over. The force eventually rises to 24,000.

June 15   US troops in first action against Viet Cong.

July 28   Johnson announces numbers of US troops in Vietnam will be increased from 75,000 to 125,000.

1966 Feb. 8   Declaration of Honolulu by Johnson and South Vietnam Premier Ky promises economic and social reforms in Vietnam.

Mar. 2   Defense Secretary Robert McNamara announces US forces in Vietnam will be increased to 235,000.

June 11   US forces in Vietnam to rise to 285,000.

1967 Jan. 27   Space Treaty with Britain and USSR outlaws use of nuclear weapons in space.

1967	June 23–25	Summit meeting between Johnson and Soviet leader Kosygin in Glassboro, New Jersey.
	July 22	Announcement of intention to deploy 525,000 US troops in Vietnam by end of 1968.
	July 27	Puerto Rico votes against independence and to remain a US commonwealth territory.
1968	Jan. 23	North Korea seizes crew of USS *Pueblo* and accuses them of spying. They are released on 22 December.
	Jan. 30	Viet Cong open 'Tet' offensive. Although a military failure for the Communists, the attack has a dramatic effect on US commitment to war in Vietnam.
	Mar. 16	US troops massacre 450 inhabitants in Vietnamese village of My Lai. News does not break until November. Lt. William Calley given life imprisonment, 29 March 1971, but sentence reduced.
	Mar. 31	Johnson announces end to bombing of North Vietnam.
	May 13	Preliminary Vietnam peace talks open in Paris.
	July 1	United States signs Nuclear Non-Proliferation Treaty with Britain and USSR.
1969	Jan. 25	Full Vietnam peace talks begin in Paris.
	Mar.	US troops in Vietnam reach their highest level at 541,000.
	Nov. 3	Nixon announces intention to withdraw US forces and to 'Vietnamize' the war.
	Nov. 25	United States renounces use of biological weapons.
1970	Apr. 16	Strategic Arms Limitation Talks (SALT) open between US and USSR in Vienna.
	Apr. 21	Nixon announces 150,000 US troop reduction in Vietnam over next year.
	Apr. 30	US troops deployed in Cambodia.
1971	June 10	United States lifts 21-year trade embargo on China.
	Oct. 25	United States signs Seabed Treaty with USSR, Britain and other states banning nuclear weapons on ocean floor.
1972	Feb. 21–25	Nixon reverses US policy by visiting Communist China.
	Apr. 6	United States resumes bombing of North Vietnam following communist offensive.

May 22–30   Nixon and Brezhnev agree to limit atomic weapon production at Moscow Summit. Senate ratifies agreement on 3 August.

1973   Jan. 28   Cease-fire ends US involvement in Vietnam War. Final combat troops leave 29 March.

June 16–24   Nixon and Brezhnev summit meeting in the United States reaches agreement on co-operation to prevent nuclear war and on future arms negotiations.

July 1   Congress orders end to US bombing of Cambodia and military action in area by 15 August.

Oct. 17   Arab states ban oil supplies to United States in protest against support for Israel. Ends 1974.

1974   Jan. 10   Defense Secretary James Schlesinger announces 'limited strategic strike options' as new nuclear doctrine.

May 7   Ford declares Vietnam War era is over a week after Saigon falls to Communists.

July 3   United States signs Threshold Test Ban Treaty with USSR, placing limits on underground nuclear testing.

1975   Aug. 1   United States signs Helsinki Treaty with USSR guaranteeing European post-war boundaries and recognizing human rights.

1977   Sept. 7   Carter signs Panama Canal Zone Treaty agreeing to evacuate Canal Zone by the year 2000.

1978   Sept. 5–17   Carter mediates at Camp David negotiations between Egyptian President Sadat and Israeli Prime Minister Begin, culminating in outline Middle East peace treaty. Treaty signed at White House 26 March 1979; effective 25 April 1979.

1979   Jan. 1   United States establishes full diplomatic relations with China and severs links with Nationalist government on Taiwan.

Feb. 8   United States withdraws support from President Somoza of Nicaragua ensuring his downfall to Sandinista revolution.

Nov. 4   Iranian students occupy US Embassy in Tehran and seize 52 American hostages.

1979 Nov. 4   United States establishes formal relations with Ger-
                    man Democratic Republic.

1980 Apr. 24–25   Eight US dead in unsuccessful helicopter attempt
                    to rescue Tehran Embassy hostages.
      Dec. 21   Iran demands $10,000 million payment for release
                    of Embassy hostages.

1981 Jan. 20   US Embassy hostages released from Tehran as
                    Reagan is sworn in as President.

1983 Oct. 23   241 US Marine members of peace-keeping force
                    killed by suicide bombers in Beirut.
      Oct. 25   US troops invade Grenada with forces of six Carib-
                    bean states to put down alleged left-wing threat.
                    Suffer 42 dead in fighting with Grenada Army and
                    Cuban construction workers.

1985 May 1   United States bans all trade with Nicaragua.
      Nov. 19–21   Reagan and Gorbachev summit in Geneva agrees
                    on future annual meetings but fails to resolve differ-
                    ences over 'Star Wars' as obstacle to arms control.

1986 Jan. 7   Reagan orders US citizens to leave Libya and bans
                    trade in retaliation for alleged Libyan involvement
                    in international terrorism.
      Feb. 18   Reagan announces $15 million military aid to anti-
                    government guerrillas in Angola.
      Mar. 20   House of Representatives rejects Reagan's $100
                    million aid package to anti-government Contra guer-
                    rillas in Nicaragua. Finally approves on 25 June and
                    Reagan signs Bill on 18 October.
      Mar. 24   US task force asserting sailing rights in Gulf of Sidra
                    attacked by Libyan missile ships. United States sinks
                    two ships and bombs coastal radar installation.
      Apr. 14   American F-111 bombers strike Tripoli and Benghazi
                    following alleged Libyan links with international
                    terrorism.
      June 18   House of Representatives votes for trade embargo
                    on South Africa and withdrawal by US companies.
      June 27   International Court rules US support of Contras in
                    Nicaragua illegal.
      July 15   US troops deployed in Bolivia to assist in opera-
                    tions against cocaine producers.

	Sept. 26	Reagan vetoes South African sanctions proposal by House of Representatives.
	Oct. 2	US Senate defies Presidential veto and imposes trade sanctions on South Africa.
	Oct. 10–11	Reagan and Gorbachev meet in Reykjavik, Iceland. Blame each other for failure to achieve arms control agreement.
1987	Nov. 24	United States reaches agreement with USSR on scrapping of intermediate-range nuclear missiles.
	Dec. 8–11	Reagan and Gorbachev summit meeting in Washington. Intermediate-range missiles treaty signed; agreement on further arms reductions proposals and for a meeting in 1988.
1988	May 29	Reagan and Gorbachev meet in Moscow and agree on further intermediate-range missile reductions.
	July 3	USS *Vincennes* shoots down Iranian Airbus over Gulf of Iran, killing 290 passengers.
	Dec. 14	United States declares willingness to talk with Palestine Liberation Organization following Yasser Arafat's 7 December acceptance of Israel's right to exist. Discussions in Tunis take place, 16 December.
1989	Jan. 4	US navy jets shoot down two Libyan aircraft over Mediterranean.
	Dec.	US forces invade Panama in operation to overthrow Noriega regime.
1990	Aug. 7	US forces embark for Saudi Arabia to repel Iraqis from Kuwait (Operation Desert Shield).
1991	Jan.–Feb.	Defeat of Iraqi forces and liberation of Kuwait (Operation Desert Storm) (see p. 277).
	July 9	Sanctions against South Africa withdrawn.
	July 10	Defense Base Closure and Realignment Commission proposals to reduce military bases accepted.
1992	Nov. 24	Americans leave base in Subic Bay in the Philippines (acquired 1898).
	Dec. 9	US forces deployed in Somalia.
	Dec. 17	USA, Canada and Mexico sign free trade treaty.
1993	May 13	America abandons Strategic Defense Initiative ('Star Wars' programme).

1993	June 26	USA missile attack on Iraq in retaliation for earlier attempt on life of George Bush.
	Oct. 3	18 US soldiers killed in Somalia.
	Dec.	Uruguay Round of GATT trade negotiations concluded on the basis of a 40% cut in tariffs.

1994	Jan. 1	North American Free Trade Area (NAFTA) comes into force.
	Feb. 3	US economic embargo on Vietnam lifted.
	Mar. 25	Last US troops leave Somalia.
	June 15	Four-day tour of North Korea by ex-President Jimmy Carter.
	Aug. 18	Anticipated influx of Cuban refugees; Clinton ends 30-year-old policy of right of asylum.
	Sept. 26	US sanctions lifted against Haiti.
	Dec. 11	United States pledges creation of free trade area of all the Americas by 2005 at Miami Summit.

1995	May 2	Agreement signed with Cuba over immigration policies.
	July 11	Full diplomatic links established with Vietnam.
	Nov. 21	Dayton Peace Accords commit 20,000 troops to peace-keeping in Bosnia.

| 1996 | Sept. 3 | Missile strikes launched against Iraq for assaults on Kurds. |
| | Nov. 15 | United States commits 5,000 troops to Rwanda peace-keeping force. |

| 1997 | Nov. | United States threatens military action against Iraq for violations of arms inspection agreements (crisis repeated in March 1998). |

Canada since 1945

1945   King's Liberal Party returned in general election (June).

1946   Arrests of Soviet spies allegedly involved in transfer of atomic secrets to Russia (Feb.). British Labour government authorizes the election of a Newfoundland Convention to discuss its future (June).

1948   Referendum on future of Newfoundland indecisive (June); second referendum (July) gives majority for federation with

Canada. Louis St Laurent becomes Liberal leader and Prime Minister in succession to MacKenzie King (Nov.).

1949   Newfoundland becomes 10th province of Canada (Mar.); Canada signs North Atlantic Treaty (Apr.). Official Languages Act establishes English and French as dual official languages. British North America Act gives federal parliament limited rights to amend constitution.

1950   Death of Mackenzie King (July).

1951   Old Age Security Act introduced.

1952   Collaboration on production of hydro-electric power with United States begins.

1953   Work begun on St Lawrence Seaway system of canals and locks linking the Atlantic and the Great Lakes. General election won by St Laurent for the Liberals.

1956   John Diefenbaker becomes leader of Progressive Conservative Party (Dec.).

1957   St Laurent loses general election to Diefenbaker and the Conservatives form minority government (June), ending 22 years of Liberal government.

1958   St Laurent hands over as leader of opposition to Lester Pearson; Conservatives obtain clear majority of 158 seats in new election (Mar.). Conference at Montreal institutes Commonwealth Assistance Loans.

1959   St Lawrence Seaway formally opened (June).

1963   Diefenbaker resigns (17 Apr.); Pearson forms Liberal government (22 Apr.).

1964   Canada adopts Maple Leaf emblem for National flag. Growing discontent between French and English-speaking Canadians and growing movement for separatism in Quebec.

1967   Diefenbaker retires from politics. De Gaulle angers Canadian government by references to autonomy for French Canada on visit to Quebec (July).

1968   Pearson resigns in favour of Pierre Trudeau (Apr.): Trudeau increases Liberal majority at general election (June).

1970   *Parti Québécois* gains six seats in Quebec National Assembly (of 110).

1972   Trudeau left as head of minority Liberal government following general election (Oct.).

1974   Trudeau regains majority in general election.

1976   *Parti Québécois* gains 70 seats in Quebec National Assembly.

1977   Visit of head of *Parti Québécois*, René Lévesque, to France with full honours (Nov.).

1979   Trudeau defeated in general election (May); Conservative government under Joe Clark.

1980   Trudeau leads Liberals to general election victory (Feb.). Trudeau proposes 'patriation' of the Constitution, severing last constitutional links with Britain, causing violent scenes in parliament. Referendum (20 May) in Quebec votes against proposal of *Parti Québécois* for negotiation for a looser political association with the rest of Canada.

1981   Canada formally asks Britain for 'patriation' of the Constitution (Dec.).

1982   Canada Bill, approving patriation, passes British House of Commons. Queen Elizabeth visits Canada to formalize complete national sovereignty for Canada (Apr.). New constitution replaces Acts of 1867 and 1949, provides a bill of rights and redefines ethnic, provincial and territorial rights.

1983   Brian Mulroney takes over as leader of Conservative Party from Joe Clark (June).

1984   John Turner succeeds Trudeau as Liberal leader and Prime Minister (June). Conservatives sweep to victory in general election (Sept.), winning 211 of 282 seats.

1988   General election on issue of Free Trade Agreement with the United States leads to further victory for Mulroney and the

Progressive Conservative Party (Nov.). Free Trade Agreement with United States enacted.

1992   A plebiscite rejects a constitutional reform package endorsed by leaders of the 10 provinces of the country in August. The new Constitution would have offered a special status to French-speaking Quebec and placed greater power into the hands of the governments and legislatures of the provinces (Oct.).
Prime Minister Mulroney, with US President Bush and Mexican President de Gortari, signs the North American Free Trade Association Treaty (NAFTA) (Dec.).

1993   In accordance with the agreement signed by Prime Minister Mulroney (May), the Canadian Eskimos will receive a 2.2 million sq. km territory called Nunavut in 1999. The name means 'our land' in the language of the Inuit tribe.
Mrs Kim Campbell, former Minister of Defense, takes over from the retiring Mulroney as the head of the Progressive Conservative Party and the government (June). Gaining only two seats, the Conservatives suffer a devastating defeat at the parliamentary elections (Oct.). Jean Chrétien, the leader of the Liberals, who have won an absolute majority, forms a government (Nov.). With 54 seats, the separatist Bloc Québécois becomes the largest opposition force.

1994   Re-election of hard-line separatist Premier Jacques Parizeau in Quebec.

1995   Federalists win narrow victory in referendum on future of Quebec (Oct.). Jacques Parizeau resigns as leader of the *Parti Québécois.*

1996   Lucien Bouchard assumes leadership of *Parti Québécois* (Jan.). Chrétien reshuffles his Cabinet with greater representation from British Columbia and Quebec.

1997   General election in June results in re-election of Chrétien's Liberal government with a slightly reduced majority.

Heads of state and selected ministers/rulers

Afghanistan

Kingdom of Afghanistan

King

Muhammad Zahir Shah   1933–73

The monarchy was overthrown in a peaceful coup in July 1973 and a republic instituted.

Republic of Afghanistan

Presidents

Lt.-Gen. M. Daoud	1973–78
D. Kadir (acting)	1978 (Apr.–May)
N. Taraki	1978–79
H. Amin	1979 (Oct.–Dec.)
B. Karmal	1979–86
M. Najibullah	1986–92
S. Majaddedi	1992 (Apr.–June)
B. Rabbani	1992–96*

Albania

Socialist Republic (until 1991), then Republic

Presidents

O. Nishani	1946–53
Maj.-Gen. H. Leshi	1953–82
R. Alia	1982–92
S. Berisha	1992–97

* Following the Taleban revolution, Afghanistan was declared an Islamic Emirate in 1997.

Prime Ministers

Col.-Gen. E. Hoxha	1946–54
Col.-Gen. M. Shehu	1954–82
A. Çarçani	1982–91
Y. Bufi	1991
V. Ahmeti	1991–92
A. Mekhi	1992–97
B. Fino	1997–

First Secretaries, Albanian Workers' Party*

Col.-Gen. E. Hoxha	1946–48
Col.-Gen. M. Shehu	1948–53
Gen. E. Hoxha	1953–85
R. Alia	1985–92

Angola

Angola became independent from Portugal as a Republic in 1975.

Presidents

A. Neto	1975–79
J. dos Santos	1979–

Prime Ministers

L. Ferreira do Nascimento	1975–78 (post temporarily abolished)
M.J.C. Moco	1990–96
F.J.F. Van Dúnem	1996–

Argentina

Presidents

Gen. E. Farrell	1944–46
Gen. J. Perón	1946–55
Gen. E. Leonardi	1955 (Sept.–Nov.)
Gen. P. Aramburu	1955–58
A. Frondizi	1958–62
J. Guido (acting)	1962–63
A. Illia	1963–66
Gen. J. Ongania	1966–70
Military junta	1970 (June)

* During communist era.

Brig.-Gen. R. Levingston	1970–71
Military junta	1971 (Mar.)
Gen. A. Lanusse	1971–73
H. Campora	1973 (May–July)
R. Lastiri (acting)	1973 (July–Oct.)
Gen. J. Perón	1973–74
M. (Isabel) Perón	1974–75
I. Luder (acting)	1975 (Sept.–Oct.)
M. (Isabel) Perón	1975–76
Military junta	1976 (March)
Gen. J. Videla	1976–81
Gen. R. Viola	1981 (Mar.–Dec.)
Gen. L. Galtieri	1981–82
Gen. R. Bignone	1982–83
R. Alfonsín Foulkes	1983–89
C. Menem	1989–

Australia

Governors-General

Henry, Duke of Gloucester	1936–47
Sir W. Dugan (acting)	1947 (Jan.–Mar.)
Sir W. McKell	1947–52
W. Slim, Viscount Slim	1952–60
W. Morrison, Viscount Dunrossil	1960–61
Sir R. Brooks (acting)	1961 (Feb.–Aug.)
Sir W. Sidney, Viscount de I'Isle	1961–65
Sir H. Smith (acting)	1965 (May–Sept.)
Sir R. Casey, Baron Casey	1965–69
Sir P. Hasluck	1969–74
Sir J. Kerr	1974–77
Z. Cohen	1977–82
Sir N. Stephen	1982–89
W. Hayden	1989–96
Sir W. Deane	1996–

Prime Ministers

F. Forde (acting	1945 (July)
J. Chifley	1945–49
Sir R. Menzies	1949–66
H. Holt	1966–67
Sir J. McEwen	1967–68
J. Gorton	1968–71

W. McMahon	1971–72
E.G. Whitlam	1972–75
J. Fraser	1975–83
R. Hawke	1983–91
P. Keating	1991–96
J. Howard	1996–

Austria

Presidents

K. Renner	1945–50
L. Figl (acting)	1950–51
T. Körner	1951–57
J. Raab	1957 (Jan.–May)
A. Schärf	1957–65
J. Klaus (acting)	1965 (Feb.–June)
F. Jonas	1965–74
B. Kreitsky (acting)	1974 (Apr.–July)
R. Kirchschläger	1974–86
K. Waldheim	1986–92
T. Klestil	1992–

Belgium

Kings

Leopold III	1934–51

There was a Regency from September 1944 to July 1950. Leopold III returned to the throne in July 1950 and abdicated in July the following year.

Prince Charles (Regent)	1944–50
Leopold III	1950–51
Baudouin I	1951–93
Albert II	1993–

Prime Ministers

A. Van Acker	1945–46
P.-H. Spaak	1946 (Mar.)
A. Van Acker	1946 (Mar.–July)
C. Huysmans	1946–47
P.-H. Spaak	1947–49
G. Eyskens	1949–50
J. Duvieusart	1950 (June–Aug.)

J. Pholien	1950–52
J. Van Houtte	1952–54
A. Van Acker	1954–58
G. Eyskens	1958–61
T. Lefevre	1961–65
P. Harmel	1965–66
P. Vanden Boeynants	1966–68
G. Eyskens	1968–72
E. Leburton	1973–74
L. Tindemans	1974–78
P. Vanden Boeynants	1978 (Nov.–Dec.)
W. Martens	1979–81
M. Eyskens	1981 (Apr.–Sept.)
W. Martens	1981–92
J.-L. Dehaene	1992–

Brazil

Presidents

J. Linhares	1945–46
Gen. E. Gaspar Dutra	1946–51
G. Dornelles Vargas	1951–54
J. Café Filho	1954–55
C. Coimbra da Luz (acting)	1955 (Nov.)
N. de Oliveira Ramos (acting)	1955–56
J. Kubitschek de Oliveira	1956–61
J. da Silva Quadros	1961 (Jan.–Aug.)
P. Ranieri Mazzilli	1961 (Aug.–Sept.)
J. Marques Goulart	1961–64
P. Ranieri Mazzilli (acting)	1964 (Apr.)
Marshal H. Castelo Branco	1964–67
Marshal A. da Costa e Silva	1967–69
Gen. E. Garrastazu	1969–74
Gen. E. Geisel	1974–79
Gen. J. Baptista de Fugueiredo	1979–85
J. Sarney	1985–89
F. Collor de Mello	1989–92
I. Franco	1992–95
H. Cardoso	1995–

Cambodia

Cambodia was a French protectorate from 1863, gained autonomy in 1945 and independence in 1953.

Kingdom of Cambodia

High Commissioners of the Indo-Chinese Federation

G. d'Argenlieu	1945–47
E. Bollaert	1947–48
L. Pignon	1948–50
J. de Lattre de Tassigny	1950–52
J. Letourneau	1952–53

Kings

(under French protection)

Norodom Sihanouk	1941–53

The Kingdom became independent in 1953.

Norodom Sihanouk	1953–55
Norodom Suramarit	1955–60
Council of Regency	1960 (Apr.–June)

Head of State

Prince Norodom Sihanouk	1960–68

State of Cambodia

Head of State

Cheng Heng	1968–70

Prime Ministers

Samdech Penn Nouth	1968–69
Gen. Lon Nol	1969–70

The Khmer Republic

Presidents

Cheng Heng	1970–72
Gen. Lon Nol	1972–75

Democratic Cambodia

Presidents

Prince Norodom Sihanouk	1975–76
Khieu Samphan	1976–81
Heng Samrin	1981–91

Prime Ministers

Samdech Penn Nouth	1975–76
Pol Pot	1976 (Apr.–Sept.)
Nuon Chea (acting)	1976–77
Pol Pot	1977–79
Khieu Samphan	1979–81
Pen Sovann	1981–82
Chan Si	1982–84
Hun Sen	1985–91

*Kingdom of Cambodia**

King

Norodom Sihanouk	1993–

Prime Ministers

Norodom Ranariddh	1993–97
Hun Sen	1993–
Ing Huot	1997–

Canada

Governors-General

A. Cambridge, Earl of Athlone	1940–46
H. Alexander, Viscount Alexander of Tunis	1946–52
V. Massey	1952–59
Maj.-Gen. G. Vanier	1959–67
D. Michener	1967–74
J. Léger	1974–79
E. Schreyer	1979–84
J. Sauvé	1984–89
R. Hnatyshyn	1989–94
R. Leblanc	1994–

Prime Ministers

W. Mackenzie King	1935–48
L. St Laurent	1948–57
J. Diefenbaker	1957–63
L. Pearson	1963–68

* Established after Interim Government, 1991–93.

P. Trudeau	1968–79
J. Clark	1979–80
P. Trudeau	1980–84
J. Turner	1984 (June–Sept.)
B. Mulroney	1984–93
K. Campbell	1993 (Feb.–Oct.)
J. Chrétien	1993–

Chile

Presidents

J. Antonio Rios	1942–46
A. Duhale (acting)	1946 (June–Aug.)
Vice-Adm. V. Merino Bielech (acting)	1946 (Aug.–Nov.)
G. González Videla	1946–52
Gen. C. Ibáñez del Campo	1952–58
J. Alessandri Rodríguez	1958–64
E. Frei Montalva	1964–70
S. Allende Gossens	1970–73
Gen. A. Pinochet Ugarte (acting)	1973–74
(President)	1974–90
Patricio Aylwin	1990–94
Eduardo Frei	1994–

China

Presidents

| Chiang Kai-shek | 1943–49 |
| Gen. Li Tsung-jen | 1949 (Jan.–Dec.) |

Presidents of the Executive Yuan (Prime Minister)

Chiang Kai-shek	1939–45
Soong Tzu-wen	1945–47
Chiang Kai-shek	1947 (Mar.–Apr.)
Gen. Chang Chun	1947–48
Wong Wen-hao	1948 (May–Nov.)
Sun Fo	1948–49
Gen. Ho Ying-chin	1949 (Mar.–June)
Marshal Yen Hsi-shan	1949 (June–Dec.)

A Communist regime took power at the end of a civil war in 1949.

Chairmen of the Republic

Mao Zedong	1949–58
Marshal Zhu De	1958–59
Liu Shaoqi	1959–68
Dong Biwu	1968–75

(The office was abolished in 1975.)

Chairmen of the Communist Party

Mao Zedong	1949–76
Hua Guofeng	1976–81
Hu Yaobang	1981–82

This office was abolished in 1982 and replaced by the post of General Secretary, which Hu Yaobang took.

Prime Ministers

Zhou Enlai	1949–76
Hua Guofeng	1976–80
Zhao Ziyang	1980–88
Li Peng	1988–98
Zhu Rongji	1998–

Congo

The Belgian Congo until independence in 1960. Under the regime of the dictator Mobutu, the country was called Zaïre (1965–97).

Governors-General

P. Ryckmans	1934–46
E. Jungers	1946–51
L. Pétillon	1951–58
H. Cornelis	1958–60

Presidents

J. Kasavubu	1960–65
J.-D. Mobutu (became Mobutu Sésé Séko Kuku Ngbendu wa Zabanga)	1965–97
L.-D. Kabila	1997–

Cuba

Presidents

R. Grau San Martin	1944–48
C. Prío Socarrás	1948–52
Gen. F. Batista y Zalvidar	1952–59
C. Piedra (acting)	1959 (Jan.)
M. Urrutia Lleo (acting)	1959 (Jan.–July)
O. Dórticos Torrado	1959–76
F. Castro Ruíz	1976–

Prime Ministers

J. Miro Cardona	1959 (Jan.–Feb.)
F. Castro Ruíz	1959–

Castro also held the post of First Secretary of the Communist Party Central Committee from 1965.

Czechoslovakia

Presidents

E. Hácha	1938–45

Czechoslovakia became a German Protectorate in March 1939. Beneš presided over a Czech government-in-exile and returned to Czechoslovakia in 1945.

E. Beneš	1945–48
K. Gottwald	1948–53
A. Zápotocky	1953–57
A. Novotny	1957–68
Gen. L. Svoboda	1968–75
G. Husák	1975–89
V. Havel	1989–92

Czechoslovakia was divided into the Czech Republic and Slovakia as of 1 January 1993.

Czech Republic

President

V. Havel	1993–

Denmark

Monarchs

Christian X	1912–47
Frederick IX	1947–72
Margarethe II	1972–

Prime Ministers

K. Kristensen	1945–47
H. Hedtoft	1947–50
E. Eriksen	1950–53
H. Hedtoft	1953–55
H. Hansen	1955–60
V. Kampmann	1960–62
J. Krag	1962–68
H. Baunsgard	1968–71
J. Krag	1971–72
A. Jorgensen	1972–73
P. Hartling	1973–75
A. Jorgensen	1978–82
P. Schlüter	1982–93
P.N. Rasmussen	1993–

Egypt

Kings

Farouk	1936–52
Regency for Ahmad Faud II	1952–53

Presidents

Gen. M. Neguib	1953–54
Col. G.A. Nasser	1954–70
A. Sadat	1970–81
S. Talib (acting)	1981 (Oct.)
Lt.-Gen. H. Mubarak	1981–

El Salvador

Presidents

O. Aguirre Salinas	1944–45
S. Castañeda Castro	1945–48

M. Cordoba	1948–49
O. Osorio	1949–56
J. Lemus	1956–60
C. Yanes Urias	1960–61
A. Portillo	1961 (Jan.–Feb.)
M. Castillo	1961–62
E. Cordón Cea	1962 (Jan.–July)
J. Rivera Carballo	1962–67
F. Sánchez Hernández	1967–72
A. Molina Barraza	1972–77
Gen. C. Romero Mena	1977–79
Civilian/military junta under A. Majano and J. Gutiérrez	1979–80
J. Napoleon Duarte	1980–82
A. Magaña	1982–84
J. Napoleon Duarte	1984–89
A. Cristiani	1989–94
Armando Calderón Sol	1994–

Ethiopia

Emperors

| Haile Selassie | 1930–74 |
| Asfa Wossen (King-designate in exile) | 1974–75 |

There was a military coup in September 1974.

Heads of Military Council

| Lt.-Gen. Aman Mikhail Andom | 1974 (Sept.–Nov.) |
| Brig.-Gen. Teferi Benti | 1974–75 |

A republic was established in March 1975.

Heads of State

Brig.-Gen. Teferi Benti	1975–77
Lt.-Col. Mengistu Haile Mariam (from 1979 known as President)	1977–91
M. Zenawi (interim)	1991–95
N. Guidada	1995–

Finland

Presidents

Field-Marshal K. Mannerheim	1944–46
J. Paasikivi	1946–56
U. Kekkonen	1956–81
M. Koivisto	1981–94
M. Ahtisaari	1994–

France

General C. de Gaulle led a National Unity government as head of state, 1945–46. The Fourth Republic was constituted in December 1946.

Fourth Republic

Presidents

V. Auriol	1947–54
R. Coty	1954–59

Prime Ministers

F. Gouin	1946 (Jan.–June)
G. Bidault	1946 (June–Dec.)
L. Blum	1946–47
P. Ramadier	1947 (Jan.–Nov.)
R. Schuman	1947–48
A. Marie	1948 (July–Sept.)
H. Queuille	1948–49
G. Bidault	1949–50
H. Queuille	1950 (July)
R. Pleven	1950–51
H. Queuille	1951 (Mar.–Aug.)
R. Pleven	1951–52
E. Fauré	1952 (Jan.–Mar.)
A. Pinay	1952–53
R. Mayer	1953 (Jan.–June)
J. Laniel	1953–54
P. Mendès-France	1954–55
E. Fauré	1955–56
G. Mollet	1956–57
M. Bourgès-Mannoury	1957 (May–Nov.)
F. Gaillard	1957–59

The Fifth Republic was constituted in October 1958.

Fifth Republic

Presidents

Gen. C. de Gaulle	1959–69
A. Poher (interim)	1969 (Apr.–June)
G. Pompidou	1969–74
A. Poher (interim)	1974 (Apr.–May)
V. Giscard d'Estaing	1974–81
F. Mitterrand	1981–95
J. Chirac	1995–

Prime Ministers

M. Debré	1959–62
G. Pompidou	1962–68
M. Couve de Murville	1968–69
J. Chaban-Delmas	1969–72
P. Messmer	1972–74
J. Chirac	1974–76
R. Barre	1976–81
P. Mauroy	1981–84
L. Fabius	1984–86
J. Chirac	1986–88
M. Rocard	1988–91
E. Cresson	1991–92
P. Bérégovoy	1992–93
E. Balladur	1993–95
A. Juppé	1995–97
L. Jospin	1997–

Germany

Germany was occupied and divided by the Allies in 1945. The Western Zone became the Federal Republic of Germany in September 1949. The Eastern Zone became the German Democratic Republic the following month. Germany was reunited in 1990.

Federal Republic of Germany

Presidents

T. Heuss	1949–59
H. Lübke	1959–69
G. Heinemann	1969–74
W. Scheel	1974–79
K. Carstens	1979–84

| R. von Weizsäcker | 1984–94 |
| R. Herzog | 1994– |

Federal Chancellors

K. Adenauer	1949–63
L. Erhard	1963–66
K. Kiesinger	1966–69
W. Brandt	1969–74
W. Scheel (acting)	1974 (May)
H. Schmidt	1974–82
H. Kohl	1982–

German Democratic Republic

President

| W. Pieck | 1949–60 |

The office of President was abolished in 1960. Its powers were transferred to that of the Chairman of the Council of State.

Chairmen of the Council of State

W. Ulbricht	1960–73
W. Stoph	1973–76
E. Honecker	1976–89*
M. Gerlach (acting)	1989–90

Ghana

Until independence in 1957 Ghana was the British colony of the Gold Coast.

Governors

A. Burns	1941–48
G. Creasy	1948–49
C. Arden-Clarke	1949–57

Governors-General

| C. Arden-Clarke | 1957 (May–Nov.) |
| Lord Listowel (W. Hare) | 1957–60 |

Ghana became a Republic in 1960.

* Replaced briefly as Communist Party leader by Egon Krenz. The reformist Hans Modrow became Prime Minister on 8 November. On 12 April 1990 he was succeeded by Lothar de Maizière, the last to hold the office in the former East Germany.

Presidents

K. Nkrumah	1960–66
Eight man National Liberation Council under J. Ankrah	1966–69
Gen. A. Afrifa	1969 (Apr.–Aug.)
Three man Presidential Commission: A. Afrifa, J. Harley, A. Kwesi-Ocran	1969–70
E. Akufo-Addo	1970–72
Col. I. Acheampong (Chairman, National Redemption Council, 1972–75; Chairman, Supreme Military Council, 1975–78)	1972–78
Lt.-Gen. F. Akuffo (Chairman, SMC)	1978–79
Flt.-Lt. J. Rawlings (Head, Armed Forces Revolutionary Council)	1979 (June–Sept.)
H. Limann	1979–81
Flt.-Lt. J. Rawlings	1981–

Prime Ministers

K. Nkrumah	1957–66

The post was abolished from 1966 to 1969.

K. Busia	1969–72

The post was effectively abolished in 1972.

Greece

Kings

George II	1935–44
Regency	1944–46
George II	1946–47
Paul I	1947–64
Constantine II	1964–74

The monarchy was abolished in the 1974 referendum.

Prime Minister of government-in-exile

E. Tsouderos	1941–44

Prime Ministers

S. Venizelis	1944 (Apr.)
G. Papandreou	1944–45
Gen. N. Plastiras	1945 (Jan.–Apr.)
Adm. P. Voulgaris	1945 (Apr.–Oct.)
Archbishop Damaskinos	1945 (Oct.–Nov.)
P. Kanellopoulos	1945 (Nov.)
T. Sofoulis	1945–46
P. Poulitsas	1946 (Apr.)
C. Tsaldaris	1946–47
D. Maximos	1947 (Jan.–Aug.)
C. Tsaldaris	1947 (Aug.–Sept.)
T. Sofoulis	1947–49
A. Diomedes	1949–50
J. Theotokis	1950 (Jan.–Mar.)
S. Venizelis	1950 (Mar.–Apr.)
Gen. N. Plastiras	1950 (Apr.–Sept.)
S. Venizelis	1950–51
Gen. N. Plastiras	1951–52
A. Papagos	1952–55
C. Karamanlis	1955–58
M. Georgakoloulos	1958 (Mar.–May)
C. Karamanlis	1958–63
G. Papandreou	1963 (Nov.–Dec.)
J. Paraskevopoulos	1963–64
G. Papandreou	1964–65
G. Athanasiadis-Novas	1965 (July–Aug.)
S. Stephanopoulos	1965–66
I. Paraskevopoulos	1966–67
P. Kanellopoulos	1967 (Apr.)

There was a military coup in April 1967.

Prime Ministers

C. Kollias	1967 (Apr.–Dec.)
Col. G. Papadopoulos	1967–73
S. Markeznis	1973 (Oct.–Nov.)
A. Androutsopoulos	1973–74

Gen. G. Zoitakis was Regent from 1967–72. Col. G. Papadopoulos became Regent in 1972. Restoration of the monarchy was rejected by plebiscite in 1974.

Presidents

G. Papadopoulos (provisional)	1973 (June–Nov.)
Gen. P. Ghizikis	1973–74
M. Stassinopoulos (interim)	1974–75
K. Tsatsos	1975–80
C. Sartzetakis	1985–90
K. Karamanlis	1990–95
C. Stephanopoulos	1995–

Prime Ministers

K. Karamanlis	1974–80
G. Rallis	1980–81
A. Papandreou	1981–89
T. Tzannetakis	1989 (July–Nov.)
X. Zolotas	1989–90
C. Mitsotakis	1990–93
A. Papandreou	1993–96
C. Simitis	1996–

Hungary

Hungary became a Republic in 1945.

Presidents*

Z. Tildy	1946–48
A. Szakasits	1948–50
S. Ronái	1950–52

Chairman of the Praesidium

I. Dobi	1952–67

Chairmen of the Presiding Council

P. Losonczi	1967–88
B. Straub	1988–89

Prime Ministers

Z. Tildy	1945–46
F. Nagy	1946–47

* After the end of the People's Republic in October 1989 Dr Arpad Goncz became interim President, then President in his own right.

L. Dinnyés	1947–48
I. Dobi	1948–52
M. Rákosi	1952–53
I. Nagy	1953–55
A. Hegedüs	1955–56
I. Nagy	1956 (Oct.–Nov.)
J. Kádár	1956–58
F. Münnich	1958–61
J. Kádár	1961–65
G. Kállai	1965–67
J. Fock	1967–75
G. Lázár	1975–87
K. Grósz	1987–89
M. Németh	1989–90
J. Antall	1990–93
P. Boross	1993–94
G. Horn	1994–

India

Viceroys

A. Wavell, Viscount Wavell	1943–47
L. Mountbatten, Earl Mountbatten	1947

Governors-General

L. Mountbatten, Earl Mountbatten	1947–48
C. Rajagopalachari	1948–49

Presidents

R. Prasad	1949–62
S. Radhakrishnan	1962–67
Z. Hussain	1967–69
V. Giri (acting)	1969 (May–Aug.)
V. Giri	1969–74
F. Ahmed	1974–77
B. Jatti	1977 (Feb.–July)
N. Reddy	1977–82
G. Singh	1982–87
R. Venkataraman	1987–92
S.D. Sharma	1992–97
K.R. Narayan	1997–

Prime Ministers

J. Nehru	1949–64
G. Nanda (acting)	1964 (May–June)
L. Shastri	1964–66
G. Nanda (acting)	1966 (Jan.)
Mrs I. Gandhi	1966–77
M. Desai	1977–79
C. Singh	1979–80
Mrs I. Gandhi	1980–84
R. Gandhi	1984–89
V.P. Singh	1989–90
C. Shekhar	1990–91
P.V. Narasimha Rao	1991–96
A.B. Vajpayee	1996 (May)
H.D. Deve Gowda	1996–97
I.K. Gujral	1997–98
A.B. Vajpayee	1998–

Indonesia

Indonesia became officially independent from the Netherlands in December 1949.

Lieutenant Governor-General

H. van Mook	1942–48

Commissioners-General

W. Schermerhorn	1946–48
M. van Poll	1946–48
F. de Boer	1946–48

Presidents

M. Sukarno	1945–67
Gen. R. Suharto	1967–98
B. Habibie	1998–

Iran

Shah

Mohammad Reza Shah Pahlevi	1941–79

The Shah fled from Iran in January 1979. Ayatollah Ruhollah Khomeini became head of a provisional government in February. As supreme religious leader he was acknowledged as the Islamic Republic of Iran's highest authority until his death in 1989.

Presidents

A. Bani-Sadr	1980–81
M. Raja'i	1981 (July–Aug.)
H. Khamenei	1981–89
H. Rafsanjani	1989–97
M. Khatami	1997–

Iraq

King

Faisal II	1939–58

The monarchy was overthrown and a republic formed in July 1958.

Presidents

Gen. M. Najib Rubai	1958–63
Col. A. Mohammed Aref	1963–66
Maj.–Gen. A. Rahman Aref	1966–68
Maj.–Gen. A. Hassan Bakr	1968–79
S. Hussein al-Takriti	1979–

Ireland

Presidents

S. O'Kelly	1945–59
E. de Valéra	1959–73
E. Childers	1973–74
C. Dalaigh	1974–76
P. Hillery	1976–90
M. Robinson	1990–97
M. McAleese	1997–

Prime Ministers

E. de Valéra	1932–48
J. Costello	1948–51
E. de Valéra	1951–54
J. Costello	1954–57

E. de Valéra	1957–59
S. Lemass	1959–66
J. Lynch	1966–73
L. Cosgrave	1973–77
J. Lynch	1977–79
C. Haughey	1979–81
G. FitzGerald	1981–82
C. Haughey	1982 (Mar.–Dec.)
G. FitzGerald	1982–87
C. Haughey	1987–92
A. Reynolds	1992–94
J. Bruton	1994–97
B. Aherne	1997–

Israel

Presidents

C. Weizmann (acting)	1948–49
C. Weizmann	1949–52
J. Springzak (acting)	1952 (Nov.–Dec.)
I. Ben-Zvi	1952–63
K. Luz	1963 (Apr.–May)
Z. Shazar	1963–68
E. Katzir	1968–78
Y. Navon	1978–83
C. Herzog	1983–93
E. Weizmann	1993–

Prime Ministers

D. Ben-Gurion	1948–53
M. Sharett	1953–55
D. Ben-Gurion	1955–63
L. Eshkol	1963–69
Mrs G. Meir	1969–74
I. Rabin	1974–77
M. Begin	1977–83
Y. Shamir	1983–84
S. Peres	1984–86
Y. Shamir	1986–92
I. Rabin	1992–95
S. Peres	1995–96
B. Netanyahu	1996–

Italy

Kings

Victor Emmanuel III (Emperor of Ethiopia 1936; King of Albania 1939)	1900–46
Umberto	1946 (May–June)

Italy became a Republic by referendum in June 1946.

Presidents

A. de Gasperi (acting)	1946 (June)
E. de Nicola	1946–48
L. Einaudi	1948–55
G. Gronchi	1955–62
A. Segni	1962–64
G. Saragat	1964–71
G. Leone	1971–78
A. Fanfani (acting)	1978 (June–July)
A. Pertini	1978–85
F. Cossiga	1985–92
O.L. Scalfaro	1992–

Prime Ministers

F. Parri	1945 (June–Nov.)
A. de Gasperi	1945–53
G. Pella	1953–54
A. Fanfani	1954 (Jan.–Feb.)
M. Scelba	1954–55
A. Segni	1955–57
A. Zoli	1957–58
A. Fanfani	1958–59
A. Segni	1959–60
F. Tambroni	1960 (Mar.–July)
A. Fanfani	1960–63
G. Leone	1963 (June–Dec.)
A. Moro	1963–68
G. Leone	1968 (June–Dec.)
M. Rumor	1968–70
E. Colombo	1970–72
G. Andreotti	1972–73
M. Rumor	1973–74
A. Moro	1974–76

G. Andreotti	1976–79
F. Cossiga	1979–80
A. Forlani	1980–81
G. Spadolini	1981–82
A. Fanfani	1982–83
B. Craxi	1983–87
G. Andreotti	1987 (Feb.–June)
G. Goria	1987–88
C. De Mita	1988–89
G. Andreotti	1989–92
G. Amato	1992–93
C. Ciampi	1993–94
S. Berlusconi	1994–95
L. Dini	1995–96
R. Prodi	1996–

Japan

Emperors

| Hirohito | 1926–89 |
| Akihito | 1989– |

Prime Ministers

Adm. K. Suzuki	1945 (Apr.–Aug.)
N. Higashikuni	1945 (Aug.–Oct.)
K. Shidehara	1945–46
S. Yoshida	1946–47
T. Katayama	1947–48
H. Ashida	1948 (Feb.–Oct.)
S. Yoshida	1948–54
I. Hatoyama	1954–56
T. Ishibashi	1956–57
N. Kishi	1957–60
H. Ikeda	1960–64
E. Sato	1964–72
K. Tanaka	1972–74
T. Miki	1974–76
T. Fukuda	1976–78
M. Ohira	1978–80
M. Ito (acting)	1980 (June–July)
Z. Suzuki	1980–82
Y. Nakasone	1982–87
N. Takeshita	1987–89

S. Uno	1989 (June–Aug.)
T. Kaifu	1989–91
K. Miyazawa	1991–93
M. Hosokawa	1993–94
T. Hata	1994 (Apr.–June)
T. Murayama	1994–95
R. Hashimoto	1995–

Jordan

Part of the Ottoman Empire until taken by Britain in the First World War. Britain occupied Transjordan from 1918 until it became a protectorate under Emir Adbullah ibn Hussein in 1923. The area gained independence in 1946 and became known as Jordan in 1949.

Resident (Transjordan)

A. Kirkbride	1939–46

Kings

Abdullah ibn Hussein	1946–51
Talal ibn Abdullah	1951–52
Hussein ibn Talal	1952–

Korea

The Empire of Ta'ehan, as Korea was known, was under Japanese occupation from 1910 to 1945. In May 1945 the country was divided into Soviet and American zones.

Republic of Korea (South Korea)

Presidents

Syngman Rhee	1948–60
Huh Chung (acting)	1960 (Apr.–Aug.)
Yoon Bo Sun	1960–62
Gen. Park Chung Hi	1962–79
Choi Kyu-hah	1979–80
Gen. Chun Doo Hwan	1980–88
Roh Tae–Woo	1988–93
Kim Young Sam	1993–98
Kim Dae Jung	1998–

Korean People's Democratic Republic (North Korea)

Presidents

Kim Du Bon	1948–57
Choi Yong Kun	1957–72
Marshal Kim Il-sung	1972–94
Kim Il-jong	1994– *

General Secretary, Korean Workers' Party

Marshal Kim Il-sung	1948–94
Kim Il-jong	1997– **

Lebanon

Originally part of the Ottoman Empire, Lebanon was a French mandate from 1920 and became independent in January 1944.

Presidents

Bishara al-Khuri	1944–52
Camille Chamoun	1952–58
Gen. Fouad Chehab	1958–64
Charles Hélou	1964–70
Suleiman Franjieh	1970–76
Elias Sarkis	1976–82
Bachir Gemayel	1982 (Aug.–Sept.)
Amin Gemayel (Resigned in 1988 with no successor appointed until 1989)	1982–88
R. Moawad	1989 (5–22 Nov.)
E. Hrawi	1989–

Libya

Libya was controlled by Italy from 1912, became a United Nations mandate in 1945 and an independent Kingdom in 1951. Libya became a republic in 1969 and has been known as the Libyan Arab Republic (1969–76), the Libyan Arab People's Republic (1976–77), and the Socialist People's Libyan Arab Jamahiriya (State of the Masses) from 1977.

* De facto head of state after the death of his father.
** Not formally appointed until 1997.

Kingdom of Libya

King

Idris I	1951–69

Prime Ministers

Mahmud Muntasser	1951–54
Mohammed Saqizly	1954 (Feb.–Apr.)
Mustafa Halim	1954–57
Abdul Majid Coobar	1957–60
Mohammed bin-Othman al Said	1960–63
Mohieddine Fekini	1963–64
Mahmud Muntasser	1964–65
Husain Maziq	1965–67
Abdel Kader al Badri	1967 (July–Oct.)
Abdel Hamid Bakkouche	1967–68
Wanis al Geddafi	1968–69

The monarchy was overthrown in September 1969.

President

Col. Mu'ammar Muhammad al-Qadhafi	1969–

Prime Ministers (until 1977, when post abolished)

Mahmoud Sulaiman al Maghrabi	1969–70
Col. Mu'ammar Muhammad al-Qadhafi	1970–72
Maj. Abdul Salam Ahmed Jallud	1972–77
Abdullah Obeidi	1977

Secretaries of the General People's Committee

Jadallah at-Talhi	1979–84
Muhammad az-Zarrouk Ragab	1984–86
Jadallah Azouz at-Talhi	1986–89
Omar al-Muntasir	1989–90
Abu Zaid Omar Dourda	1990–96
Abd al-Majid al-Qaud	1996–

Malawi

The country was known as Nyasaland from 1907 and was under British control. It was federated with Rhodesia between 1953 and 1963 and became independent in 1964.

Governors

E. Richards	1942–47
G. Colby	1948–56
R. Armitage	1956–61
G. Jones	1961–64

Federation of Rhodesia and Nyasaland (1953–63)

Prime Ministers

Sir G. Higgins	1953–56
Sir R. Welensky	1956–63

Governor-General

Sir G. Jones	1964–66

Prime Minister

H. Banda	1964–66

Malawi became a Republic in 1966.

Presidents

H. Banda	1966–94
B. Muluzi	1994–

Malaysia

Malaya became independent from Britain in 1957. It federated with Sabah, Sarawak and Singapore to form Malaysia in 1963. Singapore seceded in 1965.

Malaya

Heads of State

Abdul Rahman	1957–60
Hisamuddin Alam Shah	1960 (Apr.–Sept.)
Syed Putra	1960–63

Prime Ministers

Abdul Rahman	1957–59
Abdul Razak	1959 (Apr.–Aug.)
Abdul Rahman	1959–63

Malaysia

Heads of State

Syed Putra	1963–65
Ismail Nasiruddin Shah	1965–70
Abdul Halim Mu'azzam Shah	1970–75
Yahya Putra	1975–79
Mahmood Iskandar ibni Sultan Ismail	1979–84
Mahmood Iskandar ibni Al-Marhum	1984–89
Azlan Muhibbuddin Shah	1989–94
Jaafar Abdul Rahman	1994–

Prime Ministers

Abdul Rahman	1963–70
Abdul Razak	1970–76
Hussein bin Onn	1976–84
Mahathir Mohamad	1984–

Mexico

Presidents

Gen. M. Avila Camacho	1940–46
M. Alemán Valdés	1946–52
A. Ruiz Cortines	1952–58
A. López Mateos	1958–64
G. Díaz Ordaz	1964–70
L. Echeverría Alvárez	1970–76
J. Portillo y Pacheco	1976–82
M. de la Madrid Hurtado	1982–88
C. de Gortari	1988–94
E. Zedillo	1994–

Mozambique

Mozambique achieved independence from Portugal in 1975.

Presidents

S. Machel	1975–86
J. Chissanó	1986–

Netherlands

Queens

Wilhelmina	1890–1948
Juliana	1948–80
Beatrix	1980–

Prime Ministers

W. Schermerhorn	1945–46
L. Beel	1946–48
W. Drees	1948–58
L. Beel	1958–59
J. de Quay	1959–63
V. Marijnen	1963–65
J. Cals	1965–66
J. Zijlstra	1966–67
P. de Jong	1967–71
B. Biesheuvel	1971–73
J. den Uyl	1973–77
A. van Agt	1977–82
R. Lubbers	1982–94
W. Kok	1994–

New Zealand

Governors-General

Sir C. Newall, Baron Newall	1941–46
Sir B. Freyberg, Baron Freyberg	1946–52
Sir C. Norrie, Baron Norrie	1952–57
Sir C. Lyttelton, Viscount Cobham	1957–62
Sir B. Fergusson	1962–67
Sir A. Porritt	1967–72
Sir E. Blundell	1972–77
Sir K. Holyoake	1977–80
Sir D. Beattie	1980–85
Sir P. Reeves	1985–90
Dame Catherine Tizard	1990–96
M.H. Boys	1996–

Prime Ministers

P. Fraser	1940–49
Sir S. Holland	1949–57

K. Holyoake	1957 (Sept.–Dec.)
Sir W. Nash	1957–60
K. Holyoake	1960–72
Sir J. Marshall	1972 (Feb.–Dec.)
N. Kirk	1972–74
H. Watt (acting)	1974 (Aug.–Sept.)
W. Rowling	1974–75
R. Muldoon	1975–84
D. Lange	1984–89
G. Palmer	1989–90
M. Moore	1990 (Sept.–Oct.)
J. Bolger	1990–97
J. Shipley	1997–

Nicaragua

Presidents

Gen. A. Somoza García	1937–47
L. Argüello	1947 (May)
B. Lescayo-Sacasa	1947 (May–Aug.)
V. Roman y Reyes	1947–50
A. Somoza García	1950–56
L. Somoza Debayle	1956–63
R. Shick Gutiérrez	1963–66
L. Guerrero Gutiérrez	1966–67
Gen. A. Somoza Debayle	1967–72
Three-member military junta (Gen. R. Martinez Laclayo, Gen. A. Lobo Cordero, E. Papua Irias)	1972–74
Gen. A. Somoza Debayle	1974–79
Five-member junta	1979–81
Three-member junta with D. Ortega Saavedra as co-ordinator	1981–85
D. Ortega Saavedra	1985–90
Violeta Barrios de Chamorro	1990–96
A. Alemán	1996–

Nigeria

Nigeria became independent from Britain in 1960 and a republic in 1963.

Governors-General

J. Macpherson	1954–55
J. Robertson	1955–60
N. Azikiwe	1960–63

Presidents

(Title not used from January 1966 to October 1977, and after 1983.)

N. Azikiwe	1963–66
N. Orizu (acting)	1966 (Jan.)
Maj.-Gen. J. Aguiyi-Ironsi	1966 (Jan.–July)
Lt.-Col. Y. Gowon	1966–75
Gen. M. Ramat Mohammed	1975–76
Lt.-Gen. O. Obasanjo	1976–79
A. Shehu Shagari	1979–83
Maj.-Gen. M. Buhari	1983–85

Prime Minister

| A. Tafawa Balewa | 1957–66 |

Under military rule from 1966.

Heads of State and Commanders-in-Chief of Armed Forces

Maj.-Gen. J. Aguiyi-Ironsi	1966–68
Lt.-Col. Y. Gowon	1968–75
Gen. M. Ramat Mohammed	1975–76
Lt.-Gen. O. Obasanjo	1976–79
A. Shehu Shagari	1979–83
Maj.-Gen. M. Buhari	1983–85
Maj.-Gen. I. Babangida	1985–93
E. Shonekan*	1993 (Aug.–Nov.)
Gen. S. Abacha**	1993–98
Gen. A. Abubakar	1998–

Norway

Kings

Haakon VII	1905–57
Olaf V	1957–91
Harald V	1991–

* Head of Interim Government.
** Chairman of the Provisional Ruling Council.

Prime Ministers

E. Gerhardsen	1945–51
O. Torp	1951–55
E. Gerhardsen	1955–63
J. Lyng	1963 (Aug.–Sept.)
E. Gerhardsen	1963–65
P. Borten	1965–71
T. Bratteli	1971–72
L. Korvald	1972–73
T. Bratteli	1973–76
O. Nordli	1976–81
G. Brundtland	1981 (Feb.–Oct.)
K. Willoch	1981–86
G. Brundtland	1986–89
J. Syse	1989–90
G. Brundtland	1990–96
T. Jagland	1996–97
K. Bondevik	1997–

Pakistan

Presidents

Q. Ali Jinnah	1947–48
K. Nazimuddin	1948–51
G. Muhammed	1951–55
Maj.-Gen. I. Mirza	1956–58
Field Marshal M. Ayub Khan	1958–69
Maj.-Gen. A. Yahya Khan	1969–71
Z. Ali Bhutto	1971–73
F. Elahi Chaudri	1973–78
Gen. M. Zia ul-Haq	1978–88
I. Khan	1988–93
S.F. Leghari	1993–97
M.R. Tarar	1997–

Philippines

Under US control from 1898. The Philippines became a commonwealth in 1935 and an independent republic in 1946.

Presidents

| M. Quezón | 1935–44 |
| (in exile 1941–44) | |

S. Osmena	1944–46
M. Roxas y Acuna	1946–48
E. Quirino	1948–53
R. Magsaysay	1953–57
C. Garcia	1957–61
D. Mascapagal	1961–65
F. Marcos	1965–86
Mrs C. Aquino	1986–92
Gen. F. Ramos	1992–98
J. Estrada	1998–

Poland

Poland was controlled by a Provisional Government of National Unity from July 1945. Elections in 1947 gave communist-socialist candidates a majority.

President

B. Bierut	1945–52

In 1952 the office of President was replaced by a Council of State (until 1989).

Chairmen of the Council of State

A. Zawadski	1952–64
E. Ochab	1964–68
Marshal M. Spychalski	1968–70
J. Cyrankiewicz	1970–72
H. Jablonski	1972–85
Gen. W. Jaruzelski	1985–89

Presidents

Gen. W. Jaruzelski	1989–90
L. Walesa	1990–95
A. Kwaśniewski	1995–

First Secretaries, Communist Party Politburo

W. Gomulka	1945–48
B. Bierut	1948–56
E. Ochab	1956 (Mar.–Oct.)
W. Gomulka	1956–70
E. Gierek	1970–80

S. Kania   1980–81
Gen. W. Jaruzelski   1981–89

Gomulka was Poland's dominant political figure, 1956–70; Gierek, 1970–1980. Jaruzelski took this position from 1981.

Prime Ministers

J. Cyrankiewicz   1954–70
P. Jaroszewicz   1970–80
E. Babiuch   1980 (Feb.–Aug.)
J. Pinkowski   1980–81
Gen. W. Jaruzelski   1981–85
Z. Messner   1985–88
M. Rakowski   1988–89
T. Mazowiecki   1989–91
J.K. Bielecki   1991 (Jan.–Dec.)
J. Olszewski   1991–92
H. Suchocka   1992–93
W. Pawlak   1993–95
J. Oleksy   1995–96
W. Cimoszewicz   1996–97
J. Buzek   1997–

Portugal

Presidents

Marshal A. Carmona   1926–51
A. Salazar (provisional)   1951 (Apr.–July)
Marshal F. Lopez   1951–58
Rear-Adm. A. Tomás   1958–74
Gen. A. de Spinola   1974 (May–Sept.)
Gen. F. Gomes   1974–76
Gen. A. Eanes   1976–86
M. Soares   1986–96
J. Sampaio   1996–

Prime Ministers

A. Salazar   1932–68
M. Caetano   1968–74
A. Carlos   1974 (May–July)
V. Goncalves   1974–75
P. de Azevedo   1975–76
M. Soares   1976–78

N. da Costa	1978 (Aug.–Oct.)
C. Pinto	1978–79
M. Pintassilgo	1979 (July–Dec.)
F. Carneiro	1979–80
D. do Amaral	1980 (Dec.)
P. Balsemão	1980–82

Balsemão resigned on 19 December 1982. P. Crespo was appointed Prime Minister but was unable to form a government. Balsemão formed a caretaker government January–June 1983.

M. Soares	1983–85
A. Silva	1985–95
A. Guterres	1995–

Romania

King

| Michael | 1940–47 |

Prime Ministers

| N. Rădescu | 1944–45 |
| P. Groza | 1945 (Mar.) |

Romania became a republic in 1947.

Presidents

C. Parhon	1948–52
P. Groza	1952–58
I. Maurer	1958–61
G. Gheorghiu-Dej	1961–65
C. Stoica	1965–67
N. Ceauçescu	1967–89*
I. Iliescu	1989–96
E. Constantinescu	1997–

Russia (USSR until 1991)

During the Soviet era, when Russia was a constituent republic of the USSR, the effective rulers of Russia were the leaders of the Soviet Union.

---

* Ceauçescu was executed on 25 December 1989 during the Romanian revolution. Iliescu became interim President.

Effective rulers

J. Stalin	1927–53
N. Khrushchev	1953–64 (deposed)
L.I. Brezhnev	1964–82
Y.V. Andropov	1982–84
K.V. Chernenko	1984–85
M. Gorbachev*	1985–91

Following the collapse of the Soviet Union in December 1991, the Russian Federation became a founder member of the Commonwealth of Independent States (see p. 213). Boris Yeltsin was directly elected President of the Russian Federation in June 1991.

President

B. Yeltsin	1991– **

Prime Ministers

B. Yeltsin	1991–92
Y. Gaidar	1992 (June–Dec.)
V. Chernomyrdin	1992–98
S. Kiriyenko***	1998–

Saudi Arabia

United as a kingdom in 1932.

Kings

Abdul Aziz ibn Abdur-Rahman al-Faisal Al Sa'ud	1932–53
Saud ibn Abdul Aziz	1953–64
Faisal ibn Abdul Aziz	1964–75
Khalid ibn Abdul Aziz	1975–82
Fahd ibn Abdul Aziz	1982–

Singapore

Singapore became independent from Britain in 1963 and almost immediately joined the Malaysian federation. It seceded in 1965.

* Gorbachev became President of the USSR in 1988 then Executive President (1990) until the collapse of the USSR. He resigned, 25 December 1991.

** Re-elected in 1996.

*** Nominated by Yeltsin and eventually accepted by the Duma on a third vote on 24 April 1998.

Head of State

Inche Yusuf bin Ishak	1963 (Aug.–Sept.)

Prime Ministers

D. Marshall	1955–56
Lim Yew Hock	1956–59
Lee Kuan Yew	1959–63

Republic of Singapore

Presidents

Inche Yusuf bin Ishak	1965–70
B. Sheares	1971–81
D. Nair	1981–85
W.K. Wee	1985–93
O.T. Cheong	1993–

Prime Ministers

Lee Kuan Yew	1965–90
Goh Chok Tong	1990–

South Africa

Governors-General

N. de Wet	1943–46
G. van Zyl	1946–50
E. Jansen	1951–59
L. Steyn (acting)	1959–60
C. Swart	1960–61

In 1961 South Africa became a republic and left the British Commonwealth.

Presidents

C. Swart	1961–67
J. Naudé (acting)	1967–68
J. Fouché	1968–75
N. Diederich	1975–78
M. Viljoen (acting)	1978 (Aug.–Oct.)
B. Vorster	1978–79
M. Viljoen	1979–84

P. Botha	1984–89
F. de Klerk (acting until Sept. 1989)	1989–94
N. Mandela	1994–

Prime Ministers

Gen. J. Smuts	1939–48
D. Malan	1948–54
J. Strijdom	1954–58
C. Swart (acting)	1958 (Aug.–Sept.)
H. Verwoerd	1958–66
B. Vorster	1966–78
P. Botha	1978–84

The post of Prime Minister was abolished in 1984 and combined with that of President.

Spain

Chief of State

Gen. F. Franco Bahamonde	1939–75

Franco designated Prince Juan Carlos as his eventual successor in 1969.

King

Juan Carlos I	1975–

Presidents of Council of Ministers (Prime Ministers)

Gen. F. Franco Bahamonde	1939–73
Adm. L. Carrero Blanco	1973–74
C. Arias Navarro	1974–75
A. Súarez Gonzalez	1975–81
L. Calvo Sotelo	1981–82
F. González Márquez	1982–96
José María Aznar	1996–

Sri Lanka

Sri Lanka was known as Ceylon while under British contol, and achieved its independence in 1948.

Governors-General

H. Moore	1948–49
H. Ramsbotham, Viscount Soulbury	1949–55
O. Goonetilleke	1955–62
W. Gopallawa	1962–72

Prime Ministers

S. Senanayake	1948–52
D. Senanayake	1952–53
Sir J. Kotelawala	1953–56
S. Bandaranaike	1956–59
W. Dahanayake	1959–60
D. Senanayake	1960 (Mar.–July)
Mrs S. Bandaranaike	1960–65
D. Senanayake	1965–70
Mrs S. Bandaranaike	1970–72

Sri Lanka became a republic in 1972.

Presidents

W. Gopallawa	1972–78
J. Jayawardene	1978–88
R. Premadasa	1988–93
D.B. Wijedunga	1993–94
C.B. Kumaratunga	1994–

Prime Ministers

Mrs S. Bandaranaike	1972–77
J. Jayawardene	1977–78
R. Premadasa	1978–89
D.B. Wijedunga	1989–93
R. Wickremasinghe	1993–94
C.B. Kumaratunga	1994 (Aug.–Nov.)
S.R.D. Bandaranaike	1994–

Sweden

Kings

Gustav V	1907–50
Gustav VI Adolf	1950–73
Charles XVI Gustav	1973–

Prime Ministers

P. Hansson	1936–46
T. Erlander	1946–69
O. Palme	1969–76
T. Fälldin	1976–78
O. Ullsten	1978–79
T. Fälldin	1979–82
O. Palme	1982–86
I. Carlsson	1986–91
C. Bildt	1991–94
I. Carlsson	1994–96
G. Persson	1996–

Syria

President

France, which held Syria as a League of Nations' mandate, suspended the constitution in 1939. Syria was under Anglo–French occupation 1941–46.

S. Shukri al Quwwatli	1943–49
Col. H. Zaim	1949 (June–Aug.)
Col. S. Hinawi (acting)	1949 (Aug.)
H. al-Atassi	1949–51
Col. A. es-Shishaqli (Dictator)	1951–53
Col. A. es-Shishaqli (President)	1953–54
H. al-Atassi	1954–55
S. Shukri al Quwwatli	1955–58

(Union with Egypt under the Egyptian head of state, 1958–61.)

N. el-Kudsi	1961–63
Maj.-Gen. L. Atassi	1963 (Mar.–July)
Gen. A. el-Hafez	1963–66
N. Atassi	1966–70
A. Khatib	1970–71
Lt.-Gen. H. al-Assad	1971–

Taiwan

Following the communist victory in the Chinese civil war in 1949, the Nationalist Government held only the island of Taiwan (Formosa).

Presidents

Gen. Li Tsung-jen	1949–50
Chiang Kai-shek	1950–75
Yen Chia-kan	1975–78
Chiang Ching-kuo	1978–87
Lee Teng-hui	1987–

Tanzania

Tanzania was made up of Tanganyika (German until the First World War; British Trust Territory until independence in 1961) and Zanzibar (British Protectorate from 1890 until independence in 1963). They combined in 1964.

Tanganyika

Governors

W. Battershill	1945–49
E. Twining	1949–58
R. Turnbull	1958–61

Dominion of Tanganyika

Governor-General

Sir R. Turnbull	1961–62

Prime Ministers

J. Nyerere	1961–62
R. Kawawa	1962 (Jan.–Dec.)

Republic of Tanganyika

President

J. Nyerere	1962–64

Prime Minister

R. Kawawa	1962–64

Zanzibar

Residents

H. Pilling	1941–46
V. Glenday	1946–51
J. Rankine	1952–54
H. Potter	1954–60
G. Mooring	1960–63

Sultanate of Zanzibar

Sultan

Seyyid Jamshid bin-Abdullah bin-Khalifah	1963–64

Prime Minister

Muhammed Shamte Hamadi	1963–64

Republic of Zanzibar

President

Abeid Amani Karume	1964 (Jan.–Apr.)

Prime Minister

Abdullah Kassim Hanga	1964 (Jan.–Apr.)

Tanzania

Presidents

J. Nyerere	1964–85
A.H. Mwinyi	1985–95
B. Mkapa	1995–

Prime Ministers

(The office was abolished until 1972)

R. Kawawa	1972–77
E. Sokoine	1977–80
C.D. Msuya	1980–83
E. Sokoine	1983–84
S.A. Salim	1984–85

J. Warioba	1985–90
J. Malecela	1990–94
C. Msuya	1994–95
F. Sumaye	1995–

Thailand

Generally known before 1939 as Siam.

Kings

Ananda Mahidol	1935–46
Bhumipol Adulyadej	1946–

Turkey

Presidents

Gen. I. Inönü	1938–50
M. Bayar	1950–60
Gen. C. Gürsel	1961–66
Gen. C. Sunay	1966–73
Adm. F. Korutürk	1973–80
I. Caplayangil	1980 (Apr.–Sept.)
Gen. K. Evren	1980–89
T. Özal	1989–93
S. Demirel	1993–

Prime Ministers

S. Saracoglu	1943–46
R. Peker	1946–47
H. Saka	1947–49
S. Gunaltay	1949–50
A. Menderes	1950–60
C. Gursel	1960–61
I. Inönü	1961–65
S. Urguplu	1965 (Feb.–Oct.)
S. Demirel	1965–71
N. Erim	1971–72
F. Melen	1972–73
N. Talû	1973–74
B. Ecevit	1974 (Jan.–Nov.)
S. Irmak	1974–75
S. Demirel	1975–77

B. Ecevit	1977 (June–July)
S. Demirel	1977–78
B. Ecevit	1978–79
S. Demirel	1979–80
B. Ülüsü	1980–83
T. Özal	1983–89
Y. Akbulut	1989–91
M. Yilmaz	1991 (June–Nov.)
S. Demirel	1991–93
T. Çiller	1993–96
M. Yilmaz	1996 (Mar.–June)
N. Erbakan	1996–

Union of Soviet Socialist Republics

Until the 1917 Revolution, Russia had been a monarchy. A Bolshevik government took power in November 1917 and adopted the constitution of a Federal Republic in July 1918. See also Russia, pp. 193–4.

Presidents

M. Kalinin	1922–46
N. Shvernik	1946–53
Marshal K. Voroshilov	1953–60
L. Brezhnev	1960–64
A. Mikoyan	1964–65
N. Podgorny	1965–77
L. Brezhnev	1977–82
Y. Andropov	1983–84
K. Chernenko	1984–85
A. Gromyko	1985–88
M. Gorbachev	1988–91

The dominant figure from 1917 to 1990 was the General Secretary of the Communist Party. From 1990 to the collapse of the Soviet Union, Gorbachev was Executive President.

General Secretaries

J. Stalin	1922–53
N. Khrushchev	1953–64
L. Brezhnev	1964–82
Y. Andropov	1982–84
K. Chernenko	1984–85
M. Gorbachev	1985–91

United Kingdom

Sovereigns

George VI	1936–52
Elizabeth II	1952–

Prime Ministers

C. Attlee	1945–51
Sir W. Churchill	1951–55
Sir A. Eden	1955–57
H. Macmillan	1957–63
Sir A. Douglas-Home	1963–64
H. Wilson	1964–70
E. Heath	1970–74
H. Wilson	1974–76
J. Callaghan	1976–79
Mrs M. Thatcher	1979–90
J. Major	1990–97
A. Blair	1997–

United States

Presidents

F. Roosevelt	1933–45
H. Truman	1945–53
D. Eisenhower	1953–61
J. Kennedy	1961–63
L. Johnson	1963–69
R. Nixon	1969–74
G. Ford	1974–77
J. Carter	1977–81
R. Reagan	1981–89
G. Bush	1989–93
W. Clinton	1993–

Vatican

Popes

Pius XII	1939–58
John XXIII	1958–63
Paul VI	1963–78
John Paul I	1978
John Paul II	1978–

Venezuela

Presidents

R. Betancourt	1945–48
R. Gallegos Freire	1948 (Feb.–Nov.)
Lt.-Col. C. Delgado Chalbaud	1948–50
G. Suárez Flamerich	1950–52
Col. M. Pérez Jiménez	1952–58
Rear-Adm. W. Larrazábal Ugueto	1958 (Jan.–Nov.)
E. Sanabria	1958–59
R. Betancourt	1959–64
R. Leoni	1964–69
R. Caldera Rodríguez	1969–74
C. Pérez Rodríguez	1974–79
L. Herrera Campins	1979–84
J. Lusinchi	1984–89
C. Pérez Rodríguez	1989–93
R. José Velásquez (interim)	1993–94
R. Caldera Rodríguez	1994–

Vietnam

The central Vietnam region of Annam was a French protectorate from 1883 and part of the Indo-Chinese Union from 1887. Between 1940 and 1945 it was controlled by Japan. French rule was restored in 1945, local autonomy within an Indochinese Federation was granted in 1946, and Vietnam became independent in 1954.

High Commissioners of Indo-Chinese Federation

G. d'Argenlieu	1945–47
E. Ballaert	1947–48
L. Pignon	1948–50
J. de Lattre de Tassigny	1950–52
J. Letourneau	1952–53

Democratic Republic of Vietnam (North Vietnam)

Presidents

Ho Chi-minh	1945–69
Ton Duc Thang	1969–76

Prime Ministers

Ho Chi-minh	1945–55
Pham Van Dong	1955–76

Empire of Vietnam

Emperor

Bao Dao	1954–55

Prime Ministers

Buu Loc	1954–55
Ngo Dinh Diem	1955 (June–Oct.)

Republic of Vietnam (South Vietnam)

Presidents

Ngo Dinh Diem	1955–63
Maj.-Gen. Duong Van Minh	1963–64
Mej.-Gen. Nguyen Khanh	1964 (Jan.–Feb.)
Maj.-Gen. Duong Van Minh	1964 (Feb.–Aug.)
Maj.-Gen. Nguyen Khanh	1964 (Aug.–Sept.)
Maj.-Gen. Duong Van Minh	1964 (Sept.–Oct.)
Phan Khac Suu	1964–65
Gen. Nguyen Van Thieu	1965–75
Tran Van Huong	1975 (Apr.)
Maj.-Gen. Duong Van Minh	1975 (Apr.)

South Vietnam fell to the North in April 1975 and the two states were united in 1976.

Socialist Republic of Vietnam

Presidents

Ton Duc Thang	1976–80
Nguyen Huu Tho	1980–81
Truong Chinh	1981–86
Nguyen Van Linh	1986–87
Vo Chi Cong	1987–92
Le Duc Anh	1992–

Prime Ministers

Pham Van Dong	1976–87
Pham Hung	1987–88
Do Muoi	1988–91
Vo Van Kiet	1991–

Secretaries-General Vietnamese Party of Labour (Communist Party)

Le Duan	1960–80
Truong Chinh	1986 (July–Dec.)
Nguyen Van Linh	1986–91
Do Muoi	1991–97
Le Kha Phieu	1997–

Yugoslavia

The Serb, Croat and Slovene State formed in December 1918 became known as Yugoslavia in October 1929. Yugoslavia was occupied by the Axis in 1941. A government-in-exile was based in London and then in Cairo. A republic was proclaimed in 1945. With the break-up of Yugoslavia a 'Federal Republic of Yugoslavia' (i.e. Serbia and Montenegro) was declared in 1992.

Presidents of the Praesidium

I. Ribar	1945–53
Marshal J. Broz Tito	1953–80

After 1980 Yugoslavia had a 'Collective Presidency'. A President was selected annually from this eight-member committee.

Heads of the Collective Presidency

L. Kolisevski	1980 (May)
C. Mijatović	1980–81
S. Krajger	1981–82
P. Stambolić	1982–83
M. Spiljak	1983–84
V. Djuranović	1984–85
R. Vlajković	1985–86
S. Hasani	1986–87
L. Mojsov	1987–88
R. Dizdarević	1988–89
J. Drnovsek	1989–90
B. Jovic	1990–91
S. Mešić	1991–92

Prime Ministers

Marshal J. Broz Tito	1945–63
P. Stambolić	1963–67
M. Spiljak	1967–69

R. Ribičić	1969–71
D. Bijedić	1971–77
V. Djuranović	1977–82
M. Planinć	1982–86
B. Mikulić	1986–89
A. Marković	1989–92

Federal Republic of Yugoslavia (since 1992)

The dominant figure in 'rump' Yuguslavia has been Milosević. The elected presidents have little real power.

Zaïre

See Congo, p. 166.

Zimbabwe

Southern Rhodesia was annexed to the British Crown in 1923. A white regime declared illegal unilateral independence in 1965 and a republic in 1970. The area became independent as Zimbabwe in 1980.

Governors

W. Tait	1944–46
J. Kennedy	1947–53
P. William-Powlett	1954–59
H. Gibbs	1959–65

Prime Ministers

Sir G. Huggins (later Lord Malvern)	1933–53
G. Todd	1953–58
Sir E. Whitehead	1958–62
W. Field	1962–64
I. Smith	1964–80

Between 1953 and 1963 Rhodesia was part of the Federation of Rhodesia and Nyasaland. The Federal Prime Ministers were:

| Sir G. Huggins | 1953–56 |
| Sir R. Welensky | 1956–63 |

Presidents (during period of illegal independence)

C. Dupont	1970–76
J. Wrathall	1976–80

Zimbabwe

President

C. Banana	1980–87

Prime Minister

R. Mugabe	1980–

(from 1987 executive President)

Wars and international affairs

Principal international organizations and groupings

Arab League (League of Arab States)

Established in 1945 to promote co-operation between member states. All the Arab countries including Mauritania, Sudan and Somalia are normally members, but Egypt was temporarily suspended in 1979 after its overtures to Israel. Palestine also holds membership. The League sent a peace-keeping force to Lebanon in June 1976, and tried to mediate in the civil war there in the 1980s.

Secretaries-General

Abdul Azzem (Egypt)	1945–52
Abdul Hassouna (Egypt)	1952–72
Mahmoud Riad (Egypt)	1972–79
Chedli Klibi (Tunisia)	1979–90
Esmat Abdel Meguid (Egypt)	1991–

Members

Algeria (1962)	Oman (1971)
Bahrain (1971)	Palestine
Comoros (n.a.)	Qatar (1971)
Djibouti (1977)	Saudi Arabia
Egypt (suspended 1979)	Somalia (1974)
Iraq	Sudan (1956)
Jordan	Syria
Kuwait (1961)	Tunisia (1958)
Lebanon	United Arab Emirates (1971)
Libya (1951)	Western Sahara (n.a.)
Mauritania (1973)	Yemen
Morocco (1958)	

Association of South-East Asian Nations (ASEAN)

This association was formed on 8 August 1967, with headquarters in Jakarta, to promote active collaboration and mutual assistance in economic, social, cultural, technical, scientific and administrative fields. The founding members were Indonesia, Thailand, the Philippines, Malaysia and Singapore. Brunei joined in 1984 and Vietnam in 1995. Future members are expected to include Cambodia, Laos and Myanmar (Burma). It was hoped through the association to increase the political stability of South-East Asia and to improve the rate of economic development. There is an annual meeting of Foreign Ministers, and progress has been made not only in economic co-operation but also in joint research, education, transport and tourism.

Secretaries-General

Hartono Dharsono (Indonesia)	1967–78
Umarjadi Njotowijona (Indonesia)	(Feb.–July) 1978
Datuk Ali bin Abdullah (Malaysia)	1978–80
Narciso Reyes (Philippines)	1980–82
Chan Kai Yau (Singapore)	1982–84
Phan Wannamethee (Thailand)	1984–89
Rusli Noor (Indonesia)	1989–91
Dato' Ajit Singh (Malaysia)	1991 (acting)
Roderick Yong (Brunei)	1991–

Members

Brunei (1984)	Singapore (1967)
Indonesia (1967)	Thailand (1967)
Malaysia (1967)	Vietnam (1995)
Philippines (1967)	

Commonwealth, the

A grouping of states, numbering 54 in 1998, which evolved from the former territories of the British Empire. The statute of Westminster (31 December 1931) defined the structure of the British Commonwealth and recognized the dominions as 'autonomous communities'. The organization works to improve economic collaboration and other forms of co-operation between member states. Not all former territories of the British Empire are members. Myanmar (Burma) never joined; the Republic of Ireland is not a member. South Africa left in 1961 but rejoined in 1994. Pakistan left in 1972 and rejoined in 1989. Fiji left after the military coup in 1987 but rejoined in 1997. Namibia (joined 1990), Cameroon (joined 1995) and Mozambique (joined 1995) are recent members.

Secretaries-General of the Commonwealth

Arnold Smith (Canada)	1965–75
Sir Shridath S Ramphal (Guyana)	1975–89
Chief Emeka Anyaoku (Nigeria)	1989–

Commonwealth of Independent States (CIS)

A voluntary association of 11 (formerly 12) states formed when the Soviet Union disintegrated. Its history to date suggests it is little more than a forum to keep alive some vague form of co-operation after the demise of the old USSR. Early 'agreements' were made at Minsk (14 February 1992, on strategic forces). Kiev (20 March 1992, on state frontiers) and Tashkent (15 May 1992, on collective security). By 1993 the Asian states were drifting away from the CIS.

Council for Mutual Economic Assistance (COMECON)

Organization established in Moscow in January 1959 to improve trade between the Soviet Union and other Eastern European states. Regarded by Stalin as an instrument to enforce an economic boycott on Yugoslavia, and also used as a Soviet response to growing Western European economic interdependence. Apart from the East European countries, Mongolia joined in 1962, Cuba in 1972 and Vietnam in 1978. Changes in Europe since 1989 left its future role uncertain and it was formally dissolved in January 1991.

Secretaries

Nikolai Faddeyev (USSR)	1949–83
Vyacheslav Sychev (USSR)	1983–91

Council of Europe

Organization established in 1949 to achieve greater European unity based on the common heritage of its member states. Matters of national defence are excluded. The original states were Belgium, Britain, Denmark, France, Ireland, Italy, the Netherlands, Norway and Sweden. They were soon joined by Greece, Iceland and Turkey later in 1949, West Germany in 1951, Austria in 1956, Cyprus in 1961, Switzerland in 1963 and Malta in 1965. With the fall of communism, and the new political order in Central and Eastern Europe, membership has grown rapidly (to 39 in 1997). It is quite separate from the European Union (q.v.).

Secretaries-General

Jacques Camille-Paris (France)	1949–53
Leon Marchal (France)	1953–57
Ludovico Benvenuti (Italy)	1957–64
Peter Smithers (UK)	1964–69
Lujo Toncic-Sorinj (Austria)	1969–74
Georg Kahn-Ackermann (Federal Republic of Germany)	1974–79
Franz Karasek (Austria)	1979–84
Marcelino Oreja Aguirre (Spain)	1984–89
Catherine Lalumière (France)	1989–94
Daniel Tarschys (Sweden)	1994–

European Union (EU) (formerly European Community)

Formerly also referred to as the Common Market. The European Community came into being on 1 January 1958, following the signing by the original six states (Belgium, France, Italy, Luxembourg, the Netherlands and West Germany) of the Treaty of Rome on 25 March 1957. The original six states, who bound themselves to work together for economic and political union, have been enlarged with the entry of Denmark, Ireland and the UK on 1 January 1973, Greece on 1 January 1981, Spain and Portugal on 1 January 1986 and Austria, Finland and Sweden on 1 January 1995. Under the original Lomé Convention of 31 October 1979, the Community negotiated trade agreements with 58 countries in Africa, the Caribbean and the Pacific. Subsequent agreements have enlarged this number.

Presidents of the European Commission

Walter Hallstein (Federal Republic of Germany)	1958–66
Jean Rey (Belgium)	1966–70
Franco Malfatti (Italy)	1970–72
Sicco Mansholt (Netherlands)	1972–73
Francois-Xavier Ortoli (France)	1973–77
Roy Jenkins (UK)	1977–81
Gaston Thorn (Luxembourg)	1981–85
Jacques Delors (France)	1985–95
Jacques Santer (Luxembourg)	1995–

Presidents of the European Parliament

Robert Schuman (France)	1958–60
Hans Furler (Federal Republic of Germany)	1960–62

Gaetano Martino (Italy)	1962–64
Jean Duvieusart (Belgium)	1964–65
Victor Leemans (Belgium)	1965–66
Alain Poher (France)	1966–69
Mario Scelba (Italy)	1969–71
Walter Behrendt (Federal Republic of Germany)	1971–73
Cornelius Berkhouwer (Netherlands)	1973–75
Georges Spénale (France)	1975–77
Emilio Colombo (Italy)	1977–79
Simone Veil (France)	1979–82
Pieter Dankert (Netherlands)	1982–84
Pierre Pflimlin (France)	1984–87
Lord Plumb (UK)	1987–89
Enrico Barón Crespo (Spain)	1989–91
Egon Klepsch (Germany)	1992–94
Klaus Hänsch (Germany)	1994–

European Free Trade Association (EFTA)

Grouping of European countries whose aims are to achieve a free trade in industrial goods between members, to help achieve the creation of a general Western European market and to expand world trade in general. Six members have left to join the European Economic Community (Denmark and the UK in 1972, Portugal in 1985, Austria, Finland and Sweden in 1994). Indeed, EFTA had arisen partly as a response to the original veto by France on Britain joining the European Community.

Secretaries-General

Frank Figgures (UK)	1960–65
John Coulson (UK)	1965–72
Bengt Rabaeus (Sweden)	1972–75
Charles Muller (Switzerland)	1976–81
Magnus Vahlquist (Sweden) (Acting)	1981 (Oct.–Nov.)
Per Kleppe (Norway)	1981–88
Georg Reisch (Austria)	1988–94
Kjartan Jóhannsson (Iceland)	1994–

League of Nations

International organization set up as an integral part of the Versailles Settlement in 1920 to preserve the peace and settle disputes by negotiation.

Although the United States refused to participate, it comprised 53 members by 1923. Based in Geneva, the League relied upon non-military means to coerce states, such as 'sanctions', but found itself virtually powerless in the face of the Japanese invasion of Manchuria and the Italian invasion of Abyssinia. The League was discredited by 1939 and was dissolved in April 1946 with the formation of the United Nations.

Secretaries-General

Sir Eric Drummond (Earl of Perth) (UK)	1919–32
Joseph Avenol (France)	1933–40
Sean Lester (Ireland) (acting)	1940–46

North Atlantic Treaty Organization (NATO)

Created by the North Atlantic Treaty of 4 April 1949. The organization represented the first US commitment to European defence in peacetime. NATO came in response to Western fears about the power of the Soviet Union and the failure of the UN Security Council to operate in the face of the Soviet veto. The treaty states are obliged to take such action as they deem necessary to assist a fellow signatory subjected to aggression, although there is no obligation to fight. The treaty states are Belgium, Luxembourg, the Netherlands, Britain, the United States, Canada, Italy, Norway, Denmark, Iceland and Portugal, who were original signatories, plus Greece and Turkey (1952) and West Germany (1955). The reunited Germany acceded in October 1990. Spain joined in 1982. With the fall of communism, the role of NATO is changing and its membership is reaching out to Central and Eastern Europe. NATO has provided support for peace-keeping operations in Bosnia. France was an original signatory, but withdrew from the organization in 1966.

Secretaries-General

Lord Ismay (UK)	1952–57
Paul-Henri Spaak (Belgium)	1957–61
Alberico Casardi (Acting)	1961 (Mar.–Apr.)
Dirk Stikker (Holland)	1961–64
Manlio Brosio (Italy)	1964–71
Joseph Luns (Holland)	1971–84
Lord Carrington (UK)	1984–88
Manfred Wörner (Federal Republic of Germany)	1988–95
Javier Solana (Spain)	1995–

Supreme Allied Commanders, Europe

Dwight D. Eisenhower (US)	1950–52
Matthew Ridgway (US)	1952–53
Alfred M. Gruenther (US)	1953–56
Lauris Norstad (US)	1956–63
Lyman L. Lemnitzer (US)	1963–69
Andrew J. Goodpaster (US)	1969–74
Alexander Haig (US)	1974–79
Bernard Rogers (US)	1979–87
John R. Galvin (US)	1987–92
John Shalikashvili (US)	1992–93
George Joulvan (US)	1993–97
Wesley Clark (US)	1997–

Organization for Economic Co-operation and Development (OECD)

The organization consists of over 20 countries, mostly the richer nations. Its aims are to encourage and co-ordinate the economic policies of members, to contribute to the expansion of developing countries and to promote the development of world trade on a multi-lateral basis. It publishes economic statistics and compiles reports on specific aspects of world economics. It is the successor to the Organization for European Economic Co-operation (OEEC).

Secretaries-General

Thorkil Kristensen (Denmark)	1961–69
Emile van Lennep (Netherlands)	1969–84
Jean-Claude Paye (France)	1984–96
Donald Johnston (Canada)	1996–

Organization of African Unity

Grouping of African states set up in 1963 after a meeting in Addis Ababa. Its formation united the rival Monrovia and Casablanca groups as well as including nearly all the independent black African states. At its first meeting the members agreed to accept inherited colonial boundaries, thus preventing many border incidents. The members also voted to boycott South Africa. It has mediated successfully in disputes among its members (as in 1972, in the dispute between Guinea and Senegal) and has campaigned against the vestiges of colonialism in southern Africa (as in Namibia in the 1980s).

Secretaries-General

Diallo Telli (Guinea)	1964–72
Nzo Ekangaki (Cameroon)	1972–74
William Eteki Mbomua (Cameroon)	1974–78
Edem Kodjo (Togo)	1978–83
Peter Onu (Nigeria) (Acting)	1983–85
Ide Oumarou (Niger)	1985–89
Salim Ahmed Salim (Tanzania)	1989–

Organization of American States (OAS)

Regional political organization consisting of the United States and over 30 Latin American and Caribbean republics, created at the Bogotá Conference in 1948. The organization has an Inter-American Conference which meets every five years to discuss general policies, and each member state is represented by an ambassador on its council, which oversees the implementation of OAS policy. There are provisions for *ad hoc* consultative meetings of foreign ministers and special conferences which promote co-operation in dealing with technical problems. The whole organization is served by a secretariat known as the Pan-American Union, which operates through its general headquarters in Washington.

Secretaries-General

Alberto Lleras Camargo (Colombia)	1948–54
Carlos Davila (Chile)	1954–56
José Mora Otero (Uruguay)	1956–68
Galo Plaza Lasso (Ecuador)	1968–75
Alejandro Orfila (Argentina)	1975–84
Valerie McComie (Barbados) (Acting)	1984 (Mar.–June)
João Clemente Baena Soares (Brazil)	1984–94
César Gavíria Trujillo (Colombia)	1994–

Organization of Petroleum Exporting Countries (OPEC)

This organization, whose membership is open to any country with substantial exports of crude petroleum, works to unify and co-ordinate the oil policies of its members, helps to stabilize prices in international oil markets and generally to safeguard the interests of its members. It originated in September 1960 when, after a Baghdad meeting, such leading oil producers as Saudi Arabia, Iran and Venezuela banded together to form OPEC. In 1973, OPEC precipitated a world economic crisis by agreeing price increases which eventually quadrupled the price of oil. Britain is not a member.

Secretaries-General

Faud Rouhani (Iran)	1961–64
Abdul Rahman Al-Bazzaz (Iraq)	1964–65
Ashraf Lutfi (Kuwait)	1965–66
Mohammed S. Joukhdar (Saudi Arabia)	1967
Francisco R. Parra (Venezuela)	1968
Elrich Sanger (Indonesia)	1969
Omar El-Badri (Libya)	1970
Nadim Pachachi (UAE)	1971–72
Abderrahman Khene (Algeria)	1973–74
M.O. Feyide (Nigeria)	1975–76
Ali M. Jaidah (Qatar)	1977–78
Rene G. Ortiz (Ecuador)	1979–81
Marc S. Nan Nguema (Gabon)	1981–83
Fadhil J. Al-Chalabi (Iraq)	1983–88
Dr Subroto (Indonesia)	1988–95
Dr Rilwanu Lukman (Nigeria)	1995–

United Nations, the

International peace-keeping organization set up in 1945 to replace the League of Nations (q.v.). From the 50 states who signed the Charter of the UN in 1945, numbers had more than doubled by 1970 with the rise of independent ex-colonial states. All states have one vote in the General Assembly and its executive, the Security Council, can call on member states to supply armed forces. UN troops have been involved in peace-keeping duties in many parts of the world since 1945, notably in the Middle East, Africa and Cyprus. (See also pp. 228–33 for a chronology of the United Nations.)

Secretaries-General

Trygve Lie (Norway)	1946–53
Dag Hammarskjöld (Sweden)	1953–61
U Thant (Burma)	1961–71

Kurt Waldheim (Austria)	1972–81
Javier Pérez de Cuellar (Peru)	1982–91
Boutros-Boutros Ghali (Egypt)	1992–96
Kofi Annan (Ghana)	1997–

Warsaw Pact, the

Military grouping of Russia and East European states, with a political consultative committee intended to meet twice a year with rotating venue and chairmanship. In fact it met every alternate year, with delegations led by first secretaries of the party. Committee of defence ministers also met annually. Committee of foreign ministers met annually from 1976. Military Council of national chiefs of staff met twice a year. Following the collapse of Communism in Eastern Europe, by late 1990 the Warsaw Pact had effectively ceased to exist as a military alliance.

Commanders-in-Chief

Marshal I.S. Konev (USSR)	1955–60
Marshal A.A. Grechko (USSR)	1960–67
Marshal I.I. Yakubovsky (USSR)	1967–76
Marshal Viktor G. Kulikov (USSR)	1977–91

Members

Albania (ceased to participate in 1961 because of Stalinist and pro-Chinese attitudes. Withdrew in 1968)
Bulgaria
Czechoslovakia
German Democratic Republic (formally withdrew on 24 September 1990)
Hungary
Poland
Romania
USSR

Major Treaties and International Agreements since 1944

1944   Bretton Woods Agreement, July, to set up a World Bank and International Monetary Fund.
        Russia signed armistice with Finland, 4 September, ending Finnish involvement in war.
        Russia signed armistice with Romania, 12 September.
        Moscow conference between Churchill and Stalin, 9–19 October.

1945   Armistice signed with Hungary, 20 January.
        Yalta Agreement, 11 February, between Britain, Russia and the United States on the future of Germany, Europe and world security.
        Pact of Union of Arab States in Cairo, 22 March, set up Arab League.
        United Nations Charter, 26 June, established new world forum with Britain, Russia, France, the United States and China as leading powers.
        Potsdam Agreement between Britain, Russia and the United States, 2 August, expanded on the Yalta Agreement.

1946   Treaty of London recognized Transjordan as independent state, 25 May.
        Linggadjati Agreement, 15 November, between Dutch and Indonesians on creation of Indonesian Republic.
        World Bank set up, 27 December.

1947   Peace Treaties, 10 February, with Italy, Finland, Hungary, Bulgaria and Romania.
        Treaty of Dunkirk, 4 March, between Britain and France promised mutual aid against German aggression.
        Benelux customs union created, 14 March, between Belgium, Holland and Luxembourg.
        Marshall Plan, 5 June; aid for reconstruction accepted by 16 European countries through European Recovery Programme.

1947   British announced Indian Independence, setting up states of India and Pakistan, 5 July.
UN voted for partition of Palestine into Jewish and Arab states, 29 November.

1948   Brussels Treaty, 17 March, between Britain, France, Belgium, Holland and Luxembourg, providing for mutual aid against aggression, and for economic and social co-operation.
Organization for European Economic Co-operation (OEEC) formed by 16 West European nations, 16 April.
Treaty forming Organization of American States (OAS) for joint resistance to attack, signed 30 April, by United States and 20 other Central and Latin American states to come into force in 1951.

1949   Comecon (Council for Mutual Economic Assistance) set up, 25 January, by USSR and communist Eastern European states for economic co-ordination and development.
North Atlantic Treaty, 4 April, between the United States, Canada, Britain, France, Belgium, Holland, Luxembourg, Norway, Denmark, Portugal and Iceland for mutual aid against aggression.
Statute of the Council of Europe, 5 May, signed by 10 West European states.
Israel signed armistice with Egypt, 24 February; Jordan, 3 April; Syria, 20 July, establishing effective borders of new Israeli state.
The Hague conference reached agreement on independence of Indonesia, 2 November.

1950   US–South Korea defence agreement, 26 January.
Colombo Plan formed, 28 November, for economic development of Commonwealth countries in Asia.

1951   Pacific Security Treaty between United States, Australia and New Zealand (ANZUS Pact), 1 September.
Japanese Peace Treaty, 8 September, with 48 other powers; Japan signed Mutual Security Pact with the United States permitting them to remain indefinitely in Japan.

1952   US–Japanese Agreement, 28 February, on bases in Japan.
Treaty between France, West Germany, Italy, Belgium, Holland and Luxembourg, 27 May, created European Defence Community.
US–Israeli defence agreement, 23 July.

1953   Armistice signed in Korean War, 27 July, at Panmunjon.
        Mutual defence agreement between United States and Spain,
        26 September, allowing US bases.
        Mutual Defence Treaty of United States with South Korea,
        1 October.

1954   Truce signed in Indo-Chinese War, 21 July, partitioning North
        and South Vietnam.
        Peace agreement in Geneva, 11 August, about future of Viet-
        nam, not signed by United States or South Vietnam.
        South-East Asia Collective Defence Treaty, 8 September, signed
        by United States and seven other nations pledging joint action
        to protect South Vietnam and other nations in the area.
        London Agreement, 3 October, extended Brussels Pact to West
        Germany and Italy, forming the West European Union.
        Mutual Defence Treaty with Nationalist China by United States,
        2 December.

1955   US–Canadian agreement on operation of Early Warning Sys-
        tem, 5 May (extended in 1958 to set up NORAD, North Amer-
        ican Air Defence Command).
        London and Paris Agreements, 5 May, gave West Germany
        full sovereignty and brought her into North Atlantic Treaty
        Organization.
        Warsaw Pact formed, 13 May, between Russia and Eastern bloc
        powers for mutual assistance in the event of war.
        Austrian State Treaty, 15 May, between Britain, the United States,
        Russia and France established Austria as neutral, sovereign state.

1957   Treaty of Rome, 22 March, between France, West Germany,
        Italy, Belgium, Holland and Luxembourg established European
        Economic Community.
        UN International Atomic Energy Agency for peaceful use of
        atomic energy set up, 29 July.

1959   Ten-Power Committee on Disarmament set up, 7 September,
        representing Britain, Canada, France, Italy, the United States,
        Bulgaria, Czechoslovakia, Poland, Romania and the Soviet Union.
        Treaty for peaceful use of Antarctica opened for signature,
        1 December.

1960   Japanese–US Treaty of mutual security, 19 January.
        Stockholm Convention, 3 May, between Britain, Denmark, Nor-
        way, Portugal, Austria, Sweden and Switzerland set up European
        Free Trade Association.
        Indus Waters Treaty, 19 September, between Pakistan and India.

1961   Organization for Economic Co-operation and Development (OECD), 30 September, replaced the OEEC and includes United States and Canada.

1963   Treaty of Co-operation between France and West Germany, 22 January.
        Partial Test-Ban Treaty, 5 August, between Britain, the United States and Russia limiting nuclear testing.
        'Hot-line' agreement reached between the United States and Soviet Union, 5 April.

1966   Malaysian–Indonesian Agreement, 1 June, ending 'confrontation'.

1967   Treaty banning nuclear weapons in space opened for signature in London, Moscow and Washington, 27 January.
        Treaty of Tlatelolco, prohibiting nuclear weapons in Latin America, agreed for signature in Mexico City, 14 February.
        Egypt and Jordan signed anti-Israel Pact, 30 May.
        Iraq joined anti-Israel Pact, 4 June.

1968   UN Security Council called for permanent peace settlement in Middle East, 22 November.
        Nuclear Non-Proliferation Treaty agreed and opened for signature, 1 July.

1969   Disarmament Committee renamed Conference of the Committee on Disarmament with 24 members, 26 August.

1970   Standstill cease-fire between Egypt and Israel in Suez Canal Zone, 7 August.
        Treaty between West Germany and Russia, 12 August, renounced use of war.
        Treaty between West Germany and Poland, 18 November, renounced use of war and confirmed existing borders.

1971   Sea-bed Treaty prohibiting use of sea-bed for nuclear weapons opened for signatures, 11 February.
        Five-power agreement of Britain, Australia, New Zealand, Singapore and Malaysia on defence of Singapore and Malaysia, 9 January.

1972   SALT I anti-ballistic missile (ABM) agreement and five-year interim agreement on limitation of strategic arms signed by US and Soviet Union, 26 May.
        Simla Peace Agreement between India and Pakistan, 3 July; 'Line of control' in Kashmir agreed, 11 December.

1973   Israeli–Egyptian agreement on cease-fire line following Yom Kippur War, 11 November.

1974   Protocol to the US–Soviet SALT ABM agreement limited deployment to a single area, 3 July; US–Soviet Threshold Test Ban Treaty signed, limiting underground nuclear tests, 3 July.
Vladivostok Accord between United States and Soviet Union, 24 November, established framework for future negotiations controlling strategic arms race.
Israeli–Egyptian Agreement on disengagement of forces on Suez Canal, 18 January.
Israeli–Syrian agreement on disengagement on Golan Heights, 5 June.

1975   Act of the Helsinki Conference, 'Helsinki Agreement', 1 August, between 35 nations regarding European security, including a reaffirmation of human rights and proposals for economic collaboration between Eastern and Western 'blocs'.
Israeli–US agreement on establishment of early warning system in Sinai, 1 September.
Israeli–Egyptian agreement for Israeli withdrawal from Sinai and establishment of a buffer zone, 4 September.

1976   US–Soviet Treaty restricting nuclear explosions for peaceful purposes, 28 May.

1978   Camp David agreements between Israel and Egypt for conclusion of peace treaty and overall Middle East settlement, 17 September.

1979   Israeli–Egyptian Peace Treaty, 26 March.
SALT II Agreement signed by United States and Soviet Union restricting numbers of strategic offensive weapons, 18 June; ratification withheld by the United States.
Lancaster House Agreement, London, 15 December, ended war in Zimbabwe and created independent state from April 1980.

1980   Agreement for normalization of US relations with China, 17 September.

1981   US, Israel and Egypt signed agreement for peace-keeping force in Sinai, 10 July.
Inhumane Weapons Convention signed in Geneva, 18 May.

1982   Israeli–Egyptian agreement on Sinai, 19 January, completed Israeli withdrawal.

1984   Lusaka Accord between Angola and South Africa, 16 February; South Africa agreed to withdraw from Angola and SWAPO to withdraw from Namibia.

Nkomati Accord between Mozambique and South Africa, 1 March; mutual non-aggression agreement and to seek end to civil war in Mozambique.

US–Soviet agreement to expand and improve 'Hot-line', 17 July.

Sino–British declaration on return of Hong Kong to China, 26 September.

1985   All Pacific nations sign Treaty of Raratonga, aimed at creating a nuclear-free zone in the Pacific.

1987   Cease-fire agreement reached in Iran–Iraq War, 20 August, policed by UN.

Arias Peace Plan signed by Presidents of Central American states to end war in Nicaragua, 1 August.

Intermediate Nuclear Force (INF) Treaty signed between United States and Soviet Union, 8 December.

1988   Geneva Accord, 14 May, for withdrawal of Soviet forces from Afghanistan, beginning 15 May 1988 and to be concluded by February 1989; Pakistan and Afghanistan agreed non-interference in each others' affairs.

Cease-fire agreement in Geneva, 1 August, reached over Namibia; timetable for withdrawal of Cuban forces from Angola reached in November; UN Transition Assistance Group to supervise progress to full Namibian independence on 1 April 1990. All Cuban forces to leave Angola by July 1991.

1989   Representatives of Algeria, Libya, Morocco, Mauritania, and Tunisia sign a treaty establishing the Arab Maghreb Union, 17 February.

1990   Treaty on the Final Settlement with Respect to Germany signed by East Germany, West Germany, France, Britain, United States and Soviet Union, 12 September.

President Gorbachev and President Bush sign an agreement to destroy chemical weapons and to discontinue their production, 1 June.

1991   Leaders of the MPLA and the UNITA sign a cease-fire agreement to end the Angolan civil war, 31 May.

Heads of states of the Organization of African Unity sign a treaty to establish the African Economic Union by the year 2025, June.

START I agreement signed, 31 July, by Bush and Gorbachev.

Treaty concluding the Cambodian civil war is signed, 23 October, in Paris.

Heads of states of Russia, Ukraine, and Belarus decide to create a commonwealth of states, the Commonwealth of Independent States (CIS), 8 December, which is later joined by the other member republics of the former Soviet Union (apart from Georgia and the Baltic States), 21 December.

1992   Treaty ending civil war in El Salvador signed in Mexico City, 16 January.

In Maastricht in Holland the leaders of the countries of the European Community (after an agreement reached in December 1991) sign a treaty preparing the way for their economic, financial and political unification, 7 February.

North American Free Trade Association (NAFTA) agreement with Canada, United States and Mexico, 17 December.

Open Skies Treaty signed in Helsinki, 24 March.

Treaty ending 15-year civil war in Mozambique signed in Rome, October.

1993   Presidents Bush and Yeltsin sign the START II Treaty, 3 January, in Moscow.

International treaty on the total abolition of chemical weapons is signed, 13 January, in Paris with representatives from 127 countries.

Gaza–Jericho Accord signed in Washington by Israeli Prime Minister Rabin and Palestinian leader Yasser Arafat, 13 September.

1994   Agreement to open US diplomatic liaison offices with Vietnam (May) following easing of economic embargo in 1992.

1995   Dayton Agreements hosted by the United States on future of Bosnia-Herzegovina.

1996   Treaty of Pelindaba signed, banning the possession and deployment of nuclear weapons on the African continent or the islands surrounding it. Comprehensive Test Ban Treaty signed by 149 states (September).

1997   Founding Treaty signed between Russia and NATO, 27 May.

Russia–Chechnya Peace Agreement, 12 May. Russo–Chinese border agreement (November). Ottowa Treaty banning landmines (December).

The United Nations

1941	June 12	Inter-Allied Declaration signed in London by all nations then at war with Germany to work for a 'world in which, relieved of the menace of aggression, all may enjoy economic and social security'.
	Aug. 14	Atlantic Charter issued by US President Franklin D. Roosevelt and British Prime Minister Winston Churchill detailing eight points to 'base their hopes for a better future for the world'.
1942	Jan. 1	Declaration by United Nations signed by 26 nations in Washington approving basic points of Atlantic Charter; first official use of name 'United Nations'.
1943	Oct. 30	Moscow Declaration on General Security signed by Britain, China, Soviet Union and United States, recognizing 'the necessity of establishing at the earliest practicable date a general international organization, based on the principle of sovereign equality'.
1944	Aug. 21	Dumbarton Oaks Conference in Washington DC at which representatives of 39 nations discuss over three months proposals for establishing United Nations organization, agreeing on Security Council as executive branch of UN.
1945	June 26	UN Charter approved by delegates of 50 nations at international conference in San Francisco.
	Oct. 16	Food and Agriculture Organization of United Nations established to improve consumption, production and distribution of food throughout world.
	Oct. 24	UN Charter goes into effect upon ratification by majority of nations, including Britain, China, France, Soviet Union, and United States. Date celebrated annually as United Nations Day.
1946	Jan. 10	UN General Assembly begins first meeting in London with delegates of 51 nations as members. Trygve

Lie of Norway is elected first Secretary-General of UN.

June 25   International Bank for Reconstruction and Development begins operations to assist nations by government loans.

Nov. 4   UNESCO, United Nations Educational, Scientific and Cultural Organization, formed to promote international co-operation in solving problems such as illiteracy.

Dec. 14   Gift of $8,500,000 from US millionaire John D. Rockefeller Jr accepted by UN to buy 18 acres in New York City as site of permanent headquarters.

1947   Apr. 4   International Civil Aviation Organization established to develop international standards and regulations for civil aviation.

1948   Apr. 7   World Health Organization established to promote world health.

Sept. 17   UN peace negotiator Count Folke Bernadotte of Sweden assassinated in Jerusalem while trying to arrange truce in fighting between Arabs and Israelis.

Dec. 10   Universal Declaration of Human Rights adopted by UN General Assembly.

1949   Jan. 1   Cease-fire between India and Pakistan obtained by UN to end two years of fighting over control of Kashmir.

Feb.–July   Cease-fire agreements arranged between Israel and Arab states by UN negotiator Ralph J. Bunche.

Dec. 27   Netherlands grants independence to Indonesia after conference arranged by UN to settle fighting.

1950   Mar. 23   World Meteorological Organization established to promote international reporting and observations of weather.

June 27   UN Security Council calls for member nations to send troops to aid South Korea, which had been attacked by communist North Korea. Soviet Union was boycotting meetings of Security Council at this time and so could not veto measure. Troops of US and 15 other nations dispatched to aid South Korea.

1953   July 27   UN signs truce with North Korea, ending over three years of fighting.

1956	Nov. 7	UN obtains cease-fire in Suez Canal fighting between Egypt and Israeli–British–French forces; sends UN Emergency Force to supervise truce.
1957	July 29	International Atomic Energy Agency created to promote peaceful uses of atomic energy.
1961	Sept. 13	UN troops begin fighting in Congo to restore order in civil war.
	Sept. 18	UN Secretary-General Dag Hammarskjöld killed in air crash in Africa while on Congo peace mission.
	Nov. 3	U Thant of Burma elected as UN's third Secretary-General to succeed Dag Hammarskjöld.
1964	Mar. 4	UN peace-keeping force sent to Cyprus to prevent fighting between Turkish and Greek forces.
1966	Dec. 16	UN Security Council asks member nations to stop trading with Rhodesia because of its policies against Blacks.
1967	June 10	UN negotiates truce in Six-Day Israeli–Arab War.
1971	Oct. 25	Communist China admitted to UN and Nationalist China expelled by 76–35 vote of General Assembly.
	Dec. 13	UN General Assembly votes 79 to 7 with 36 abstentions for Israel to restore to Arab countries territories acquired by force.
1972		Kurt Waldheim appointed UN Secretary-General on resignation of U Thant.
1973	Oct. 22	Cease-fire in 17-day-old Middle East War ordered by UN Security Council.
	Oct. 25	UN peace-keeping force sent to Middle East to prevent further fighting between Arab nations and Israel.
1974		Special session of UN General Assembly establishes emergency relief fund for poor nations of world.
1975		International Women's Year declared by UN to promote women's equality.

1977	Nov. 4	Mandatory embargo on military supply shipments to South Africa ordered by UN; first such action against UN member.
1978		UN 6,100-man peace-keeping force stationed in southern Lebanon: brings withdrawal of Israeli troops that invaded in March.
1982		Pérez de Cuellar becomes Secretary-General.
1987	Aug. 20	UN Secretary-General, Pérez de Cuellar, negotiates cease-fire in Iran–Iraq War. UN observer group police the truce.
1988		UN Transition Assistance Group supervise cease-fire in Namibia and elections prior to independence.
1990		UN Security Council endorses sanctions against Iraq because of the Iraqi invasion of Kuwait (6 Aug.) To secure the compliance of its resolution, the Security Council endorses the creation of a blockade around Iraq (25 Aug.). In an ultimatum, the UN Security Council demands that Iraq withdraw its troops from Kuwait by 15 January 1991. At the same time, the UN authorizes its member states to use force against the aggressor if Iraq does not comply with the resolution. (28 Nov.).
1991		UN-brokered cease-fire agreement is signed to conclude the Angolan civil war. In order to monitor disarmament and the coming free elections, the UN sends peace-keeping forces to Angola (31 May).
	July 26	UN observers arrive in El Salvador in order to monitor the disarmament process after the endorsement of an agreement concluding the civil war (January 1992).
	Oct. 23	Treaty bringing an end to the Cambodian civil war is signed in Paris. (In order to monitor the disarmament of the opposing sides and to organize free elections, UN peace-keeping forces are sent to Cambodia in 1992.)
	Dec. 16	The UN General Assembly withdraws its resolution endorsed in 1975 which branded Zionism as racism.

1992   Jan. 1   The Egyptian Boutros-Boutros Ghali replaces Pérez
                    de Cuellar as the Secretary-General of the UN.

       Feb. 21   The UN Security Council passes a resolution to send
                    peace-keeping forces to the former Yugoslavia.

       Apr.   The UN Security Council orders economic sanc-
                    tions against Libya since Libya has refused to hand
                    over to the United States and Britain the two Libyan
                    men who are charged with having bombed PanAm
                    Flight 103 in December 1988.

       May 30   The UN Security Council orders comprehensive eco-
                    nomic sanctions against 'rump' Yugoslavia (Serbia
                    and Montenegro).

       Sept. 23   Due to the break-up of the country, the UN Secur-
                    ity Council declares the dissolution of Yugoslavia;
                    and does not recognize 'rump' Yugoslavia as the
                    legal successor of the former Yugoslavia.

       Dec. 9   With the authorization of the UN Security Council,
                    the landing of US forces in Somalia commences.
                    (On 4 May 1993 troops from 20 countries replace
                    the US peace-keepers.)

1993   Jan.   According to statistics, approximately 80,000 UN
                    peace-keepers are stationed at 12 locations in the
                    world.

       May 24   The UN Security Council extends the deadline
                    of the sanctions introduced against Iraq in August
                    1990.

       May 26   The UN Security Council adopts a resolution to set
                    up an international court for the prosecution of
                    war criminals in the Yugoslavian war. Since the
                    Nuremberg trials, this has been the first court of
                    this nature. (The court is officially set up on 17
                    November 1993.)

       June 14–25   Organized by the UN, and with the participation of
                    166 countries, a world human rights conference is
                    held in Vienna.

       July 28   With the acceptance of Andorra into the UN, the
                    number of member states of the United Nations is
                    raised to 184.

       Oct. 5   The UN Security Council extends the mandate of
                    the UN peace-keeping forces stationed in the former
                    Yugoslavia until 31 March 1994.

       Oct. 8   The General Assembly of the UN cancels the eco-
                    nomic sanctions against South Africa (the arms

embargo remains valid until the general elections in South Africa in April 1994.)

Oct. 18   The UN Security Council introduces an arms and oil embargo against Haiti and freezes Haiti's foreign assets in order to force the military leadership of the country to allow the banished President Jean-Bertrand Aristide to return to Haiti. The UN orders a naval blockade against Haiti.

Nov. 18   The UN Security Council extends the mandate of the UN peace-keeping forces stationed in Somalia until 31 May 1994.

1995   UN peace-keeping efforts in Bosnia (see pp. 277–8).

1997 Sept. 22   Kofi Annan becomes Secretary-General.
            The United States agrees settlement in principle of its UN debt.
            Crisis over UN inspection teams in Iraq.

1998 Feb. 23   Renewed crisis over Iraq defused by visit of Kofi Annan to Baghdad.

      Mar.   Agreement reached on UN inspection of presidential sites in Iraq.

The new nations since 1945[1]

Algeria	French Algeria until 1962.
Angola	Portuguese Angola until 1975.
Armenia	an independent state since 1991, before which it was a member state of the Soviet Union.
Austria	rump state, created in 1918 from German-speaking part of former Austro-Hungarian Empire.
Azerbaijan	an independent state since 1991, before which it was a member state of the Soviet Union.
Bangladesh	prior to 1947 part of British Indian Empire; 1947–71 known as East Pakistan.
Belarus	an independent state since 1991, before which it was a member state of the Soviet Union (and known as Belorussia).
Belize	British Honduras until 1973, independent in 1981.
Benin	until 1960 part of French West Africa; then Dahomey until 1975.
Bhutan	former semi-autonomous kingdom linked to British Indian Empire.
Bosnia-Herzegovina	an independent state since 1992, before which it was a member state of Yugoslavia.
Botswana	British Bechuanaland until 1966.
Brunei	former British protectorate in British Borneo.
Burkina Faso	formerly French Upper Volta; then Upper Volta until 1984.
Burundi	formerly part of German East Africa (to 1919), thereafter part of Belgian controlled Ruanda-Urundi. Urundi become Burundi in 1962.
Cameroon	formerly French and British Cameroon. French Cameroon became independent in 1960, and in 1961 part of British Cameroon acceded to the independent, former French Cameroon to form a two-state Federal Republic, the United Republic of Cameroon in 1972 and the Republic of Cameroon in 1984.

[1] Some of the 'micro-states' (e.g. the Pacific Island republics) have been excluded from this list.

Cape Verde	Portuguese Cape Verde until 1975.
Central African Republic	formerly part of French Equatorial Africa.
Chad	formerly part of French Equatorial Africa.
Congo (Brazzaville)	formerly part of French Equatorial Africa.
Congo	formerly Belgian Congo until independence in 1959; name changed to Zaïre in 1971 but reverted to Congo in 1997.
Croatia	an independent state since 1991, before which it was a member state of Yugoslavia.
Czechoslovakia	formerly part of Austro-Hungarian Empire (pre-1918). Split in 1993 into Czech Republic and Slovakia.
Czech Republic	An independent state since 1993; part of Czechoslovakia (1918–93).
Djibouti	French Somaliland until 1967, then French territory of Afars and Issas. Independent in 1977.
Egypt	British Protectorate until 1922.
Equatorial Guinea	formerly Spanish Territory of the Gulf of Guinea.
Eritrea	an independent state since 1993; part of Ethiopia (1952–93); before the Second World War it was an Italian colony.
Estonia	an independent state from 1918 to 1940, and again since 1991. It was a part of Russia before 1918 and a member state of the Soviet Union (1940–91).
Finland	part of Russian Empire until 1917 as autonomous Grand Duchy.
Gabon	formerly part of French Equatorial Africa.
Gambia	formerly British Gambia, now part of Confederation of Senegambia (with Senegal).
Georgia	an independent state since 1991, before which it was a member state of the Soviet Union.
German Democratic Republic	(East Germany) formerly part of the united German state, divided as a result of the Second World War, but excluding part of former German state lost to present state of Poland. Reunited with Germany, 1990.
German Federal Republic	(1948–90, West Germany; from 1990, united Germany) formerly part of the united German state divided as a result of the Second World War.
Ghana	formerly British Gold Coast, including British Togoland, formerly German Togoland (to 1922).
Greenland	formerly a province of Denmark (to 1979).
Grenada	formerly part of British Windward Islands.

Guinea	formerly French Guinea.
Guinea-Bissau	formerly Portuguese Guinea.
Guyana	formerly British Guiana.
Hungary	up to 1918 part of the dual monarchy of Austria-Hungary and the Austro-Hungarian Empire.
India	formerly part of the British Indian Empire, then also comprising present-day Pakistan and Bangladesh.
Indonesia	formerly Dutch East Indies.
Ireland, Republic of	formerly the Irish Free State, a dominion of Great Britain (1921–48), prior to 1921 part of the United Kingdom. Also known as Eire, 1921–48.
Israel	created in 1948 out of Palestine, a British mandated territory from 1920, previously part of Ottoman Empire.
Ivory Coast	formerly French Ivory Coast.
Jamaica	British colony of Jamaica until 1962.
Jordan	formerly Transjordan (from 1922), part of the united Palestine mandate of Britain (1920–22), previously part of Ottoman Empire.
Kampuchea	formerly Cambodia (from 1953), previously part of French Indo-China. Now reverted to Cambodia.
Kenya	formerly British colony of Kenya (to 1963), known as British East Africa to 1920.
Kirghizia	an independent state since 1991, before which it was a member state of the Soviet Union.
Korea, North	formerly part of Japanese-controlled Korea (1910–45); created separate state in 1948.
Korea, South	formerly part of Japanese-controlled Korea (1910–45); created separate state in 1948.
Kuwait	protected status under Britain until independent state in 1961.
Laos	formerly part of French Indo-China.
Latvia	an independent state from 1918 to 1940, and again since 1991. It was a part of Russia before 1918 and a member state of the Soviet Union (1940–91).
Lebanon	French mandated territory (1920–43), previously part of Ottoman empire.
Lesotho	British protectorate of Basutoland until 1966.
Libya	formerly Tripoli (as Italian colony, 1911–45).
Lithuania	an independent state from 1918 to 1940, and again since 1991. It was a part of Russia before 1918 and a member state of the Soviet Union (1940–91).
Macedonia	an independent state since 1991, before which it was a member state of Yugoslavia.

Madagascar	an independent state since 1960, before which it was a French colony. Known also as the Malagasy Republic.
Malawi	formerly part of Federation of Rhodesia and Nyasaland (1953–64), previously British protectorate of Nyasaland.
Malaysia	formerly the Federation of Malaya (to 1963), previously known as the Straits Settlements and the Federated Malay States.
Mali	formerly (with Senegal) the Federation of Mali (1959–60); previously part of French West Africa.
Mauritania	French colony of Mauritania until 1960.
Moldova	an independent state since 1991. Major parts of Moldova belonged to Romania (1918–40). It was a member state of the Soviet Union (1940–91) when it was known as Moldavia.
Mongolia	prior to 1924 Outer Mongolia.
Morocco	formerly French Morocco (to 1956) and Spanish Morocco which became part of independent Morocco in 1969.
Mozambique	Portuguese Mozambique until 1975.
Myanmar	formerly Burma until 1989. Burma was part of British India before Independence in 1948.
Namibia	formerly South-West Africa (to 1990), prior to 1920 German South-West Africa.
Niger	formerly French West Africa.
Nigeria	an independent state since 1960, before which it was a British protectorate.
Pakistan	prior to 1947 part of British Indian Empire.
Papua New Guinea	formerly (1920–45) Australian mandated territory, thereafter Australian-governed to 1975. Prior to 1920 the area comprised German New Guinea and Australian-run Papua.
Philippines	American colony from 1898 until independence in 1946.
Poland	an ancient kingdom, but prior to 1918 Poland's territory formed part of the German, Austro-Hungarian and Russian Empires. In 1945 its boundaries were substantially altered.
Russia	an ancient monarchy which became an independent state once again in 1991. It was the leading member republic of the Soviet Union (1922–91).
Rwanda	part of German East Africa to 1919, then mandated to Belgium as part of Ruanda-Urundi. Following the

Second World War part of United Nations trust territory of Ruanda-Urundi under Belgian administration. In 1962 Ruanda became the separate state of Rwanda.

Saudi Arabia   proclaimed the kingdom of Saudi Arabia in 1932, previously comprising kingdom of Hejaz and Arabia.

Senegal   formerly part of French West Africa, in 1959 joined with French Sudan, present-day Mali, in Federation of Mali, but from 1960 independent. In 1982 formed brief Confederation of Senegambia with Gambia.

Sierra Leone   British Sierra Leone until 1961.

Singapore   British Crown Colony, then part of Malaysia 1963–65.

Slovakia   an independent state since 1993; it was a part of Czechoslovakia (1918–92).

Slovenia   an independent state since 1991, before which it was part of Yugoslavia. Prior to 1918 it was part of the Austro-Hungarian Empire.

Somalia   formerly British and Italian Somaliland, united as an independent state in 1960.

Sri Lanka   British colony of Ceylon to independence in 1948; in 1972 changed name to Sri Lanka.

Sudan   Anglo–Egyptian Sudan until independence in 1956.

Surinam   Dutch Guiana to 1954 when became an autonomous part of the Netherlands, independent from 1975.

Syria   prior to 1918 part of Ottoman Empire, then placed under French League of Nations mandate until independence in 1946.

Taiwan   ceded to Japan in 1895, the island of Formosa returned to China in 1945, but from 1949 became base for Nationalist Chinese State under Chiang Kai-shek.

Tajikistan   an independent state since 1991, before which it was a member state of the Soviet Union.

Tanzania   formerly German East Africa (to 1918), then League of Nations mandated territory of Tanganyika under British control. Following independence in 1961, it joined with Zanzibar (independent in 1963) in 1964 to form Tanzania.

Thailand   known as Siam until 1939.

Togo   German Togoland until 1918 when mandated under British and French control, then United Nations trust territory. In 1957 British Togoland joined with the Gold Coast and became part of independent Ghana. French Togoland became independent in 1960.

Trinidad and Tobago	British colony of Trinidad and Tobago until 1962.
Tunisia	French protectorate until independence in 1956.
Turkey	formerly the central part of the Ottoman Empire which included much of the Middle East and Arabia. The Turkish Republic was founded in 1923, comprising most of the modern area of Turkey.
Turkmenistan	an independent state since 1991, before which it was a member state of the Soviet Union.
Uganda	British protectorate until independence in 1962.
Ukraine	an independent state since 1991, before which it was a member state of the Soviet Union.
Union of Soviet Socialist Republics	formerly the Russian Empire (to 1917); broke up in 1991 and replaced by loose Commonwealth of Independent States (CIS) containing only part of the former USSR.
United Arab Emirates	known as the Trucial States prior to 1971.
Uzbekistan	an independent state since 1991, before which it was a member state of the Soviet Union.
Vietnam	part of French Indo-China to 1954 when separated into North and South Vietnam, reunited as a single state in 1975.
Western Sahara	formerly known as Spanish Morocco to 1956 when divided between Mauritania and Morocco; in 1979 Mauritania relinquished its claim but it remains disputed between Morocco and an independence movement, the Polisario Front.
Yemen Arab Republic[1]	part of the Ottoman Empire until 1918, when passed to local tribal control, becoming the Yemen Arab Republic in 1962.
Yemen, Peoples' Democratic Republic[1]	formerly under British control, including part of Aden as the protectorate of Aden; independent from 1967.
Yugoslavia	before 1918 the independent kingdom of Serbia and parts of the Austro-Hungarian Empire and Bulgaria. In 1918 Yugoslavia created as kingdom of Serbs, Croats and Slovenes. After its disintegration in the 1990s, a 'rump' Yugoslavia of Serbia and Montenegro was created.
Zaïre	see Congo.

[1] In 1990 the two Yemens united as a single country.

Zambia   formerly known as Northern Rhodesia and a British protectorate; in 1953 combined with Southern Rhodesia and Nyasaland in a Federation, dissolved in 1963, becoming independent Republic of Zambia in 1964.

Zimbabwe   formerly known as British Southern Rhodesia; in 1953 combined with Northern Rhodesia and Nyasaland in a Federation, dissolved in 1963, becoming British colony of Rhodesia. It declared independence in 1965 as Rhodesia, but following the war and agreement of 1979 became Zimbabwe.

Foreign Ministers of the Great Powers since 1945

China

Zhou Enlai	1949–58
Chen Yi	1958–72
Ji Bengfei	1972–74
Qiao Guanhua	1974–76
Huang Hua	1976–82
Wu Xueqian	1982–88
Qian Qichen	1988–

France

Georges Bidault	1944–46
Léon Blum	1946–47
Georges Bidault	1947–48
Robert Schuman	1948–53
Georges Bidault	1953–54
Pierre Mendès-France	1954–55
Edgar Faure	1955 (Jan.–Feb.)
Antoine Pinay	1955–56
Christian Pineau	1956–58
René Pleven	1958 (May–June)
Maurice Couve de Murville	1958–68
Michel Debré	1968–69
Maurice Schumann	1969–73
Michel Jobert	1973–74
Jean Sauvagnargues	1974–76
Louis de Guiringaud	1976–78
Jean François-Poncet	1978–81
Claude Cheysson	1981–84
Roland Dumas	1984–86
Jean Raimond	1986–88
Roland Dumas	1988–93
Alain Juppé	1993–95
Hervé de Charette	1995–97
Hubert Védrine	1997–

Germany (West Germany until 1990)

Konrad Adenauer	1951–55
Heinrich von Brentano	1955–61
Gerhard Schröder	1961–66
Willy Brandt	1966–69
Walter Scheel	1969–74
Hans-Dietrich Genscher	1974–92
Klaus Kinkel	1992–

Russia (after 1991) (for Soviet Union, see below)

Andrei Kozyrev	1991–96
Yevgeni Primakov	1996–

Union of Soviet Socialist Republics (USSR)

Vyacheslav M. Molotov	1939–49
Andrel Y. Vyshinsky	1949–53
Vyacheslav M. Molotov	1953–56
Dimitri T. Shepilov	1956–57
Andrei A. Gromyko	1957–85
Edvard Shevardnadze	1985–91
Alexander Bessmertnykh	1991 (Jan.–Aug.)
Boris Pankin	1991 (Aug.–Nov.)
Eduard Shevardnadze	1991 (Nov.–Dec.)

United Kingdom

Anthony Eden	1940–45
Ernest Bevin	1945–51
Herbert S. Morrison	1951 (Mar.–Oct.)
Anthony Eden	1951–55
Harold Macmillan	1955 (Apr.–Dec.)
Selwyn Lloyd	1955–60
Sir Alec Douglas-Home	1960–63
R.A. Butler	1963–64
Patrick Gordon-Walker	1964–65
Michael Stewart	1965–66
George Brown	1966–68
Michael Stewart	1968–70
Sir Alec Douglas-Home	1970–74
James Callaghan	1974–76
Anthony Crosland	1976–77

David Owen	1977–79
Lord Carrington	1979–82
Francis Pym	1982–83
Sir Geoffrey Howe	1983–89
John Major	1989 (July–Oct.)
Douglas Hurd	1989–95
Malcolm Rifkind	1995–97
Robin Cook	1997–

United States (Secretaries of State)

Edward Stettinius	1944–45
James Byrnes	1945–47
George Marshall	1947–49
Dean Acheson	1949–53
John Dulles	1953–59
Christian Herter	1959–61
Dean Rusk	1961–69
William Rogers	1969–73
Henry Kissinger	1973–77
Cyrus Vance	1977–80
Edmund Muskie	1980–81
Alexander Haig	1981–82
George Schultz	1982–89
James Baker	1989–92
Lawrence Eagleburger	1992–93
Warren Christopher	1993–97
Madeleine Albright	1997–

Wars and Major Armed Conflicts

Second World War, 1939–45

German forces invaded Poland on 1 September 1939, which led to declarations of war by Britain and France on 3 September. The Germans invaded the Low Countries on 10 May 1940, and France was compelled to sign an armistice on 22 June. The British army was evacuated from Dunkirk, while in the 'Battle of Britain' the German Luftwaffe failed to defeat the RAF and establish air superiority which would have made an attempted invasion of Britain possible. Italy declared war on 10 June 1940, and Britain attacked Italian forces in North Africa. For over a year Britain and her Empire stood alone against the Axis powers. In 1941, however, the war was vastly extended, Japan joining the Axis and Russia, China and America joining Britain. The Japanese rapidly overran many of the European colonies in South-East Asia, but Hitler's invasion of Russia (June 1941) eventually proved a decisive mistake. In 1942 the Germans were defeated in North Africa and Russia, in 1943 the Allies invaded Italy, and in 1944 Britain and America opened the 'Second Front' in France. The Allies linked up with the Russians on the Elbe on 28 April 1945 and the Germans accepted unconditional surrender terms on 7 May. In the Far East, major Japanese forces remained committed to the indecisive war in China, but American forces in the 'island-hopping' campaign in the Pacific, and British forces via Burma, inflicted defeats on the Japanese forces. A huge bombing and submarine offensive had brought Japan near to defeat when atomic bombs were dropped on Hiroshima and Nagasaki in early August 1945. Japan surrendered on 14 August 1945.

The Greek Civil War, 1944–49

The Greek Civil War developed out of the rivalry between communist and monarchist partisans for control of Greece as the Axis forces retreated at the end of the Second World War. British troops were sent to aid the pro-monarchist forces in 1944, while the Soviet Union took the side of the communist insurgents. After 1945, American aid enabled British troops to remain in Greece and assist the return of the monarchy. Communist resistance was seriously weakened by the break between Yugoslavia and Russia in 1948, resulting in the closure of much of Greece's northern border to infiltration and aid. The Greek communists announced an end to open conflict in October 1949.

Palestine, 1945–48

Guerrilla warfare was waged by Jewish Zionists against British mandate forces and the Arab population to achieve an independent Jewish nation. On 22 July 1945 the King David Hotel in Jerusalem, housing the British headquarters, was blown up, leaving 92 dead or missing. With the proclamation of the independence of Israel on 14 May 1948, Britain surrendered her League of Nations mandate over Palestine and withdrew her armed forces.

Indonesian War of Independence, 1945–49

The independence of the Republic of Indonesia (formerly Netherlands East Indies) was proclaimed by the nationalist leaders, Sukarno and Hatta, on 17 August 1945. British, Indian and Dutch troops began to arrive on 29 September 1945. British troops captured the rebel capital of Surabaya on 29 November 1945. The Dutch recognized the Indonesian Republic (comprising Java, Sumatra and Madura) on 13 November 1946. The withdrawal of British troops was completed on 30 November 1946. A nationalist uprising on West Java on 4 May 1947 led to Dutch military action on Java on 20 July 1947. A truce, arranged under UN auspices on 17 January 1948 broke down, and the Dutch occupied the rebel capital, Jogjakarta, on 19 December 1948. International opposition and guerrilla warfare led to the Dutch decision to withdraw, and to the independence of Indonesia on 27 December 1949.

Chinese Civil War, 1946–49

Civil war between the national government under Chiang Kai-shek and the communist forces resumed after the defeat of Japan in August 1945. Through the mediation of General George C. Marshall, a truce was arranged on 14 January 1946. It broke down and American supplies to the nationalists were halted on 29 July 1946. A nationalist offensive in Shaahxi took the communist capital, Yenan, on 19 March 1947, but it was retaken in April 1948. As communist forces advanced, Beijing fell on 22 January 1949, Nanjing on 22 April 1949 and Shanghai on 27 May 1949. Mao Zedong proclaimed the People's Republic of China on 1 October 1949. The nationalists withdrew to Taiwan on 7 December 1949.

Philippines, Hukbalahap Insurgency, 1946–54

When the Philippines became independent on 4 July 1946, the war-time communist Anti-Japanese People's Liberation Army, or Hukbalahaps, waged a guerrilla campaign against the government of the republic. By 1950 the Hukbalahaps, with an army of 15,000 men and support of the peasantry, had established control over central Luzón. With American backing, however, a new Defence Secretary, Ramón Magsaysay, revitalized the Philippine armed forces. Counter-insurgency operations, together with a programme of land reform and the resettlement of dissidents, meant that by 1954 the revolt had petered out. The Hukbalahap leader, Luís Taruc, surrendered on 17 May 1954.

First Indo-China War, 1946–54

Following the surrender of Japan, Ho Chi-minh proclaimed the Democratic Republic of Vietnam at Hanoi on 2 September 1945. French and British forces regained control in Saigon, and after negotiations, French troops entered Hanoi on 16 March 1946. After French naval forces shelled the Vietnamese quarter of Haiphong on 23 November 1946, an abortive Viet Minh uprising took place in Hanoi on 19 December 1946. Guerrilla warfare grew into full-scale conflict between the French and the Viet Minh forces under General Giap. On 20 November 1953 the French established a forward base at Dien Bien Phu to lure the Viet Minh into a set-piece battle, but the garrison of 15,000 men was overwhelmed on 7 May 1954. An agreement for a cease-fire and the division of the country at latitude 17°N was signed at the Geneva Conference on 27 July 1954.

Indo-Pakistan War, 1947–49

A rebellion by the Muslim majority in Kashmir led the Hindu maharajah to accede to the Indian Union, and Indian troops were flown into Kashmir on 27 October 1947. Pakistan sent aid to the Muslim Azad ('free') Kashmir irregulars, and Pakistani army units crossed into Kashmir in March 1948. An undeclared state of war between India and Pakistan continued until UN mediation brought about a cease-fire on 1 January 1949. India formally annexed Kashmir on 26 January 1957.

Israeli War of Independence, 1948–49

Israel was invaded by the armies of its Arab neighbours on the day the British mandate ended, 15 May 1948. After initial Arab gains, Israel counter-attacked successfully, enlarging its national territory. Only the

British-trained Arab Legion of Jordan offered effective opposition. Separate armistices were agreed with Egypt (23 February 1949), Jordan (3 April 1949) and Syria (20 July 1949).

Burmese Civil War, 1948–55

In the year after gaining independence on 4 January 1948, the Burmese government faced armed opposition from a wide range of dissident groups: the communists, themselves divided into the White Flag Stalinists and the Red Flag Trotskyites; a private army of war-time 'old comrades' known as the People's Volunteer Organization, who made common cause with army mutineers; ethnic minorities seeking autonomy, such as the Mons and Karens; and bands of Muslim terrorists, Mujahids, in the north of Arakan. By 12 March 1949, when Mandalay fell to the Karen National Defence Organization and the communists, most of Burma was in rebel hands. But the rebels were disunited, and Mandalay was retaken by government forces on 24 April 1949. The rebel capital, Toungoo, was captured on 19 March 1950. The government held the initiative and was able to deal with a new threat posed by Chinese Kuomintang refugees in the eastern Shan states. An offensive in November 1954 reduced the Mujahid menace, and Operation 'Final Victory' was launched against the Karens on 21 January 1955. Outbreaks of fighting have occurred since 1955, but never on the scale of the early years of independence.

Colombian Guerrilla Wars, 1948 – continuing

Civil war – 'La Violencia' – in 1948 allowed the military wing of the Communist Party, the Colombian Revolutionary Armed Forces (FARC), to establish itself. It was joined by other guerrilla groups from the 1960s, including the pro-Cuban ELN, the Maoist APL, the Leftist M-19, and the Trotskyite ADO. Guerrilla warfare in the hinterland tied down over 57,000 troops and 50,000 paramilitary police. Attempts at a peace accord collapsed after a cease-fire in 1984–85 with all groups except the ELN. Financed by cocaine profits, the guerrilla groups have carried out kidnappings, murders and robberies, but also have fought pitched battles with Colombian troops. In the mid-1990s two Marxist insurgent guerrilla groups remained active. A National Conciliation Committee was established in August 1995 to formulate peace proposals. The war has been estimated to have cost over 200,000 lives since 1948.

Karen Insurgency in Burma, 1948 – continuing

Since independence in 1948 the Burmese state has been faced with guerrilla insurgency from the four-million-strong Karen population, based near the Thai border, as well as by other ethnic minorities. The Karen

National Liberation Army is one of six groups fighting for autonomy or complete independence. Drug traffic via Thailand supplies funds for the Karen forces, who are opposed by 170,000 men of the Burmese forces. Guerrilla attacks, mainly in the Irrawaddy Delta, have been countered by 'search and destroy' missions by the Burmese army. The insurgency had been contained by the 1990s.

Malayan Emergency, 1948–60

The Federation of Malaya was proclaimed on 1 February 1948. Communist guerrilla activity began, and on 16 June a state of emergency was declared. In April 1950 General Sir Harold Briggs was appointed to co-ordinate anti-communist operations by Commonwealth forces. He inaugurated the Briggs Plan for resettling Chinese squatters in new villages to cut them off from the guerrillas. After the murder of the British High Commissioner, Sir Henry Gurney, on 6 October 1951, General Sir Gerald Templer was appointed High Commissioner and director of military operations on 15 January 1952, and on 7 February a new offensive was launched. On 8 February 1954 British authorities announced that the Communist Party's high command in Malaya had withdrawn to Sumatra. The emergency was officially ended on 31 July 1960.

Costa Rican Civil War and rebel invasion, 1948

Civil war broke out in March 1948 when President Teodoro Picado attempted to annul the elections. He allowed the communists to organize a 2,000-strong militia to support the regular army. But the forces of the National Liberation Party, led by Colonel José Figueres, gradually took control of the country and entered the capital, San José, on 24 April 1948. President Picado resigned and the regular army was disbanded. On 10 December 1948 Costa Rica was invaded from Nicaragua by 1,000 armed supporters of the ex-President, Calderón Guardia. The town of La Cruz fell, but the rebels had been driven out by 17 December 1948.

Korean War, 1950–53

North Korean troops invaded the South on 25 June 1950. The United Nations decided to intervene following an emergency session of the Security Council, which was being boycotted by the Soviet Union. The first American troops landed at Pusan airport on 1 July 1950. General MacArthur mounted an amphibious landing at Inchon on 15 September 1950, and Seoul was recaptured on 26 September. The advance of the UN forces into North Korea on 1 October 1950 led to the entry of China into the war on 25 November 1950. Seoul fell to the Chinese on 4 January 1951, but was retaken by UN forces on 14 March 1951. General MacArthur was relieved of his command on 11 April 1951 after expressing his desire to expand the war into China. Truce talks began on 10 July 1951, and an armistice was finally signed at Panmunjon on 27 July 1953.

Chinese Invasion of Tibet, 1950–59

The Chinese invaded across the eastern frontier of Tibet on 7 October 1950. An agreement was signed on 23 May 1951, giving China control of Tibet's affairs, and Chinese troops entered Lhasa in September 1951. The Dalai Lama remained as a figurehead ruler, but there was widespread guerrilla activity against the Chinese forces of occupation. The last serious resistance came in 1959. On 10 March 1959 an uprising took place in Lhasa, but it was suppressed by Chinese tanks, and on 30 March the Dalai Lama fled to asylum in India.

Indonesian Civil War, 1950–62

In 1950 prolonged guerrilla campaigns began by a fanatical Muslim sect, Darul Islam, and by the South Moluccans, who proclaimed their independence on 26 April 1950. In 1957 objections to Javanese domination of Indonesian affairs and suspicion of Dr Sukarno's left-wing policies led the military commanders in Borneo, Sumatra and Celebes to refuse to acknowledge the authority of the Cabinet. A Revolutionary Government of the Indonesian Republic was proclaimed on 15 February 1958. The authorities took military action against the right-wing rebels, capturing their headquarters at Bukittingi on 5 May 1958, and their capital, Menado, on 26 June 1958. The rebel movement finally collapsed when an amnesty was offered on 31 July 1961, and the civilian leaders surrendered. Opposition from Darul Islam was also suppressed by 1962.

Tunisian War of Independence, 1952–56

In February 1952 Habib Bourguiba and other leaders of the New Constitution Party were arrested, and the ensuing disorders led to the introduction of martial law. In the countryside the Tunisian nationalists waged a guerrilla campaign, while in the towns there were terrorist outrages by nationalists and by the 'Red Hand', a secret settler organization. Preoccupied with the Algerian revolt, France granted Tunisia independence on 20 March 1956.

Mau Mau Revolt, 1952–60

Violence by the Mau Mau, an African secret society in Kenya, led to a British declaration of a state of emergency on 20 October 1952. Leading Kikuyu nationalists were arrested and Jomo Kenyatta was given a seven-year prison sentence in October 1953. A separate East African command consisting of Kenya, Uganda and Tanganyika was set up under General Sir George Erskine. In campaigns in the first half of 1955 some 4,000 Mau Mau in the Mount Kenya and Aberdare regions were dispersed. Britain began to reduce her forces in September 1955; the state of emergency in Kenya ended on 12 January 1960.

East German Workers' Uprising, 1953

Demonstrations by building workers in East Berlin on 16 June 1953 spread to a number of factories the following day. More than 300 places in East Germany were affected, including major towns such as Magdeburg, Jena, Görlitz and Brandenburg. The disorders were suppressed by security police, and curfew and martial law restrictions remained in force until 12 July 1953.

Moroccan War of Independence, 1953–56

Nationalist agitation grew when Sultan Muhammad V was forced into exile on 20 August 1953 after refusing to co-operate with the French authorities. The Army of National Liberation, composed of Berber tribesmen who had seen service with the French army during the Second World War and the First Indo-China War, began a large-scale guerrilla campaign in 1955. The Sultan returned on 5 November 1955, and a Franco–Moroccan declaration on 2 March 1956 ended the French protectorate and established the independence of Morocco.

Cuban Revolution, 1953–59

An attempted uprising led by Fidel Castro in Santiago and Bayamo on 26 July 1953 was suppressed. Castro was imprisoned but granted an amnesty in May 1955. He led an unsuccessful landing in Oriente Province on 30 November 1955, but commenced a successful guerrilla campaign based in the Sierra Maestra. Castro launched a final offensive in October 1958, and General Batista fled the country on 1 January 1959.

Guatemalan Invasion, 1954

An army of liberation, composed of Guatemala exiles and supported by the US Central Intelligence Agency, invaded Guatemala from Honduras and Nicaragua on 18 June 1954. The left-wing government of President Arbenz was overthrown by 27 June and the leader of the exiles, Colonel Carlos Castillo Armas, was declared President on 8 July 1954.

Costa Rican Invasion, 1954

On 25 July 1954 Costa Rican exiles based in Nicaragua crossed the border, but were repelled. A Nicaraguan plane was hit and both sides mobilized on the border, but the United States sent planes to Costa Rica to deter further Nicaraguan action.

Algerian War of Independence, 1954–62

Algerian nationalists staged attacks on French military and civilian targets on 1 November 1954. In August 1956 the guerrilla groups formed the Armée de Libération Nationale. The French army conducted a brutal counter-insurgency campaign, which, while effective, alienated its supporters. On 13 May 1956 criticism of army methods led the Commander-in-Chief in Algeria, General Massu, to refuse to recognize the government of France. General de Gaulle, returned to power on 1 June 1958, set a course for Algerian self-determination. A mutiny by the French army in Algeria, led by generals Challe and Salan, began on 22 April 1961, but was suppressed. Despite terrorism by French settlers of the OAS, peace talks began at Evian-les-Bains in May 1961, and a cease-fire was agreed on 18 March 1962. Algeria was declared independent on 3 July 1962.

Cyprus Emergency, 1955–59

Agitation for union with Greece (Enosis) led in April 1955 to the start of a campaign of terrorism and guerrilla warfare by EOKA, the militant wing of the Enosis movement. A state of emergency was declared on 27 November 1955. Archbishop Makarios of Cyprus was deported to the Seychelles on 9 March 1956. A cease-fire came into effect on 13 March 1959, and the state of emergency was lifted on 4 December 1959. Cyprus became an independent republic on 16 August 1960.

Sudanese Civil War, 1955 – continuing

The conflict began in 1955 with riots in Yambio in July and mutinies by southern troops in August. The Anya Nya rebels, demanding secession for southern Sudan, began a guerrilla campaign in 1963. Peace talks between the insurgents and the government began in Addis Ababa in February 1972. A cease-fire came into effect on 12 March 1972 and the south was granted a measure of autonomy. However, a mutiny of southern troops in May 1983 and opposition to President Nimeiri's imposition of Islamic law on the country in September 1983 led to renewed civil war. The Sudan People's Liberation Army was formed under Colonel John Garang and President Nimeiri declared a state of emergency on 29 April 1984. The rebel Sudanese People's Liberation Army (SPLA) in the south and the National Democratic Alliance (NDA) in the north are still a potent force in the 1990s.

Costa Rican rebel invasion, 1955

On 11 January 1955 a 500-strong force of rebels invaded from Nicaragua. After an 11-day campaign, and pressure brought to bear on the Nicaraguan government through the council of the Organization of American States, the invaders were driven out.

Polish Workers' Uprising, 1956

A revolt of workers seeking better conditions broke out in Poznan on 28 June 1956. It was suppressed by the security forces.

Hungarian Uprising, 1956

Student demonstrations in Budapest on 23 October 1956 led to a general uprising against the government of Erno Gero. The Stalin statue was torn down and the radio headquarters were seized by the crowds. The insurgents fought against the troops of the State Defence Authority (ÁVH) and the intervening Soviet troops. On 25 October, the ÁVH troops, hiding on rooftops around Kossuth Square, shot into the peaceful demonstrators, thus causing more people to join the insurgents. At dawn on 24 October, Imre Nagy became the Prime Minister and gradually a supporter of the revolution. On 26 October, he invited non-communist politicians into the government. On 27 October Soviet troops were withdrawn from Budapest. On 1 November 1956 Imre Nagy announced Hungary's withdrawal from the Warsaw Pact and asked the United Nations to recognize its neutrality. Soviet reinforcements surrounded Budapest and entered the city early on 4 November. Resistance ended on 14 November 1956.

Suez Invasion, 1956

Egypt nationalized the Suez Canal on 26 July 1956. After secret talks with Britain and France, Israel invaded Sinai on 29 October 1956. When Egypt rejected a cease-fire ultimatum by France and Britain, their air forces began to attack Egyptian air bases on 31 October. On 5 November British and French forces invaded the Canal Zone. Pressure from the United Nations and world opinion forced a cease-fire at midnight on 6/7 November 1956.

Honduras border conflict with Nicaragua, 1957

On 18 April 1957 Nicaraguan troops crossed the Coco River and invaded Honduras to seize disputed border territory. Honduras recaptured the town of Morocon on 1 May. The Organization of American States arranged a cease-fire and withdrawal of forces on 6 May 1957.

Ifni Incident (Morocco), 1957

On 23 November 1957, some 1,200 Moroccan irregulars attacked the Spanish territory of Ifni. The Spanish garrison was strengthened and Madrid announced that order had been restored on 8 December 1957.

Lebanese Civil War, 1958

Civil war broke out in Lebanon in April 1958 between the pro-Western government of President Chamoun, dominated by Maronite Christians, and pro-Nasserite Muslims. Following the overthrow of the monarchy in an army coup in Iraq on 14 July 1958, President Chamoun appealed for aid, and on 15 July American troops landed in Beirut. On 23 September 1958, the neutralist General Chehab took over from President Chamoun. The last American troops were withdrawn from Lebanon on 25 October 1958.

Tunisian conflict with France, 1958–61

On 8 February 1958 the French air force bombed the Tunisian town of Sakiet, killing 79 people, in retaliation for Tunisian assistance to the Algerian rebels. Clashes took place as Tunisia demanded the evacuation of French bases. On 17 June 1958 the French agreed to withdraw from all bases except Bizerte. On 5 July 1961 Tunisia made a formal claim to the French Bizerte base and imposed a blockade on 17 July. France sent reinforcements, who occupied the town of Bizerte in heavy fighting on 19–22 July. An agreement for the withdrawal of French troops from the town was signed on 29 September 1961, and the French base was evacuated by 15 October 1963.

Laotian Civil War, 1959–75

The arrest of Prince Souphanouvong and other leaders of the communist Pathet Lao on 28 July 1959 marked the end of attempts at coalition government and the beginning of a three-way conflict between neutralists under Premier Prince Souvanna Phouma, rightists under General Nosavan, and the Pathet Lao. International efforts to find a settlement led to a cease-fire on 3 May 1961 and recognition of the neutrality of Laos at a conference in Geneva on 23 July 1962. But fighting resumed in Laos, with growing involvement by North Vietnam, Thailand and the United States. The South Vietnamese army attacked Laos on 8 February 1971 to disrupt the Ho Chi-minh Trail. A new cease-fire agreement was reached on 21 February 1973, and a coalition government formed in 1974. But communist victories in Vietnam and Cambodia in April 1975 opened the door to a takeover by the Pathet Lao in Laos. The Pathet Lao declared Vientiane liberated on 23 August 1975, and Laos was proclaimed the Lao People's Democratic Republic on 2 December 1975, with Prince Souphanouvong as President.

Vietnam War, 1959–75

Following the division of Vietnam at the Geneva Conference in 1954, Ngo Dinh Diem became President of South Vietnam and secured American support. His government became increasingly authoritarian and repressive, and unrest grew. The communists in South Vietnam (the Viet Cong) built up their strength and launched their first attack on the South Vietnamese armed forces on 8 July 1959 near Bien Hoa, killing two American advisers. A state of emergency was proclaimed in the south on 19 October 1961. After attacks on the USS *Maddox* and *Turner Joy*, the US Congress passed the Gulf of Tonkin resolution on 7 August 1964, giving President Johnson wide military powers in South Vietnam. The sustained bombing of North Vietnam by US aircraft (Operation 'Rolling Thunder') began on 7 February 1965. The first American combat troops landed at Da Nang on 8 March 1965 and engaged the Viet Cong on 15 June. On 30 January 1968, communist forces launched their Tet Offensive with heavy attacks on Saigon, Hue and 30 provincial capitals. On 31 March 1968 President Johnson announced the end of the bombing of the North, and on 13 May 1968 peace discussions began in Paris. On 25 January 1969 these discussions were transformed into a formal conference. American and South Vietnamese troops invaded Cambodia in 1970, and the South Vietnamese made an incursion into Laos in 1971. A new communist offensive against the South began on 30 March 1972, and this led to a resumption of American bombing of the North on 6 April. The last American ground combat units were withdrawn on 11 August 1972. American bombing was halted on 15 January 1973, and a peace agreement was signed in Paris on 27 January. Two years later, a North Vietnamese offensive, which began on 6 January, overran the South, and Saigon was occupied on 30 April 1975.

Congolese Civil War, 1960-67

Belgium granted independence to its Congo colony on 30 June 1960. Widespread disorder soon followed. The army mutinied, and on 11 July 1960 Moise Tshombe declared the rich mining province of Katanga an independent state. The Prime Minister of the Congo, Patrice Lumumba, appealed to the United Nations and the establishment of a peace-keeping force was approved by the Security Council on 14 July 1960. On 14 September 1960 the army chief of staff, Colonel Mobutu, seized power. Lumumba was seized by Mobutu's troops, handed over to the Katangese and murdered on 9 February 1961. For the next two years, periods of armed conflict and negotiation (during which Dag Hammarskjöld, UN Secretary-General, was killed in a plane crash on 18 September 1961) failed to solve the Congo's problems. Katanga's secession eventually ended when a UN offensive in December 1962 forced Tshombe into exile (15 January 1963). The last UN forces left the Congo on 30 June 1964. Violence continued until November 1967, when a revolt by mercenaries in the eastern provinces, which had begun on 5 July, was finally suppressed.

Revolt of the Kurds in Iraq, 1961 – continuing

The Kurdish minority in north-east Iraq, led by General Mustafa Barzani, rose in revolt in March 1961 after the failure of negotiations on autonomy with General Kassem's regime. The Kurdish militia, the Pesh Merga ('Forward to Death'), fought a prolonged campaign, growing in strength up to 1974, thanks to support from Iran. Then on 13 June 1975 Iran and Iraq signed the Algiers Pact, by which Iran agreed to stop its supplies and close its borders to the Kurds. The revolt collapsed and although guerrilla warfare continued, it was on a much-reduced scale. Fighting was renewed during the Iran–Iraq War (see p. 272) when Iraq was widely condemned for using chemical weapons against Kurdish insurgents, many of whom fled across the Turkish border. The Iraqi invasion of Kuwait (see Gulf War, p. 277), also brought a resurgence of fighting. The defeat of Iraq led to a Kurdish revolt in the north, which was suppressed. The Allies imposed a military exclusion zone north of the 36th parallel, but Saddam Hussein was able to use Kurdish divisions to re-assert his authority.

Angolan War of Independence, 1961–75

The liberation struggle commenced in Portuguese Angola on 3 February 1961, when insurgents attempted to free political prisoners in Luanda. The risings were suppressed with great bloodshed, but a guerrilla campaign developed, and by 1974 Portugal was maintaining an army in Angola of 25,000 white and 38,000 locally enlisted troops. After the coup in Portugal on 25 April 1974, negotiations began, and on 15 January 1975 the Portuguese agreed to Angolan independence. As rival liberation groups fought for control of the country, the independence of Angola was proclaimed on 11 November 1975.

Bay of Pigs Invasion, 1961 (Cuba)

Some 1,500 anti-Castro exiles landed in the Bay of Pigs, Cuba, on 17 April 1961, in an operation sponsored by the US Central Intelligence Agency. The invasion was defeated after three days' fighting, when the expected general anti-Castro uprising failed to take place.

Guerrilla Insurgency in Guatemala, 1960–96

Guerrilla warfare began after the revolt against the government of President Ydigoras Fuentes on 13 November 1960 by junior army officers, who objected to the presence of American-sponsored training camps for Cuban exiles. The rebels were defeated, but soon launched a guerrilla campaign. In the late 1960s they allied themselves with the Guatemalan Communist Party to form the Fuerzas Armadas Rebeldes (Insurgent Armed Forces), a name later changed to the Guerrilla Army of the Poor. American special forces assisted in government operations against the insurgents, who were forced to switch their attacks from the countryside to the cities for a time. Retaliation by right-wing death squads resulted in thousands of deaths on both sides. In 1977 the United States halted military aid to Guatemala over human rights violations, but the embargo was lifted on 17 January 1982. A state of siege was introduced on 1 July 1982. However, in December 1996, after 36 years of conflict, a peace treaty was signed by the major guerrilla groups with the conservative government of President Arzu. Since the war began in November 1960, an estimated 150,000 people have died and 50,000 have disappeared. Hundreds of thousands of Guatemalans, most of them indigenous, have been displaced or forced into exile.

Conflict on Irian Jaya (West New Guinea), 1962 – continuing

Following a clash between Indonesian and Dutch naval forces on 15 January 1962, President Sukarno ordered military mobilization and sent armed units into West New Guinea. In a settlement negotiated through the United Nations, the Dutch agreed on 15 August 1962 to hand over West New Guinea, which was incorporated into Indonesia as Irian Barat on 1 May 1963. The Free Papua Movement, opposed to Indonesian control and desiring unification with Papua New Guinea, undertook small-scale guerrilla operations. Fighting in 1984 led to the movement of over 11,000 refugees to Papua New Guinea. A 1990 peace agreement has not ended the fighting against the Indonesian regime.

Indo-Chinese War ('Himalayan War'), 1962

After a series of incidents in the disputed border areas, Chinese forces attacked on 20 October 1962 and drove the Indian forces back on the north-east frontier and in the Ladakh region. India declared a state of emergency on 26 October 1962, and launched an unsuccessful counter-offensive on 14 November 1962. On 21 November, the Chinese announced that they would cease fire all along the border and withdraw 12.5 miles behind the line of actual control that existed on 7 November 1959.

North Yemen Civil War, 1962–70

The royal government of North Yemen was overthrown in an army coup led by Colonel Sallal on 26 September 1962. A civil war began, in which the republican regime was supported by up to 70,000 Egyptian troops and the royalist tribesmen were assisted by arms supplies and technicians from Saudi Arabia. Egypt's defeat in the Six-Day War in 1967 led to an agreement with Saudi Arabia for a disengagement of forces from North Yemen, signed at a meeting of Arab heads of state in Khartoum on 31 August 1967. Sporadic fighting continued until Saudi Arabian mediation secured the formation of a coalition government on 23 May 1970.

Algerian conflict with Morocco, 1963

A series of border clashes between Moroccan and Algerian forces in the Atlas mountains took place in September and October 1963. Ethiopia and Mali mediated a cease-fire on 30 October 1963, and an agreement for the establishment of a demilitarized zone was signed on 20 February 1964.

'Confrontation' between Indonesia and Malaysia, 1963–66

When the Federation of Malaysia was established on 16 September 1963, President Sukarno of Indonesia announced a policy of 'confrontation' on the grounds that the federation was 'neo-colonialist'. There followed a campaign of propaganda, sabotage and guerrilla raids into Sarawak and Sabah. An agreement ending 'confrontation' was signed in Bangkok on 1 June 1966 (ratified 11 August).

Cypriot Civil War, 1963–68

President Makarios's proposals for constitutional reform led to fighting between Greek and Turkish Cypriots on 21 December 1963. There was a cease-fire on 25 December. A United Nations peace-keeping force was established in Cyprus on 27 March 1964. On 7–9 August 1964, Turkish planes attacked Greek Cypriot positions on the north-west coast in retaliation for attacks on Turkish Cypriots. There was renewed fighting between Turkish and Greek communities in 1967. A settlement was reached after mediation by the UN and the United States on 3 December 1967, and the withdrawal of Greek regulars from Cyprus and the demobilization of Turkish forces held in readiness to invade was completed by 16 January 1968.

Kenyan conflict with Somalia, 1963–67

The 1960 independence constitution of the Somali Democratic Republic contained a commitment to recover its 'lost territories', which included the northern frontier district of Kenya. Serious border clashes between the Kenyans and Somalis began in March 1963 and diplomatic relations were broken off in December. Sporadic fighting continued until the two countries agreed to end the dispute by the Declaration of Arusha on 28 October 1967.

Guinea–Bissau War of Independence, 1963–74

Armed resistance to Portuguese rule was launched by PAIGC in 1963. PAIGC proclaimed the independence of the republic on 24 September 1973. Following the *coup d'état* in Lisbon on 25 April 1974, led by General Antonio de Spinola (who had been Governor and Commander-in-Chief in Guinea), the Portuguese recognized the independence of Guinea on 10 September 1974.

Eritrean Revolt, 1963–94

Eritrea was integrated into the Ethiopian Empire on 14 November 1962, and a separatist movement, the Eritrean Liberation Front, took up arms the following year. Taking advantage of the instability caused by the overthrow of Haile Selassie on 12 September 1974, separatist guerrillas succeeded in taking control of most of Eritrea except the capital, Asmara, by the end of 1977. The conclusion of the Ogaden War in March 1978 (see p. 270) enabled the Ethiopian army, with Cuban and Soviet assistance, to launch a major counter-offensive in Eritrea on 15 May 1978. The last major town in rebel hands, Keren, fell to government troops in

November 1978. In 1984 the Eritrean People's Liberation Front (EPLF) launched a new offensive (and in 1987 they were joined by a guerrilla revolt in Tigré province). Faced by rising guerrilla successes, the Marxist dictator Mengistu fled Ethiopia in 1991. The Eritrean capital, Asmara, fell to the guerrillas. Independence was proclaimed. This was overwhelmingly confirmed in a referendum on 25 April 1993.

Ethiopia, invasion by Somalia, 1964

After a series of border clashes, Somali armed forces crossed into Ethiopia on 7 February 1964 to assert the Somali Republic's claim to the Ogaden desert region. The Organization of African Unity called for an end to hostilities, and President Abboud of Sudan secured a cease-fire based on the original boundary on 30 March 1964.

Mozambique War of Independence, 1964–74

FRELIMO launched its first attacks in September 1964, and gradually took control of large areas of the countryside. By 1974 Portugal was forced to maintain an army in Mozambique of 24,000 white and 20,000 locally enlisted troops. After the coup in Portugal of 25 April 1974, negotiations were opened with FRELIMO. Despite a violent revolt by white settlers in Lourenço Marques (now Maputo) on 3 September 1974, a cease-fire agreement was signed on 7 September 1974 and Mozambique officially became independent on 25 June 1975.

Aden, 1964–67

On 18 January 1963 Aden acceded to the South Arabian Federation. British troops were involved in frontier fighting with the Yemen, and in suppressing internal disorders in Aden. A large-scale security operation was launched in January 1964 in the Radfan region, north of Aden. On 26 November 1967 the People's Republic of South Yemen was proclaimed, and the British military withdrawal from Aden was completed on 29 November. In the period 1964–67, British security forces lost 57 killed and 651 wounded in Aden.

Indo-Pakistan War, 1965

Border clashes took place in the Rann of Kutch in April 1965, but a cease-fire agreement came into effect on 1 July. More serious fighting in Kashmir and the Punjab began on 5 August 1965, when Muslim irregulars invaded east Kashmir. The Indian army contained these incursions, but on 1 September 1965 Pakistani regular forces crossed the frontier.

India launched a three-pronged attack towards Lahore on 6 September. As a military stalemate developed, the UN Security Council called for a cease-fire which came into effect on 23 September 1965.

Indonesia, attempted communist rising, 1965–66

An attempted coup by the '30th September Movement', apparently led by Colonel Untung, was launched on 1 October 1965. Details remain very obscure. The coup was crushed in Jakarta (but only after six loyalist generals were murdered). However, in parts of Java the communists took control (the city of Jogjakarta in central Java was briefly seized). Fighting was subsequently reported in north Sumatra, Celebes and Kalimantan (Borneo). Blood-letting and civil war continued into 1966 in central Java, especially around Jogjakarta, Surakarta and Semarang. The massacres of 'communists' left an estimated 500,000 dead as the government regained control.

Dominican Civil War, 1965

Civil war broke out on 24 April 1965 between the Constitutionalists, supporting former President Bosch, and the Loyalist forces of President Reid Cabral. On 28 April 1965, 400 US marines were sent in to prevent a left-wing takeover and during the next month a further 24,000 American troops were landed. A cease-fire was signed on 6 May and at the end of May an Inter-American peace-keeping force, comprising units from the United States, Honduras, Nicaragua, Costa Rica, Brazil and El Salvador, under the auspices of the Organization of American States, was formed to keep the warring factions apart.

Oman, war in the Dhofar, 1965–75

Civil war broke out in 1965 between the Sultan's armed forces and dissident tribesmen in the Dhofar, who had won control of most of the region by 1970. On 23 July 1970 Sultan Said bin Taimur was deposed by his son, Qaboos, who greatly strengthened the armed forces. With foreign assistance, including an Iranian expeditionary force of 2,000 men, the revolt was suppressed and the Sultan officially declared the war ended on 11 December 1975.

Rhodesia (Zimbabwe) War of Independence, 1965–79

Black nationalist guerrilla activity in Southern Rhodesia grew after the unilateral declaration of independence by Ian Smith's white minority regime on 11 November 1965. Two guerrilla forces were operating: ZIPRA, the military wing of Joshua Nkomo's Zimbabwe African People's Union, based in Zambia and recruiting from the Ndebele peoples; and ZANLA, the military wing of Robert Mugabe's Zimbabwe African National Union, based in Mozambique and recruiting from the Shona peoples. These two groupings united to form the Patriotic Front on 9 October 1976. A settlement for an end to the conflict based on a new constitution was reached at the conclusion of a conference at Lancaster House, London, on 15 December 1979. Zimbabwe became an independent republic on 18 April 1980.

Chad Civil War, 1965–90

The civil war in Chad originated in the mid-1960s as a conflict between the French-backed government of President Tombalbaye and a number of separatist factions in the Muslim north of the country, grouped into the Front de Libération Nationale and supported by Libya. By the mid-1970s FROLINAT controlled three-quarters of the country. On 6 February 1978 the head of state, General Malloum, who had overthrown President Tombalbaye in 1975, announced a cease-fire with FROLINAT. Conflict then developed between two factions in FROLINAT: FAN, under Hissène Habré, and the more militant FAP, under Goukouni Oueddei, backed by Libya. Habré's army defeated FAP and captured the capital, N'Djamena, on 7 June 1982. Fighting resumed in 1983 when FAP and Libyan troops advanced and took the strategically important town of Faya-Largeau on 24 June. Habré appealed for foreign assistance and troops were sent by Zaïre on 3 July and France on 14 August. The Libyan advance was halted, and France and Libya signed a withdrawal agreement on 17 September 1984. Libyan troops remained in the north of Chad, however, and created a *de facto* partition of the country until Goukouni Oueddei was shot and wounded in an argument with Libyan troops, and his men changed sides in 1986. A united Chadian force mounted a surprise attack and captured the Libyan air base at Ouadi Doum in March 1987, forcing the Libyans to evacuate most of the territory they had occupied. In 1990 rebels of the Popular Salvation Movement, led by Idris Deby, overthrew the government of Hissène Habré and took power.

Namibian War of Independence, 1966–89

Namibia was mandated to South Africa by the League of Nations on 17 December 1920. South Africa refused to recognize the South West Africa People's Organization, which was designated the 'sole authentic representative of the Namibian people' by the United Nations in 1973.

SWAPO launched a guerrilla campaign in October 1966 and this was stepped up in 1978 from bases in Angola and Zambia. South Africa carried out a series of attacks on SWAPO camps in Angola. SWAPO guerrilla activity in Namibia continued, despite the non-aggression pact signed by Angola and South Africa on 16 February 1984. A cease-fire supervised by the UN took effect from 1989, providing for the withdrawal of Cuban and South African forces from the region to be followed by elections in Namibia and independence in 1990.

Israeli–Arab Six-Day War, 1967

Israel decided on a pre-emptive strike following Egypt's request for the withdrawal of the UN peace-keeping force from Sinai on 16 May, the closure of the Gulf of Aqaba to Israeli shipping on 22 May, and the signature of an Egyptian–Jordanian defence pact on 30 May. On 5 June 1967 Israel launched devastating air attacks on Egyptian air bases. Israeli forces then invaded Sinai and reached the Suez Canal on 7 June. By nightfall on 7 June Jordan had been defeated and Jerusalem and the West Bank were in Israeli hands. On 9 June Israeli troops attacked Syria and occupied the Golan Heights. A cease-fire was agreed on 10 June 1967.

Nigerian Civil War, 1967–70

On 30 May 1967 the military governor of the Eastern Region of Nigeria, Colonel Ojukwu, declared the Ibo homeland an independent sovereign state under the name of the Republic of Biafra. Troops of the Nigerian federal army attacked across the northern border of Biafra on 7 July 1967. The Biafrans invaded the neighbouring Mid-West Region on 9 August 1967. The federal army recaptured Biafra on 22 September 1967, and Port Harcourt fell on 20 May 1968. Supply shortages and starvation finally led to the collapse of Biafran resistance after a four-pronged federal attack in December 1969. The Biafran army surrendered on 15 January 1970.

Philippine Communist and Muslim Insurgency, 1968–96

The Hakbalahap insurgency (see p. 246) had declined by the mid-1950s, but in December 1968 a congress of re-establishment was held on Luzon, which reconstituted the Communist Party. Its New People's Army (NPA) began a guerrilla campaign. The government also faced armed opposition from Muslim separatists of the Moro National Liberation Front (MNLF) on Mindanao. President Marcos declared martial law on 23 September 1972. A cease-fire with the MNLF was announced on 22 December 1976 after talks held in Libya, but fighting continued. President Aquino signed a 60-day truce with the NPA on 27 November 1986, but fighting resumed when it expired in 1987. In September 1996 a peace agreement was signed providing for the establishment of a Muslim autonomous region covering 14 provinces and 9 cities on Mindanao.

Soviet Invasion of Czechoslovakia, 1968

During the night of 20/21 August 1968 some 250,000 Soviet troops, accompanied by token contingents from Warsaw Pact allies Poland, Hungary and Bulgaria, crossed the Czech frontier and occupied Prague and other leading cities to reverse the liberalizing reforms of Alexander Dubček's government, the so-called 'Prague Spring'. The Czech army was ordered to offer no resistance, but there were extensive civilian demonstrations against the occupying forces. The Soviet invasion led to the installation of a new Soviet-backed government and the end of the 'Prague Spring'.

Honduran 'Soccer' War with El Salvador, 1969

Hostilities were sparked off by the harassment of a visiting Honduran soccer team in San Salvador (in retaliation for the treatment of the Salvadorean team in Honduras) and the victory of El Salvador over Honduras in a World Cup soccer match on 15 June 1969. The underlying cause was the presence of some 300,000 Salvadorean workers living, many illegally, in Honduras. Riots led to the deaths of two Salvadoreans and the expulsion of 11,000 others. In response, the Salvadorean army crossed the border at several points on 14 July 1969. Honduras accepted an Organization of American States cease-fire call on 16 July, but El Salvador continued fighting. The OAS formally branded El Salvador as the aggressor and voted to impose sanctions on 29 July. El Salvador began to withdraw on 30 July and withdrawal was completed by 5 August.

Chinese border conflict with Soviet Union, 1969

Long-standing Sino–Soviet border disputes erupted into serious fighting on Damansky Island in the Ussuri river on 2 March 1969. Each side blamed the other for the clash, in which 31 Soviet frontier-guards were killed. The fighting spread further west to the border between Xinjiang (Sinkiang) and Kazakhstan. On 11 September 1969 the Soviet Prime Minister, Alexei Kosygin, who was returning from the funeral of Ho Chi-minh in Hanoi, stopped briefly at Beijing airport for a meeting with Zhou Enlai. Talks were arranged and tension on the border subsided.

Northern Ireland, civil insurgency, 1969–98

In 1968 long-standing sectarian animosity between the Catholic and Protestant communities in Northern Ireland degenerated into violent conflict, sparked by the campaign for Catholic civil rights. British troops were deployed in Londonderry on 14 August 1969 and Belfast on 15 August at the request of the government of Northern Ireland. The first British soldier to be killed was shot by an IRA sniper in Belfast on 6 February 1971. Internment without trial was introduced on 6 August 1971, and direct rule from London was imposed on 30 March 1972. On 'Bloody Sunday', 30 January 1972, British troops opened fire on a Catholic civil rights march, and 13 people were killed. At the peak, in August 1972, there were 21,500 British soldiers in Northern Ireland, but this was reduced to 10,000 by the mid-1980s. Over 3,160 persons had died in the conflict by the end of August 1994, when the IRA called a 'Complete Cessation' of Military Operations. The cease-fire was ended in February 1996. It was resumed in 1997 as the political wing of the IRA, Sinn Féin, entered the peace process (which culminated in the April 1998 agreement).

South Yemen conflicts with Saudi Arabia and rebel exiles, 1969–72

An unsuccessful attempt by the new left-wing government in South Yemen to assert a claim to disputed border territory led to clashes with Saudi Arabia in November 1969. Saudi Arabia provided training and a base at ash-Sharawrah for South Yemeni exiles, organized into an 'Army of Deliverance', which raided into South Yemen. In 1972 fighting spread to the border between North and South Yemen. In August 1972 South Yemeni exiles in the north formed a United National Front of South Yemen. Their forces, supplied by Saudi Arabia, mounted attacks on 26 September 1972, which led to full-scale fighting. Arab mediation brought agreement between North and South Yemen in Cairo on 28 October 1972 to meet for discussions on a merger of the two countries.

Kampuchean Civil War, 1970–75

On 18 March 1970, Lieutenant General Lon Nol ousted the head of state, Prince Norodom Sihanouk, who was out of the country. Sihanouk allied himself with his former enemies, the Marxist Khmer Rouge, to form the National United Front of Cambodia. Lon Nol appealed for aid on 14 April 1970, and on 29 April, American and South Vietnamese troops mounted an incursion into Kampuchea to attack North Vietnamese Viet Cong and Khmer Rouge forces. The last American troops withdrew on 29 June 1970. The communists took control of the countryside, and in 1975 cut supply routes to the capital, Phnom Penh. Lon Nol left the country on 1 April 1975 and the Khmer Rouge occupied Phnom Penh on 17 April.

Jordanian Civil War, 1970–71

After serious clashes between Palestinian guerrillas and the Jordanian army, King Hussein declared martial law on 16 September 1970. Civil war broke out in Amman on 19 September as the army attacked the Palestinian refugee camps. Some 250 Syrian tanks entered Jordan in support of the Palestinians, but suffered losses in Jordanian air strikes and withdrew on 23 September 1970. A cease-fire was agreed on 25 September 1970. Further heavy fighting took place early in 1971 and the PLO guerrillas withdrew from Amman on 13 April. Their expulsion from Jordan was completed by 18 July 1971.

Indo-Pakistan War and Bangladeshi War of Independence, 1971

Elections in December 1970 resulted in a landslide victory in East Pakistan for the Awami League. On 26 March 1971 Sheikh Mujibur Rahman, the head of the League, proclaimed East Pakistan an independent republic under the name of Bangladesh. He was arrested, and West Pakistani troops and locally raised irregulars, *razakars*, put down large-scale resistance by 10 May 1971. Awami League fighters, the Mukti Bahini, began a guerrilla campaign, and clashes between India and Pakistan increased as millions of refugees fled into India. President Yahya Khan declared a state of emergency in Pakistan on 23 November 1971. On 3 December 1971 the Pakistani air force launched surprise attacks on Indian airfields. On 4 December some 160,000 Indian troops invaded East Pakistan. Pakistani forces in East Pakistan surrendered on 16 December 1971, and a general cease-fire came into effect the following day.

Burundi Civil War, 1972–73

On 29 April 1972 guerrillas from the majority Hutu tribe in Burundi attacked the ruling Tutsi minority, killing between 5,000 and 15,000 in an abortive coup. The Burundi armed forces, under Tutsi command, retaliated with assistance from Zaïre, and by the end of May 1972 the death toll among the Hutu had risen to an estimated 100,000. Refugees poured into neighbouring states. On 10 May 1973 Hutu rebels from Rwanda and Tanzania invaded Burundi. The Burundi army in response crossed into Tanzania on 29 June and killed 10 people. President Mobutu of Zaïre mediated an accord between the presidents of Tanzania and Burundi on 21 July, 1973.

Uganda rebel invasion, 1972

On 17 September 1972 some 1,000 armed supporters of ex-President Milton Obote, who had been overthrown by General Amin in January 1971, invaded Uganda from Tanzania. The guerrillas were easily repulsed, and the Ugandan air force bombed the Tanzanian towns of Bukoba and Mwanza in reprisal. The Organization of African Unity and the Somali Foreign Minister mediated a peace agreement between Uganda and Tanzania, which was signed on 5 October 1972.

Yom Kippur War, 1973

On 6 October 1973, the day of a Jewish religious holiday, Egyptian forces crossed the Suez Canal, overwhelming Israel's Bar-Lev defence line in a well-planned surprise attack. Syrian forces attacked the Golan Heights, but initial gains were surrendered by 12 October. In a daring counter-stroke on 15 October 1973, Israeli forces crossed to the west bank of the Suez Canal and encircled the Egyptian Third Army. A cease-fire became effective on 24 October 1973.

Turkish invasion of Cyprus, 1974

In July 1974 a coup in Cyprus brought to power a government favouring 'enosis' (union) with Greece, but Turkey quickly responded by invading the island to safeguard the Turkish half of the population. An armistice was agreed on 16 August, which left Turkish rule over one-third of the island.

Western Sahara, Polisario Insurgency, 1975 – continuing

The Spanish colony of Western Sahara was claimed by both Morocco and Mauritania, while there was also an independence movement, the Polisario, formed in 1973 and supported by Algeria. On 6 November 1975 King Hassan of Morocco sent 350,000 unarmed Moroccans in a 'Green March' into the Western Sahara. They were recalled after three days, but agreement was reached in Madrid on 14 November 1975 for a Spanish withdrawal and joint administration of the territory after 28 February 1976 by Morocco and Mauritania. Their armed forces came into conflict with the Polisario, which proclaimed the Saharan Arab Democratic Republic. The Polisario concentrated on Mauritanian targets, mounting a daring raid on the capital, Nouakchott, on 7 June 1976. Morocco and Mauritania formed a joint military command on 13 May 1977, and Mauritania received support from the French air force. On 5 August 1979 Mauritania came to terms with Polisario, but Morocco moved to occupy the whole of the Western Sahara. Libya recognized the Polisario in April 1980. In 1984 Morocco built a 1,600-mile defensive wall from the Moroccan town of Zag to Dakhla on the Atlantic coast, protecting the economically important north of the territory and creating an effective stalemate. After repeated UN efforts, a cease-fire came into effect on 6 September 1991 and a referendum on the future of the territory was to be held. This has not yet taken place.

Lebanese Civil War and invasions, 1975–96

Tensions between the Christian and Muslim communities in Lebanon were exacerbated by the influx of Palestinian guerrillas expelled from Jordan in 1971. A state of civil war existed after a massacre of Palestinians by Phalangist gunmen on 13 April 1975. Syrian forces were drawn into the conflict on 1 June 1976. A cease-fire was agreed on 17 October 1976, backed by an Arab Deterrent Force consisting mainly of Syrian troops, but fighting soon resumed. Palestinian raids into Israel led to an Israeli incursion into the Lebanon 15 March–13 June 1978. Israel launched a full-scale invasion of Lebanon on 6 June 1982 and forced a Palestinian evacuation from Beirut, beginning on 22 August 1982. An agreement between Israel and the Lebanese government on 17 May 1983 proved a dead letter, but Israel withdrew its forces from the Lebanon during 1985. Fighting between the various factions continued unabated. Eventually, Syrian forces occupied West Beirut in strength on 22 February 1987 to separate the warring militias, but a Christian attempt to resist Syrian domination led to renewed bitter fighting in 1989. Eventually, the warring militias were replaced by a new Government of National Reconciliation, declared in December 1990. However, Israeli military operations in Lebanon have continued in the 1990s in response to bombardment of northern Israel by Hizbollah guerrillas. In 1993 Israel launched an offensive against Lebanon code-named 'Operation Accountability'. On 11 April 1996, Israel launched 'Operation Grapes of Wrath', a major attack on Lebanon intended to ensure the safety of Israeli citizens.

East Timor, Indonesian annexation and guerrilla war, 1975 – continuing

In June 1975 Portugal announced its intention of holding independence elections in its colony of East Timor. On 11 August 1975 the moderate UDT, which favoured continuing links with Portugal, attempted to stage a coup, but by 20 August civil war had broken out with the communist group FRETILIN. As increasing numbers of refugees fled into Indonesian West Timor, Indonesian troops entered East Timor on 7 December 1975 to forestall a left-wing takeover. By 28 December, the Indonesians were in control, and East Timor was officially integrated into Indonesia on 17 July 1976. Guerrilla war by FRETILIN continued against Indonesian forces, with harsh reprisals leading to a death toll well in excess of 100,000 by the 1990s. The guerrilla leader, Xanana Gusmao, was captured in 1993. Earlier, the massacre of civilians at the Santa Cruz Cemetery, perpetrated by Indonesian forces, had provoked international condemnation.

Angolan Civil War, 1975 – continuing

The three rival liberation movements signed an agreement with Portugal on 15 January 1976 regarding Angolan independence, but were soon engaged in a civil war for control of the country. Major fighting between the MPLA and FNLA broke out in the capital, Luanda, on 27 March 1975. During July 1975 the MPLA gained control of Luanda. In the ensuing conflict the Marxist MPLA received aid from the Soviet Union and was supported by some 15,000 Cuban troops, while the FNLA/UNITA alignment received supplies from the US via Zaïre, and South African military support from October 1975. When independence was declared on 11 November 1975, FNLA/UNITA established a rival government in Huambo. The MPLA drove FNLA forces into Zaïre and captured Huambo on 8 February 1976. The United States had halted its aid to FNLA/UNITA on 27 January 1976. The Organization of African Unity recognized the MPLA government on 11 February 1976, and South Africa announced the withdrawal of its forces on 25 March 1976. UNITA continued to wage a guerrilla campaign in Angola with aid from South Africa, which sought a counter to Angola's support for the South West Africa People's Organization guerrillas fighting for the independence of Namibia. In April 1989 a cease-fire was arranged, leading to the withdrawal of Cuban and South African forces and a cessation of UNITA attacks. However, the cease-fire failed to hold, but a further peace agreement was signed between UNITA and the government in May 1991. No real solution emerged and a UN peace-keeping force was despatched.

Mozambique Civil War, 1976–92

From 1976 Rhodesia fostered a guerrilla campaign by anti-FRELIMO dissidents in Mozambique, which was harbouring Robert Mugabe's ZANLA fighters (see p. 261). After 1980, South Africa took over the support of the MNRM as part of its policy of 'destabilizing' its neighbours. The MNRM concentrated on sabotage and guerrilla raids on communications, power lines and foreign-aided development projects. Mozambique and South Africa signed a non-aggression pact, the Nkomati accord, on 16 March 1984, but MNRM activity had scarcely slackened by the end of the 1980s. However, on 4 October 1992 President Chissano and Afonso Dhlakama (the MNRM leader) signed a treaty in Rome ending the civil war.

Soweto Uprising, 1976

Large-scale rioting in the black townships of South Africa, triggered by measures to enforce learning of Afrikaans in schools, led to over 500 African deaths in the ensuing repression.

Bangladesh, separatist guerrilla campaign, 1976–97

In 1976 guerrilla troops supporting The Hill Tracts Peoples' Solidarity Committee (PCJSS), an alliance of the Chakma people and 12 other groups seeking autonomy, opened a campaign against Bengali settlers in the east of the country. Despite a cease-fire negotiated in 1992, several thousand people were killed in sporadic ambushes mounted by Shanti Bahini guerrillas estimated to be 5,000 strong, until negotiations opened on a draft peace treaty in September 1997. At the height of the campaign, Bangladesh deployed 70,000 troops in the area.

Libyan conflict with Egypt, 1977

Strained relations and border incidents led Egypt to mount a limited punitive action against Libya on 21 July 1977 in the shape of an armed incursion and air attacks on the major Libyan air-base at Al Adem. A cease-fire was agreed, through the mediation of Yasser Arafat, Chairman of the PLO, and others, on 24 July, 1977.

Zaïre, rebel invasions from Angola, 1977–78

On 8 March 1977 Zaïre's Shaba province (formerly Katanga) was invaded from Angola by some 2,000 insurgents claiming to be members of the Congolese National Liberation Front. President Mobutu accused Cuban troops of leading the invasion and appealed for African support on 2 April 1977. On 10 April French transport aircraft carried 1,500 Moroccan troops to Zaïre and they helped the Zaïre army to repel the invasion. On 11 May 1978 a second invasion from Angola by some 3,000 rebels took place. French and Belgian paratroopers were sent to Kolwezi to rescue white hostages on 19 May 1978 and the invaders were dispersed. Zaïre and Angola signed a non-aggression pact on 12 October 1979.

Ethiopian conflict in the Ogaden, 1977–78

The turmoil in Ethiopia after the overthrow of Emperor Haile Selassie on 12 September 1974 led the Somali Republic to pursue its claim to the Ogaden by fostering a guerrilla movement in the area, the Western Somali Liberation Front. A Somali-backed offensive in 1977 gave the guerrillas control of the southern desert area, and an attack launched against Harar on 23 November 1977 narrowly failed. With Cuban and Soviet support, Ethiopia launched a counter-offensive on 7 February 1978 and recovered control of the Ogaden. On 9 March 1978 Somalia announced the withdrawal of its forces from the Ogaden.

Sri Lanka, communal strife, 1977 – continuing

Tension between the Tamil minority and the Sinhalese majority in Sri Lanka led to rioting in the northern town of Jaffna, beginning on 14 August 1977, in which 125 people died. The situation grew more serious in the 1980s. Acts of terrorism by the Tamil Liberation Tigers provoked violence by the army against the Tamil community. A state of emergency was declared on 4 June 1981. Two soldiers, the first military victims, were killed in an ambush in Jaffna in October 1981. Talks between President Jayawardene and the Tamil United Liberation Front failed to find a political solution. In 1987 Indian troops were requested to assist the Sri Lankan government and a force of 100,000 Indian troops attacked Tamil positions in the Jaffna peninsula. Guerrilla war continued and in 1989 Indian troops began to withdraw. In the south the ultra-left JVP movement active from 1971 conducted an increasingly bitter terror campaign after 1987. During the 1990s violence continued. President Ranasinghe Premadasa was assassinated on 1 May 1993, but a cease-fire with the Tamils was signed in January 1995. It did not hold and violence continues.

Vietnamese Invasion of Kampuchea, 1978–89

After a series of clashes on the border, Vietnamese forces and Kampuchean rebels launched an invasion of Kampuchea on 25 December 1978. The capital, Phnom Penh, was occupied on 7 January 1979, and a People's Republic of Kampuchea was proclaimed, with Heng Samrin as President. Guerrilla operations against the Vietnamese occupying forces were carried out by three groups: the Khmer Rouge; guerrillas loyal to the former head of state, Prince Sihanouk; and the non-communist Khmer People's National Liberation Front. These groups formed a loose coalition in Kuala Lumpur, Malaysia, on 22 June 1982. Warfare continued, especially on the Thai border, although talks aiming at a settlement began in 1987, leading to agreement on a withdrawal of Vietnamese forces in 1989.

Ugandan conflict with Tanzania, 1978–79

On 27 October 1978 Uganda invaded Tanzania and occupied some 700 square miles of Tanzanian territory known as the Kagera salient. A Tanzanian counter-offensive on 12 November 1978 ejected the Ugandans from the salient. In January 1979, Tanzanian forces, with armed Ugandan exiles, advanced into Uganda. Kampala fell on 11 April 1979 and President Amin fled the country.

Nicaraguan Civil War, 1978–90

Civil war was precipitated by the murder of President Anastasio Somoza's leading opponent, newspaper editor Pedro Joaquín Chamorro, on 10 January 1978. The FSLN made steady advances, and Somoza finally fled the country on 17 July 1979. Civil war continued as the Sandinista government faced two military threats: the first, the Democratic Revolutionary Front, a group of rebels led by dissident Sandinist Eden Pastora, mounted raids from its base in Costa Rica; the second, the Nicaraguan Democratic Front or 'Contras', was a force of ex-National Guardsmen who operated from their exile in Honduras and who received extensive American aid until the US Congress halted funding on 25 June 1984. The Sandinista regime declared a state of emergency in May 1982, but disunity among its enemies enabled it to function despite the guerrilla threat. On 8 August 1987 leaders of the five Central American countries, including Nicaragua, met in Guatemala City to sign a peace accord calling for the democratization of Nicaragua and for Contra–Sandinista negotiations. A 60-day cease-fire was announced in Sapoa on 23 March 1988. With the election defeat of the Sandinistas in 1990, the civil war effectively ended.

El Salvador Guerrilla Insurgency, 1979–92

Guerrilla activity by the left-wing Farabundo Marti National Liberation Front (FMLN) intensified after 1979. Conflict between the 40,000-strong Salvadorean army, backed by the United States, and 9,000 Liberation Front guerrillas reached a stalemate during the 1980s. A peace agreement was signed between the government and the FMLN in January 1992 under which both sides would report their full strength of troops and weapons to ONUSAL (the UN Observer Mission in El Salvador).

Chinese Invasion of Vietnam, 1979

Chinese forces launched an invasion of Vietnam on 17 February 1979 in retaliation for Vietnam's intervention in Kampuchea (see p. 270). Following the fall of the provincial capital, Lang Son, on 3 March 1979, the Chinese government announced that it had accomplished its aims, and the withdrawal of its forces was completed by 16 March 1979.

Soviet Invasion of Afghanistan and Civil War, 1979 – continuing

The instability of the Soviet-backed regime and growing resistance to reforms led to a full-scale Soviet invasion of Afghanistan on 27 December 1979. A new government was installed under Babrak Karmal, but a considerable Soviet military presence had to be maintained in the country to combat the Mujaheddin guerrillas. Following Babrak Karmal's resignation on 4 May 1986, his successor, Major-General Najibullah, announced a six-months' cease-fire on 15 January 1987, but this was rejected by the Mujaheddin. Russian troops began to withdraw in 1988 and completed withdrawal in early 1989, having lost 15,000 dead. Contrary to expectation the Kabul regime did not collapse, and attempts by the Mujaheddin forces to take Kabul and other principal cities were repulsed. Civil war continued. Renewed fighting raged in early 1993. Fighting had claimed 3,000 lives by February in a struggle between the government of President Burhanuddin Rabbani and the Hezb-i-Islami of Gulbuddin Hekmatyar, and the pro-Iranian, mainly Shi'ite, Islamic Unity Party (Hezb-i-Wahdat). A new military force, the student revolutionary Taliban, entered the fray in 1994. Despite seizing Kabul in 1997, they have failed to win total control of the country.

Iran–Iraq War, 1980–88

Hoping to exploit the instability of Iran after the fall of the Shah, Iraq abrogated the Algiers Pact of 1975, by which it had been forced to accept joint control of the Shatt al-Arab waterway, and invaded Iran on 12 September 1980. Khorramshahr fell on 13 October 1980, but the Iranian government did not collapse and its armed forces began to counterattack successfully. Each side bombed the other's oil installations and attacked international shipping in the Gulf. Iran rejected Iraq's cease-fire overtures as the military stalemate deepened. On 9 January 1987 Iran launched a major offensive – codenamed Karbala-5 – with the aim of capturing Basra. The Iranians advanced some distance towards their objective, while suffering heavy casualties. In 1987 and 1988 Iraq made major advances and a cease-fire was organized in August 1988. The war is estimated to have cost almost a million casualties, with some of the heaviest land-fighting since the Second World War.

Somalian Civil War, 1981 – continuing

Following protracted civil war which had originally begun in 1981, law and order broke down completely. President Mohammed Siad Barre was overthrown in a coup in 1991 and an interim government appointed under Ali Mahdi Mohammed. However, by the end of the year fighting between clan-based factions developed into renewed civil war. Following widespread famine, a US-led UN force landed in Somalia in December 1991 but withdrew in 1995. In January 1997 leaders of the 26 factions competing for dominance in and around the capital Mogadishu agreed on the formation of a National Salvation Council to lay the ground for a government of national unity.

Falkland Islands (Malvinas), 1982

Argentina maintained a long-standing claim to the sovereignty of the Falkland Islands and on 2 April 1982 the Argentine dictatorship, under General Galtieri, launched a successful invasion of the islands, forcing its garrison of 18 Royal Marines to surrender. Argentine forces also seized the island of South Georgia. On 5 April a British Task Force set sail to recapture the islands and on 7 April an exclusion zone of 200 miles was declared around the island. On 25 April South Georgia was recaptured and on 1 May air attacks began on the Argentine garrison on the Falklands. The next day the Argentine cruiser *Belgrano* was sunk by a British submarine and on 4 May HMS *Sheffield* was hit by an Exocet missile. On 21 May British troops went ashore at San Carlos. Two British frigates, the *Ardent* and *Antelope*, were sunk and others damaged by air attack, but British troops took Darwin and Goose Green by the end of May and on 11–14 June an attack on Port Stanley led to the surrender of the Argentine forces. During the conflict 255 British and 720 Argentine troops were killed. A large permanent garrison and modern airstrip have been placed on the island for its future security.

Invasion of Grenada, 1983

On 19 October 1983 the army took control in Grenada after a power struggle led to the murder of Prime Minister Maurice Bishop. On 21 October the Organization of Eastern Caribbean States appealed to the United States to intervene, and on 25 October US marines and airborne troops invaded Grenada, together with token contingents from six other

Caribbean countries. Resistance from the Grenadian army and 700 Cuban construction workers with paramilitary training was overcome, and order restored by 27 October 1983.

Sikh separatist unrest, 1984 – continuing

Separatist unrest among Sikhs had led to several hundred deaths in the Punjab by early 1984 and the introduction of emergency rule. Following the stock-piling of arms at the Golden Temple, Amritsar, the Sikhs' holiest shrine, the Indian army stormed the complex and in fierce fighting killed the leading Sikh militant Jarnail Sing Bhindranwale and over 700 of his followers. On 31 October the Indian Prime Minister, Indira Gandhi, was assassinated by two Sikh bodyguards and in ensuing 'revenge' attacks over 2,000 Sikhs were killed. Terrorism by Sikh extremists and communal riots had led to several thousand deaths by 1990 and the reintroduction of emergency rule in the Punjab. The conflict remains unresolved.

Indo-Pakistan conflict in Kashmir, 1984 – continuing

The UN has policed the cease-fire line established in the wake of the 1971 Indo-Pakistan War, but in the high Himalayan ranges, sporadic fighting has taken place, principally around the Sianchin glacier. In May 1984 the Pakistanis launched a major infantry-artillery attack to dislodge Indian troops who had moved on to the glacier. In 1985 Pakistani planes bombed Indian positions and air combat took place. Renewed tension brought India and Pakistan to the verge of war in 1990. Sporadic fighting and artillery exchanges have continued in the 1990s.

New Caledonia Separatist Movement, 1984–87

In 1984 the indigenous Melanesian population, the Kanaks, began violent resistance to elections which it was expected would confirm in power French settlers opposed to independence. Kanak separatists resisted any compromise short of a referendum on independence among the indigenous population. As violence spread, 7,000 French soldiers and riot police were sent to New Caledonia in 1987 to allow a referendum election to take place. In September 1987 residents of New Caledonia, including the 40% who are French, voted to remain a French territory.

Burkina Faso (Upper Volta) conflict with Mali, 1985

In December 1985 Burkina Faso forces invaded northern Mali over a border dispute, with each side backed respectively by Libya and Algeria.

Three days of fighting left 400 dead, but arbitration by the international court at the Hague was accepted.

Turkey, Revolt of the Kurds, 1986 – continuing

Since the mid-1980s the outlawed Kurdistan Workers' Party (PKK), a Marxist-Leninist group led by Abdullah Ocalan, has fought for an independent Kurdish state in the south-east of Turkey (where some 12 million Kurds are located). An estimated 10,000 guerrillas confront about 200,000 Turkish soldiers. It is now (1998) the bloodiest conflict in the Middle East after the Algerian Civil War.

Uprising or 'Intifada' in Arab West Bank and Gaza, 1987 – continuing

In December 1987, widespread unrest among Palestinian refugees erupted in the Israeli-occupied West Bank and Gaza strip against Israeli security forces. Rioting and terrorist incidents had led to over 600 dead by end 1989. In April 1988, an Israeli special unit assassinated the PLO military commander, Abu Jihad, believing he was masterminding the violence. The intifada eventually led to progress towards the creation of a Palestinian authority.

The Soviet Union, disintegration and ethnic conflict, 1988–91

During the final days of the Soviet Union, ethnic clashes were already developing. Rioting between Armenians and Azerbaijanis, sparked by a dispute over control of the Nagorno-Karabakh region, began on 20 February 1988. In Uzbekistan, fighting between Uzbeks and Meskhetian Turks began on 4 June 1989. The armed forces also moved against nationalist movements in Georgia, Moldova, Azerbaijan and the Baltic Republics. After the collapse of the Soviet Union, serious conflicts developed in the following areas: Azerbaijan-Armenia; the Abkhazia region of Georgia; Moldova and Tajikistan. (See also Chechnya, p. 279).

Papua New Guinea, Bougainville Secession of, 1988–97

The island of Bougainville, with rich reserves of copper, renewed its attempted secession from Papua New Guinea in 1988. The conflict became the longest-running confrontation in the Pacific since the Second World War. The fighting claimed an estimated 10,000 lives and destroyed much of the economic life of the island. A truce was signed on 10 October 1997 after talks in Christchurch, New Zealand.

Romanian Revolution and Civil War, 1989

On 17 December 1989 security forces fired on protesters in the Romanian city of Timisoara. On 18 December, Romania closed its frontiers. On 20 December, troops surrendered in Timisoara. Fighting spread to Bucharest and other major cities. The army switched sides, joining the popular uprising against the Ceauçescu (q.v.) dictatorship and the hated security police (the Securitate). By 24 December all strategic points were controlled by the revolutionary National Salvation Front. Ceauçescu and his wife were executed by firing squad on 25 December 1989, having been found guilty of genocide by a military court. Provisional casualty figures gave 689 dead and 1,200 injured in the revolution.

Liberian Civil War, 1989 – continuing

What began in December 1989 as an invasion by the National Patriotic Front of Liberia (NPLF) against President Samuel Doe degenerated within five years to chaos as eight war lords competed for power. A breakaway Independent NPLF, which was formed in February 1990, murdered President Doe in September. By April 1991 the NPLF controlled 90% of the country, but its refusal to join an interim government of national unity thwarted attempts by the Economic Community of West African States (ECOWAS) to restore peace. A United Liberia Movement for Democracy (ULIMO) appeared on the scene in 1992. An estimated 150,000 had died and over 750,000 had been forced to flee as refugees as the factions attempted to agree on an ECOWAS peace plan at the end of 1996.

Panama, US invasion of, 1989

Tension between America and the corrupt Noriega (q.v.) dictatorship mounted during 1989, especially after the annulment of the May elections. On 20 December, US forces launched a ground and air invasion to overthrow the Panamanian regime and seize Noriega. Despite some resistance from the Panamanian Defence Forces and the pro-Noriega civilian militia (the 'Dignity Battalions'), US forces rapidly occupied Panama City and other key areas. Noriega fled, finding refuge in the Vatican embassy, before surrendering and being extradited to the United States. By 31 December 1989, 23 Americans had died and 320 had been wounded in the invasion.

Rwandan Civil War, 1990 – continuing

Despite attempts by President Juvénal Habyarimana, who had seized power in 1973, to allow the Tutsis a political role in Hutu-dominated Rwanda, a Tutsi force invaded the country from neighbouring Uganda in September 1990 but was defeated within a month. In January 1991 the predominantly Tutsi Rwandan Patriotic Front (FPR) guerrillas renewed the attack. Despite a cease-fire in March, an estimated 15,000 Tutsis were massacred by the Hutu militia between 1991 and 1993. In February 1993 the FPR launched a new offensive which culminated in July 1994 – following the death of President Habyarimana in a suspicious air crash – in the capture of the capital Kigali and the formation of a government of national unity. However, following the flight of 800,000 Hutu refugees in 1994, FPR attacks on both Hutus and Tutsis continued.

The Gulf War, 1990–91

On 2 August 1990 Iraqi troops launched a surprise attack on Kuwait and invaded the country, which President Saddam Hussein then annexed on 7 August, and on 28 August declared it to be the 19th province of Iraq. The UN Security Council condemned the invasion and demanded the immediate withdrawal of the Iraqi troops. On 10 August, a similar declaration was made by the Arab League (only Libya and the Palestine Liberation Organization voted against the declaration). Due to the failure of diplomatic means, the UN voted for economic sanctions against Iraq (6 August) and the United States – in alliance with other countries – started to build up their military forces in the area. On 28 November, the UN Security Council authorized its member states to use force against the aggressors if Iraq did not withdraw its troops from Kuwait by 15 January 1991. After acquiring an absolute supremacy in the air within a matter of days, the US air force, together with its allies, bombed Iraqi positions and major cities for more than a month – carrying out a vast air offensive. In response, Saddam Hussein launched 'Scud' air missiles on Israel and Saudi Arabia, had hundreds of thousands of tons of oil poured into the Persian Gulf, and set 500 Kuwaiti oil wells on fire. On 23 February, a land offensive was also launched and by 26 February Kuwait was fully liberated. On 28 February – after Iraq's total defeat – US President Bush ordered a cease-fire.

Yugoslavian Civil War (Serbo–Croat War), 1991–95

Declarations of independence by the former Yugoslav Republics of Slovenia and Croatia led to clashes on Slovenian borders from July 1991, followed by heavy fighting on Croatian territory between Croatian militia and Serbian irregulars (chetniks) backed by the Yugoslav Federal Army. Main centres of fighting were eastern and central Croatia and the Adriatic coast around Dubrovnik. Yugoslavia officially ceased to exist in January 1992 and Slovenia and Croatia were recognized as independent states. On 29 February 1992 Muslim leaders in Bosnia-Herzegovina declared independence. Bosnian Serbs and the Serbian leadership in Belgrade rejected this, and war began on 6 April with the opening of the siege of the capital Sarajevo. Serbs were accused of 'ethnic cleansing' to secure territorial domination, and a UN trade embargo was imposed on Serbia on 31 May. Peace talks in Geneva, mediated by Lord Owen and Cyrus Vance, began on 26 August. On 16 November a UN naval blockade was mounted against Serbia and Montenegro. Fighting continued as a further peace conference was held in Geneva on 22–23 January 1993. Serbs attacked Muslim enclaves at Srebenica and Goradze. Numerous peace talks collapsed. In 1995 Croatia launched major offensives and an uneasy peace accord was signed at Dayton, Ohio. An estimated 200,000 people died in the Yugoslavian Civil War.

Sierra Leone Civil War, 1991–98

In March 1991 a Revolutionary United Front (RUF) force – supported by mercenaries from Burkina Faso – advanced in two columns into Sierra Leone. The northern force was halted by government troops with assistance from Guinea but the southern force came close to the capital Freetown. However, by 1996 the RUF had weakened as it collapsed into competing factions. Renewed conflict came in May 1997 when the elected government of President Kabbah was overthrown by the RUF in a military coup. Kabbah was restored in March 1998.

Algerian Civil War, 1992 – continuing

An army-dominated High State Council took power in Algeria when it appeared that the fundamentalist Islamic Salvation Front (FIS) would be successful in the January 1992 elections, provoking rioting and terrorism. By the end of 1993 this had developed into full-scale civil war between government troops, the FIS armed wing – the Islamic Salvation Army (AIS) – and the Armed Islamic Group (GIA). In an attempt to weaken the government's position, Islamic guerrillas attacked the oil industry and mounted attacks on foreigners. The war was also marked by a number of massacres of civilians. By the beginning of 1998, an estimated 65,000 people had been killed in the conflict.

Nigerian conflict with Cameroon, 1993 – continuing

A dispute between the two states over ownership of the Bakassi Peninsula in the Gulf of Guinea, apparently settled by an agreement in 1987 on joint border patrols, erupted into clashes in 1993 and 1994 in which at least 12 soldiers were killed. Further clashes in February 1996 were followed by negotiations which remain inconclusive.

Yemen War, 1994

Following the unification of the Yemen, tensions continued between the northern GPC and the southern YSP and full-scale war erupted in February 1994. The southern forces were able to hold off their northern opponents and in May declared secession from the union. However, the YSP leaders fled in July as the northern troops captured Aden. A new government excluding the YSP was formed. An estimated 7,000 were killed in the fighting.

Burundi Civil War, 1994 – continuing

Fighting between Hutu and dominant Tutsi factions which broke out in February 1994 intensified following the death in an air crash of President Cyprien Ntaryamira in April. The orders of his successor, interim President Sylvestre Ntibantunganya, for both sides to disarm were ignored. Ethnic tension was increased by an influx of 200,000 Hutu refugees from neighbouring Rwanda. Government forces, allegedly co-operating with Tutsi extremists, attacked the Hutu suburbs of the capital Bujumbura, killing hundreds of civilians. By the end of 1995, an estimated 150,000 civilians had died and, as conflict heightened, refugees fled to Rwanda, Tanzania and Zaïre. Threats from extremist factions prevented the deployment of an Organization of African Unity (OAU) peace-keeping force and the overthrow of President Ntibantunganya by Pierre Buyoya in July 1996 blocked hopes that an East African force would be accepted.

Russia–Chechnya War, 1994–96

Russian troops were ordered into Chechnya in December 1994 to end the rebel republic's bid for independence. Fighting ensued for 21 months as Russian troops failed to subdue the population. The fighting was the worst on Russian soil since the Second World War, with Grozny, the Chechnya capital, razed to the ground. The Russian army suffered a major loss of face. On 31 August 1996 Russia and Chechnya signed a peace deal, freezing the issue of independence for five years. In January 1997 the withdrawal of all Russian troops from Chechnya was completed.

Peru–Ecuador Border War, 1995

In January 1995 fighting broke out between Peru and Ecuador over 320 square kilometres of border land believed to contain valuable oil and gold resources. Under a treaty negotiated in 1942 following a ten-day war, Peru had occupied 40% of the territory, but in 1960 Ecuador repudiated the territory and there were clashes in 1981. By the end of February 27

Ecuador troops and 46 Peruvians had died, but in April both sides agreed to withdraw from the area and to attempt a peaceful resolution of the dispute negotiated by Argentina, Brazil, Chile and the United States.

Eritrean conflict with Yemen, 1995

In November 1995 Eritrea attempted to assert its claim to three Yemeni-occupied islands in the Red Sea Bab el Manded Strait by landing a naval patrol. Eritrea claimed the islands on the grounds that they had formerly belonged to the colonial powers, Britain and Italy, and then to Ethiopia. Negotiations followed the mobilization of Yemen forces, but on 15 December Eritrea captured the largest of the islands following a three-day battle in which six Eritrean and three Yemeni soldiers were killed. UN Secretary-General Boutros Boutros-Ghali secured a Yemen agreement to withdraw from the area on 31 December but in January 1996 Eritrea expelled the Yemeni ambassador.

Zaïre Civil War, 1996–97

In October 1996 the Alliance of Democratic Forces for the Liberation of Congo-Zaïre – led by President Mobutu Sésé Séko's long-term opponent Laurent Kabila – launched an attack on the Zaïreian army in alliance with anti-Mobutu Tutsi guerrillas, and forces seeking autonomy for the Shaba and Kasai provinces. Kabila's troops were supported during the campaign by Rwanda and Uganda while Mobutu strengthened his army with white mercenaries. After a rapid advance through the country, the capital Kinshasa fell to Alliance forces in May 1997. Kabila declared himself head of state, renaming the country the Democratic Republic of the Congo. Mobutu Sésé Séko fled to Morocco where he died in September.

Indonesian civil unrest, 1998

In May 1998, after the killing of six students in anti-government protests, a popular uprising swept Jakarta, Medan, Jogyakarta and other cities. In rioting and looting (especially of ethnic Chinese areas) over 500 people were reported killed.

Nuclear development and arms control since 1939

1940   Professors Peierls and Frisch at Birmingham University in Britain produce memorandum on the design of an atomic bomb (Feb.); increased support given to research.

Soviet Union sets up committee to investigate the 'uranium problem'.

Germans set up research institute in Berlin, code-named 'The Virus House' to explore atomic developments.

1941   British Maud Committee reports favourably on possibility of atomic weapon (June).

Russian programme disrupted by German invasion and removed beyond the Urals (July).

1942   Anglo–Norwegian sabotage team wreck German 'heavy water' plant at Rjukan in Norway, crucial to German atomic research (Apr.).

Americans set up 'Manhattan Project' under US Army Corps of Engineers to administer work on the production of an atomic bomb (June). Several processes tried to achieve separation of fissile Uranium 235 from Uranium 238.

First nuclear chain reaction using plutonium takes place at the University of Chicago under direction of Fermi (Dec.).

1943   Quebec agreement between Churchill and Roosevelt agrees co-operation on atomic bomb programme (Aug.).

1944   Both uranium enrichment and plutonium reaction developed in the United States to produce atomic weapons.

Discovery of captured German documents reveals lack of progress in their atomic research.

1945   The first successful explosion of an experimental atomic device takes place at Alamogordo, New Mexico (16 July).

USAAF B29 bomber, *Enola Gay*, dropped the first atomic bomb, nicknamed 'Little Boy', on the Japanese city of Hiroshima (6 Aug.). Second atomic bomb, nicknamed 'Fat Man', dropped on Nagasaki (9 Aug.).

1946   United Nations General Assembly passes a resolution to establish an Atomic Energy Commission (Jan.).

At the first meeting of the Atomic Energy Commission, the American delegate, Bernard M. Baruch, puts forward a plan by which the United States would surrender its atomic weapons and reveal the secrets of controlling atomic energy to an International Control Agency. The Baruch Plan rejected by the Soviet Union (June).

United States carries out the first nuclear test in peace-time at Bikini Atoll in the Marshall Islands (1 July).

President Truman signs the Atomic Energy Act, restricting exchange of information with other nations on atomic energy, thus ending co-operation between the United States and Britain in the development of nuclear weapons (6 Aug.).

1949   Soviet Union explodes an atomic bomb, ending the American monopoly of nuclear weapons (29 Aug.).

1950   Soviet Union withdraws from the Atomic Energy Commission (Jan.).

1952   Britain tests its first atomic bomb (3 Oct.).

United States explodes the first hydrogen device at Eniwetok Atoll in the Marshall Islands (1 Nov.).

1953   Soviet Union tests its first hydrogen bomb in Siberia (12 Aug.).

'Atoms for Peace': President Eisenhower announces a plan at the UN General Assembly for a pool of fissile material to be available for peaceful purposes (Dec.).

1954   'Massive retaliation': in the aftermath of the Korean War, John Foster Dulles, US Secretary of State, announces that 'Local defence must be reinforced by the further deterrent of massive retaliatory power', that is, by the threat of nuclear weapons (12 Jan.).

First atomic power station opened at Obninsk, USSR (27 June).

USS *Nautilus*, first American atomic powered submarine, commissioned (Sept.).

1955   At the Geneva Summit, President Eisenhower puts forward his 'open skies' proposal for mutual aerial photography of each other's territory by the Soviet Union and United States as a step towards disarmament (July).

1956   Britain opens first large-scale commercial nuclear power station at Calder Hall, Cumbria (23 Oct.), but mainly used for defence purposes.

1957   First British hydrogen bomb exploded near Christmas Island (15 Aug.).
        UN International Atomic Energy Agency established to promote the safe use of atomic energy for peaceful purposes (July).
        Soviet Union announces the successful launch of an inter-continental ballistic missile (26 Aug.).
        Adam Rapacki, Foreign Minister of Poland, proposes in a speech to the UN General Assembly the creation of a nuclear-free zone in central Europe. Plan rejected by NATO on the grounds that nuclear weapons are essential to offset Soviet superiority in conventional forces (2 Oct.).

1958   First meeting of Britain's Campaign for Nuclear Disarmament (CND) held in London (17 Feb.).
        Successful firing of America's first inter-continental ballistic missile (ICBM), the liquid-fuelled Atlas (Nov.).

1959   Establishment of the Ten-Power Committee on Disarmament, comprising representatives from Britain, Canada, France, Italy, United States, Bulgaria, Czechoslovakia, Poland, Romania and Soviet Union (7 Sept.). Treaty for the peaceful use of Antarctica opened for signature in Washington.

1960   France explodes its first atomic device in the Sahara (13 Feb.).
        First successful underwater firing of a Polaris missile from the USS *George Washington* (20 July).
        First Polaris nuclear submarine, USS *George Washington*, becomes operational (15 Nov.).
        United States offers five submarines with 80 Polaris missiles to create a NATO Multilateral Nuclear Force at the NATO ministerial meeting in Paris (Dec.).

1962   First meeting in Geneva of the Eighteen Nation Disarmament Committee, the former Ten-Power Committee with the addition of Brazil, Burma, Egypt, Ethiopia, India, Mexico, Nigeria and Sweden (14 Mar.).
        US Secretary of Defense, Robert McNamara, announces in a speech at the University of Michigan, Ann Arbor, a new strategy of 'flexible response' to replace that of 'massive retaliation' (June).

1962   Cuban Missile Crisis: President Kennedy announces that aerial reconnaissance has established that offensive missile sites are being constructed by the Soviet Union in Cuba and that a naval and air 'quarantine' is being imposed until the sites are dismantled (22 Oct.).
Khrushchev agrees to remove the missiles from Cuba in return for an American guarantee not to invade (28 Oct.).
President Kennedy meets British Prime Minister, Harold Macmillan, at Nassau in the Bahamas and agrees to make US Polaris missiles available to Britain for use with British warheads (Dec.).

1963   'Hot-line' agreement between the United States and the Soviet Union (5 Apr.).
Partial Test-Ban Treaty, outlawing nuclear tests in the atmosphere and outer space and underwater (5 Aug.).

1964   First Chinese atomic explosion takes place at Lop Nor in Sinkiang province (16 Oct.).

1965   US Secretary of Defense, Robert McNamara, announces that the United States would rely on threat of 'assured destruction' to deter a Soviet attack (18 Feb.).

1966   NATO establishes the Nuclear Defence Affairs Committee (all members except France, Iceland and Luxembourg) and the Nuclear Planning Group (all members except France and Iceland) (14 Dec.).

1967   Treaty banning all nuclear weapons in outer space opened for signature in London, Moscow and Washington (28 Jan.).
Treaty of Tlatelolco, prohibiting nuclear weapons in Latin America, opened for signature in Mexico (14 Feb.).
First Chinese hydrogen bomb test carried out (17 June).

1968   Non-Proliferation Treaty opened for signature in London, Moscow and Washington (1 July).
France explodes its first hydrogen bomb (25 Aug.).

1969   President Nixon announces the decision to deploy a ballistic missile defence system, 'Safeguard', primarily to defend ICBM sites (14 Mar.). Eight new members join the Eighteen Nation Disarmament Committee, renamed the Conference of the Committee on Disarmament (Aug.).
Five additional members join on 1 Jan. 1975.

Preparatory negotiations on Strategic Arms Limitation Talks (SALT) between the United States and the Soviet Union begin in Helsinki (17 Nov.).

1970   Strategic Arms Limitation Talks open in Vienna (16 Apr.).
First Minuteman III missiles to be equipped with multiple independently targeted re-entry vehicles (MIRVs) become operational in the United States (June).
First successful underwater launch of a Poseidon missile from USS *James Madison* (Aug.).

1971   Sea-bed Treaty prohibiting the emplacement of nuclear weapons on the sea-bed opened for signature in London, Moscow and Washington (11 Feb.).

1972   SALT I anti-ballistic missile (ABM) agreement and five-year interim agreement on the limitation of strategic arms signed by the United States and the Soviet Union (26 May).

1973   Mutual and Balanced Force Reduction talks between NATO and the Warsaw Pact begin in Vienna (30 Oct.).

1974   US Secretary of Defense, James Schlesinger, announces new doctrine of 'limited strategic strike options' in the event of a nuclear war, in which a broad spectrum of deterrence would be available before the resort to large-scale strategic strikes (10 Jan.).
India explodes its first atomic device at Pokharan in the Rajasthan desert (18 May).
Protocol to the US–Soviet SALT ABM agreement, limiting ABM deployment to a single area (3 July).
US–Soviet Threshhold Test Ban Treaty signed, limiting underground nuclear tests (3 July).
Vladivostok Accord between the United States and the Soviet Union, setting out the framework for future negotiations on controlling the strategic arms race (24 Nov.).

1976   US–Soviet treaty restricting nuclear explosions for peaceful purposes (28 May).

1977   United States announces that it had tested an Enhanced Radiation Weapon or 'neutron bomb' (7 July).

1978   President Carter announces the postponement of a decision on the production and deployment of the neutron bomb (7 Apr.).

1979   Major nuclear accident in the United States at Three Mile Island, Harrisburg, Pennsylvania: thousands of gallons of radioactive water and a plume of radioactive gas released (28 Mar.).

SALT II agreement signed by United States and Soviet Union, restricting numbers of strategic offensive weapons (18 June). United States withholds ratification of the treaty following the Soviet invasion of Afghanistan in December 1979.

NATO announces its intention to modernize its long-range theatre nuclear systems by the deployment of 464 ground-launched Cruise missiles and 108 Pershing II medium-range ballistic missiles in Europe (12 Dec.).

1980   Agreement to site 'Cruise missiles' in Europe (June).

President Carter signs Presidential Directive 59, emphasizing the possibility of flexible, controlled retaliation against a range of military and political targets in a prolonged nuclear war (25 July).

US Department of Defense announces its intention to build an Advanced Technology, or 'stealth', bomber with a greatly reduced radar detectability (22 Aug.).

1981   In Operation BABYLON Israeli F-16 aircraft drop 16 tons of explosives on Iraq's Osirak nuclear plant on the grounds that Iraq is manufacturing nuclear weapons (7 June).

President Reagan orders the production and stockpiling of the neutron bomb, but says that it would not be deployed in Europe without NATO's consent (6 Aug.).

President Reagan authorizes the updating of US strategic forces, including the production of 100 MX missiles and the new B-1 bomber (2 Oct.).

US–Soviet negotiations on intermediate-range nuclear forces open at Geneva (30 Nov.).

1982   Strategic Arms Reduction Talks (START) between United States and Soviet Union begin at Geneva (29 June).

1983   President Reagan announces the Strategic Defense Initiative, or 'Star Wars' project, which aims to employ lasers and satellite technology to neutralize a missile attack on the United States (23 June).

Intermediate-range 'Cruise missiles' deployed in Britain, Holland and Germany (Nov.).

1986   Major nuclear accident in the Soviet Union at the Chernobyl site, north of Kiev, involving explosions, fire and release of radioactivity from No. 4 Reactor (26 Apr.).

Summit meeting on arms control between Presidents Reagan and Gorbachev at Reykjavik, Iceland, founders on the issue of the US Strategic Defense Initiative (11–12 Oct.).

1987   President Reagan announces imminent arms control deal and super-power summit with Gorbachev (18 Sept.).
Deployment of Cruise missiles halted in NATO countries (Nov.).
US and USSR reach historic agreement to scrap intermediate range nuclear weapons (24 Nov.), when INF Treaty signed in Washington (8 Dec.).

1988   Moscow summit talks between Reagan and Gorbachev (29 May).

1989   Gorbachev offers unilateral cuts in short-range missiles (10 May).
Cruise missiles removed from NATO countries (June), including the Greenham Common site in England, the scene of continuous women's demonstrations in the 1980s. President Bush announces cuts in Strategic Defense Initiative programme; 'stealth bomber' unveiled (July).

1990   At the Ottawa round of the conference series on establishing the 'Open Sky' system (an idea that was renewed by US President Bush), the representatives of the United States and the Soviet Union signed an agreement on the level of reduction of troops stationed in Europe (195,000 soldiers per side) (12–13 Feb.).
President Gorbachev and President Bush sign an agreement to destroy chemical weapons and to discontinue their production (1 June).

1991   South Africa joins the Anti-Nuclear Proliferation Treaty (8 July).
President Gorbachev and President Bush sign the START I Treaty (31 July).

1992   China joins the Anti-Nuclear Proliferation Treaty (9 Mar.).
'Open Sky' Treaty signed in Helsinki (24 Mar.).

1993   President Bush and President Yeltsin sign the START II Treaty in Moscow (3 Jan.).
As a result of the Geneva Conference on Disarmament – in the presence of representatives from 127 countries – a multilateral international treaty on the total abolition of chemical weapons is signed in Paris (13 Jan.).

1993   The People's Democratic Republic of Korea publicly denounces the Anti-Nuclear Proliferation Treaty (12 Mar.).

US Defense Secretary Les Aspin announces that the United States is abandoning the approximately $30-billion SDI programme (May).

Violating the unspoken moratorium, China carries out an underground nuclear weapons test (5 Oct.).

Comprehensive Test Ban Treaty signed (Sept.).

1998   Nuclear tests carried out by India and Pakistan.

Strategic nuclear weapons of the super-powers since 1963

	1963	1968	1976	1980	1985
United States					
ICBM	424	1054	1054	1054	1026
SLBM	224	656	656	656	640
LRB	630	600	373	338	241
Soviet Union					
ICBM	90	858	1477	1398	1398
SLBM	107	121	845	1028	979
LRB	190	155	135	156	170

Key: ICBM Inter-continental ballistic missiles
SLBM Submarine-launched ballistic missiles
LRB Long-range bombers (range over 6,000 miles)

Sources: The International Institute for Strategic Studies, *The Military Balance, 1976–1977* (London, 1976), p. 75; *The Military Balance, 1985–1986* (London, 1986).

Strategic nuclear arsenals of other states since 1960

	1960	1976	1986
United Kingdom			
Aircraft	50	50	—[1]
Land-based missiles	—	—	—
SLBM	—	64	64
France			
Aircraft	—	36	34[1]
Land-based missiles	—	18	18
SLBM	—	48	80
China			
Aircraft	—	65	110
Land-based missiles	—	50–80 (est.)	140–180 (est.)
SLBM	—	—	26

Note: SLBM: Submarine-launched ballistic missiles.
[1] Aircraft designated for strategic nuclear role only. In 1986 the United Kingdom possessed 201 land-based, short-range aircraft capable of carrying a nuclear payload plus 30 carrier-borne aircraft; France had 75 land-based, short-range aircraft, plus 36 carrier-borne.

Source: The International Institute for Strategic Studies, *The Military Balance, 1976–1977* (London, 1976), pp. 18, 21, 50; *Royal United Services Institute and Brassey's Defence Yearbook, 1987* (London, 1987), pp. 462, 465.

Economic and social

Estimated world population, 1950–2000

Year	Millions
1950	2,516
1955	2,751
1960	3,019
1965	3,335
1970	3,693
1975	4,076
1980	4,450
1985	4,837
1990	5,246[1]
1995	5,678[1]
2000	6,122[1]

[1] Medium variant of estimated population. High and Low variants are:

Year	High	Low
1990	5,334	5,189
1995	5,827	5,562
2000	6,340	5,927

Source: United Nations, *World Population Prospects: Estimates and Projections as assessed in 1984* (New York, 1986)

World population and estimates by major areas, 1950–2000

(millions)

	Africa	Latin America	North America	Far East[1]	South Asia[2]	Europe	Oceania	USSR
1950	224	165	166	671	704	392	13	180
1960	280	217	199	791	877	425	16	214
1970	361	283	227	986	1,116	459	19	242
1980	479	361	252	1,176	1,408	485	23	265
1985	555	405	264	1,250	1,568	492	25	279
1990	645	451	275	1,324	1,734	499	26	292
2000[3]	872	546	297	1,475	2,074	512	30	315

[1] China, Japan, Korea

[2] India, Pakistan, Bangladesh, South-East Asia

[3] Projected

Source: United Nations, *World Population Prospects: Estimates and Projections as assessed in 1984* (New York, 1986)

Population of individual countries

(millions, rounded to nearest thousand)

Afghanistan	1950	8,420
	1960	10,016
	1970	12,457
	1980	14,607
	1988	19,340
	1994	20,500
Algeria	1950	9,000 (est.)
	1966	11,822
	1972	15,270
	1977	17,422
	1988	23,820
	1995	28,580
Argentina	1947	15,894
	1960	20,011
	1970	23,362
	1980	27,947
	1985	31,730
	1995	34,590
Australia	1947	7,561
	1961	10,508
	1971	12,756
	1984	15,540
	1994	17,980
Bangladesh	1961	50,854 (East Pakistan)
	1974	71,479
	1981	87,120
	1988	103,630
	1993	118,700

Brazil	1950	51,976	
	1960	79,967	
	1970	92,342	
	1980	118,675	
	1994	159,100	

Canada	1951	14,009	
	1971	21,568	
	1981	24,343	
	1985	25,660	
	1995	28,500	

China	1953	590,195	
	1965	700,000	(est.)
	1975	933,000	(est.)
	1985	1,080,920	
	1996	1,240,000	

Cuba	1950	5,858
	1960	7,029
	1970	8,572
	1985	10,038
	1994	10,980

Egypt	1947	18,967
	1957	22,997
	1966	30,076
	1976	36,626
	1988	51,320
	1996	60,240

France	1946	40,507
	1962	46,510
	1975	52,656
	1985	55,730
	1995	58,172

Germany	1939	69,500	
		West Germany	*East Germany*
	1950	47,696	17,199
	1961	53,977	15,940
	1984	61,675	16,660
	1995	81,912	

Ghana	1950	4,242
	1960	6,772
	1970	8,614
	1980	11,457
	1988	14,045
	1995	16,470
India	1951	356,879
	1961	435,512
	1971	548,160
	1981	685,120
	1988	789,120
	1994	913,070
Indonesia	1950	79,538
	1960	96,194
	1970	120,280
	1980	150,958
	1988	172,450
	1996	203,300
Iran	1956	18,955
	1966	25,785
	1976	33,708
	1988	47,680
	1996	63,500
Iraq	1947	4,816
	1957	6,317
	1965	8,047
	1977	12,030
	1988	16,745
	1996	22,900
Israel	1950	1,748
	1961	2,183
	1972	3,148
	1985	4,315
	1994	5,470
Italy	1951	47,159
	1961	49,904
	1971	53,745
	1985	57,115
	1995	57,386

Japan	1950	83,200
	1960	93,419
	1970	103,720
	1980	117,060
	1988	122,603
	1996	126,300

Korea, South	1950	20,357
	1960	25,003
	1970	31,923
	1980	38,124
	1985	42,130
	1996	45,600

Korea, North	1965	11,100
	1975	16,000 (est.)
	1985	21,185
	1994	23,030

Malaysia	1960	10,992[1]
	1970	8,809[2]
	1980	14,157
	1989	16,640
	1996	21,200

[1] Includes Singapore, Sarawak and Sabah
[2] Excludes Singapore which became a separate state, 1965

Mexico	1950	25,791
	1960	34,923
	1970	48,225
	1980	67,396
	1988	83,040
	1996	97,100

Netherlands	1947	9,625
	1960	11,462
	1971	13,061
	1985	14,454
	1995	15,487

Nigeria	1953	30,418
	1963	55,670
	1975	74,870

	1985	95,690
	1996	104,600
Pakistan	1951	75,842[1]
	1961	93,832[1]
	1972	64,980
	1981	83,782
	1989	105,720
	1996	136,800

[1] Includes the population of East Pakistan which in 1971 became Bangladesh

Philippines	1950	20,551
	1960	27,904
	1970	37,540
	1980	48,317
	1988	57,410
	1996	71,200

Poland	1946	23,900[1]
	1960	29,776
	1985	38,060
	1996	38,700

[1] The boundaries of the Polish state were substantially altered in 1945.

Russia	1996	148,000[1]

[1] Formerly part of USSR

South Africa	1946	11,416
	1960	16,003
	1970	21,488
	1980	24,886
	1989	34,335
	1996	43,500

Spain	1950	27,977
	1960	30,431
	1970	34,041
	1981	37,746
	1989	39,690
	1995	39,188

Sri Lanka	1960	10,965
	1971	12,711
	1981	14,850
	1987	16,550
	1992	17,400
Sudan	1955	10,260
	1973	12,428
	1983	20,564
	1988	24,235
	1994	28,200
Taiwan	1953	7,591
	1960	12,345
	1982	18,271
	1996	21,600
Tanzania	1948	7,596
	1967	12,231
	1978	17,552
	1985	21,733
	1996	29,700
Thailand	1950	19,635
	1967	29,700
	1979	45,221
	1985	50,610
	1996	62,100
Turkey	1955	24,065
	1965	31,391
	1975	40,348
	1988	53,230
	1994	61,180
Ukraine	1996	51,700[1]

[1] Formerly part of USSR

United Kingdom	1951	50,225
	1961	52,709
	1971	55,907
	1985	56,618
	1996	58,900

USSR[1]	1959	208,800
	1970	241,700
	1987	284,580

United States of	1940	131,669
America	1950	151,868
	1960	179,979
	1970	203,984
	1980	227,236
	1987	245,650
	1996	268,700

Vietnam	1950	26,000[1]	
		North	*South*
	1964	17,900	15,715
	1970	23,787	21,154 (est.)
	1979	52,742[2]	
	1988	64,120[2]	
	1996	77,100[2]	

[1] As part of French Indo-China
[2] North and South Vietnam were united in 1975

Yugoslavia	1948	15,700[1]
	1961	18,549
	1971	20,523
	1981	22,428[2]

[1] Includes territory annexed in 1945
[2] Broken up into constituent elements after 1989

Zaïre[2]	1947	10,805[1]
	1958	12,769[1]
	1970	21,637
	1983	31,944
	1994	43,800

[1] As Belgian Congo
[2] Renamed the Democratic Republic of Congo, 1997

Zambia	1950	2,000
	1974	4,751
	1982	6,242
	1993	8,940

Zimbabwe	1951	2,320
	1974	6,100
	1982	7,532
	1996	12,200

Source: United Nations, *Demographic Yearbook* (New York, 1996)

Population density and urbanization: selected countries

	Population density (per sq. km.)			Urban population (percentage)			
	1975	1985	1995[1]	1950[1]	1970[1]	1985[1]	1995[1]
Afghanistan	30	30	25	5.8	11.0	18.5	21.0
Algeria	7	10	12	—	—	43.0	44.3
Angola	5	8	9	—	—	25.0	50.0
Argentina	9	11	12	62.5	80.7	85.0	86.6
Australia	2	2	2	68.9	85.6	86.0	85.4
Bangladesh	533	720	740	—	—	12.0	14.0
Bolivia	4	6	7	—	—	48.0	52.0
Brazil	13	17	17	36.2	55.9	73.0	76.0
Burma (Myanmar)	45	57	62	—	—	24.0	26.0
Canada	2	2	2	62.9	76.1	76.0	76.0
Chad	3	4	4	—	—	27.0	27.0
Chile	14	17	17	60.2	76.0	84.0	84.0
China	86	112	129	13.5	16.7	21.0	33.8
Colombia	18	26	40.2	37.1	57.2	67.4	70.0
Cuba	81	94	99	49.4	60.2	71.8	74.0
Czechoslovakia	116	126	131[2]	51.2	55.5	65.0	75.0[2]
Ecuador	24	35	40	—	—	52.0	60.0
Egypt	37	51	63	30.1	39.8	46.0	47.0
Ethiopia	23	37	38	—	—	12.0	15.0
France	96	102	104	55.9	70.0	73.0	73.0
Germany E.	156	153 } 228[3]		68.8	73.8	77.0 } 84.0[3]	
Germany W.	249	245		71.1	—	86.0	
Ghana	41	59	69	14.5	29.1	39.6	35.0
Greece	69	76	79	36.8	64.7	69.7	71.0
Guatemala	57	79	87	30.5	35.7	41.4	39.0
Haiti	165	197	244	—	—	20.0	21.0

	Population density (per sq. km.)			Urban population (percentage)			
	1975	1985	1995[1]	1950[1]	1970[1]	1985[1]	1995[1]
Hong Kong	4,179	5,337	5,400	—	—	92.0	93.0
Hungary	113	114	110	36.5	45.2	54.3	55.0
India	182	246	274	17.3	19.9	24.0	24.7
Indonesia	69	90	102	12.4	17.1	25.3	42.0
Iran	20	29	37	30.1	44.0	52.0	58.0
Iraq	26	38	45	33.8	51.1	71.0	74.0
Israel	162	212	249	71.7	85.3	90.0	92.0
Italy	185	190	189	—	47.7	67.0	72.0
Japan	297	324	332	37.5	72.1	77.0	81.0
Kampuchea	45	37	32	—	—	11.0	12.0
Kenya	23	39	50	—	—	20.0	20.0
Korea N.	132	176	188	—	—	64.0	64.0
Korea S.	352	428	451	21.4	40.7	65.0	84.0
Laos	14	16	19	—	—	16.0	19.0
Libya	2	2	2	—	—	65.0	68.0
Madagascar	11	18	23	—	—	22.0	25.0
Malawi	43	64	81	—	—	12.0	12.0
Malaysia	36	50	59	—	—	38.0	45.0
Mexico	30	39	42	42.6	58.7	70.0	73.0
Morocco	30	35	38	—	—	45.0	50.0
Mozambique	12	18	18	—	—	19.0	30.0
Nepal	89	122	125	—	—	8.0	9.6
Netherlands	334	351	356	54.6	78.0	88.4	90.0
New Zealand	11	12	12	—	—	84.0	84.0
Nicaragua	17	27	36	34.9	47.0	59.4	61.0
Niger	4	6	7	—	—	16.0	19.0
Nigeria	68	89	96	10.2	16.1	23.0	36.0
Pakistan	87	120	150	10.4	25.5	29.1	32.0
Peru	12	16	19	—	—	67.0	70.0
Philippines	142	191	228	27.1	33.0	39.6	53.0
Poland	109	122	123	39.8	52.3	61.0	61.0
Portugal	103	106	107	19.3	26.2	31.2	32.0
Romania	89	97	96	31.3	38.2	49.0	55.0
Russia	—	—	86	—	—	—	73.0
Saudi Arabia	3	6	8	—	20.8	25.0	33.0
Senegal	26	34	41	—	—	36.0	40.0
Serbia	—	—	111	—	—	—	40.0
Sierra Leone	43	54	64	—	—	28.0	32.0
Singapore	3,872	4,274	4,568	—	—	100.0	100.0
Somalia	5	13	13	—	—	15.0	25.0

	Population density (per sq. km.)			Urban population (percentage)			
	1975	1985	1995[1]	1950[1]	1970[1]	1985[1]	1995[1]
South Africa	20	31	34	42.6	47.9	49.0	50.0
Soviet Union	11	13	—[4]	47.9	56.3	66.0	—
Spain	70	79	82	37.0	54.7	76.0	80.0
Sri Lanka	213	256	272	—	—	21.0	21.0
Sudan	6	8	11	—	—	21.0	24.0
Sweden	18	19	19	47.5	81.4	83.0	83.0
Switzerland	155	158	158	—	—	58.0	58.0
Syria	40	60	65	—	43.5	50.0	50.0
Taiwan	—	550	585	—	—	66.0	72.0
Tanzania	16	25	32	—	—	22.0	30.0
Thailand	81	99	114	—	—	20.0	27.0
Tunisia	35	47	51	—	—	47.0	53.0
Turkey	51	68	73	28.8	34.4	46.0	60.0
Uganda	49	67	84	—	—	10.0	11.3
Ukraine	—	—	86	—	—	—	68.0
United Kingdom	229	236	240	80.8	78.0	92.0	90.0
United States	23	26	28	64.0	73.5	74.0	75.0
Uruguay	16	18	18	—	—	85.0	87.0
Venezuela	13	20	22	53.8	75.7	82.0	84.0
Vietnam	136	195	195	—	—	20.0	20.0
Yemen	27	50	21[5]	—	—	20.0	14.0[5]
Yugoslavia	83	92	—[6]	18.5	38.6	46.0	—[6]
Zaïre	11	14	18	15.8	21.6	27.0	30.0
Zambia	6.5	10	12	—	—	50.0	56.0
Zimbabwe	16	22	30	—	—	25.0	32.0

[1] Or nearest equivalent date
[2] Czech Republic
[3] Federal Republic of Germany from 1990
[4] See under Russia, Ukraine for populations of major constituent nations of the former USSR
[5] Unified State of Republic of Yemen, created in 1990
[6] Broken into constituent republics after 1989

Population of major world cities*

(thousands)

	1951	1956	1960	1966	1971	1981	1985	1995[1]
Accra	136	—	338	—	564	—	860	950
Addis Adaba	—	—	—	—	1,083	—	1,408	1,700
Alexandria	919	1,278	—	1,081	—	2,576	—	2,917
Ankara	—	451	—	971	1,553	—	1,877	2,542
Athens	1,379	—	1,853	—	2,101	3,027	—	3,072
Auckland	—	—	—	—	797	—	—	929
Baghdad	—	656	—	1,657	2,184	—	2,200	3,841
Beijing (Peking)	—	4,010	—	—	7,570	—	9,452	10,870
Belgrade	368	—	585	—	746	—	936	970
Berlin	3,337[1]	—	3,261[1]	3,268	—	—	3,049	3,472[1]
Bogota	648	—	—	1,681	2,978	—	3,968	4,819
Bombay (Mumbai)	2,839	—	4,152	—	5,971	8,227	—	9,925
Brussels	956	—	1,020	1,075	—	997	982	951
Bucharest	—	1,237	—	1,519	—	1,979	1,995	2,343
Budapest	—	1,850	—	1,960	—	—	2,071	1,930
Buenos Aires	4,603	—	7,000	—	8,925	9,927	—	11,662

City								
Cairo	—	2,877	—	4,220	—	5,650	—	6,452
Calcutta	4,578	—	4,405	—	7,031	9,166	—	11,022
Cape Town	578	—	807	—	1,108	—	—	2,350
Caracas	694	—	—	1,764	—	2,944	—	1,824
Chicago	3,621	—	3,550	—	3,369	3,005	2,992	2,783
Colombo	—	409	—	618	—	—	—	588
Damascus	—	—	—	—	923	1,251	—	1,489
Delhi	1,384	—	2,359	—	3,647	5,714	—	7,207
Dhaka	—	—	—	—	—	—	—	3,397
Guatemala City	284	—	439	—	707	793	—	2,000 (est.)
Hamburg	—	1,760	—	1,851	—	—	1,600	1,701
Hanoi	—	—	644	—	1,400	—	—	1,088
Ho Chi-minh City[2]	—	—	—	—	1,825	—	—	3,169
Hong Kong	2,240	—	—	—	—	5,109	5,364	6,170
Houston	596	—	938	—	1,234	1,595	—	1,630
Istanbul	—	1,269	—	2,053	3,135	2,948	—	6,293
Jakarta	—	1,865	2,907	—	4,576	6,503	—	9,000 (est.)
Johannesburg	884	—	1,153	—	1,441	1,534	—	1,916
Kabul	154	—	—	400	318	377	913	700 (est.)
Karachi	1,126	—	—	2,721	3,499	5,103	—	—

[1] East and West Berlin   [2] Previously known as Saigon

* The definition of urban areas for individual countries is often at variance with that of other countries; also, the definition of urban areas concerned has sometimes changed in the course of the past century. Figures here are for urban agglomeration unless otherwise stated

(thousands)

	1951	1956	1960	1966	1971	1981	1985	1995
Khartoum	—	—	—	—	228	—	476	476
Kiev	—	—	1,104	1,413	—	2,355	—	2,600
Kinshasa	—	290	—	508	2,008	—	2,654	3,804
Kuala Lumpur	—	—	665	—	452	—	938	937
Lagos	272	—	—	—	1,080	—	1,404	1,347
Lahore	849	—	—	1,674	2,165	2,922	—	2,922
Leningrad	—	—	3,300	3,706	—	4,779	—	4,883[1]
Lima	—	—	—	—	3,318	5,259	—	5,706
Lisbon	790	—	817	—	762	—	807	823
London	8,348	—	8,172	7,914	7,281	6,754	6,851	6,679
Los Angeles	1,970	—	2,479	—	2,812	2,967	3,097	3,485
Madras	1,416	—	1,729	—	3,170	4,277	—	5,422
Madrid	—	1,775	2,260	2,559	—	3,188	3,217	2,909
Managua	109	—	235	—	399	608	644	682
Manila	984	—	1,139	—	1,436	1,630	—	1,601
Melbourne	—	1,524	—	2,108	2,584	2,604	—	3,198
Mexico	2,335	—	2,698	—	7,315	—	8,831	15,047
Montreal	—	1,621	—	2,437	—	2,862	—	3,127
Moscow	—	—	5,032	5,507	—	8,396	8,408	8,793
New York	7,892	—	7,782	—	7,896	7,072	7,165	7,322
Osaka	—	2,547	—	3,133	—	—	2,632	2,481

Paris	2,850	4,823	2,790	—	—	8,510	—	9,318
Pusan	474	—	1,271	—	1,842	3,160	—	3,797
Rio de Janeiro	2,303	150	3,124	—	4,252	5,093	—	5,480
Riyadh	—	150	—	225	668	—	1,250	1,800
Rome	1,652	2,188	—	2,485	—	2,840	2,832	2,723
Rotterdam	—	712	—	1,048	—	—	1,021	—
São Paulo	2,017	—	3,674	—	5,870	7,034	—	9,646
Santiago	—	1,539	—	2,314	—	4,132	—	5,181
Seoul	1,446	—	2,983	—	5,433	8,364	9,646	10,628
Shanghai	—	6,900	—	—	10,820	—	12,048	8,760
Singapore	—	—	—	—	2,278	—	2,529	2,930
Stockholm	744	—	809	1,262	1,493	—	1,562	1,577
Sydney	—	1,863	—	2,445	2,874	3,022	—	3,738
Tehran	—	1,512	—	2,695	3,150	—	5,734	6,476
Tel Aviv	—	364	—	392	1,091	1,305	—	1,140
Tokyo	—	7,867	—	11,005	—	—	8,389	7,874
Toronto	—	1,358	—	2,158	—	3,067	—	3,893
Vancouver	—	665	—	892	—	1,311	—	1,602
Vienna	1,766	—	1,628	—	1,615	1,516	1,531	1,596
Warsaw	804	—	—	1,261	—	1,621	1,649	1,653

[1] Name changed in 1991 back to pre-1914 name of St Petersburg.

Sources: B.R. Mitchell, *European Historical Statistics, 1750–1975* 2nd edn (Macmillan, 1980), pp. 76–8; B. Hunter (ed.), *The Statesman's Year-Book, 1996–97* (Macmillan, 1996)

Output of wheat, 1950–94: selected countries

(millions of metric tons)

	1950	1962	1972	1983	1994
Argentina	—	7.5	7.9	11.7	10.7
Australia	—	8.2	8.4	21.7	16.5
China	14.5	16.7	36.0	81.4	101.2
Canada	—	15.4	14.5	26.9	23.4
France	7.7	14.1	17.9	24.8	30.7
Germany[1]	2.6	4.6	7.1	9.0	16.5
India	—	11.2	26.4	42.5	59.1
Italy	7.8	9.5	9.4	8.5	7.8
Pakistan	—	4.2	6.9	12.4	15.2
Turkey	—	8.6	12.3	16.4	17.5
USSR	31.0	70.8	86.0	82.0	32.1[2]
USA	—	33.0	42.0	66.0	63.1

[1] West Germany only 1945–83
[2] Russia

Sources: B.R. Mitchell, *European Historical Statistics, 1750–1970* (Macmillan, 1975), pp. 249–75; J. Paxton (ed.), *The Statesman's Year-Book, 1985–86* (Macmillan, 1985), p. xiii; B. Hunter (ed.) *The Statesman's Year-Book, 1996–97* (Macmillan, 1996), p. xix

Output of rice, 1962–94: major producers

(in thousand metric tons)

	1962	1972	1980	1985	1994
Bangladesh	15,034	15,134	20,821	21,700	27,537
Brazil	6,123	6,761	9,776	7,760	10,499
Burma (Myanmar)	7,786	7,361	13,100	14,500	19,057
China	86,038	105,197	142,993	172,184	178,251
India	52,733	58,868	80,312	90,000	118,400
Indonesia	12,393	18,031	29,652	34,300	46,245
Japan	16,444	15,319	12,189	12,958	11,918
Korea, South	4,809	5,500	5,311	7,608	7,058
Korea, North	—	3,783	4,960	5,200	2,104
Pakistan	1,824	3,495	4,679	5,210	3,995
Philippines	3,957	4,898	7,836	8,150	10,150
Thailand	11,267	12,413	17,368	18,535	18,447
USA	3,084	3,875	6,629	4,523	8,972
Vietnam, North	4,600	4,400 ⎫	11,679	14,500	24,500
Vietnam, South	6,029	6,348 ⎭			

Sources: J. Paxton (ed.), *The Statesman's Year-Book, 1977–78* (Macmillan, 1977), p. xviii; *The Statesman's Year-Book, 1985–86* (Macmillan, 1985), p. xviii; B. Hunter (ed.), *The Statesman's Year-Book, 1996–97* (Macmillan, 1996), p. xxiv

Output of coal and lignite, 1950–94: selected countries

(in million metric tons)

	1950	1960	1975	1985	1994[1]
United States[2]	468	377	643	828	1,034
United Kingdom	220	197	124	91	68
USSR	261	509	701	716	306[3]
Japan	49	51	20	17	7
Germany	188	240	214	207 ⎫	259
(E. Germany 1950–85)	140	228	245	278 ⎭	
India	n.a.	n.a.	92	125	263
Australia	—	—	70	107	285
China	—	—	425	715	1,150
South Africa	—	—	70	146	196
Poland	83	114	211	117	197
Ukraine	—	—	—	—	192
Kazakhstan	—	—	—	—	112

[1] Or nearest available year
[2] Short tons
[3] Russia only

Sources: B.R. Mitchell, *European Historical Statistics, 1750–1970* (Macmillan, 1975), pp. 365–8; B. Hunter (ed.), *The Statesman's Year-Book, 1996–97* (Macmillan, 1996)

Output of steel, 1950–94: selected countries

(annual production in million metric tons)

	1950	1960	1975	1985	1994
United States[1]	96.4	99.3	116.6	84.6	100.6
United Kingdom	16.6	24.7	20.2	15.1	17.3
Germany[2]	12.1	34.1	40.4	35.7	40.8
USSR	27.3	65.2	141.3	154.0	58.3[4]
France	8.7	17.3	27.0	23.3	17.1
Japan	4.8	22.1	114.0	99.5[3]	98.3
Italy	2.4	8.2	21.8	21.7	24.8
India	—	—	4.9	10.9[3]	13.9
China	—	—	25.0	29.0	89.6
Brazil	—	—	7.5	14.7	25.2
Ukraine	—	—	—	—	24.0 (est.)

[1] Figures in net tons of 2,000 lb
[2] West Germany only 1945–85
[3] 1982 figures
[4] Russia only

Sources: B.R. Mitchell, *European Historical Statistics, 1750–1970* (Macmillan, 1975), pp. 399–402; J. Paxton (ed.), *The Statesman's Year-Book, 1985–86* (Macmillan, 1985); B. Hunter (ed.), *The Statesman's Year-Book, 1996–97* (Macmillan, 1996)

Motor vehicles produced, 1965–95: selected countries

(in thousands, commercial and private)

	1965	1975	1985	1995
Brazil[3]	—	—	—	1,391[2]
Canada[3]	—	—	—	2,010
France	1,616	1,694	3,148	2,836[2]
Germany[1]	3,063	3,172	3,334	3,497[2]
India[3]	—	—	—	399
Italy	1,186	1,459	1,575	1,684
Japan	1,876	6,942	11,122	—
Mexico[3]	—	—	—	681
South Korea[3]	—	—	—	1,900
Spain	234	967	1,226	1,843
USSR	814	—	1,300	—
United Kingdom	2,180	1,647	1,313	1,375[2]
USA	9,306[2]	6,713[2]	6,739[2]	—

[1] West Germany only, 1965–85

[2] Passenger cars only

[3] Figures before 1995 not available

Sources: B.R. Mitchell, *European Historical Statistics, 1750–1970* (Macmillan, 1975), pp. 467–9; J. Paxton (ed.), *The Statesman's Year-Book, 1996–97* (Macmillan, 1996)

Output of electricity, 1955–94: selected countries

(in million kWh)

	1955	1975	1985	1994
France	49.6	180.0	262.8[1]	454.1
Germany[2]	78.9	301.8	366.9	452.7
Italy	25.6	140.8	182.9[3]	226.2
Russia	170.2	1,039.0	1,418.0[3]	956.6
Spain	11.9	76.3	117.3[3]	165.4
Sweden	24.7	80.6	100.1[1]	137.7
United Kingdom	89.0	272.1	297.3	302.8
China	55.0	121.0	—	839.5
India	25.5[4]	54.6	122.0[1]	350.5
United States	—	—	—	2,910.7
Canada	—	263.3	395.4[3]	511.3
Brazil	—	56.3[5]	152.0[1]	237.6
Japan	65.2	459.0	581.1[1]	906.7

[1] 1982

[2] West Germany only 1948–90

[3] 1983

[4] 1964

[5] 1972

Sources: B.R. Mitchell, *European Historical Statistics, 1750–1970* (Macmillan, 1975), pp. 479–82; J. Paxton (ed.), *The Statesman's Year-Book, 1985–86* (Macmillan, 1985); B. Hunter (ed.), *The Statesman's Year-Book, 1996–97* (Macmillan, 1996)

Output of crude oil, 1950–95: selected countries

(million metric tons)

	1950	1960	1975	1984	1995[1]
Americas					
USA	285.2	384.1	411.4	487.0	—
Canada	3.8	27.5	70.0	82.0	—
Mexico	10.3	14.1	41.4	150.0	—
Trinidad	3.0	6.1	11.1	8.0	7.13
Venezuela	78.2	148.7	122.1	95.0	—
Argentina	3.5	9.2	20.2	24.0	—
Brazil	0.1	4.0	9.4	24.0	—
Middle East					
Iraq	6.7	47.5	111.0	58.5	—
Iran	32.3	52.1	266.7	105.0	—
Saudi Arabia	26.6	61.1	352.1	235.0	—
Kuwait	17.3	81.7	104.8	58.0	—
Abu Dhabi	—	—	67.3	36.0	—
Qatar	1.6	8.2	20.8	18.8	—
Egypt	2.4	3.6	11.7	36.0[1]	44.8
Kazakhstan	—	—	—	—	23.0
Africa					
Nigeria	—	1.0	88.0	68.0	69.0
Libya	—	—	72.4	52.5	—
Algeria	—	8.6	88.0	29.5	—
Angola	—	—	8.4	9.5	25.5
Gabon	—	1.0	13.1	8.0	—
Far East & Australasia					
China	—	5.0	77.0	110.0	—
Indonesia	6.5	20.6	65.5	70.5	—
India	—	—	8.1	28.0	32.2
Brunei	4.3	4.7	9.5	8.0	8.85
Malaysia	—	—	—	21.0	30.0
Australia	—	—	19.3	23.0	31.7

(million metric tons)

	1950	1960	1975	1984	1995[1]
Europe					
United Kingdom	—	—	1.6	125.0	96.2
Norway	—	—	1.6	34.5	—
Romania	4.1	11.5	14.6	12.0	6.7
USSR[2]	37.5	148.0	489.8	615.0	354.0

[1] Or nearest available date
[2] Russia in 1995

Sources: J. Paxton (ed.), *The Statesman's Year-Book, 1977–78* (Macmillan, 1977), pp. xxv–xxiii; *The Statesman's Year-Book, 1985–86* (Macmillan, 1985), pp. xxii–xxiii; B. Hunter (ed.), *The Statesman's Year-Book, 1996–97* (Macmillan, 1996)

World oil reserves: 1985 and 1994

(Billions of barrels)

	1985	1994
Gulf States and Middle East		
Neutral Zone	5.4	(see Kuwait)
Iran	48.5	92.8
Iraq	44.5[1]	100.0 (est.)
Kuwait	92.7[1]	96.5
Oman	3.5	4.7
Qatar	3.35	3.7
United Arab Emirates	32.49	98.1
Saudi Arabia	171.7[1]	261.2
Syria	1.45	1.5
Africa		
Algeria	9.0	9.2
Angola	1.8	—
Egypt	3.2	—
Libya	21.1	22.8
Nigeria	16.7	17.9
Western Hemisphere		
USA	27.3	23.7
Mexico	48.6	50.9
Canada	7.1	5.1
Venezuela	25.9	63.3
Western Europe		
United Kingdom	13.6	4.5
Norway	8.3	9.3
Asia-Pacific		
Australia	1.5	1.6
Brunei	1.4	1.3[2]
India	3.0	8.0[2]

(Billions of barrels)

	1985	1994
Indonesia	8.7	11.0[2]
Malaysia	3.5	2.9[2]
China	19.1	24.0[2]
USSR	63.0	57.0
Other	2.0	—

[1] These figures are believed to represent a considerable underestimation

[2] 1991

Sources: Adapted from *Oil and Gas Journal,* December 1984 and December 1985; B. Hunter (ed.), *The Statesman's Year-Book, 1996–97* (Macmillan, 1996), p. xxvii

Gross national product per capita: selected countries

(US $)

	1982	1995
Afghanistan	184	—
Albania	840	360
Algeria	2,140	1,690
Argentina	2,560	8,060
Australia	11,080	17,980
Austria	10,210	24,950
Bangladesh	140	230
Brazil	2,220	3,370
Bulgaria	4,150	1,160
Burkina Faso	240	300
Burundi	230	150
Canada	11,400	19,570
Chad	110	190
Chile	1,965	3,560
China	300	530
Colombia	1,380	1,620
Congo	1,110	640
Cuba	2,696	—
Czechoslovakia	5,820	3,210[1]
Denmark	13,120	28,110
Egypt	650	710
Ethiopia	140	130
France	12,190	23,470
Germany	13,450[2]	25,580
Greece	3,540	7,710
Guatemala	1,140	1,190
Hong Kong	5,738	21,650
Hungary	2,100	3,840
India	260	310
Indonesia	520	880
Iran	2,160	2,190
Iraq	3,020	2,140
Ireland	4,855	13,630
Israel	5,160	14,410

(US $)

	1982	1995
Italy	6,960	19,270
Japan	9,706	34,630
Kenya	420	260
South Korea	1,700	8,483
North Korea	736	923
Libya	8,540	5,410
Malawi	200	140
Malaysia	1,840	3,520
Mexico	2,250	4,010
Mozambique	270	80
Nepal	150	200
Netherlands	11,790	21,970
New Zealand	7,700	13,190
Nicaragua	860	330
Nigeria	870	280
Norway	12,023	26,480
Pakistan	350	440
Peru	1,170	1,890
Philippines	790	960
Poland	3,900	2,470
Rwanda	250	210
Saudi Arabia	12,600	7,240
South Africa	2,770	3,010
Spain	4,173	13,280
Sri Lanka	300	640
Syria	1,570	1,110
Tanzania	280	90
Thailand	770	2,210
Turkey	1,540	2,450
Uganda	220	200
USSR	—	2,650[3]
UK	9,110	18,410
USA	12,820	25,860
Venezuela	4,644	2,760
Zaïre	210	220
Zambia	600	350
Zimbabwe	780	490

[1] Czech Republic   [2] West Germany only   [3] Russia

Sources: J. Paxton (ed.), *The Statesman's Year-Book, 1985–86* (Macmillan, 1986); B. Hunter (ed.), *The Statesman's Year-Book, 1996–97* (Macmillan, 1996)

Famines and major natural disasters

1945	Tidal wave in East Pakistan (now called Bangladesh) kills 4,000.
1948	4,000 killed in earthquake in Japan.
1949	7,000 killed in earthquake in Ecuador.
1950	Three earthquakes in Iran kill 1,500.
1953	Over 1,200 people die in coastal floods in Low Countries and Britain (Feb.); 1,000 killed by tidal wave in Greek isles (Aug.).
1954	1,600 killed at Orleansville, Algeria, in earthquake.
1956	Typhoon in China kills over 2,000.
1957	Earthquake in northern Iran kills 2,000 people.
1958	Typhoon in Japan kills 1,300 people.
1959	Over 3,000 killed in typhoon in Madagascar.
1960	Earthquake at Agadir, Morocco, kills 12,500 (Feb.); 1,500 die in earthquake at Lars, Iran (April): 3,000 die in East Pakistan floods (Oct.).
1962	Avalanche in the Peruvian Andes kills 3,000 people (Jan.); over 12,000 killed in Iranian earthquake (Sept.).
1963	10,000 die in East Pakistan hurricane (May); Skopje earthquake kills 1,000 people in southern Yugoslavia (July); dam burst in Italy kills 3,000 (Oct.); 4,000 die in Haiti hurricane (Oct.).
1964	Burst reservoir kills 1,000 people in India; typhoon kills 7,000 in Ceylon and Madras.
1965	Typhoon kills 10,000 in East Pakistan.

1966   2,000 die in Turkish earthquake.

1968   Iranian earthquake kills between 11,000 and 20,000 people.

1970   Massive floods in East Pakistan kill between 250,000 and 500,000 people (Nov.); Peruvian earthquake kills an estimated 70,000 people.

1971   5,000 killed by typhoon floods in India.

1972   Earthquake in Managua, Nicaragua, kills 10,000 people.

1973   Drought and famine in Sahel area of Mauritania, Senegal, the Gambia, Upper Volta, Mali, Niger and Chad kill an estimated 250,000 people; 100,000 die in Ethiopia.

1974   20,000 feared dead in Chinese earthquake (May); monsoon floods in Bangladesh kill 2,000 (Aug.); typhoon floods in Honduras kill 8,000 (Sept.); earthquake in Pakistan kills 4,000 (Dec.).

1975   Earthquake centred on Lice, Turkey, kills 3,000 people.

1976   Earthquake in Guatemala kills 22,000 people (Feb.); almost a 1,000 killed in Italy by earthquake (May); earthquake in Philippines kills 3,000 (Aug.); 3,700 killed at Van, Turkey, by earthquake (Nov.).

1977   Romanian earthquake kills 1,570 people.

1978   Flood of Jumna river in India kills 10,000 (Sept.); between 5,000 and 20,000 killed in Iranian earthquake (Sept.).

1978–80 Drought and famine in East Africa threaten estimated 10 million with starvation in Sudan, Ethiopia, Somalia and Djibouti.

1979   1,000 killed in hurricanes on Dominica.

1980   Algerian earthquake at El Asnam kills between 2,000 and 20,000 people (Oct.); earthquake in southern Italy kills 3,000–4,000 people (Nov.); UN relief agencies estimate 2 million facing starvation in Cambodia.

1981   Floods in Shansi province, China, kill 5,000 people.

1982   Monsoon floods in India kill several hundred and leave millions homeless (Sept.); earthquake in Yemen kills nearly 3,000 people (Dec.).

1983   2,000 killed in Turkish earthquake.

1984   10,000 killed in typhoon floods in Philippines.

1984–85 Famine in Ethiopia and neighbouring area affects millions, prompting huge relief effort.

1985   10,000 killed in typhoon floods in Bangladesh (May); Mexican earthquake kills 2,000 people (Sept.).

1987   Failure of Ethiopian harvest prompts fresh famine scare.

1988   Armenian earthquake kills thousands.

1989   San Francisco earthquake causes major structural damage (Oct.).

1990   Iranian earthquake kills 35,000 (June).

1991   Eruption of Pinatubo volcano causes death of 700 (June); tropical storm Thelma kills 5,000 (Nov.).

1992   In Somalia, civil war and natural disaster threaten 4.5 million with famine (Aug.); Nicaraguan earthquake kills and injures several hundred (Sept.); Egyptian earthquake kills 200 and injures 2,000 (Oct.)

1993   Indian earthquake kills 22,000 in Maharashtra state (Sept.).

1995   6,000 killed in Kobe earthquake in Japan (Jan.); 1,600 killed in Sakhalin earthquake (May); floods in central China kill 1,200 (July).

1996   Earthquake in south China kills several hundred.

1997   Growing evidence of famine in North Korea following floods and bad harvests since 1995. Eruptions of volcanic island of Montserrat forces thousands of refugees to flee the south of the island. Forest fires rage in south-east Asia.

World health, disease and medicine

1941   Successful use of first antibiotic, penicillin; becomes widely available within next three years for dealing with infections.

1944   Quinine artificially produced.

1946   US research links smoking to cancer.

1948   Antibiotic streptomycin introduced for treatment of tuberculosis. World Health Organization established, based in Geneva with offices in New York and regional offices elsewhere. WHO launches campaign against TB.

1949   Cause of sickle cell anaemia found.

1950   First kidney transplant carried out in Chicago.

1952   Artificial heart pump first used to keep patient alive in United States.

1953   Dr Salk produces successful vaccine against polio. First full chemical analysis of a protein, insulin, carried out by Dr Sanger at Cambridge. Watson and Crick discover structure of DNA. Drs Bunge and Sherman demonstrate that deep-frozen sperm remains fertile, paving way for sperm banks.

1957   Asian flu epidemic.

1958   First heart 'pacemaker' implanted in patient. The drug Thalidomide is associated with birth defects in children. Oral contraceptive – 'The Pill' – becomes available.

1963   First successful kidney transplant to overcome rejection problems.

1966   WHO campaign against TB has completed 400 million tests and 180 million vaccinations.

1967   First heart transplant by Dr Christiaan Barnard in South Africa.

1969   Human egg fertilized in test tube for first time.

1971   First heart-lung transplant.

1975   WHO announces smallpox eradicated from Bangladesh, leaving Ethiopia only infected area.

1978   First 'test-tube baby' born with use of egg and sperm fertilized outside the womb.

1979   'Body-scanner' for diagnosis developed in Britain.

1980   WHO announces eradication of smallpox.

1981   Identification of an immune deficiency disease, AIDS, affecting homosexual groups in the United States.

1984   AIDS-causing virus discovered. World Health Organization estimates potential deaths at several million, with deaths affecting the heterosexual community also.

1985   Gorbachev launches anti-alcohol campaign in USSR.

1987   Widespread anti-AIDS campaign begun in several countries.

1989   World-wide research on anti-AIDS drugs produces first treatments likely to slow progress of disease. Some 200,000 full-blown cases reported spread over 150 countries; 6–10 million estimated to be infected by the HIV virus.

1990   First successful gene therapy carried out on four-year old girl suffering from DNA defect.

1996   Cloning of a sheep opens the way to widespread reproduction of complex organisms.

1998   New plague fears as a result of drug-resistant organisms.

Major population and refugee movements

1944–45   1.2 million Germans flee westward in face of Russian advance.

1945–50   An estimated 1 million German POWs remain in the USSR after peace. 1.4 million 'displaced persons' in Germany, mainly consisting of persons unwilling or unable to return to their home country. Continued flight from east into Allied-occupied Germany; approximately one-third of West German population by 1950 consists of people not born in its territory. Repatriation of approximately 3 million Japanese from Co-Prosperity Sphere, Manchuria, Korea and China to Japanese mainland.

1947   At partition of India over 17 million Hindu and Muslim refugees flee to join co-religionists in the new independent states of India and Pakistan. First major arrivals of West Indian immigrants to United Kingdom.

1948   Jewish population of Palestine rises to 800,000 from 84,000 in 1922 as a result of increased flow of immigrants.

1948–49   Creation of state of Israel and Arab–Israeli War lead to displacement of about a million Palestinian Arab refugees to Syria, Lebanon, Jordan and Egypt.

1948–60   Almost a million Jews, many from Eastern Europe and north Africa, emigrate to Israel.

1948–62   Period of mass migration to United Kingdom from West Indies and Indian sub-continent, approximately 1.5 million people.

1949   Approximately 2 million Nationalist Chinese under Chiang Kai-shek flee to Formosa (Taiwan) after communist victory in Chinese Civil War.

1950–53   Korean War displaces approximately 3 million Koreans from North to South Korea.

1956   Approximately 200,000 Hungarians flee to West following uprising.

1959   Australia alters immigration rules to facilitate non-English-speaking immigrants; by 1963 there are 250,000 Italian immigrants. Dalai Lama heads flight of Tibetan refugees to India after Chinese crush revolt.

1960   Beginning of 'guest-worker' system in Germany; by 1970s approximately 2.5 million workers come from Yugoslavia and Turkey.

1971   Thousands of Bangladeshis flee into India to escape fighting in aftermath of declaration of independence.

1972   Ugandan ruler Idi Imin expels 50,000 Ugandan Asians.

1975   Communist victory in Vietnam leads to exodus of 'boat people' to other countries of South-East Asia.

1979   Soviet invasion of Afghanistan leads to an estimated 2 million Afghan refugees in camps in Pakistan.
        Thousands of refugees flee Cambodia for Thailand following Vietnamese invasion to end Pol Pot regime; Red Cross estimates 2 million people in danger inside and outside Cambodia as a result of disruption.

1980   Relief agencies report two million refugees in East Africa, mainly in Somalia, Ethiopia and Sudan, as a result of war and drought. Somalia estimated to have biggest refugee problem in the world and a million refugees have fled to Sudan from Ethiopia, Zaïre, Chad and Uganda.

1985   Massive drought in East Africa uproots millions of people.

1987   400,000 refugees flee from Somalia to Ethiopia to escape fighting.

1989   Opening of Hungarian part of 'iron curtain' with Austria permits start of exodus of East Europeans to West. This gathers momentum with the lifting of similar restrictions in Czechoslovakia, East Germany, etc. and the symbolic opening of the Brandenburg Gate in December 1989.

1991   From the introduction of passports (July 1990) to the first free elections (Mar. 1991), more than 56,000 Albanians emigrate from their home country. The Greek and Italian authorities turn the majority of the emigrants back to Albania. Approximately 1.5–2 million Kurds escape from Saddam Hussein's Iraq to neighbouring Turkey and Iran. After the Gulf War, approximately 300,000 Palestinians are expelled from Kuwait because they are accused of having collaborated with the invaders.

1992   By the end of the year, 650,000 (among them 300,000 Bosnian) refugees have moved to Croatia.

1993   According to official statistics, from April 1991, 500,000 Serbs emigrated from various parts of the former Yugoslavia to Serbia (Nov.).

1994   An estimated 330,000 Rwandan refugees are believed to have fled the country (April).

1996   400,000 refugees flee from South Lebanon (April). Several thousand Kurdish refugees flee to Iran (Sept.). 400,000 Rwandan refugees begin to return to their country (Nov.).

1998   Exodus from Indonesia (hit by financial collapse) to Malaysia.

The environment and pollution: major events since 1945

1945   First atomic explosions in New Mexico and at Hiroshima and Nagasaki.

1946   First nuclear test at Bikini Atoll in the Marshall Islands.

1952–53   First hydrogen bomb tests in the Pacific Marshall Islands by the United States, and in Siberia by the USSR.

1952   London 'smog' kills an estimated 4,000 people; beginning of serious action to tackle air pollution in United Kingdom; London declared a smokeless zone (1955); Clean Air Act passed (1956). Britain explodes atomic bomb off Western Australia.

1957   Major radioactive leak at Windscale nuclear plant in Cumbria, Britain.

1959   Treaty for peaceful use of Antarctica opened for signature.

1960   France begins atomic bomb testing in the Sahara.

1961   World Wildlife Fund opened.

1962   Recognition of the effects of Strontium 90.

1967   *Torrey Canyon* oil spillage off south-western Britain reveals first major concern with effects of pollution on marine environment. Treaty banning nuclear weapons from space.

1971   Sea-bed Treaty prohibits the emplacement of nuclear weapons on the sea-bed. Friends of the Earth founded.

1972   UN Conference on the Human Environment held at Stockholm.

1975   Greenpeace organization founded.

1976   Explosion at chemical plant at Seveso, Italy, releases dioxins into a large area; town evacuated and massive clean-up operation involving removal of thousands of tons of top-soil.

1977   UNESCO sets up fund to save the Acropolis, Athens, from effects of air pollution.

1979   International agreement on transnational air pollution signed. A major nuclear accident in the United States at Three Mile Island, near Harrisburg, Pennsylvania; thousands of gallons of radio-active water and a plume of radio-active gas released. Temporary evacuation of population puts effective end to nuclear power station construction in United States.

1983   First Green deputies elected to West German parliament; first representation of specific environmental party in Western Europe.

1984   240 killed by gas explosion in Mexico (Nov.); explosion at Bhopal, India, and gas leak kills 3,000 people and injures 200,000 more (Dec.).

1986   Explosion at Chernobyl nuclear reactor in USSR spreads radio-active pollution over wide area of the Soviet Union and Western Europe. Population of Chernobyl evacuated and emergency action taken to seal the nuclear core.

1987   Widespread concern about effects of 'acid rain' on Western European forest areas and waters; agreements to reduce some emissions of sulphur dioxide by power stations. Nimbus 7 satellite confirms hole in ozone layer over Antarctica (Oct.).

1988   Widespread deaths of seals in North Sea from viral infection claimed as result of growing pollution. Explosion from leak in trans-Siberian pipeline in the Urals, USSR, kills several thousand people in railway trains. International recognition of global climatic change in depletion of 'ozone layer' and 'greenhouse effect'. First measures to reduce use of harmful CFC gases and to encourage further research.

1989   Massive spillage from oil-tanker *Exxon Valdez* off Alaska contaminates large area of coastline. Euro-elections show continued

·   growth of Green Movement as a political force. Crippled
Iranian oil-tanker *Kharg V* creates 260 square km oil slick off
coast of Morocco (Dec.).

1991   Iraq pours oil into the Persian Gulf which threatens the Gulf's
living creatures with extinction (Jan.). Iraq sets 500 of the 950
Kuwaiti oil wells on fire in the war; the consequences can be
felt even in Europe (Feb.). Because of an explosion on board
the tanker *Haven*, 50,000 tons of oil flow into the ocean off
the shores of Guinea (April).

1993   When the Liberian tanker *Braer* sinks, 85,000 tons of oil flow
into the sea off the shores of Scotland. In Rio de Janeiro –
under the auspices of the UN – an environment world conference is held, with representatives from 178 countries parti-
cipating (June). The break-down of the ozone layer protecting
the Earth from ultraviolet radiation becomes more and more
severe.

1997   Tokyo summit agrees reduction of gases harmful to the earth's
atmosphere.
Smog from forest fires casts pall over south-east Asia.

1998   Forest fires out of control in Amazonia.

SECTION FOUR

Biographies

Abbas, Ferhat (1899–1985): Algerian nationalist. One of the leaders of the Algerian independence movement. Prime Minister of the provisional government-in-exile in Tunisia, 1958–61. President of the National Assembly, 1962–63, after independence, but after mounting differences with Ben Bella he resigned.

Acheampong, Ignatius Kutu (1931–   ): Ghanaian military leader who led the coup which overthrew Kofi Busia (q.v.) in 1972. He became Chairman of the National Redemption Council government with responsibility also for defence and finance. On 9 October 1975 he became Chairman of the Supreme Military Council. He was deposed in the coup of July 1978.

Acheson, Dean (1893–1971): American statesman. As US Secretary of State from 1949 to 1955 played a key role in establishing NATO (q.v.) and in formulating American policy during the Korean War (q.v.).

Adenauer, Konrad (1876–1967): German statesman. Mayor of Cologne, 1917–33. Removed by Nazis. Prominent member of Catholic Centre Party in Weimar Republic. President of Prussian State Council, 1920–33. Twice imprisoned by Nazis. Founded Christian Democratic Union, 1945. Elected first Chancellor of Federal Republic, 1949; re-elected 1953, 1957. Also Foreign Minister, 1951–55. Negotiated German entry into NATO, EEC. Established diplomatic relations with USSR, 1955. Resigned 1963.

Agnew, Spiro (1918–96): Vice-President of the United States, 1969–73. Republican politician, distinguished only as Nixon's (q.v.) surprise running-mate (chosen to secure the Southern vote) and also for his forced resignation in 1973 over his financial affairs.

Allende, Salvador (1908–73): A founder member of the Chilean Socialist Party, he became its General Secretary in 1942. In 1945 he was elected to the Senate and served as its Vice-President and President. In 1970, as the candidate for the Popular Unity Front, he was narrowly elected as President. His policies 'to open the road to socialism' included land reforms, nationalization of industry and the mines, and opposition to American economic dominance. Following a worsening economic situation and considerable opposition to these policies, a right-wing military junta, backed by the US, overthrew his government in September 1973. Allende died while being overthrown in the coup.

Amin, Idi (1925–   ): Ugandan dictator. As Uganda's army commander he overthrew the government of Milton Obote (q.v.) on 25 January 1971. His period as dictator (1971–79) was marked by massacres and brutality. In 1972 he ordered the mass expulsion of Asians from Uganda. Fled to Libya in 1979 after his overthrow following a Tanzanian invasion.

Aquino, Corazón (1932–   ): Philippine politician. Entered politics in 1985 following the 1983 assassination of her husband, opposition leader Benigno Aquino. Won 1986 Presidential election despite rigging attempt by Marcos (q.v.). Pro-Aquino demonstrations and the withdrawal of US support forced Marcos's flight. Faced five early attempted coups, but success in a 1987 plebiscite confirmed her as President until 1992. A further coup attempt occurred in 1989.

Arafat, Yasser (1929–   ): Chairman of the PLO (q.v.) since 1969 and head of the Executive Committee of al-Fatah (q.v.) since 1968. Founding member of al-Fatah in 1956 and worked as an engineer in Kuwait between 1957 and 1965. He steered the PLO in a moderate direction following the October 1973 War, leading ultimately to successful talks which led to the creation of a Palestinian Authority, of which he became Chairman and Minister of the Interior in May 1994. He became President of the Palestine Legislative Council in 1996. Accused by Israel of being soft on his own militants, his efforts to achieve peace were opposed by Hamas (q.v.) and Islamic Jihad who continued terrorist action against Israeli settlers.

Assad, Hafez Ali (1928–   ): President of Syria since 1971; he has shown extraordinary political longevity for a Syrian ruler. He is a member of the Ba'ath Party (q.v.) and became Defence Minister and Commander of the Air Force in 1966. In 1970 mounted a coup which placed him in office. He has ruled an authoritarian regime opposed to the state of Israel, but which was worsted in the October 1973 War. His support for terrorists led to a breach with the West in the mid-1980s but he has recently played the role of power-broker to end the civil war in Lebanon, to secure the release of Western hostages, and sided with the West in the Gulf War of 1992. His co-operation with the West since the break-up of the Soviet Union has been one of the key factors in leading to a Middle East settlement.

Attlee, Clement Richard, 1st Earl Attlee (1883–1967): Elected leader of the Labour Party in 1935. In the war-time coalition government he took office as Lord Privy Seal, 1940–42, Secretary for the Dominions, 1942–43 and Lord President of the Council, 1943–45. He was Deputy Prime Minister, 1943–45 and Prime Minister from 1945 to 1951. As Labour Prime Minister he presided over an active and able Cabinet which introduced the National Health Service, comprehensive social welfare and nationalized many basic industries. He presided over the granting of independence to India, Pakistan, Ceylon (Sri Lanka) and Burma (Myanmar), the British withdrawal from Palestine and the onset of the Cold War.

Ayub Khan, Mohammed (1907–74): Commander-in-Chief of the Pakistani army and Minister of Defence from 1954 to 1955. He became President in 1958. He was re-elected in January 1965, but after widespread strikes and riots, especially in East Pakistan, he resigned in March 1969.

Azikiwe, Mhamdi (1904–96): Premier of Eastern Nigeria from 1954 to 1959, he became Nigeria's Governor-General in 1960 after independence. When Nigeria became a Republic on 1 October 1963 he was its first President. He was deposed in a military coup which occurred while he was in Britain in January 1966.

Balewa, Sir Abubakar Tafawa (1912–66): Nigerian statesman. The first federal Prime Minister of independent Nigeria, 1960–66. On 15 January 1966 he was murdered in a military *coup d'état.*

Banda, Hastings Kamazu (1906–97): African nationalist. Practised as a doctor in Britain and Ghana before returning to Nyasaland, where he became President-General of the African National Congress in 1958. Riots led to the declaration of a state of emergency, and the arrest of Banda. He was released in April 1960 and became leader of the Malawi Congress Party and first Prime Minister on independence. He was President of Malawi for three decades after independence.

Bandaranaike, Mrs Sirimavo (1916–   ): Sri Lankan politician. Prime Minister, 1960–65, the first woman Prime Minister. Prime Minister again from 1970 to 1977, and since 1994; responsible for the 1972 constitution by which Ceylon became the Republic of Sri Lanka.

Batista, Fulgencio (1901–73): Cuban politician. Army sergeant. Joined a coup against President Machado in 1933, took rank of colonel and attempted to develop a fascist state. Allowed formation of opposition parties, 1937; elected President, 1939. Voluntary exile in Dominican Republic, 1944. Returned as dictator after coup, 1952. Increasingly unpopular with the army and harried by guerrilla forces under Fidel Castro (q.v.), he fled from Cuba in 1958.

Begin, Menachem (1913–92): Israeli politician. Prime Minister, 1977–83. Became Prime Minister of Israel when his right-wing Likud alignment won a greater number of seats than any other political party in the May 1977 elections. However, since Likud did not gain a majority, it was necessary to form a coalition with other groups represented in Parliament. Begin had commanded the Irgun, a terrorist group operating first against the British in the 1940s. After independence he led the Herut party which became part of the Likud group. He was minister without portfolio in the National Unity government formed just before the Six Day War. He opposed any withdrawal from the West Bank but presided over relaxation of tension with Egypt. Joint recipient of Nobel Peace Prize with Sadat (q.v.) in 1978.

Ben Bella, Mohammed Ahmed (1916–   ): Algerian revolutionary leader. Imprisoned by French for political activities, 1950; escaped in 1952. Founded and led *Front de la Libération Nationale* (FLN) in armed struggle against France, 1954. Arrested in 1956, he was freed under terms of Evian Agreements in 1962 to become Algerian President. Overthrown in 1965 and under house arrest till 1979.

Beneš, Eduard (1884–1948): Czech statesman. Worked with Masaryk in Paris during First World War, seeking Czech independence. Principal Czech representative at Paris Peace Conference. Prime Minister, 1921–22, Foreign Minister, 1918–35. Active diplomat, chief proponent of Little Entente (Czechoslovakia, Romania and Yugoslavia, with French support). President of League of Nations Assembly, 1935. Succeeded Masaryk as President, 1935. Resigned, 1938, following Munich Agreement. President of Czech government-in-exile in London, 1941–45. Re-elected president, 1946. Resigned shortly after Communist coup, 1948.

Ben Gurion, David (1886–1973): Zionist leader. Chairman of the Jewish Agency, 1935–48. Proclaimed the independence of the state of Israel and subsequently became its first Prime Minister (1948–53). He was a key figure in the creation of the modern democratic state of Israel.

Beria, Lavrenti Pavlovich (1899–1953): Soviet secret police chief. Bolshevik organizer in Russian Revolution. Led secret police in Georgia, 1921–31. First Secretary of Georgian Communist Party, 1931. Appointed by Stalin (q.v.) to head Commissariat for Internal Security (NKVD), 1938–53. Deputy Prime Minister, 1941. Politburo member, 1946. Arrested and executed by rivals in Party power struggle following Stalin's death.

Berlusconi, Silvio (1936–   ): Italian politician. Originally a business tycoon, the owner of the Fininvest group (with massive TV and newspaper interests, real estate, etc., and ownership of the AC Milan football club). Founder of *Forza Italia*. Headed right-wing alliance which won March 1994 election. Became Prime Minister and survived a Senate confidence vote on 18 May; pro free market, anti immigration and pro decentralization, his government fell from power in December 1994 and he then faced charges of corruption.

Bernadotte, Count Folke (1895–1948): Swedish Red Cross president and United Nations mediator. Arranged exchanges of wounded Allied and German prisoners, 1943–44. Involved by Himmler in rejected peace approaches to Western Allies, January 1945. Appointed UN mediator between Arabs and Jews in Palestine. May 1948. Assassinated by Jewish terrorists, September 1948.

Bhutto, Benazir (1953–   ): Pakistani politician; Prime Minister, 1988–90, 1993–96. American and Oxford-educated daughter of Zulfikar Ali Bhutto (see below). She returned from exile in 1986 and became premier following the Pakistan People's Party success in the November 1988 elections. She was dismissed for alleged corruption in August 1990 against a growing background of violence and military influence, but in 1993 formed a new coalition government. Renewed violence, strikes and charges of corruption overshadowed her attempts to seek rapprochement with India and ease militant Islamic tensions. She was dismissed again in November 1996, followed by the resounding defeat of her Pakistan People's Party by the Muslim League in the February 1997 elections.

Bhutto, Zulfikar Ali (1928–79): Pakistani politician. Appointed Prime Minister in December 1971 after India's victory over Pakistan. As Foreign Minister, 1963–66, he had favoured close links with China and urged a tough line with India over the disputed state of Kashmir. After a period marked by political and social reforms, he was ousted from power in 1977. Executed in 1979; his daughter, Benazir Bhutto, became Prime Minister nine years later.

Biko, Steve Bantu (1946–73): South African black nationalist leader. Medical student. Helped found South African Students' Organization in 1968, becoming its President, and the Black People's Convention. Organized Black Community Programme to encourage black pride and opposition to apartheid. Banned by South African government, 1973. Death in police custody aroused international condemnation.

Botha, Pieter Willem (1916–   ): South African politician. Entered National Party government in 1958. Held a number of posts, becoming party leader and Prime Minister in 1978. He became state President in 1984. His policy of modifying apartheid failed to satisfy black aspirations and international opinion but increasingly alienated his own right wing. Relinquished party leadership following a stroke in January 1989, retaining presidency until his angry resignation, August 1989. Resigned from National Party, May 1990, in protest at talks with ANC.

Boumediene, Colonel Houari (1925–78): Algerian Prime Minister and head of government, 1965–78. Ousted Ben Bella (q.v.) from power in 1965. From 1960 to 1962 he was chief-of-staff of the Algerian forces fighting for independence from France. In 1962, after independence, he became Defence Minister and Vice Premier, 1963–65.

Bourguiba, Habib (1902–   ): President of Tunisia, 1957–88. A leading Tunisian nationalist, in 1934 he formed the Neo-Destour Party which was outlawed by France. He spent several years in prison during the struggle for independence. Bourguiba has favoured close relations with the West. In 1975 he was elected President for Life. Deposed in 1988 after he became increasingly senile.

Brandt, Willy (1913–92): West German Social Democratic statesman. Active in opposition to Hitler. Member of Bundestag, 1949–57. President of Bundesrat, 1955–57. Mayor of West Berlin, 1957–66. Chairman of Social Democratic Party, 1964. Joined coalition with Christian Democrats under Chancellor Kiesinger, 1966. Chancellor in SPD–Free Democrat coalition, 1969. Awarded Nobel Peace Prize, 1971. Resigned following spy scandal, 1974, remaining Chairman of SPD. Consistent advocate of improved relations with Eastern Europe ('*Ostpolitik*').

Brezhnev, Leonid Ilyich (1906–82): Soviet politician. Communist Party official in Ukraine and Moldavia. Held military posts, 1933–34. Member of Praesidium of Supreme Soviet, 1952–57. President of Praesidium, 1960–64, succeeding Marshal Voroshilov. Succeeded Khrushchev as First Secretary of Central Committee, 1964. General Secretary of Central Committee, 1966. Chairman of Praesidium, 1977.

Bunche, Ralph (1904–71): United Nations official. Academic turned State Department official. Involved in establishing the United Nations; Director of Trusteeship Division, 1947; UN Under-Secretary, 1955–71. First black American to be awarded Nobel Peace Prize for work in Palestine, 1950. Led UN peace-keeping operations in Suez (1956), the Congo (1960) and Cyprus (1964).

Bush, George Herbert Walker (1924–   ): 41st President of the United States. Republican politician. Gained lengthy experience as Vice-President, 1981–89, serving under Reagan (q.v.). The first Vice-President to be elected President since Martin van Buren in 1836. Inherited Reagan's legacy of massive budget deficit, a drugs crisis and external problems in Panama. Bush ordered the December 1989 invasion of Panama to overthrow the Noriega (q.v.) regime and seize the dictator. He successfully negotiated the end of the Cold War with Gorbachev (q.v.) and successfully pursued the Gulf War against Saddam Hussein (q.v.) in 1992. Lack of identifiable policies to woo the electorate and budgetary crises led to the victory of Clinton (q.v.) in the 1992 election.

Busia, Kofi Abrefa (1913–78): Nigerian politician. After the deposition of Nkrumah (q.v.) in 1966 he was made adviser to the National Liberation Council. On 1 October 1969 he became Prime Minister when power

was handed over to civilian government again. His government encouraged the Africanization of foreign firms. On 13 January 1972 he was
overthrown by the military and went into voluntary exile.

Caetano, Marcelo (1906–80): Portuguese politician. Minister under Salazar
(q.v.) in the 1940s and 1950s; retired to academic life in 1959. Following
Salazar's retirement was Prime Minister, 1966–74. Attempted liberalization, but its limited nature and his failure to resolve colonial wars in
Angola and Mozambique led to 1974 revolution and his exile.

Carter, James Earl (Jimmy) (1924–   ): 39th US President. Democrat Senator for Georgia, 1962–66. Elected Governor of Georgia 1971. Defeated
Ford (q.v.) in Presidential election, 1976. Negotiated Panama Canal
Treaty, treaty between Egypt and Israel at Camp David (see p. 225) and
the unratified SALT II. Weakened by bad relations with Congress, failure to surmount world oil crisis and economic recession. Bungled rescue
attempt of American Embassy hostages in Iran contributed to defeat by
Reagan (q.v.) in Presidential election, 1980. He has subsequently played
a major part in peace initiatives around the world.

Castro, Fidel (1927–   ): Cuban revolutionary leader. Prime Minister
since 1959. Formerly a lawyer, he was imprisoned in 1953 for an attack
on an army barracks in Cuba. Following his release during an amnesty,
he went to Mexico and organized the Cuban revolutionary movement.
After attempts in 1956 and 1958, the rebels finally occupied Havana in
1959 and overthrew President Batista. He became Prime Minister and
head of the armed forces on 16 February 1959. A Marxist, he instituted
reforms in agriculture, industry and education and broke away from
American economic dominance. In 1961 he routed an invasion of US-
supported exiles at the Bay of Pigs (q.v.). The following year his acceptance of Russian help and the installation of Soviet rockets led to the
so-called 'Cuban missile crisis'. In 1976 he became head of State and
President of the Council of State, but has faced increasing economic
difficulties since the cutting off of Soviet aid following the breakup of
the Soviet Union.

Ceauçescu, Nicolae (1918–89): Romanian dictator. Member of underground Communist Party, 1936. Party Secretariat member, 1954. Deputy
leader, 1957–65. General Secretary, 1965. Head of State, 1967. Combined independent foreign policy, notably criticism of the 1968 Warsaw
Pact invasion of Czechoslovakia, with authoritarian regime, massive repression and personality cult. Repressed demonstrations prompted by
economic crisis, 1967. Showed little sympathy for the Soviet line instituted by Gorbachev (q.v.). His corrupt regime and bankrupt economy

provoked riots in 1989. Their savage repression led to the December 1989 'winter revolution' (see p. 276). Executed by firing squad after secret trial, 25 December 1989.

Chernomyrdin, Viktor (1938–   ): Russian prime minister from 1992 to April 1998. Joined the Communist Party in 1961 and was a Central Committee functionary, 1978–83. He was a Deputy Minister from 1983 to 1985, when he was appointed Gas Minister. Member of the centrist Civic Union, which advocates gradual change, with the state playing a major role. He supported Yeltsin against the September 1993 constitutional coup but was dismissed by him in April 1998.

Chiang Kai-shek (1887–1975): Chinese general and statesman. He took part in the 1911 Chinese revolution and became chief-of-staff to the revolutionary leader Sun Yat-sen. In 1928 he became commander of the Guomindang army and head of the government established at Nanking. His forces fought local war-lords, Japanese invaders and communists. He led the government during the Second World War but in 1949 was defeated by the communists and retired to Formosa (Taiwan), from where he continued to lead the Nationalist government until 1975.

Chiluba, Frederick (1933–   ): President of Zambia since 1991. He became chairman of the Zambia Congress of Trade Unions in 1974 and was a leading opponent of the one-party state of President Kaunda (q.v.), becoming leader of the Movement for Parliamentary Democracy (MPD) formed in July 1991. He was elected to the presidency in November 1991.

Chou En-lai, (1898–1976): Chinese communist leader. He organized the revolt in Shanghai in 1927, established a partnership with Mao in 1931 and took part in the Long March of 1934–35. After talks with Chiang Kai-shek (q.v.) to establish a coalition failed, he became Prime Minister and Foreign Minister of the new China in 1949. During the Cultural Revolution he used his influence to restrain extremists. He died in office in January 1976.

Chrétien, (Joseph Jacques) Jean (1934–   ): Canadian politician and lawyer. Prime Minister since October 1993. Liberal politician with extensive ministerial experience. Secretary of State for External Affairs and Deputy Prime Minister, June–September 1984. First elected to Commons in 1963.

Churchill, Sir Winston (1874–1965): British statesman. Conservative MP, 1900–4. Became a Liberal in protest at Tariff Reform policies. Liberal MP, 1906–8, 1908–22. Constitutionalist, later Conservative MP, 1924–

45. Conservative MP for Woodford, 1945–64. Under-secretary at Colonial Office, 1906–8. President of the Board of Trade, 1908–10. Home Secretary, 1910–11. First Lord of the Admiralty, 1911–15. Chancellor of the Duchy of Lancaster, 1915. Minister of Munitions, 1917–19. Secretary for War and Air, 1919–21. Secretary for Air and Colonies, 1921. Colonial Secretary, 1921–22. Chancellor of the Exchequer, 1924–29. First Lord of the Admiralty, 1939–40. Prime Minister and Minister of Defence, 1940–45. Leader of the Opposition, 1945–51. Prime Minister, 1951–55. Minister of Defence, 1951–52. Knighted, 1953. Resigned 1955. Chequered career. During First World War was involved in disputes over Admiralty policy and Gallipoli campaign. Opposed Conservative policies over India and rearmament during 1930s. Advocated prevention of German expansion. War-time leadership earned him legendary status, though not returned to power in 1945. Negotiated war-time alliance with the United States and USSR. After Second World War, favoured alliance with the United States against USSR.

Clinton, William Jefferson (Bill) (1946–   ): 42nd President of the United States, having defeated George Bush in the November 1992 presidential elections. Inaugurated in January 1993. Governor of Arkansas, 1979–80 and 1983–92. His immediate policy concerns as his administration began were the economy, the health-care system and foreign trade. His first administration suffered several setbacks – the failure of health-care reform, the advent of the right-wing Republican 'Contract with America', the widespread mid-term Democratic losses of 1994 and the continuing allegations arising from the Whitewater affair. His wife, Hillary, played an important political role. Re-elected in November 1996 (defeating Republican Bob Dole) he faced but survived numerous scandals.

Collor de Mello, Fernando (1950–   ): President of Brazil, 1990–92. Elected mayor of Maceió in 1979, federal deputy for Alagoas in 1982, state governor in 1986. Left the Brazilian Democratic Movement (PMDB) to form the National Renovation Party as a vehicle for his presidential ambitions. He campaigned in 1990 pledging to end inflation, poverty and corruption. Despite his initial radical rhetoric, poverty, crime and inflation all increased during his period in office. He resigned in December 1992 following a congressional investigation into his and his family's alleged involvement in corruption.

Cuellar, Pérez de: *See* Pérez de Cuellar

D'Aubuisson, Roberto (1943–92): El Salvador politician, founder of the right-wing Arena party. He joined the National Guard, moving to the armed forces general command in 1975. Dismissed following alleged involvement with right-wing paramilitary organizations, d'Aubuisson went into exile in Guatemala. He was acquitted on charges of attempting a coup in El Salvador in 1980. He formed Arena (Alianza Republicana Nacionalista) in 1981 and was President of the National Assembly from 1982 to 1983. He won 46% of the votes in the 1984 presidential election, his party gaining control of the National Assembly in 1988. He was unable to gain financial support for the 1988 presidential campaign because of persistent allegations of his involvement in political murders.

Dayan, Moshe (1915–81): Israeli politician and defence chief. Foreign Secretary under Begin, 1978–79. Defence Minister between 1967 and 1974, he was blamed for being caught unprepared when the 1973 October War came. From 1953 to 1957 he was chief-of-staff of the Israeli Defence Forces. He left the army to be active in the Labour Party and he served as the Agriculture Minister from 1959 to 1964. A member of Ben Gurion's faction, he left the Labour Party with Ben Gurion (q.v.) in 1965 but rejoined the government after the 1967 Arab–Israeli War. He opposed the return of the Arab territory occupied in 1967.

de Gaulle, Charles (1890–1970): French soldier and statesman. Member of French military mission to Poland, 1919–20. Lectured at Staff College. Sought to modernize Army. Published 'The Army of the Future', 1932–34. Ideas subsequently employed by German Army. Briefly a member of Reynaud's government, 1940. Fled to Britain after fall of France. Became head of Committee of National Liberation ('Free French'), 1943. Claimed status of head of government. Led unsuccessful attempt to recapture Dakar. Entered Paris, August 1944. President of provisional government, 1945. Suspected of authoritarian ambitions. Resigned, 1946. Founded political group *Rassemblement du Peuple Français* (RPF), retiring from its leadership in 1953. During Algerian Crisis, 1958, invited by President Coty to form temporary government with wide executive powers. Won overwhelming victory in referendum on new Constitution. Elected first President of Fifth Republic, 1959. Granted independence to former French colonies in Africa, 1959–60. Granted Algeria independence, 1962. Developed independent nuclear deterrent. Encouraged closer ties with Federal Germany. Twice vetoed British entry to EEC, 1962–63. 1967. Re-elected on second ballot, 1965. Re-elected after May 1968 'Events', but resigned in 1969, following opposition to his plans to reform Constitution.

de Valera, Eamon (1882–1975): Irish statesman. Led group of Irish volunteers in Easter Rising, 1916. Imprisoned, released 1917. Elected MP, 1917. Leader of Sinn Fein, 1917–26. Elected president of Dáil Eireann. Opposed 1921 treaty with Britain. Led extreme nationalists during Civil War, 1922–23. Leader of Fianna Fail, winning 1932 elections. Between

1932 and 1938 reduced links with Britain. After 1937, Prime Minister under revised Constitution. Maintained Irish neutrality during Second World War. Lost power, 1948. Re-elected, 1951–54, 1957–59. President, 1959–73.

Deng Xiaoping (1904–97): Veteran Chinese politician. Secretary-General of the Chinese Communist Party. Purged during the Cultural Revolution, but reinstated in 1973. Fell from power again, 1976. Reinstated and led attack on 'Gang of Four'. Ordered army to attack democracy gathering in Tiananmen Square, June 1989. Retired from sole remaining formal Communist Party post, November 1989, though retained considerable backstairs influence until his death. Seen as the architect of economic transformation in China to a form of 'totalitarian capitalism'.

Desai, Morarji (1896–   ): Indian politician. Long-serving Congress politician. Deputy Prime Minister, 1967. Out of favour with Indira Gandhi (q.v.). Formed Janata Party, leading it to victory in March 1977 general election. Became Prime Minister of India at the age of 81.

d'Estaing, Valéry Giscard (1926–   ): French politician. National Assembly member, 1956–74. Led Independent Republicans. Finance Minister, 1962–74. Defeated Gaullist and Left opponents in Presidential election, 1974. Gaullist backing gave him a National Assembly majority but this weakened in the face of scandals, including one over gifts received from Central African President, Bokassa. Defeated in Presidential election by Mitterrand (q.v.), 1981.

Diem, Ngo Dinh: *See* Ngo Dinh Diem

Dubček, Alexander (1921–92): Czech politician. First Secretary of the Czechoslovak Communist Party and key figure in the 'Prague Spring' (q.v.) reform movement, which culminated in the Soviet invasion of Czechoslovakia in August 1968; dismissed from his post, he was first President of the New Federal Assembly (August 1968–September 1969) then ambassador to Turkey (December 1969–June 1970) before being expelled from the Communist Party. This attempt to build a national socialism with a 'human face' posed a threat to Soviet control of Eastern Europe. By 1989, however, circumstances had changed. In December 1989 Dubček was elected Chairman (Speaker) of the Czech parliament.

Dulles, John Foster (1888–1959): American Secretary of State, 1953–59. An advocate of a hard line against Communism, his foreign policy was obdurately opposed to negotiation with Russia and to American recognition of Communist China. Strongly opposed the Anglo–French invasion of Egypt in 1956 – the 'Suez Crisis' (q.v.). *See also* massive retaliation.

Eden, Sir Robert Anthony, 1st Earl of Avon (1897–1977): Conservative politician. Eden sat as Conservative MP for Warwick and Leamington from 1925 until he retired in 1957. He acted as parliamentary private secretary to Sir Austen Chamberlain (Foreign Secretary), 1926–29, was Under-secretary at the Foreign Office, 1931–33, Lord Privy Seal, 1934–35, minister without portfolio for League of Nations Affairs, 1935 and Foreign Secretary 1935–38. In 1938 he resigned in protest at the government's policy of appeasement. War-time Foreign Secretary, 1940–45. From 1942 to 1945 he was also Leader of the Commons. He returned to the Foreign Office in 1951 and remained there until 1955. He was Prime Minister from 1955 to 1957, resigning in 1957 because of ill-health. Eden was an extremely experienced diplomat but he miscalculated domestic and world opinion when authorizing the ill-fated invasion of Suez in 1956.

Eisenhower, Dwight David (1890–1969): American statesman and military commander. After the Japanese attack on Pearl Harbor on 7 December, 1941, he became assistant chief-of-staff in charge of the Operations division in Washington. He was in command of the European theatre of operations in 1942, and successively Commander of the Allied forces in north Africa, 1942–44, Supreme Commander of the Allied Expeditionary Force in the Western Zone of Europe, 1944–45, Commander of the US Occupation Zone in Germany in 1945, Chief of Staff of the United States Army, 1945–48, and Supreme Commander of the North Atlantic Treaty Forces in Europe, 1950–52. In 1952, Eisenhower won the Republican nomination for the Presidency, and then the Presidency itself. In September 1955 he suffered a severe heart attack, and in June 1956 underwent a serious operation for intestinal disorder. He nevertheless secured re-election in November 1956. He was succeeded in office by President John F. Kennedy (q.v.) in February 1961.

Faisal, Abdul Aziz Saud Al- (1905–75): King of Saudi Arabia. After filling various government posts he became Crown Prince and Prime Minister in 1953. He competed with King Saud for power and between 1958 and 1964, when Saud was deposed, he had full control of the Saudi government. In 1964 he was proclaimed king. A conservative monarch, he had no sympathy with radical Arab regimes and maintained close relations with the United States. It was under his rule that Saudi Arabia first claimed huge profits from oil and began to use that resource for political purposes.

Farouk, King (1920–65): King of Egypt, 1936–52. His attempts at land reform and economic development failed in the face of institutional corruption. Appointed increasingly anti-British governments, 1944–52. Egypt's military failure against Israel in 1948 and Farouk's personal extravagance led to his overthrow and exile, 1952.

Ford, Gerald Rudolph (1913–   ): 38th US President. Michigan Republican Congressman, 1948–73. Nixon's Vice-President on resignation of Agnew (q.v.), 1973. Appointed President following Nixon's resignation over the Watergate scandal, 1974. Unique in holding both offices without election. Pardoned Nixon and amnestied Vietnam War draft evaders, 1974. Defeated by Carter (q.v.) in Presidential election, 1976.

Franco, Francisco (1892–1975): Spanish soldier and military dictator. Held command of Foreign Legion in Morocco. Chief-of-Staff, 1935. Governor of Canaries, 1936. On outbreak of Civil War, integrated Foreign Legion and Moorish troops into rebel army. Became leader of nationalist forces, 1936. Defeated Republican Government, 1939. Established corporatist, authoritarian state, acting as 'Caudillo' (Leader), and ruling Spain as absolutist leader until his death.

Fujimori, Alberto (1939–   ); President of Peru from 1990. Born of Japanese immigrant parents, he was a university rector with no political experience before becoming the independent Cambio '90 group's 1990 presidential election candidate. Instituted an austerity programme to deal with Peru's inflation and debt crisis. In April 1992 he closed parliament and began ruling with military backing. His New Majority–Cambio '90 coalition emerged as the leading party in November 1992 elections to a Democratic Constituent Congress to replace parliament and draft a new constitution.

Galtieri, Lieut.-Gen. Leopoldo Fortunato (1926–   ): Argentinian dictator, December 1981 to June 1982. President of Argentina during the invasion of the Falklands (Malvinas) in May 1982. The military failure of the policy led to his removal in June 1982.

Gandhi, Indira (1917–84): The daughter of Nehru (q.v.), she joined the Congress Party in 1938. In 1964 she became Minister of Information and in 1966 succeeded Shastri, becoming India's first woman Prime Minister. She survived temporary expulsion from the party leadership in 1969 and in 1971 was re-elected. In 1975 a crisis developed when the High Court declared her election invalid. This led to the declaration of a state of emergency. Her unpopular measures resulted in an overwhelming defeat for the Congress Party in the March 1977 elections and the loss of her seat. This loss of power was only temporary. Returned as Prime Minister in 1980. Assassinated by Sikh extremists, 1984. Succeeded by her son, Rajiv (q.v.).

Gandhi, Mohandas (Mahatma) (1869–1948): Indian patriot, social reformer and moral teacher. He lived in South Africa from 1893 to 1914, before returning to India to lead the independence movement. He was a dominating influence in Congress with his policies of non-violence and civil disobedience and was frequently arrested. After independence he continued his fight to rid India of the caste system and to unite Hindu and Muslim, but was assassinated in 1948 on his way to a prayer meeting.

Gandhi, Rajiv (1944–91): Indian politician. An airline pilot, he entered politics on the death in 1981 of his elder brother, Sanjay. Held a number of offices under his mother, Indira Gandhi, before succeeding her as Prime Minister at her assassination, 1984. Despatched troops to Sri Lanka to quell militant Tamil separatists, 1987. Defeated by a relatively united opposition in December 1989 elections, he was assassinated while electioneering in May 1991.

Giap, Vo Nguyen (1912–86): Vietnamese general who defeated the French at Dien Bien Phu (q.v.). Withstood American intervention in the Vietnam War which followed. Deputy Prime Minister and Commander-in-Chief, North Vietnam.

Gorbachev, Mikhail (1931–   ): Soviet statesman who succeeded Chernenko as General Secretary of the Communist Party in 1985. His advent to power after a succession of ailing, old-guard leaders marked a major departure in the Soviet leadership. Succeeded Gromyko as President, 1988. His reforming policies, especially *perestroika* and *glasnost* were increasingly threatened by nationalism in such areas as Azerbaijan and the Baltic. His policy of non-interference was vital in the 1989 revolutions in Eastern Europe which overthrew the old Communist regimes. Became Executive President, 1990, but faced increasing opposition as his reform programme became bogged down and nationalist forces grew in strength. In August 1991 a coup against him, though defeated, completely undermined his authority and led to the break-up of the Soviet Union and the formation of the Commonwealth of Independent States (q.v.). Overshadowed by the rise of Yeltsin (q.v.), he resigned as President in December 1991.

Gowon, Yakubu (1934–   ): Nigerian officer and politician. Heal of Federal Military Government, 1966–75. On 29 July 1966 he became Head of State of Nigeria and Commander-in-Chief of the army, following a coup which overthrew the regime of General Ironsi. He led the federal troops in the civil war (1967–70) but was overthrown in a coup on 29 July 1975.

Grivas, George (1898–1974): Greek army officer. Served in Second World War; supported royalists in Greek Civil War. Led EOKA guerrilla movement in Cyprus from 1953 in fight for independence from Britain and union with Greece (Enosis). Commander of post-independence Greek Cypriot National Guard. Recalled to Greece, 1967. Returned to Cyprus to wage underground struggle for Enosis which alienated Turkish Cypriot community, leading to 1975 Turkish invasion and partition of Cyprus.

Gromyko, Andrei Andreevich (1909–89): Soviet statesman. Attached to Soviet embassy in Washington, 1939. Ambassador in Washington, 1943. Attended Tehran, Yalta and Potsdam Conferences. Elected Deputy of Supreme Soviet, 1946. Became Deputy Foreign Minister, and permanent delegate to United Nations Security Council, using veto frequently. Ambassador to Britain, 1952–53. Foreign Minister, 1957–85. Signed partial nuclear test ban agreement, 1963. President of the USSR, 1985–88.

Guevara, Ernesto (Che) (1928–67): Latin American revolutionary and guerrilla fighter who became a cult figure in the 1960s. Che Guevara was born in Argentina in 1928 and trained as a doctor. He joined Castro's revolutionary army and landed in Cuba in 1956. After the overthrow of Batista in 1959, he acted as a diplomat and administrator in Cuba, and wrote a book analysing the principles and practice of guerrilla warfare. In 1966 he launched a guerrilla campaign in Bolivia, but was captured and executed by Bolivian government forces on 9 October 1967. He became a symbol and martyr for radical students world-wide. His remains were returned to Cuba, 1997.

Haig, Alexander Meigs (1924–   ): American soldier and politician. Brigade commander in Vietnam, 1966–67. President Nixon's military adviser, 1969–73, and White House chief-of-staff, 1973–74. Supreme Allied Commander, NATO Forces Europe, 1974–78, where he survived an assassination attempt. Appointed Reagan's Secretary of State, 1981, he resigned in 1982 after increasing conflict with the administration.

Haile Selassie (1892–1975): Emperor of Ethiopia, 1930–74. He was exiled to Britain, 1936–41, during the Italian occupation. He was an active supporter of Pan-African unity and was a President of the Organization of African Unity (q.v.) whose headquarters are in Addis Ababa. He acted as mediator in the Sudanese and Nigerian civil wars but was himself deposed and stripped of his powers by the army in 1974.

Hammarskjöld, Dag (1905–61): Swedish statesman. Became Secretary-General of the United Nations in 1953. Killed in an air crash while attempting to mediate in the Congo. Posthumously awarded the 1961 Nobel Peace Prize. He previously conducted the UN through the 1956 Suez Crisis with skill and impartiality.

Hassan II (1929–   ): King of Morocco since 1961. Exiled with his father by the French, he returned to Morocco in 1955 and assumed command of the armed forces. He became Prime Minister in 1960. He has survived *coup d'état* and assassination attempts and gradually has assumed wider powers. He has consistently maintained pro-Western policies.

Havel, Václav (1936–   ): President of Czechoslovakia after unanimous election, 29 December 1989, and subsequently of Czech Republic since January 1993. Former dissident and political prisoner. Born Prague; playright; co-founder of Charter 77. Jailed for 4 months. Victim of smear campaign. Jailed again, 1979, for $4\frac{1}{2}$ years for subversion. Co-founder of Civic Forum, November 1989. Reluctantly accepted popular draft as presidential candidate, December 1989.

Heath, Sir Edward (1916–   ): British Conservative politician. Entered Parliament, 1950. Party Whip, 1951–55. Chief Whip, 1955–59. Minister of Labour, 1959–60. Lord Privy Seal, 1960–63. Secretary for Trade and Industry, 1963–64. First leader of Conservative Party to be elected by ballot, 1965. Prime Minister, 1970–74. Proponent of European integration. Achieved British entry into EEC, January 1973. Failed to tackle problems of inflation and industrial relations. Improved British relations with China. Following electoral defeats of 1974, replaced as leader of Party by Margaret Thatcher, 1975. Frequently attacked 'anti-European' policies of Thatcher from back benches.

Hirohito (1901–89): Emperor of Japan. Regent, 1921; survived assassination attempt, 1924; succeeded to throne, 1926. Backed Tojo's urging of war against Britain and the United States, 1941. Threw weight behind those arguing for peace in 1945, accepting Allied unconditional surrender demand in August. Avoided trial as war criminal because General Douglas MacArthur saw him as crucial factor in post-1945 Japanese political stability. Discarded traditional divine status, 1946. Official visits abroad in the 1970s marked recognition of Japan's growing economic status. His culpability in Japan's road to war still disputed by historians.

Ho Chi-minh (1890–1969): Vietnamese nationalist and revolutionary. Leader of the Vietnam revolutionary nationalist party of Indo-China, which struggled for independence from France during and after the Second World War. In 1945 the independent republic of Vietnam was formed with Ho Chi-minh as President. In 1954 the decisive victory over the French at Dien Bien Phu (q.v.) led to the Indo-China armistice and the Geneva Agreements. Holding power until his death in 1969, he succeeded in welding together the elements of nationalism and communism in North Vietnam. Troops were sent against South Vietnam and, largely through his efforts, a unified socialist Vietnam was brought about in 1975.

Hoover, (John) Edgar (1895–1972): Head of US Federal Bureau of Investigation. Lawyer in Department of Justice, 1917. Special assistant to Attorney General, 1919. FBI Assistant Director, 1921; Director, 1924–72, serving under eight Presidents. Reorganized the Bureau, concentrating on gangsters in the 1930s, enemy spies in the 1940s and communist subversion after 1945. His role became increasingly controversial in the 1960s, when the FBI was accused of harassing anti-Vietnam War and black civil rights activists.

Hoxha, Enver (1908–85): Albanian politician. Joint founder and General Secretary of the Albanian Communist Party (now the Albanian Labour Party) from 1941 to 1985. His significance in the international communist movement was his support of China in the Sino–Soviet dispute. He broke diplomatic relations with the USSR in 1961; officially withdrew Albania from the Warsaw Pact in 1968. He kept Albania in isolation under a rigid Stalinist regime.

Hua Kuo-feng (1922–   ): Chinese Communist leader. Rapid rise to power from the obscurity of party secretary in a part of Hunan in 1955 to membership of the Central Committee in 1969 and the Ministry of Public Security. In 1973 he moved up to the politburo. Following Chou's death in January 1976 he was a surprise appointment as acting Prime Minister. This post was confirmed in April. After the death of Chairman Mao in October 1976 he became Chairman of the Central Committee of the Chinese Communist Party.

Hussein, King Ibn Talal (1935–   ): King of Jordan since 1952. Succeeded to the throne upon the abdication of his father. His crown is supported primarily by the tribes and the army as well as subsidies from the United States. His pro-Western sympathies have often been at odds with his more radical neighbours although during the Gulf War (q.v.) he sided with Iraq.

Hussein, Saddam (1937–   ): Iraqi dictator. Born in Takrit, 150 miles north of Baghdad. Joined the Ba'ath Party (q.v.). Involved in October 1959 assassination attempt against Brigadier Qassem. Fled to Egypt, before returning to Syria and entering (by marriage) the Syrian Ba'athist leadership. Became President of Iraq, July 1979. Has run Iraq through a clique of Takriti family relations and by the ruthless use of terror. He has suppressed the Kurds (by use of gas and chemical weapons), launched an enormously bloody war against Iran (see pp. 272–3) and provoked a major crisis by the invasion and annexation of Kuwait in August 1990 (see p. 277). He has continued to flout UN inspection teams monitoring Iraq's weapons of mass destruction.

Jagan, Dr Cheddi (1918–94): Guyanese nationalist. The first Prime Minister of independent Guyana.

Jaruzelski, General Wojciecj (1923–   ): Polish soldier and politician. Long and distinguished army career. Became Chief of General Staff, 1965, Minister of Defence, 1968, and member of Politburo, 1971. Became Prime Minister after resignation of Pinkowski, 1981. Declared martial law in effort to tackle economic crisis and to counter growth of Solidarity (q.v.) movement. Solidarity banned and its leaders detained and tried. Lifted martial law, July 1983. Elected President, 1989, but resigned following the return of multi-party elections.

Jiang Zemin (1926–   ): Chinese Communist leader. As the party leader in Shanghai he was appointed Party Secretary by Deng Xiaoping (q.v.) following the ousting of Zhao Ziyang after the Tiananmen Square massacre. As State President and General Secretary of the Communist Party he has presided over rapid economic modernization and the return of Hong Kong while maintaining political authority in the hands of the party and army.

Jinnah, Mohammed Ali (1876–1948): Pakistani statesman. One of the makers of modern Pakistan. President of the Muslim League. First Governor-General of independent Pakistan.

John Paul II, Pope (1920–   ): Born Karol Wojtyla. Student and actor, 1938. Quarry-worker in German-occupied Poland. Ordained as priest, 1946; appointed bishop, 1958; Archbishop of Cracow, 1964; Cardinal, 1967. In October 1978 elected as first non-Italian Pope since 1552. Doctrinally conservative, an extensive world traveller, his popular appeal much in evidence at mass rallies. Survived assassination attempts in May 1981, when he suffered gunshot wounds, and in 1982.

Johnson, Lyndon Baines (1908–73): 36th President of the United States, 1963–68. Elected to the House of Representatives in 1938 and to the Senate in 1948. Became Democratic leader in the Senate in 1953. Despite suffering a severe heart attack in 1955, he held the post until he became Vice-President of the United States in January, 1961. After completing the presidential term to which the assassinated President Kennedy had been elected, he was nominated to run as Democratic candidate for the presidency in 1964, an election which he won by a large majority.

Because of disenchantment within the Democratic Party over his administration's policies towards Vietnam, he did not run for re-election in 1968. He was succeeded by Richard M. Nixon (q.v.).

Kasavubu, Joseph Ileo (1910–69): Congolese politician who favoured a federal state. He became President in 1960 with Lumumba (q.v.) as Prime Minister after a post-independence election gave neither a majority. He was deposed by the army in November 1965 in a military coup led by Mobutu (q.v.).

Kaunda, Kenneth David (1924–   ): Zambian politician. President of Zambia, 1964–91. As leader of the Zambia National Congress, he was imprisoned for nine months, but released in 1960 and became leader of the United National Independence Party (UNIP). As first President of Zambia, he assumed virtually autocratic powers in 1972 to prevent tribal break-up of the country. After a new constitution his presidency was confirmed and he played a major part in the independence negotiations for both Mozambique and Rhodesia (Zimbabwe). Charges of corruption and authoritarianism undermined his position, leading to the formation of a rival Movement for Multi-Party Democracy which defeated UNIP in elections in 1991 and saw its leader Frederick Chiluba (q.v.) win the Presidential elections, deposing Kaunda. Kaunda returned to politics in 1995, resuming leadership of UNIP though faced by threats of arrest or deportation.

Kennedy, John Fitzgerald (1917–63): American statesman and 35th President of the United States. Born May 1917 in Boston, Massachusetts. The son of Joseph Kennedy, a successful businessman and ambassador to the United Kingdom, and a Roman Catholic. He graduated from Harvard University in 1940 and served in the US Navy. Elected to the House of Representatives in 1946. He defeated Henry Cabot Lodge for one of the Massachusetts Senate seats in 1952, and in November 1960 defeated Richard Nixon (q.v.) in the presidential election by a narrow margin. On 22 November 1963 he was assassinated in Dallas, Texas. A commission under the Chief Justice of the United States Supreme Court, Earl Warren, concluded that he had been killed by one Lee Harvey Oswald, acting alone. He was succeeded by the Vice-President, Lyndon Baines Johnson, on the afternoon of his death. His short period as President witnessed the Cuban Missile Crisis. His style and charisma made him one of the most admired and popular presidents of modern times.

Kennedy, Robert Francis (1925–68): American politician. Presidential campaign manager for his brother, John F. Kennedy, 1960. US Attorney General, emphasizing civil rights and investigating institutionalized crime,

1961–64. Democratic Senator for New York, 1965–68. Assassinated in Los Angeles, June 1968, while campaigning for Democratic presidential nomination on black rights and anti-Vietnam War platform.

Kenyatta, Mzee Jomo (1893–1978): Kenyan national leader. President of Kenya, 1964–78. In 1952 he was arrested on suspicion of leading the Mau Mau rebellion (q.v.) and sentenced to seven years' imprisonment followed by detention. He was released in 1961 and as President of the Kenya African National Union became Prime Minister in 1963 and President in December 1964.

Keynes, John Maynard, 1st Baron Keynes (1883–1946): British economist. Worked at Treasury during First World War. Chief representative at negotiations prior to Treaty of Versailles. Criticized reparations plans in *The Economic Consequences of the Peace*, 1919. Made radical proposals for dealing with unemployment by provision of public works. Ideas influenced Liberal Party's election manifesto, 1929. Full proposals on economic controls in interests of maintaining full employment appeared in *The General Theory of Employment, Interest and Money*, 1936. Inspired 'Keynesian Revolution' during and after Second World War. Rejected classical belief in self-regulating economy. Argued need for government expenditure to be adjusted to control level of public demand. Advised Chancellor of the Exchequer during Second World War. Chief British delegate at Bretton Woods Conference, 1944. Involved in discussions leading to creation of International Monetary Fund and World Bank.

Khama, Sir Seretse (1921–   ): Botswana national leader. A lawyer exiled from Botswana, 1950–56, he founded the Botswana Democratic Party in 1962 and in 1966 became the first President of Botswana at independence. As a front-line president (q.v.) he played a leading role in Rhodesian independence negotiations and in discussions of the subsequent problems of Southern Africa.

Khomeini, Ayatollah Ruholla (1900–89): Iranian religious leader of Shi'ite Muslims. His denunciation of the Shah's westernizing reforms and female emancipation led to arrest and exile in France. Urged Iranian army to overthrow Shah and institute Islamic republic. Returned to Tehran when the Shah fled, 1979, and remained the dominant figure until his death, severing relations with the West, enforcing religious fundamentalism, and waging 1980–88 war with Iraq. Issued death threat against Salman Rushdie, British author of *The Satanic Verses*.

Khrushchev, Nikita Sergeyevich (1894–1971): Soviet politician. Joined Communist Party, 1918. Fought in Civil War. Member of Central Committee of Party, 1934. Full member of Politburo and of Praesidium of Supreme Soviet, 1939. Organized guerrilla warfare against Germans during Second World War. Premier of Ukraine, 1944–47. Undertook major restructuring of agriculture, 1949. Became First Secretary of All Union Party on death of Stalin, 1953. Sensational denunciation of Stalinism, 1956. Relegated Molotov, Kaganovich and Malenkov (potential rivals), 1957. Succeeded Bulganin as Prime Minister, 1958–64. Official visits to the United States, 1959, India and China, 1960. Deposed, 1964, after criticism of his reforms.

Kim Il-sung (1912–94): Korean communist. Communist leader of the Democratic Republic of Korea from 1948 to 1994. He took the title of President in 1972 and became the centre of an ever-growing personality cult. With Soviet backing he instigated the Korean War (q.v.) in 1950 and presided over a stern, communist autocracy until his death. Succeeded by his son, Kim Jong-il, thereby creating the first Communist 'dynasty'.

King, Martin Luther (1929–68): American black civil rights leader. Ordained as Baptist minister, 1947. Began non-violent civil rights campaign in Montgomery, Alabama, leading boycott of racially segregated buses, 1955–56. Founded Southern Christian Leadership Conference, 1957. An effective orator, notably in his Washington 'I have a dream' speech, 1963. Awarded Nobel Peace Prize, 1964. His assassination in Memphis, Tennessee, April 1968, provoked widespread black riots throughout America.

Kissinger, Henry (1923–): American academic and politician. German-born; US citizen, 1943. Professor of Government, Harvard, 1958–71. Adviser in Nixon's (q.v.) Presidential campaign, 1968. White House National Security Adviser, 1969–73, playing a greater foreign policy role than the Secretary of State. Conducted diplomatic missions in Middle East, Southern Africa and Vietnam. Joint Nobel Peace Prize winner with Vietnamese negotiator Le Duc Tho for extricating US from Vietnam. Secretary of State under Nixon and Ford (q.v.), 1973–77.

Klerk, Frederik Willem de (1936–): South African politician. He was a representative of the National Party after 1972 and was also a state minister several times after 1978 (Minister of Home Affairs, 1982–86, Minister of Education and Planning, 1986–89). He was a leader of the National Party from February 1989 and the President of the Republic from August 1989 to 1994. As President, he played a crucial role in the elimination of the apartheid system and in creating a South Africa free from racial discrimination. Together with Nelson Mandela (q.v.), he received the Nobel Peace Prize. After the election victory of the African National Congress in May 1994, he became a Vice-President of South Africa. Announced his retirement from active politics, 1997.

Kohl, Helmut (1930–   ): German politician. In the Parliament of the Rhineland-Palatinate, he was the leader of the Christian Democratic Union (CDU) faction from 1963 to 1969, and became leader of the CDU organization in the province from 1967 to 1973. He became the President of the federal organization of the CDU in 1973. From 1969 to 1976, he was the Prime Minister of the Rhineland-Palatinate. In 1976, he became a member of the Federal Assembly (Bundestag), and he was president of the parliamentary group of the CDU/CSU until 1982; he has been Chancellor of the Federal Republic of Germany since 1982. He played a crucial role in the rapid realization of the reunification of the two Germanys, which significantly contributed to his party's victory in December 1990, and allowed his party to stay in power, following victories in 1983 and 1987, after the first all-German national elections. He has subsequently, at great cost, sought to rebuild the economy of the former East Germany, leading to economic cuts and a loss of support in the 1994 elections, though retaining power. He has played an active role in the drive for European Unity and in the expansion of the EU to include former EFTA and Comecon countries.

Kosygin, Alexei (1904–80): Soviet politician. Communist Party Central Committee member, 1939. Minister for Economic Planning, 1956–57. State economic planning commission chairman and first Deputy Prime Minister, 1960. Succeeded Khrushchev as Chairman of the Council of Ministers (Prime Minister), 1964. Increasingly overshadowed by Brezhnev (q.v.), his moves towards industrial and agricultural decentralization and consumer goods production largely failed. Resigned on health grounds, 1980.

Le Duc Tho (1911–90): Veteran Vietnamese nationalist. A founder member of the Viet Minh (q.v.), he led the North Vietnamese delegation at the Paris peace talks. Joint winner of Nobel Peace Prize.

Lee Kuan Yew (1923–   ): Singapore elder statesman. He was one of the founders of the Singapore Socialist People's Action Party in 1954 and was the long-serving Prime Minister, 1959–90. Under his leadership, Singapore has seen remarkable economic development, but political opposition has often been stifled.

Liaquat Ali Khan (1896–1951): Pakistan politician. Prominent pre-Second World War member of Muslim League. First Prime Minister of independent Pakistan, 1947–51, and after death of Jinnah (q.v.) in 1948, the nation's dominant figure. His refusal to declare Pakistan an Islamic state and attempts at friendlier relations with India aroused extremist anger, and he was assassinated in 1951.

Lie, Trygve (1896–1968): Norwegian social democratic politician. First Secretary-General of the United Nations, 1946–53. Advocated admission of Communist China to UN. Helped secure UN aid for South Korea to fight aggression by North Korea.

Lin Biao (1908–71): Chinese Communist military leader. Party member, 1927. Led an army on the Long March and against the Japanese. Waged successful campaign against Guomindang forces, 1948. Led Chinese armies in Korean War, 1950–52. Appointed Marshal, 1955, and Minister of Defence, 1959. Co-operated with Mao in Cultural Revolution and nominated at 1969 Party Congress as his eventual successor. Reportedly died in a plane crash in Mongolia, after attempting a coup in Beijing, September 1971.

Liu Shao-chi   (1898–1974): Chinese Communist leader. Elected to Party Central Committee, 1927. Party principal vice-chairman on establishment of People's Republic, 1949. Chairman of People's Republic, 1959. His position weakened in the Cultural Revolution when he faced criticism for viewing workers as the main revolutionary force rather than, as Mao argued, the peasantry. Stripped of all political posts, October 1968.

Lon Nol, General (1913–85): Former Prime Minister and Minister of Defence in Cambodia. Leader of the coup which overthrew Prince Sihanouk (q.v.) in March 1970. He headed the right-wing forces in the civil war, as well as holding the office of President, but was exiled following their defeat by the Khmer Rouge (q.v.) in 1975.

Lumumba, Patrice (1925–61): Congolese politician who favoured central government as opposed to a federation. He became Prime Minister and Minister of Defence in 1960, with Kasavubu (q.v.) as President, after a post-independence election gave neither side a majority. He was dismissed by Kasavubu in September 1960, and captured and reportedly shot by Katangan rebels.

Luthuli, Albert (1899–1967): African Nationalist. Former Zulu chief who became a leading figure in the ranks of the African non-violent resistance leadership. Awarded Nobel Prize for Peace in 1960.

MacArthur, Douglas (1880–1964): US General. Army Chief of Staff, 1930–35. Supreme Allied Commander, South West Pacific, Second World War.

Received Japanese surrender, 1945. Led occupation forces in Japan, 1945–51, playing a decisive role in preserving Japanese stability. Commander-in-Chief UN forces in Korean War, 1950–51. Dismissed by Truman (q.v.) for urging spread of war into China, contrary to official policy. Failed to win nomination as candidate in 1952 Presidential election.

McCarthy, Joseph (1908–57): American politician. Republican Senator for Wisconsin. McCarthy alleged in 1950 that over 200 government employees were either Communist Party members or sympathizers, though he provided no evidence. Chairman of the Senate Sub-committee on Investigations, 1953, where he accused numerous Democrats and Liberals of communist sympathies. His attacks on the Army aroused President Eisenhower's antagonism, leading to a Senate motion of censure against McCarthy in 1954 which ended his career.

Machel, Samora (1933–86): Mozambique nationalist leader. First President of Mozambique, 1975–86. President of Frelimo from 1970, Machel became President of the transitional government in Mozambique in 1974 and President on independence in 1975. As one of the front-line presidents (q.v.), he was involved in Rhodesian independence negotiations. Killed in plane crash, 1986.

Macmillan, (Maurice) Harold, Earl of Stockton (1894–1987): Conservative politician. Macmillan was Conservative MP for Stockton-on-Tees, 1924–29, 1931–45, and for Bromley 1945–64. Served as minister resident at Allied HQ in NW Africa, 1942–45, Secretary for Air, 1945, Minister for Housing and Local Government, 1951–54, Minister of Defence, 1954–55, Foreign Secretary, 1955, Chancellor of the Exchequer, 1955–57 and Prime Minister, 1957–63. As early as the 1930s Macmillan revealed himself as an advocate of the Tory paternalist tradition in the Conservative Party, a stance which suited the mood of the 1950s and facilitated his rise to the premiership. His term in Downing Street was seen as something of a high point of post-war prosperity. But by the time of his resignation in 1963, it appeared to many people that Macmillan's style of leadership was dated and out of touch with the new decade. He retired due to ill-health. Famous also for his 'Wind of Change' speech, recognizing the need for decolonization in Africa.

Makarios, Archbishop (1913–77): President of Cyprus from 1960 to his death, except for a short interval in 1974. Also, head of the Greek Orthodox Church in Cyprus. Originally a supporter of enosis, or union with Greece, he conducted negotiations with the British in the mid-1950s and was deported by them in 1956. He was released in 1957 but did not return to Cyprus until 1959. He was elected President in 1960 and during his time in office supported Cypriot independence. Forced into five-month exile after attack on presidential palace in 1974. He returned to a divided island, and was unable to reassert Greek supremacy over the Turkish Cypriot minority.

Malan, Daniel (1874–1959): South African politician. Dutch Reformed Church preacher, 1905–15. Elected as Nationalist MP, 1918. Intense Afrikaner nationalist, opposed South African involvement in Second World War. Prime Minister, 1948–54. Instituted apartheid, dividing South Africa on racial lines between black, coloured and white.

Mandela, Nelson Rolihlahla (1918–   ): South African nationalist leader and President since 1994. A lawyer, member of the African National Congress (ANC) executive, 1952; advocated multi-racial democracy. Went underground on banning of the ANC, 1961; organized *Umkonto we Sizwe* ('Spear of the Nation') for non-terrorist violent action. Arrested and imprisoned for five years, 1962. Life imprisonment at trial for sabotage under Suppression of Communism Act, 1963. Remained a national symbol of resistance to apartheid. Rejected offer of release in return for renouncing political violence, 1986. His (now former) wife, Winnie, also played an active (if controversial) political role in South Africa and internationally. Finally released in February 1990, and assumed role of primary negotiator in the dismantling of apartheid with De Klerk (q.v.). Swept to victory in 1994 elections as leader of the ANC and first black President of South Africa.

Mao Tse-tung: *See* Mao Zedong

Mao Zedong (1893–1976): Chinese Communist leader. Full-time revolutionary, 1923. Saw the peasantry as the main revolutionary force rather than, as in classical Marxism, the urban working class. Chairman of Kiangsi Soviet Republic, 1931. Driven out by Guomindang forces, led the Long March to north-west China. Allied with Guomindang against Japanese, 1937. Rejected Stalin's post-war urging to continue alliance with Guomindang, and won a civil war, becoming People's Republic Chairman, 1949. Initially followed Soviet model of agricultural collectivization and industrial development. 'Let a hundred flowers bloom' policy, 1956, sought intellectual support by encouraging ultimately unwelcome criticism of Party. The 1958 'Great Leap Forward' was a turn to small-scale labour intensive programmes and was followed by a bitter ideological split with the Soviet Union. The 1966–69 'Great Proletarian Cultural Revolution' attempted to accelerate radicalism by rallying the masses and students against the Party bureaucracy. The ensuing chaos and its consequent brake on Chinese development remained unresolved at Mao's death.

Marcos, Ferdinand Edralin (1917–89): Philippine politician. President of the Philippines, 1965–86; also Prime Minister, 1973–86. His regime was marked by massive corruption. Ousted from power in a peaceful coup by Corazón Aquino (q.v.) after rigged elections in February 1986. Given exile haven in Hawaii by the United States, where he died in 1989. His wife Imelda was also renowned for extravagance.

Mariam, Lt.-Col. Mengistu Haile (1937–   ): Ethiopian leader. Came to power in the 1971 revolution which overthrew Emperor Haile Selassie. Mengistu became first President of Ethiopia in 1987 after a plebiscite approved the country's new constitution. His Marxist dictatorship collapsed in 1991.

Meir, Golda (1898–1978): Israeli Prime Minister from 1969 to 1974. After independence, she was very active in the Labour Party and was appointed Minister to the Soviet Union in 1948. In 1949 she became the Minister of Labour, a post she held until she was appointed Minister for Foreign Affairs in 1956. She resigned as minister in 1965 and served as Secretary of the Labour Party until 1968. Elected Prime Minister, 1969. Resigned unexpectedly, 1974.

Menzies, Robert Gordon (1894–1978): Australian politician. Member of Victoria Legislative Assembly, 1928–34. United Australia Party MP, 1934. Appointed Attorney-General, 1935. Resigned, becoming party leader and Prime Minister, 1939. His concentration on the war lost him his party's leadership in 1941. Transformed the UAP into the conservative Liberal Party, 1943–45. Prime Minister, 1949–66, encouraging industrial development and an active foreign policy. Succeeded Churchill as Lord Warden of the Cinque Ports, 1965.

Mitterrand, François Maurice (1916–96): French politician. Socialist deputy, 1946. Ministerial office in 11 governments under the 4th Republic. Unsuccessful Left candidate against de Gaulle (q.v.) in Presidential election, 1965. Socialist Party secretary, 1971. Defeated in Presidential election, 1974. Elected President, defeating Giscard d'Estaing (q.v.), 1981. Backed by a National Assembly Socialist majority, attempted radical economic policy, 1981–83. After 1986 Assembly elections, shared power with Gaullist majority led by Chirac and moderated policy. Re-elected President, 1988, defeating Chirac. Failed to win Socialist majority in ensuing Assembly elections.

Mobutu Sésé Séko (1930–97): Congolese politician. President of Zaïre since 1965. At the independence of Congo he was colonel chief-of-staff of the army. Following the dismissal of Lumumba (q.v.) by Kasavubu (q.v.) he set up a caretaker government, and in 1961 he restored Kasavubu and led attacks on Katanga. In 1965 he deposed Kasavubu and became President and in 1966 Prime Minister and Minister of Defence. He was deposed in 1997 after presiding over one of the most corrupt regimes of modern Africa. Congo was known as Zaïre during his long dictatorship.

Moi, Daniel arap (1924–   ): Kenyan politician. Legislative Council member, 1957. Chairman, Kenya African Democratic Union, 1960–61. Minister for Education, 1961–62; Local Government, 1962–64; Home Affairs, 1964–68. Vice-President, 1967–78. President following death of Kenyatta (q.v.), 1978. Instituted one-party state and survived coup attempt, 1982. As increased power shifted to the Presidency, faced growing international accusations of human rights abuses.

Molotov, Vyacheslav Mikhailovich (1890–1986): Soviet politician. Emerged as prominent Bolshevik during November Revolution, 1917. Loyal colleague of Stalin, 1921 onwards. Member of Politburo, 1926–57. Helped implement Five Year Plan, 1928. Premier, 1930–41. Foreign Minister, 1939–49. Negotiated Pact with Ribbentrop, August 1939. Deputy premier, 1941–57. Negotiated treaties with Eastern Bloc countries, 1945–49. Became member of ruling triumvirate following death of Stalin, 1953. Negotiated Austrian State Treaty, 1955. Minister of State Control, 1956–57. Became Foreign Minister again, 1957. Influence declined with rise of Khrushchev. Ambassador to Mongolia, 1957–60. Retired, 1961–62.

Monnet, Jean (1888–1979): French politician, economist and diplomat. Member of Inter-Allied Maritime Commission, 1915–17. First deputy Secretary-General of League of Nations, 1919–23. Chairman, Franco-British Economic Co-ordination Committee, 1939–40. Became Minister of Commerce, 1944. Fostered establishment of National Planning Council, becoming head of Council, 1945–47. Architect of European Community. Chairman, Action Committee for United States of Europe, 1955–75. Instrumental in foundation of European Coal and Steel Community. President of ECSC, 1952–55.

Mountbatten (of Burma), Louis Mountbatten, 1st Earl (1900–79): Naval commander. At the outbreak of the Second World War Mountbatten was commanding the Fifth Destroyer Flotilla. In 1941 his ship, HMS *Kelly*, was sunk in the Mediterranean and he was nearly drowned. He was then appointed adviser on combined operations. His largest operation was the Dieppe Raid in August 1942, which though a failure, taught valuable lessons. Mountbatten was then appointed supreme commander in South-East Asia, arriving in India in October 1943 to find a diversity of problems. After the war he was Viceroy of India, and presided over the partition of the sub-continent and the independence of India and Pakistan. He later returned to a naval career. In 1955 he was First Sea Lord and in 1959 Chief of the Defence Staff. He was assassinated by Irish extremists in 1979.

Mubarak, Hosni (1928–   ): Egyptian politician. Air Force Chief-of-Staff 1969–72, Commander-in-Chief, 1972–75. Vice-President, 1975–81. Vice-Chairman of National Democratic Party (NDP), 1976–81; NDP Secretary General, 1981–82. President following assassination of Sadat (q.v.) 1981. Renewed relations with Jordan and the Palestine Liberation Organization. Faced rioting over economic problems, 1986. Further six-year term as President confirmed by referenda, 1987 and 1993.

Mugabe, Robert Gabriel (1924–   ): Zimbabwean politician. Entered politics, 1960. Deputy Secretary-General of Zimbabwe African People's Union (ZAPU), 1961. Arrested, 1962; fled to Tanzania, formed Zimbabwe African National Union (ZANU), 1963. Detained in Rhodesia, 1964–74. Joint leader with Nkomo (q.v.) of Mozambique-based Patriotic Front guerrilla campaign, 1976–79. Attended Lancaster House independence conference, 1979. First Prime Minister of Zimbabwe following election victory over Nkomo and Muzorewa (q.v.), 1980. Moved towards one-party state. Merged ZANU and ZAPU, 1987. Executive President since 1987.

Mujibur Rahman, Sheikh (1920–75): Bangladeshi politician who led the Awami League (q.v.) to victory in the 1970 general election. In March 1971 he proclaimed the independence of Bangladesh and was arrested and convicted of treason. After the intervention of India in the civil war he was released and became Prime Minister and later President of the new nation. In August 1975 he and his family were assassinated.

Mussadeq, Mohammed (1880–1967): Iranian politician. Foreign Minister, 1922–24. Withdrew from politics but returned to Parliament, 1942. Violently nationalist speeches against Anglo-Iranian Oil Company carried him into office as Prime Minister, 1951. Falling output following nationalization of company and loss of Western expert advisers prevented promised social reforms. Overthrown in coup encouraged by Shah, with CIA support, and arrested, 1953.

Muzorewa, Bishop Abel (1925–   ): Zimbabwean bishop of the United Methodist Church and nationalist leader. Led the ANC (q.v.) opposition to the Smith–Home proposals in 1971. In 1975 he led the ANC delegation at the Victoria Falls talks and in 1976 represented them at Geneva. Formerly in exile in Lusaka, he returned to Rhodesia to lead the internal group of the ANC after the split in 1977, and in March 1978 was one of the nationalist leaders to sign the internal Rhodesian settlement. Member, transitional government, Zimbabwe–Rhodesia, 1978–80. Heavily defeated by Mugabe (q.v.) in 1980 elections.

Nagy, Imre (1896–1958): Hungarian politician. Lived in USSR, 1930–44. Reforming Agriculture Minister in Hungarian Provisional Government, 1945–46. Prime Minister, 1953–55. Attempted liberalization led to loss of office and expulsion from Communist Party. Re-appointed in October 1956 Hungarian Rising; overthrown by Soviet intervention, November 1956. Arrested and secretly executed, 1958. Officially rehabilitated, 1988.

Nasser, Gamal Abdel (1918–70): Leading Arab Nationalist. President of Egypt, 1954–70. Educated at the Royal Military Academy, he fought in the 1948 Arab–Israeli War and, like all officers, was disgusted with King Farouk's provision of faulty arms to his troops. Founded the Free Officers group which overthrew the monarchy in 1952. For the first two years, Nasser hid behind the figurehead of Neguib. But as Neguib was building a popular following and demanding more power, Nasser ousted him in 1954. Nasser then became Prime Minister and Chairman of the Revolutionary Command Council, Egypt's governing body. After decades of unstable governments, Nasser did bring political stability to Egypt although this was done at the cost of increasing government control. The economy, under constant strain from the Arab–Israeli conflict and a rapidly increasing population, was quite another matter. Nasser committed Egypt to a course of socialism and nationalized first foreign firms and then Egyptian ones. His policies contributed to the 1956 Suez Crisis (q.v.). State planning controlled most of the economy. Nasser had an active Middle Eastern policy and sought to foster Arab unity and lead the Arabs. This often caused bad relations with the more conservative Arab states, and involved him in a misbegotten unity with Syria and in the Yemen misadventure. Despite this, he was a widely-respected figure in the Arab world for the pride he had brought to its people. He tried to resign after the June 1967 defeat, but his people refused to permit it.

Ne Win, U (1911–90): Burmese political leader. Member of anti-British 'We Burmans Association' in 1930s. Chief-of-staff of collaborationist army in Japanese-occupied Burma, 1942–44. Led guerrilla force supporting Allies against Japan, 1944. General and second in command of army on Burmese independence, 1948. Caretaker Prime Minister, 1958–60. Seized power in coup, 1962, leading the Burmese Socialist Programme Party (BSSP) to create a one-party state. President, 1974–81. Faced increasing resistance from communist and minority groups. Resigned as BSSP Chairman following violently suppressed anti-government demonstrations, 1988.

Neguib, Mohammed (1901–84): Egyptian general and politician. As member of Free Officers Movement overthrew King Farouk (q.v.), 1952. President of Egypt, 1952–54. Forced to resign and placed under temporary house arrest by young officers led by Nasser (q.v.), 1954.

Nehru, Pandit Jawaharlal (1889–1964): Indian national leader and statesman. First Prime Minister and Minister of Foreign Affairs when India became independent in 1947. A leading member of the Congress Party, he had been frequently imprisoned for political activity. Under his leadership India progressed, and in world affairs his influence was for peace and non-alignment.

Netanyahu, Benjamin (1950–   ): Prime Minister of Israel since 1995. Israeli ambassador to the United Nations, 1982–84; Deputy Foreign Minister, 1988–91. Became leader of Likud in 1993. Known to oppose return of the occupied territories and the formation of a Palestinian state, he has been accused of retarding the peace process both by allowing fresh Jewish settlement in occupied territory and for his general hard-line stance.

Neto, Agostino (1922–79): Angolan politician. Imprisoned four times between 1952 and 1960 and from 1960 to 1962 for nationalist activities. Led guerrilla war against Portugal as President of People's Movement for the Liberation of Angola (MPLA), 1962–74. President of Angola since 1975. Defeated South African backed rivals with Cuban assistance, 1976.

Ngo Dinh Diem (1901–63): First President of South Vietnam. Provincial Governor, 1929–32, but became increasingly anti-French. Founded anticolonialist and anti-communist National Union Front, 1947. Banned and exiled by French. Following 1954 Geneva Agreements, he returned to become Prime Minister of an anti-communist government. President of South Vietnam following a rigged election in 1955, his authoritarian regime was increasingly unpopular. Victim of a CIA-engineered coup, he was assassinated, 1963.

Nguyen Van Thieu (1923–   ): President of South Vietnam, 1967–75. Previously he had pursued an army career, becoming Chief-of-Staff in 1963. His period in office saw the fall of Saigon and the final communist takeover of South Vietnam.

Nimeiri, Gaafar Mohamad al- (1930–   ): President of the Sudan, 1969–85. Educated in the Military Academy, he served in the army and became its Commander-in-Chief. In 1969 he mounted a *coup d'état* and became

Prime Minister and President of the Revolutionary Command Council. He survived several attempts to oust him from power until his overthrow in a military coup in April 1985.

Nixon, Richard Milhouse (1913–94): 37th US President. Elected as Republican to House of Representatives, 1946; Senate, 1950. Vice-President under Eisenhower (q.v.), 1953–61. Narrowly defeated by Kennedy (q.v.) in Presidential election, 1960. Won Presidential election, 1968. Ended American involvement in Vietnam, eased US–Soviet relations and opened diplomatic links with Communist China. Re-elected President, 1972. Controversial second term saw resignation of Vice-President Agnew (q.v.), 1973, and Nixon's own resignation, 1974, under threat of impeachment for involvement in Watergate conspiracy.

Nkomo, Joshua (1917–   ): Zimbabwean politician. President, African National Congress, 1957–59. In exile, 1959–60. President, National Democratic Party, 1960. Helped found and became President of Zimbabwe African People's Union, 1962. Imprisoned, 1964–74. Joint leader with Mugabe (q.v.) of Patriotic Front guerrilla movement, 1976–79. ZAPU defeated by Mugabe's Zimbabwe African National Union (ZANU) in post-independence elections, 1980. Minister of Home Affairs in coalition government, 1980–81. Co-operation with Mugabe ended by violent tribal differences, 1982. Party Vice-President on merger of ZANU and ZAPU, 1987.

Nkrumah, Kwame (1909–72): African Nationalist. President of Ghana, 1960–66. He became Prime Minister of Ghana in 1951 and was Prime Minister at independence in 1957. On 1 July 1960 he became first President of the Republic of Ghana and was a leading advocate of Pan-Africanism. His government, hit by economic depression and an increasingly dictatorial nature, was overthrown by a military coup in February 1966. He took refuge in Guinea until his death.

Noriega, General Manuel Antonio (1938–   ): Panamanian dictator. Military background. Became chief of G-2, the Panama intelligence agency in 1969. After President Torrijos was killed in an air crash in 1981, took over control of armed forces, becoming in 1983 *de facto* ruler of Panama. Subverted 1984 Presidential election. Indicted by US juries of drug trafficking and racketeering, 1988. Survived coup attempt, October 1989. Fled US invasion force seeking to capture him, December 1989, taking refuge in Vatican embassy. Surrendered to US forces, 3 January 1990. Flown to Florida to face drug trafficking charges.

Nyerere, Julius Kambarage (1922–   ): President of Tanzania, 1964–85. He was a founder member of the Tanganyika African National Union,

Prime Minister at independence and in 1964 became President of Tanzania. Internationally known as a political philosopher, putting forward many of his views on the theory and practice of socialism in the Arusha Declaration (q.v.). One of the most respected African nationalists and Commonwealth statesmen until his retirement in 1985.

Obasanjo, Olusegun (1937–   ): Nigerian politician. Became Nigerian head of state in February 1976 after an unsuccessful coup in which President Mohammed was killed.

Obote, Opolo Milton (1924–   ): Ugandan politician. President of Uganda, 1966–71 and 1980–85. Led the opposition party in Uganda before becoming Prime Minister in 1962. Deposed by Idi Amin (q.v.) while attending the Commonwealth Conference in Singapore, he was exiled to Tanzania. Following the invasion by Ugandan dissidents in 1979, aided by the Tanzanian army, he was elected President in 1980. Deposed, 1985.

Ojukwu, Chukwuemeka Odumegwu (1933–   ): President of Biafra, 1967–70. As military governor of the Eastern states of Nigeria he announced their secession as Biafra. In January 1970, as the rebellion collapsed, he escaped to the Ivory Coast, leaving Colonel Effiong to surrender.

Ortega Saavedra, Daniel (1945–   ): Nicaraguan politician. Underground activist against Somoza (q.v.) regime, 1959. Member, National Directorate of Sandinista Liberation Front (FSLN), 1966–67. Imprisoned, 1967–74. Resumed anti-Somoza activity, fighting successful guerrilla campaign, 1977–79. Member of the Junta of National Reconstruction, 1979. President, 1981–90.

Pahlevi, Muhammed Reza Shah (1919–80): Ruler of Iran after his father's abdication in 1941, until 1979. His coronation was not until 1967. His position during the early years of his reign was precarious, and in 1953 he was forced to flee Iran for a short time. He later became an absolute ruler. In 1962, to gain popular support, he decreed the White Revolution, an extensive reform programme which included such items as land reform, a literacy campaign and the emancipation of women. He maintained close relations with the United States and built up a formidable defence capacity with her help. However, his dictatorial rule, and the excesses of the Savak (the secret police) helped fuel the fundamentalist Islamic movement led by Ayatollah Khomeini (q.v.), which overthrew him in a mass popular uprising in 1979.

Park, General Chung Hee (1917–79): South Korean general. Led the military coup in South Korea in 1961. He was at first Acting President but was elected to office in 1963 and was re-elected in 1967 and 1971.

Peres, Shimon (1923–   ): Prime Minister of Israel, 1984–86; Acting Prime Minister, 1995–96. Israeli Defence Minister from 1974 to 1977 and Labour Party candidate for Prime Minister in the May 1977 elections. During the 1948 war, Peres commanded the Israeli navy, and afterwards became an arms purchaser for the new state. He remained a member of Ben Gurion's faction, and when Ben Gurion left the ruling Labour Party in 1965, Peres followed. He helped the faction return to power after the 1967 Arab–Israeli War. In 1974 and 1977 he narrowly lost the nomination for Prime Minister to Rabin (q.v.), but with Rabin's resignation as leader of the party in April 1977, Peres achieved the nomination. Considered moderate on the Arab–Israeli conflict. Following Labour's victory in the 1992 election he was appointed Foreign Minister and was involved in talks with the Palestine Liberation Organization (PLO) in Norway in 1993. He was a prime mover behind the Israeli–PLO accord of September 1993 and the Jordanian–Israeli peace treaty of 1994. Shared the Nobel Peace Prize in 1994.

Pérez de Cuellar, Javier (1920–   ): Peruvian diplomat. Peru's United Nations representative, 1971–75, presiding over the UN Security Council in 1974. From 1979 to 1981 he was UN Under-Secretary-General for special political affairs and became Secretary-General in 1982. Successfully negotiated cease-fire between Iran and Iraq in their eight-year war, August 1988.

Perón, Juan Domingo (1895–1974): Argentine general and President. Influenced by fascism, participated in a military coup, 1943, becoming Minister of Labour and Social Security. Elected President, 1946 and 1951. Attempted to rally urban working class against traditional landed interests with anti-American nationalism and welfare policies. Eva Duarte de Perón (1919–52), his politically astute wife, played a central role. Her death, and growing confrontation with the Church, weakened his popularity. Ousted by the military and exiled, 1955. A *peronista* revival encouraged his return to victory in the 1973 Presidential election.

Pinochet, Augusto (1915–   ): Chilean general. Led right-wing military coup against socialist President Allende, 1973. Outlawed political parties and repressed Left and liberals. Commander-in-Chief of armed forces, 1973–80. President of Government Council, 1973–74. President of Chile, 1974–89. An October 1988 referendum calling for elections represented a personal rejection of Pinochet. Stood down as President but retained control over armed forces.

Pol Pot, Saloth Sar (1928–98): Kampuchean political leader. Joined underground Communist Party, 1946. Student in Paris, 1950–53. Became

Kampuchean Communist Party Secretary in 1963 and organized Khmer Rouge guerrillas who captured capital Phnom Penh in April 1975. His programme to destroy Western influence and return to agricultural society led to 2–3 million deaths. Prime Minister, 1976–79. Overthrown by invading Vietnamese army, sentenced to death in absence. Reformed guerrilla army with Chinese support, but believed to have given up leadership in 1985. His supporters active after Vietnam's withdrawal from Kampuchea in 1989. His death was confirmed in 1998.

Pompidou, Georges (1911–74): French politician. Member of Resistance during Second World War. Aide to General de Gaulle, 1944–46. Member of Council of State, 1946–54. Deputy Director-General of Tourism, 1946–49. Director-General of Rothschild's (banking house), 1954–58. Chief of de Gaulle's personal staff, 1958–59. Involved in drafting of Constitution of Fifth Republic. Negotiated cease-fire agreement with Algerian nationalists, 1961. Prime Minister, 1962–68. President, 1969–74. Pursued policies similar to those of de Gaulle (q.v.).

Qadhafi, Colonel Muammar al- (1941–   ): Libyan leader. Entered the Libyan army in 1965 and overthrew the monarchy in a coup in 1969. He has headed the Libyan government since. Of fundamentalist religious beliefs, he has sought to remould Libyan society in accordance with socialist Islamic beliefs. He supports the Palestinian hard-line approach, and also funds other radical movements abroad, such as the IRA in Ulster. He has been the architect of many unsuccessful schemes to unite with his neighbours.

Rabin, Itzhak (1922–95): Israeli politician. Prime Minister, 1974–77 and 1992–95. He resigned in April 1977 as head of the Labour Party and its candidate for Prime Minister over his wife's illegal bank account in the United States. Two weeks earlier he had defeated Shimon Peres (q.v.) for the Labour nomination. Rabin had a long career in the army and served as its chief-of-staff between 1960 and 1964. He was ambassador to the United States from 1968 to 1973. Returned as Minister of Defence, 1984; then as Prime Minister, 1992. Took a leading part in the peace accords in the Middle East but was widely criticized for being 'soft' on the PLO. He was assassinated on 4 November 1995 by a right-wing Jewish extremist.

Rahman, Tunku Abdul (1903–90): First Prime Minister and Minister of External Affairs in the Federation of Malaya. He became first Prime Minister of Malaysia in 1963. Following rioting and the declaration of a state of emergency, he resigned in 1970. The 'founding father' of independent Malaysia.

Reagan, Ronald (1911–   ): 40th US President. Film actor. Republican Governor of California, 1967–74. Defeated Carter (q.v.) in 1980 Presidential election; re-elected, 1984. First term marked by 'Reaganomics': tax-cutting, reductions in public spending which hit the poor, and maintenance of high military expenditure. Expressed intense anti-Soviet rhetoric. Military intervention in Grenada, 1983. In second term developed warmer relations with Soviet Union under Gorbachev (q.v.), with summit meetings at Geneva and Reykjavik. Reagan's hitherto impregnable personal popularity was undermined from 1986 by controversy over covert arms sales to Iran and support for Contra forces in Nicaragua.

Roosevelt, Franklin Delano (1882–1945): 32nd US President. Democrat State Senator, New York, 1911–12. Assistant Secretary to the Navy, 1913–20. Crippled by polio, 1921. Governor of New York, 1928. Defeated Hoover in Presidential election, 1932. Instituted 'New Deal' to counter Depression, with 'Hundred Days' of legislation, 1932. Devalued dollar and extended federal government role through public works, agricultural support, labour legislation and business protection. Re-elected 1936, 1940, 1944. Attacked for radicalism, some legislation was declared unconstitutional by the Supreme Court, 1937. Maintained war-time neutrality, 1939–41, but supported Britain materially through Lend-Lease. Declared war on Axis powers, December 1941. Attended war-time conferences with Stalin and Churchill, notably Yalta, which delineated East–West post-war spheres of European influence. Died in office at moment of victory over Germany.

Sadat, Anwar al- (1919–81): President of Egypt, 1970–81. Joined the Free Officers (q.v.) in 1950 and participated in the 1952 coup which overthrew the constitutional monarchy. Sadat held various important positions in the government, and was Vice-President at the time of Nasser's death. He was one of the very few of the Free Officers left in power at this point, probably because he had never sought to build a following of his own and so constituted no threat to Nasser. He became provisional President at Nasser's death and later was elected to the post. His dramatic peace initiative, including an historic visit to Jerusalem, altered the diplomatic *status quo* in the Middle East, and led to the Camp David peace treaty of 1978. Sadat was assassinated in 1981.

Sakharov, Andrei Dimitrievich (1921–89): Russian nuclear physicist. Achieved international fame as a human rights campaigner and dissident. Awarded Nobel Prize, 1975. Rehabilitated by Gorbachev, 1988.

Salazar, Antonio de Oliveira (1889–1970): Portuguese dictator. Professor of economics at Coimbra University, 1916. Minister of Finance, 1926,

1928–32. Prime Minister, 1932–68. Also Minister of War, 1936–44, Foreign Minister, 1936–37. Principal architect of authoritarian constitution introduced in 1933. Implemented fascist-type government on virtually dictatorial lines, stifling political opposition. Restored public finances and modernized transport system. Organized public works schemes. Maintained Portuguese neutrality during Second World War and maintained Portuguese empire in Angola and Mozambique.

Shamir, Yitzhak (1915–   ): Israeli politician. Served as Prime Minister after Begin's resignation in 1983. In 1984, entered into a coalition with the Labour Party, sharing the position of Prime Minister with Peres on a rotating basis. Foreign Minister, 1984 to 1986, then Prime Minister again according to the agreement. Adopted hard-line repressive policies against the *intifada*, the uprising of the Arabs in the occupied territories.

Shastri, Shri Lal Bahadur (1904–66): Indian politician. Succeeded Nehru (q.v.) as Prime Minister in 1964. Died of a heart attack after the Soviet-backed Tashkent talks aimed at bringing about peace between India and Pakistan.

Sihanouk, Prince Norodom (1922–   ): Cambodian leader. Elected head of state in Cambodia following the death of his father in 1960. He was deposed in 1970 and set up the Royal Government of National Union for Cambodia (GRUNC) in exile in Beijing. He returned to power in April 1975, following the defeat of the Republican forces, but resigned on 5 April 1976.

Singh, Vishwanath Pratap (1931–   ): Prime Minister of India from 1989 to 1990. Former Congress (I) politician. Held various posts, including Defence Minister, under Indira Gandhi. Broke with Congress Party, 1987. President, Janata Dal coalition which ousted Rajiv Gandhi from power in 1989 election, but his government fell in 1990.

Sithole, Revd Ndabaningi (1920–   ): Zimbabwean churchman and nationalist. A Congregational minister, he was originally Chairman of ZAPU (q.v.). When it split in August 1963, he became leader of ZANU (q.v.). He spent ten years in gaol and after his release in the 1974 amnesty, went into exile in Zambia with a section of the ANC led by Muzorewa (q.v.). In 1976 he withdrew a section of ZANU from the ANC and attended the Geneva Conference, contesting with Mugabe the claim to be leader of ZANU. He returned to Rhodesia in July 1977 and allied himself with Muzorewa again. In March 1978 he became a party to the internal Rhodesian agreement.

Smith, Ian Douglas (1919–   ): Leader of White Rhodesia. After posts as Deputy Prime Minister, Minister of Treasury, Defence and External Affairs he became leader of the ruling Rhodesia Front and Prime Minister in 1964. After winning an overwhelming majority in the general election in May 1965 he made a Unilateral Declaration of Independence (UDI) on 11 November 1965. In June 1969 his decision to declare a Republic and introduce an apartheid-type constitution was endorsed by a referendum. Forced to negotiate an internal settlement with Bishop Muzorewa (q.v.) in 1978. Smith became minister without portfolio in the Zimbabwe–Rhodesia government of Muzorewa. Came to London in 1979 for the talks which settled the Rhodesia crisis.

Smuts, Jan Christian (1870–1950): South African statesman and soldier. Fought on behalf of the Boers in the Boer War (1899–1902). Prime Minister of the Union of South Africa, 1919–24 and again 1939–48. Worked to heal differences within South Africa and maintain membership of the Commonwealth. Seen as too pro-British by Afrikaners. Defeated in 1948 by the National Party under Malan (q.v.).

Solzhenitsyn, Alexander Isayevich (1918–   ): Russian novelist and leading dissident. Author of *One Day in the Life of Ivan Denisovich*, a damning indictment of life in one of Stalin's prison camps (where Solzhenitsyn himself was imprisoned). Expelled from Soviet Writer's Union, 1969. Nobel Prize for Literature, 1970. Expelled from Russia in 1974, he lived in the United States before returning to Russia in 1994.

Somoza, Anastasio (1925–80): Nicaraguan general and politician. Member of family ruling Nicaragua from 1936 to 1979. President, 1967–73, 1974–79. Imposed martial law, 1972. Lost US support through human rights violations. Overthrown by Sandinista Liberation Front guerrilla forces, 1979. Assassinated in Paraguay, 1980.

Souphanouvong, Prince (1902–97): Laotian leader. Fought with independence troops against the French in Laos and later led the Pathet Lao (q.v.) in their struggle against the government of Souvanna Phouma. In the 1974 coalition government he led the Joint National Political Council and became President of the Lao People's Democratic Republic in December 1975.

Stalin, Josef Visarionovitch (J.V. Djugashvili) (1879–1953): Soviet leader. Expelled from seminary for political activities, 1899. Exiled to Siberia twice. Attended conferences of Russian Social Democrats in Stockholm, 1906, and London, 1907. Expert on racial minorities in Bolshevik Central Committee, 1912. Became editor of *Pravda*, 1917. Worked with Lenin in Petrograd during Revolution, 1917. Member of Revolutionary Military Council, 1920–23. People's Commissar for Nationalities, 1921–23. General Secretary of Central Committee of Communist Party, 1922–53. During Civil War, supervised defence of Petrograd. Co-operated with Kamenev and Zinoviev to exclude Trotsky from office, 1923. (Secured Trotsky's exile, 1929). Gained control of Party at Fifteenth Congress, 1927. Embarked on policy of 'Socialism in One Country' through Five Year Plans, 1928. Achieved rapid economic development. Eliminated political opponents in series of 'show trials', 1936–38. Massive machinery of repression created. Chairman of Council of Ministers, 1941–53. During Second World War, as Commissar of Defence and Marshal of the Soviet Union, took over direction of war effort. Present at Tehran, Yalta and Potsdam conferences. Established firm control of Eastern European Communist 'satellites', with exception of Yugoslavia, during post-war period. 'Personality cult' of Stalin officially condemned by Khrushchev at Party Congress, 1956.

Stevens, Siaka Probyn (1905–88): Sierra Leone politician. Elected Prime Minister of Sierra Leone on 21 March 1967, but was overthrown and exiled without taking office. He was restored to power on 26 April 1968, and became President when Sierra Leone became a Republic in 1971.

Stevenson, Adlai Ewing (1900–65): American politician. Democrat Governor of Illinois, 1949–53. Unsuccessful Democrat candidate against Eisenhower in Presidential elections, 1952 and 1956. US Ambassador to the United Nations, 1960–65.

Strijdom, Johannes (1893–1958): South African politician. Elected Nationalist MP, 1929; acknowledged by 1934 as an ultra-Afrikaner leader. Prime Minister following the death of Malan (q.v.), 1954–58. Extreme advocate of apartheid, responsible for legislation removing voting rights from Cape Coloureds, for undermining liberal multi-racial universities, and for the 1956–58 Treason Trial.

Suharto, General (1921–   ): Indonesian general and politician. Leader of the army who took over control in Indonesia in March 1966. Power was handed over to him by Sukarno (q.v.) in February 1967. He was acting President until March 1968, when he was elected to office by the People's Consultative Assembly. He was re-elected in March 1973 and also became Prime Minister and Minister of Defence. His authoritarian regime (and a financial collapse) brought an uprising in 1998 (see p. 280).

Sukarno, Ahmed (1901–70): Indonesian nationalist leader. First President of Indonesia. After an abortive communist coup in 1965 in which he was implicated, the army took over in March 1966. He nominally held power until February 1967, when he handed over to General Suharto (q.v.).

Syngman Rhee (1875–1965): South Korean politician. Elected President of the Republic of Korea (South Korea) in 1948 and held office until April 1960 when he was forced to resign and leave the country. His regime was corrupt and authoritarian.

Thant, Sithu U (1909–74): Burmese diplomat. Secretary-General of the United Nations, 1962–72.

Thatcher, Baroness, Margaret Hilda (*née* Roberts) (1925–): Mrs Thatcher was Conservative MP for Finchley from 1959 to 1992. She was parliamentary secretary to the Ministry of Pensions and National Insurance, 1961–64, and Secretary of State for Education and Science, 1970–74. In 1975 she was elected leader of the Conservative Party. Between 1975 and 1979 she led the party away from the centrist policies of Heath (q.v.) and adopted a monetarist stance on economic problems and a tough line on law and order, defence and immigration. In May 1979 she became Britain's first woman Prime Minister, following her election victory. In spite of considerable unpopularity and very high unemployment, Mrs Thatcher's conduct of the Falklands War and Labour's disarray led to a landslide victory at the polls in 1983. Her second term was marked by growing emphasis on liberalizing the economy, especially the privatization of major public concerns. In 1987 she achieved a record third term of office with a majority of over 100 in parliament, but rapidly encountered mounting political and economic difficulties and was forced from office in 1990. Out of office, she has continued to mount attacks on the European Union.

Tito, Josip Broz (1892–1980): Yugoslav statesman. Member of Yugoslav Communist Party since early 1920s, becoming its Secretary-General, 1937. Led Yugoslav partisan forces during Second World War. Become Marshal, 1943. After war, pursued independence from USSR, 1948. First President of Yugoslav Republic, 1953–80. Pursued independent foreign policy, encouraging co-operation among non-aligned nations.

Todd, Reginald Stephen Garfield (1908–92): Prime Minister of Southern Rhodesia in 1953 at the formation of the Federation with Northern Rhodesia and Nyasaland. In 1958 his liberal policies led to his rejection by his party, the United Federal Party. Between 1965–66 and 1972–76 he was under government restriction orders. At the Geneva talks in 1976 he was adviser to Joshua Nkomo (q.v.).

Touré, Sekou (1922–84): Guinean politician and trade unionist. Became head of state in Guinea in October 1958 on independence. He was awarded the Lenin Peace Prize in 1960.

Trudeau, Pierre (1919–   ): Canadian politician. Elected as Liberal member of the Federal Parliament, 1965. Minister of Justice and Attorney General, 1967. Succeeded Lester Pearson as Prime Minister, 1968. Strong opponent of separatism for French-speaking Quebec. Defeated in 1979 election. Returned to office as Prime Minister, 1980–84.

Truman, Harry S. (1884–1972): 33rd US President. Served in US Army in France, 1918. Democratic Senator, Missouri, 1935–44. Elected as Roosevelt's Vice-President 1944; succeeded him on death in April 1945. Authorized dropping of atomic bombs on Japan, August 1945. Surprise victor in 1948 Presidential election on 'Fair Deal' civil rights and social reform platform, but unable to push legislation through conservative Congress. Vigorous anti-communist foreign policy: Truman Doctrine; Marshall Plan for European recovery; Berlin airlift; creation of NATO, and US participation in UN forces in Korea.

Tshombe, Moise Kapenda (1919–69): Congolese Prime Minister and President, 1964–65. He announced the secession of Katanga from Congo in July 1960 and led the Katanga forces until 1963, when UN forces took control and he went into exile. In 1964 he was recalled to lead the central government, but was dismissed in 1965 and again went into exile. Having been sentenced to death by the Kinshasa High Court, his plane was hijacked to Algiers where he was placed under house arrest until his death.

Verwoerd, Hendrik Frensch (1901–66): South African Prime Minister, 1958–66. In 1950 he became Minister of Native Affairs in South Africa, where he was responsible for putting apartheid (q.v.) into practice. He then became leader of the Nationalist Party and on 2 September 1958 became Prime Minister. He was assassinated on 6 September 1966. Strong advocate of a South African Republic outside the Commonwealth (which South Africa left in 1961).

Vorster, Balthazar Johannes (1915–83): South African Prime Minister, 1966–78. Formerly Minister of Justice, he became South African Prime Minister in 1966 following the assassination of Verwoerd (q.v.). As Prime Minister he tried to make diplomatic contacts with black African states and attempted to help solve both the Rhodesian and Namibian problems. He maintained strict apartheid, winning a landslide victory from the white electorate in 1977. Forced to resign by the Muldergate scandal (q.v.).

Waldheim, Kurt (1918–   ): Austrian diplomat and politician. Diplomat, 1945–64, mainly at United Nations. Foreign Minister, 1968–70. Failed to win Presidential election, 1971. UN Secretary-General, 1971–82. Largely unsuccessful term because of East–West mutual mistrust. President of Austria, 1986–92. During election campaign reputation was undermined by questions about his war-time activities and the extent of his awareness of Nazi atrocities.

Walesa, Lech (1943–   ): Polish trade unionist. Former Gdansk shipyard worker. Emerged as leader of independent 'Solidarity' trade union. Solidarity comprised some 40% of Polish workers by late 1980. Mounted outspoken opposition to economic and social policies of government. Detained following imposition of martial law, December 1981. Released 11 months later. During his detention, Solidarity was banned. Continued to hold prominent position. Granted audience with Pope John Paul II, 1983. Awarded Nobel Peace Prize, 1983. Guided Solidarity throughout 1980s, but declined to hold office when, in September 1989, Solidarity became part of Poland's first non-Communist government for 40 years. President of Poland from 1990 until his defeat in the 1995 presidential election.

Weizmann, Chaim (1874–1952): Zionist leader. Headed British Zionist movement before First World War. Advised Foreign Office during planning of Balfour Declaration, 1917. Head of World Zionist Movement after 1920. Became head of Jewish Agency for Palestine, 1929. Elected first President of Israel, 1948.

Welensky, Roland (Roy) (1907–91): Deputy Prime Minister and Minister of Transport of the Central African Federation from 1953 to 1956 when he became Prime Minister and Minister of External Affairs. He remained Prime Minister until the break-up of the Federation in 1963.

Yeltsin, Boris Nikolaievich (1931–   ): Russian politician. From 1961 he was a member of the Soviet Communist Party, and from 1976 to 1985 Chief Secretary of the Party Committee of the Sverdlovsk region. As a secretary of the Central Committee (1985–86), the Chief Secretary of the Party Committee of Moscow, and a member of the Politburo (1985–86), he fought against the corruption, unrestricted power and privileges of the Party administration. He also spoke up for the consistent application of reforms introduced by President Gorbachev (q.v.). Appointed Vice-President, then President (1989), of the State Committee of Building and Construction. In May 1990, he was elected as the President of the Supreme Soviet of the Russian Federation (parliament); in July of the same year, he resigned his membership of the Soviet Communist

Party. As a result of direct elections, he became the first President of the Russian Federation in June 1991. In August 1991, he played a significant role in the interception of the conservative communist-led coup attempt. In November 1991, he abolished the Communist Party in the territory of the Federation; in December, together with the Ukrainian and Belarusian presidents, he established the Commonwealth of Independent States and announced the dissolution of the Soviet Union. From November 1991 to June 1992 he was also the provisional Prime Minister. In January 1992, under the direction of his Finance Minister Yegor Gaidar, he launched a radical economic reform programme. Because of this, and partly due to his autocratic style of rule, he was confronted by the generally conservative Parliament. In September 1993, with a coup-like measure, he dissolved both houses of the Parliament and – with the aid of armed forces – suppressed the 'White House' rebellion (October). The plebiscite, held simultaneously with the December Presidential elections, accepted the reformed constitution which widened the scope of Presidential powers. Although dogged by ill-health and criticism of his style of leadership, he has retained his position as the leading ex-Communist politician.

SECTION FIVE

Glossary of terms

Affirmative action   Term used to describe attempts in the United States by the 1943 Fair Employment Practices Commission and the 1960s Equal Opportunities Commission (EOC) to counter discrimination in employment and education against ethnic minorities and women. Affirmative action was weakened under the Reagan and Bush administrations in the 1980s and by Supreme Court decisions in the 1990s following criticism of the policy's allegedly discriminatory effect against the white population.

African National Congress (ANC)   Black South African pressure group, formed in 1912 at Bloemfontein to promote the welfare of Blacks in South Africa. Its origins date from the formation in Cape Colony in 1882 of the Native Education Association. Banned from South Africa in 1961. Its leader, Nelson Mandela (q.v.) the symbol of black African hopes, was convicted of sabotage in 1964 and sentenced to life imprisonment. Mandela was released in 1990 and the ANC ban was lifted. The ANC went on to emerge victorious from the multi-party elections of April 1994.

African National Council (ANC)   Black Rhodesian pressure group, initially set up in 1971 to oppose the Smith–Home settlement proposals for Rhodesia. In 1975, with the backing of the Organization of African Unity (q.v.), Muzorewa (q.v.) led an ANC delegation to the Victoria Falls conference representing all the nationalist groups. This unity did not last and, by 1977, after groupings and regroupings, the ANC was divided into two main wings, led respectively by Muzorewa and Nkomo.

al-Fatah   The Syrian branch of the Palestinian liberation movement. It became the most powerful force in the Palestine Liberation Organization (q.v.) after the Arab–Israeli War of 1967.

Alliance for Progress   Conceived and implemented during the Kennedy administration (1961–63). An attempt to promote economic development in Latin America through extensive and varied United States' assistance. The Alliance for Progress began in August 1961 with the signature of a charter by representatives of 20 American states at Punta del Este in Uruguay. Action began in March 1962, with the declared aim of increasing living standards in these countries by 2.5% per annum.

Amethyst incident   Incident on 20 April 1949 when HMS *Amethyst*, a British naval frigate engaged in carrying supplies to the British community in Nanking, was fired upon by communist guns sailing up the Yangtze-Kiang. Some 17 men were killed and a further 30 wounded. The ship was trapped off an island in the river for 14 weeks, attempts by other vessels to rescue her being unsuccessful. On the night of 30–31 July, Lieut.-Commander J.S. Kerans succeeded in getting 140 miles downriver to the

sea: by sailing at over 22 knots the ship managed to avoid the guns of
five forts on the way to the coast. The reason for the detention of the
Amethyst remains unclear, but it was presumably an attempt to assert
Chinese sovereignty over an international river on the part of the revolutionary authorities.

ANC   *See* African National Congress.

anti-Semitism   Term used to describe animosity towards the Jews, either
on a religious or a racial basis. Originally coined by racial theorists of
the late nineteenth century, anti-Semitism can take a number of different political, economic or racial forms. A number of political parties in
Germany and Austria were based on anti-Semitism, and it also appeared
in France via the *Action Française*. Economic and political anti-Semitism
was also a feature of Tsarist Russia with frequent pogroms against Jewish
communities, a form of activity which seems to have recurred in the
Soviet Union in 1958–59 and 1962–63.

Anzus Pact   Name given to the Pacific Security Treaty signed by Australia, New Zealand and the United States on 1 September 1951. It is
of indefinite duration, and marked a reorientation and new independence in defence policy by Australia and New Zealand towards the United
States and away from the United Kingdom. New Zealand later withdrew
from the Pact as part of its anti-nuclear policy.

apartheid   The South African doctrine of racial segregation, put forward
by the National Party under Dr Malan in 1948, and subsequently practised under successive governments of Strydom, Verwoerd, Vorster and
Botha. Although virtually universally condemned by the world outside,
the South African defence of apartheid was that it allowed for the separate development of the Bantu population along their own lines ultimately
leading to self-governing African states (Bantustans, q.v.) in South Africa.
In practice, under apartheid the Black African population was the subject of a continuing stream of discriminatory legislation, including the
1949 Prohibition of Mixed Marriages Act, the 1950 Suppression of Communism Act, the 1950 Group Areas Act, and the much-criticized 1963
'Ninety-Day Law' under which the police were given powers of arbitrary
confinement without recourse to the courts. The result was the suppression of all internal opposition to White supremacy. The Africans were
consigned to a role as a disenfranchised and politically powerless labour
force. During the 1980s, as South Africa became increasingly isolated
from the rest of the world, the political climate within the country began
to change. On 11 February 1990 the leader of the ANC, Nelson Mandela,
was released from prison. Earlier, in 1989, the government had an-

nounced the end of segregated beaches and a moderation of the Group Areas Act, a cornerstone of apartheid. One by one, the pillars of apartheid began to crumble. In April 1994 multi-party elections heralded the birth of a new South Africa. Nelson Mandela became President. The new situation was reflected in the return of South Africa to the Commonwealth.

arms race   The Cold War rivalry between the USSR and the Western powers, particularly the United States, to establish supremacy in arms production.

Arusha Declaration   Socialist theory of development put forward by President Nyerere (q.v.) of Tanzania in February 1967. He was sceptical about the motives of countries offering aid in Africa and felt that a developing country should control its own resources and encourage self-reliance. His theories have been put into practice in Tanzania through nationalization of banks and insurance companies, Africanization of foreign assets and nationalization of many European-owned firms, as well as the setting up of 'Ujamaa' villages which concentrate people into co-operative settlements.

ASEAN   Association of South-East Asian Nations (*see* pp. 211–12).

Atlantic Charter   Agreement reached in August 1941 between US President Franklin Roosevelt and British Prime Minister Winston Churchill which set out the basis upon which the two powers would co-operate internationally after the conclusion of the Second World War. The terms included recognizing the right of all peoples to consent to their own government and the establishment of a system of collective security. The Charter formed the basis of the subsequent alliance of the United Nations against Germany and Japan, and was endorsed by the other Allied combatants.

Atom spies   Alleged members of a Soviet spy ring which had penetrated the Manhattan Project. Following the confession in Great Britain in 1950 of the Anglo-German scientist Karl Fuchs, the FBI arrested eight persons named in the press as having supplied nuclear secrets to the USSR. Two of that number, Julius Rosenberg and his wife Ethel, were tried for conspiracy and sentenced to death. The Supreme Court considered their case five times but they were finally executed in 1953, the only persons ever sentenced to death in the USA for espionage in peace-time.

August Revolution   Term for the successful uprising against the Japanese occupation forces in Vietnam, launched by the Viet Minh (q.v.) in August

1945. The revolt met little resistance from the Japanese in the north and the Democratic Republic of Vietnam was proclaimed in Hanoi in September. In the south, the returning French successfully regained control in Saigon.

Awami League   A political party proposing independence for East Pakistan, which won 167 seats out of 300 in the Pakistan general election held in December 1970. The Pakistan authorities refused to open the new National Assembly and civil war broke out. The leader of the Awami League, Sheikh Mujibur Rahman (q.v.), became Prime Minister of the new nation of Bangladesh but in January 1975 abolished all political parties and replaced them by a single party.

ayatollah   Islamic title, given to the most learned teachers and scholars in Shi'ite Iran. The title came into prominence to refer to Ayatollah Khomeini (q.v.), the leader of the 1979 Islamic revolution in Iran.

Azania   Term used by black nationalists to denote South Africa.

AZAPO   Azanian People's Organization. Black consciousness movement formed in South Africa in 1977.

Baader-Meinhof Group   An anarchist terrorist group active in West Germany in the 1970s. It was led by Andreas Baader (1943–77) and Ulrike Meinhof (1934–76) with funds channelled via East Germany. Both were captured, and died in high-security prisons.

Ba'ath Party   Syrian political party founded in 1941, whose name means 'renaissance' in Arabic; its goals are Arab unity, socialism and freedom. It has branches in several Arab countries but has seen its greatest power in Iraq and Syria. Its support has come mainly from the military, intellectuals and the middle class.

Baghdad Pact   *See* Central Treaty Organization.

bamboo curtain   Term used to describe the isolation of Communist China from 1948 to 1971 when, with the admission of China to the United Nations and the visit of Nixon (q.v.) to Beijing, the 'bamboo curtain' was lifted. The term is analogous to 'Iron Curtain' (q.v.) used to denote Russia and Eastern Europe during the Communist era.

Bandung Conference   Conference in 1955 largely organized at the initiative of the Colombo Powers and China, to herald a new era of Afro–Asian solidarity. Its guiding principles were the 'Five Principles' of Peaceful Coexistence which had emerged from the settlement of the Sino–Indian conflict over Tibet (29 April 1954). These were: mutual respect for territorial integrity and sovereignty; non-aggression; non-interference in each other's internal affairs; equality and mutual benefit; peaceful co-existence and economic co-operation. Despite general agreement, not all countries accepted the neutralist position in world affairs advocated by China. Division and dissent marked the Second Bandung Conference in 1965.

banning order   An order used in South Africa under the apartheid regime to prohibit a person engaging in, say, political activity, being interviewed or quoted by the media.

Bantustan   The supposedly independent tribal homelands in South Africa (e.g. Transkei) established under the apartheid regime. None received international recognition.

Baruch Plan   Proposal made in June 1946 by Bernard Baruch, US representative to the UN Atomic Energy Commission, to place all sources of nuclear power under international control. It was rejected by the USSR.

Bay of Pigs   (Cochinos Bay) A coastal area in southern Cuba. On 17 April 1961, Cuban exiles trained and assisted by the US Central Intelligence Agency (CIA) landed at the Bay of Pigs in an attempt to overthrow the communist regime of Fidel Castro. The operation was planned during the later stages of the Eisenhower administration, but inherited and implemented by the Kennedy administration. The failure of the insurgents was due to many factors: the unfavourable terrain surrounding the Bay of Pigs; lack of support from local inhabitants, and the absence of sufficient military support for those who landed on the island. The result of the attempt was disastrous for the Cuban exiles, of whom more than 80 were killed and over 1000 captured; it also represented the first, and most serious, diplomatic failure of the Kennedy administration. The claims of the United States of non-involvement in the affair were scarcely credible, and the Castro regime was made to appear stronger and less vulnerable.

Biafra   The name given to the eastern region of Nigeria on its attempted secession in 1967.

'Big Five'   Permanent members of the UN Security Council: the United States, Britain, China, France and Russia (formerly the Soviet Union).

Black Monday   Term applied to the collapse of the New York Stock Exchange on 19 October 1987, when the Dow Jones Industrial Average fell by 22.6%, bringing major falls in other markets around the world. It was the worst fall since 1929.

Black Muslims   Puritanical movement of black Americans, also known as the Nation of Islam, whose twin pillars of belief are Negro superiority and racial separation. It was founded in 1933 and led by Elijah Muhammad; the most influential member was Malcolm X, who was assassinated in February 1965 after he had broken with the group to found his own internationalist Organization for Afro–American Unity. The Nation of Islam was influential again during the 1980s under Louis Farrakhan. *See* Black Power.

Black Panther Party   Name derived from the symbol used by Black Power candidates in 1966 when fighting elections in Alabama. *See* Black Power.

Black Power   Radical black movement which emerged in the United States, partly reflecting dissatisfaction with the lack of progress of the civil rights movement. It was at its most aggressive in the late 1960s, and there were fears in the United States that inter-racial strife of civil war dimensions might erupt in the cities. However, the 1970s saw some improvement in the position of American Blacks and that, together with the deaths of Black Power leaders such as George Jackson and Malcolm X, weakened the movement.

Black September   Extremist Palestinian terrorist group founded in 1971 and named after the Black September of 1970, during which King Hussein (q.v.) virtually eliminated the guerrilla presence in Jordan. The commando group organised a long series of outrages, among them the assassination of the Jordanian Prime Minister, Wasif al-Tell and the attempted assassinations of the Jordanian ambassadors to Switzerland and the United Kingdom in 1971; the murder of a number of Israeli athletes at the Munich Olympics in 1972; and the murder of the American ambassador and two other foreign diplomats in Khartoum in 1973.

boat people   Term used to describe those persons, both Chinese and non-communist Vietnamese, seeking to escape from Vietnam after 1975 when South Vietnam fell to communist North Vietnam. Many escaped, in overladen small boats, to Malaysia, Hong Kong, etc. Many fell prey to pirates. The problem became acute again in the 1980s as economic hardship in Vietnam provoked further waves of refugees into Hong Kong. Against an international outcry, Britain began repatriation to Vietnam in December 1989.

BOSS   Bureau of State Security, the South African Secret police force accused of many illegal actions both inside and outside South Africa during the era of White Supremacy.

brainwashing Term originating from the mental and frequently physical torture used by the communists in the Korean War (*see* p. 248) to persuade their captured prisoners to alter their view of society.

Bretton Woods Conference Town in New Hampshire where representatives of 28 nations attended a conference called by President Franklin Roosevelt in July 1944 to organize a system of monetary co-operation in order to prevent financial crises such as that which had triggered the Great Depression. The final agreement was largely based on the American plans on proposed convertibility of currencies and fixed exchange rates to encourage trade. The Conference also led to the establishment of the International Bank for Reconstruction and Development (the World Bank) and the International Monetary Fund.

Brezhnev Doctrine The doctrine was developed by Leonid Brezhnev, First Secretary of the Communist Party of the Soviet Union, as a justification for the invasion of Czechoslovakia by five Warsaw Pact countries in 1968; it maintained that the Socialist community of nations may intervene in the affairs of one of its members, if it sees it as necessary and for the public good. Under Gorbachev, the doctrine was abandoned and there was no intervention in 1989 as Eastern Europe reshaped its political system.

brinkmanship Term used to describe the policy of going to the brink (i.e. of nuclear war) to force another power to climb down or seek a negotiated settlement. An example is the policy of Kennedy during the Cuban Missile Crisis (q.v.). The term originated with John Foster Dulles, American Secretary of State, 1953–59.

Broederbond White secret society formed after the Boer War to maintain Afrikaner dominance in South African cultural, economic and political life, and which influenced National Party policy.

buffer state A small state established or maintained between two larger states to prevent clashes between them or to prevent either taking control of strategic territory.

Bundestag The West German federal parliament established in May 1949, elected for a four-year term by universal suffrage. Since 1990, the parliament of the reunited Germany.

Bussing American practice of moving children by bus to schools in different areas, to prevent educational facilities in the 1970s becoming entirely black or white. The intention was to encourage racial harmony, but many white parents complained the practice infringed the right to choose where their children were educated.

Camp David   The US Presidential retreat in Maryland. On 5–17 September 1978 President Carter chaired talks at Camp David between President Sadat of Egypt and Prime Minister Begin of Israel and agreement was reached on a treaty finally signed on 26 March 1979. Israel pledged to withdraw from Sinai; to stop settlement on the West Bank and the Gaza Strip; and to end their military government of the West Bank within five years, after which the Palestinian inhabitants of the area would elect a government. Syria and the PLO rejected the agreement.

Canal Zone   An area five miles each side of the 40-mile-long Panama Canal in Central America, granted to the United States in 1903. The zone is administered by a United States governor and controlled by the US army. Following increasing agitation for return of the zone, President Carter and Panamanian General Torrijos signed a treaty on 7 September 1977 promising its return by 1 January 2000.

CAP   *See* Common Agricultural Policy.

Casablanca Powers   A loose association of more radical African states consisting of Ghana, Guinea, Mali, Morocco, UAR and Algeria, set up in 1961. They combined with the Monrovia states to form the Organization of African Unity (q.v.).

caudillismo   Term used in Spanish and Latin American politics denoting the almost absolute power of the head of state and the personal loyalty of his supporters. Examples are Franco in Spain (*see* El Caudillo, below), and Perón in Argentina.

Caudillo, El (Sp: the leader)   Title assumed by Francisco Franco in 1937 as head of the insurgent nationalist forces in the Spanish Civil War, and of the so-called Burgos Government. His authority was reinforced in July 1947 with the declaration that he should remain 'Caudillo' or head of state for life, pending the restoration of the monarchy.

Central Intelligence Agency (CIA)   An American agency, headed by a director appointed by the President with Senate approval, that works under the National Security Council to co-ordinate intelligence activities in the interest of national security. The CIA evaluates intelligence information supplied by the Army, Navy, Air Force, State Department and other intelligence-gathering civilian and military agencies. This information is disseminated among various units of the national government to aid the formulation of foreign and defence policy. The CIA also engages in world-wide intelligence-gathering activities. The Congressional Charter establishing the CIA specifically prohibits the use of its resources for internal surveillance. As a result of alleged breaches of the charter, Congress has created a 'watchdog' select committee to oversee CIA operations.

Central Treaty Organization (CENTO)   The Baghdad Pact was signed by Turkey and Iraq on 24 February 1955. The Pact was joined by the United Kingdom on 4 April 1955, by Pakistan on 23 September 1955 and by Iran on 3 November 1955. Iraq withdrew on 24 March 1959, and the name was changed to the Central Treaty Organization on 21 August 1959. The United States signed bilateral defence agreements with Iran, Turkey and Pakistan on 5 March 1959. The Treaty provides for mutual co-operation for security and defence. The Islamic Revolution in Iran dealt a major blow to the organization.

Charter 77   Group of civil rights activists formed in Czechoslovakia in 1977 in the wake of the Helsinki Agreement (*see* p. 401) to monitor abuses by the authorities. They were themselves subject to imprisonment and harassment.

Chicago Seven   Leaders of disturbances at the 1968 Democratic National Convention, held in Chicago. The convention was the scene of street protests against the Vietnam War (q.v.) which were violently suppressed by the police. The leaders were tried for incitement to riot in September 1969 and five were goaled; they were originally eight in number but Bobby Seale, chairman of the Black Panther Party (q.v.), was tried separately.

Chimurenga (Zimb. 'uprising')   Term used to describe the wars of independence fought in the area of modern Zimbabwe. The first was the unsuccessful struggle by the Mashona and Ndebele people against Britain in 1893–97 and the second was the successful 1966–79 campaign against the white Rhodesian regime which culminated in independence in 1980. Chimurenga Day is celebrated on 28 April.

China lobby   Supporters in US politics of Chiang Kai-shek's Nationalist regime on Formosa (later Taiwan) following his defeat on the Chinese mainland by Mao Zedong's communist forces in 1949. The lobby successfully insisted that Chiang's Kuomintang government should continue to hold China's seat at the United Nations until 1971 when, following US President Richard Nixon's 'opening to China', the Communist regime took the position.

Christian Democracy Anti-communist, moderate political movement formed in many European countries with the development of a mass electorate in the late nineteenth and twentieth centuries. Among the largest was the Italian Christian Democrat Party founded in 1919, and the major representative of Catholic, moderate opinion. The German National People's Party, formed in 1918, and the German Centre Party, formed in 1870, also represent this tradition, latterly taken up by Adenauer's Christian Democratic Union, formed in 1945. Many other European countries have political parties with this or similar labels.

CIA *See* Central Intelligence Agency.

civil rights movement Movement to secure access for American blacks to voting and citizenship rights guaranteed by the 14th and 15th amendments to the US Constitution in 1868 and 1870. A National Association for the Advancement of Colored People was formed in 1909, but little progress was made for 50 years. In 1957 Federal troops were used in Little Rock, Arkansas, to enforce a 1954 Supreme Court ruling banning segregated education. A black campaign of sit-ins, boycotts and demonstrations in which Dr Martin Luther King (1929–68) emerged as a leader prompted civil rights legislation by the 1960s Kennedy and Johnson administrations. Riots in Harlem (1964) and Watts (1965) revealed dissatisfaction with the pace of achievement and encouraged the growth of black militancy. In the 1970s and 1980s many Blacks felt their progress towards full equality, particularly in education and employment, was weakened by what they saw as unsympathetic Republican administrations.

Cod War Popular term for the fishing dispute between Iceland and Great Britain between 1972 and 1976.

Cold War Protracted state of tension between countries, falling short of actual war. The term was first used in a US Congress debate on 12 March 1947 on the doctrine expounded by Harry S. Truman (1894–1972) promising aid to 'free peoples who are resisting attempted subjugation by armed minorities or by outside pressures'. A direct product of the civil war in Greece (1946–49), the doctrine bore the wider implication that the United States would actively respond anywhere in the world to what it saw as direct encroachment by the USSR. The practical division of Europe occurred as a result of the Eastern European states' rejection of the Marshall Plan (q.v.), often under pressure from the Soviet Union, and their subsequent membership of Comecon. This division into two hostile camps was completed by the creation of NATO (q.v.) in 1949–50 and the Warsaw Pact (q.v.) in 1955. The Cold War between the Soviet Union and the United States continued into the 1970s before being superceded by a period of detente. The main crises within the Cold War period were the Russian invasion of Hungary in 1956; of Czechoslovakia in 1968; the Berlin Blockade of 1948, and the Cuban Missile Crisis of 1962. Western outrage at these supposed manifestations of Soviet expansion was tempered by the British and French involvement in Suez in 1956, and the US involvement in Vietnam during the 1960s and early 1970s. The advent of Gorbachev in Russia and the events of 1989 in Eastern Europe are regarded as marking the end of the Cold War.

Collective security Term widely used in international diplomacy and first coined at the Geneva Conference of 1924 to denote a policy whereby the security of individual countries was guaranteed jointly by others. Under the Charter of the United Nations (q.v.) power to meet threats to peace is invested in the Security Council, whose permanent members are the United States, Russia, the United Kingdom, France and China. However as the Council cannot act if a member dissents, the principle of collective security is not fully established.

collectivism Political concept which demands that the state plays a more interventionist role in the society to promote the development of the society along collectivist lines. Rights and obligations in collectivist theory are socially derived and are based upon the conception that a notion of common good pervades, or ought to pervade, the society.

Colombo Plan Coming into force on 1 July 1951, the plan was a co-operative attempt by both developed and developing countries to further the economies and raise living standards in South and South-East Asia. It was originally intended to last until 1957, but has been successively extended.

Colonels, Greek Term applied to the Greek right-wing military junta led by two colonels who seized power in April 1967. The authoritarian regime collapsed in 1974, after the failure of its intervention in Cyprus.

colour bar The separation of people along racial divisions. Usually manifested, as formerly in South Africa, by prohibiting black people from entering white-only areas. *See* apartheid.

Command economy A centralized national economy which operates under state control rather than functioning through market forces. Prime examples of command economies were the former Soviet Union and its East European satellites before the collapse of communism in the late 1980s and, to a lesser extent, the Western powers during the Second World War. China, while remaining under Communist Party control, has gradually introduced market mechanisms into its economy.

Common Agricultural Policy (CAP)   The controversial policy of the European Community which subsidizes farmers from a Common Agricultural Fund contributed to by member states.

Common Market   *See* p. 214 under European Union.

Commonwealth   *See* p. 212.

Comrades   Radical Black militants in the townships of South Africa, e.g. Soweto. The more moderate Blacks were known as the 'Fathers'.

Conducator (leader, führer)   Title used by the Romanian communist dictator Nicolae Ceauçescu (q.v.).

Confrontation   Term applied to the armed conflict between Indonesia and Malaysia in the 1960s. In 1963 President Sukarno of Indonesia (q.v.) threatened action against Malaysia on the grounds that Malaysia was neo-colonialist. Trade with Singapore was halted, British businesses in Indonesia taken over and diplomatic relations broken off. There were Indonesian guerrilla raids into Sarawak and Sabah, and landings and airdrops across the Straits of Malacca. Hostilities ended in August 1966 when an agreement was signed in Jakarta.

Congress   (1) the two chambers of the US legislature – i.e. the more powerful Senate, and the 435-member House of Representatives. (2) Common abbreviation for the Indian National Congress, formed in 1885 and the main vehicle of Indian nationalism. *See* p. 402.

containment   US policy aimed at preventing the extension of communist influence. George Kennan argued in 1947 that the USSR should be faced with a 'patient but firm and vigilant containment of Russian expansive tendencies.' Examples in practice have been economic aid to Europe under the Marshall Plan, and military engagement in Korea and Vietnam.

continuismo   Term for presidents who remain in office beyond their constitutional period by *de facto* power, a common feature of authoritarian rule in Latin America.

Contract with America   The right-wing Republican agenda which produced victory in the mid-term elections of 1994. The agenda is most closely associated with Newt Gingrich.

Contras   Exiles from Nicaragua after the 1979 victory of the Sandinista revolution, who continued to support former right-wing dictator Anastasio

Somoza Debayle from neighbouring Honduras and mounted armed attacks in north-west Nicaragua. After Somoza's death in 1980 the Contras continued their anti-Sandinista campaign with American backing, but the electoral defeat of the Sandinistas in 1990 effectively ended their activities.

CORE   Congress of Racial Equality (CORE) was founded in 1942 and advocated non-violent civil disobedience in order to obtain civil rights for black Americans.

Crony capitalism   Term commonly used for the system of financial corruption in the mid-1990s in such countries as South Korea and Indonesia where money was invested, not for sound business reasons, but to political or family friends. It contributed to the collapse of the 'Asian Tigers' in 1997.

Cuban Missile Crisis   On 22 October 1962 President Kennedy (q.v.) announced on television that United States surveillance had established the presence of Soviet missile sites in Cuba, and that he was imposing a quarantine on Cuba to prevent the shipment of further offensive weapons. With the threat of nuclear war imminent, tense negotiations took place. On 28 October Khrushchev agreed to remove the missiles, and in return Kennedy lifted the blockade and agreed not to invade Cuba.

Cultural Revolution   The term used to describe the convulsions in Chinese society caused in 1965 by Mao Zedong's movement to purge the country of his opponents and to bring about a revolution in popular ideology.

Dalai Lama   The spiritual and also temporal leader of the Tibetan people. After Chinese troops occupied Tibet in 1951, a major rebellion took place in 1959. The Dalai Lama subsequently fled to India. He was awarded the Nobel Peace Prize, 1989.

decolonization   The European withdrawal from overseas possessions after the Second World War. Britain withdrew from India and Pakistan in 1947, and the majority of her African colonies gained independence by the 1960s. France freed Indo-China, Algeria and Tunisia after liberation wars in the 1950s. Belgium, the Netherlands and Portugal had relinquished the last of their colonies by the 1970s.

Demilitarized Zone   An area following approximately the 38th parallel which divides North and South Korea. Following cessation of hostilities in the 1950–53 Korean War, it was agreed that no military forces should enter the area. A similar zone divided Vietnam along the 17th parallel.

Dengism   Chinese economic modernization programme introduced by Deng Xiaoping in 1984. China turned to decentralized management in industry, the encouragement of market forces, individual enterprise and foreign investment. By the late 1980s there were fears of inflation and unemployment and complaints of corruption. Harshly suppressed demands for political liberalization in 1989 appeared to force a step back in the programme, but in the 1990s the modernization of the Chinese economy continued rapidly.

Dergue, the   (Amharic, 'shadow')   The name taken by the 120-strong Co-ordinating Committee of the Armed Forces which overthrew Emperor Haile Selassie of Ethiopia in 1974. On taking power, the Dergue renamed itself the Provisional Military Administrative Council and was increasingly dominated by Lieutenant Colonel Mengistu Haile Mariam (b. 1937). The Dergue was dissolved in 1980 and, following Mengistu's overthrow in 1991, many of its former members were placed on trial for crimes against humanity in 1994.

Destalinization   The overturning of the 'cult of personality' that had surrounded Soviet dictator Stalin (q.v.) who died in 1953. At the 20th Party Congress in Russia, the attack on Stalin and his purges was led by Khrushchev (q.v.). The process included renaming Stalingrad (which became Volgograd in 1961). Since the fall of communism, there have been further revelations of the evils of the Stalin era.

détente   A French diplomatic term meaning a reduction in tension between two adversary states, widely used to describe Soviet–American and Sino–American relations since 1968. The policy of detente has been characterized by a large number of personal summit meetings between US and Soviet and US and Chinese leaders which have resulted in agreements on trade, cultural exchanges and limited arms control. The Helsinki Agreement of 1975 represented the existence of a more general detente between the Western and communist nations. With the advent of Gorbachev in Russia, detente and co-operation had effectively ended the Cold War (q.v.) by the end of the 1980s.

deterrence   Strategy by which one country deters an adversary from launching a nuclear attack by the threat of instant nuclear retaliation. A so-called 'balance of terror' exists between two countries when both have a high level of assured destruction capability – that is, when neither can expect by a first strike against the enemy's nuclear force to do sufficient damage to prevent a retaliatory second strike causing unacceptable destruction to its own cities. The United States and the Soviet Union operated a range of retaliatory systems to ensure that they maintained this assured destruction capability.

Dewline   Acronym for the Distant Early Warning Viewing Line, a comprehensive radar system established in 1957 by the North American Air Defence Command (NORAD) across the northern reaches of the hemisphere to detect the approach of Soviet nuclear missiles or aircraft. By the 1970s it had been rendered obsolete by the use of satellites in space to detect military movements.

Dien Bien Phu, Battle of   The crucial battle which lost the French Empire in Indo-China. In November 1953, the French commander in Indo-China, General Navarre, fortified Dien Bien Phu, a valley 200 miles west of Hanoi, with 15,000 men to cut the supply routes of the Viet Minh guerrillas (q.v.) into Laos and to draw them into a pitched battle. But the French had underestimated the capability of General Giap (q.v.), the Viet Minh commander, to concentrate men and heavy artillery on the hills overlooking Dien Bien Phu. The vital airfield was rendered unusable, and the French garrison was overwhelmed on 7 May 1954. The defeat ended French power in Indo-China, and this was confirmed at the conference taking place in Geneva. *See also* p. 246.

Dignity battalions   Ten thousand strong paramilitary force set up by Panamanian dictator General Manuel Noriega in 1988, ostensibly to protect the country from US invasion but to intimidate the regime's opponents. The force harassed participants in the May 1989 elections but did not mount resistance to the December 1989 US invasion.

DINA   Secret police operating in Chile during the 1970s under the military dictatorship of President Pinochet. The assassination of a pre-coup defence minister, Orlando Letelier, by DINA operatives in Washington in 1976 led to difficulties in relations with the United States and the replacement of the organization by a new body, the CNI.

Dirty War   Term applied to the vicious Argentine military campaign used against such left-wing guerrilla groups as the Monteneros from 1976 to 1978.

dissidents   Term used particularly in the context of Communist Russia, Eastern Europe and China to refer to those who refuse to conform to the politics and beliefs of the society in which they live. They have frequently been imprisoned and persecuted. Among the most famous are Alexander Solzhenitsyn, the Nobel Prize-winning novelist, expelled from Russia in 1974. Under *glasnost* a new, more liberal climate developed and with the fall of Communism the term is now applied more readily to China.

Doi moi (Viet. 'renovation')   Programme of economic liberalization in Vietnam introduced in the 1980s by Communist Party General Secretary Nguyen Van Linh. *Doi moi* followed the lines of the Soviet Union's *perestroika* (q.v.) and included the abandonment of agricultural collectivism, the introduction of the free market in agricultural produce, the establishment of a private sector and the encouragement of foreign investment.

dollar diplomacy   Term used first by Latin Americans, later more generally, to refer disapprovingly to the use of economic influence by the United States in promoting its overseas interests.

domino theory   Refers to the existence of relations of political dependence between several states. Should any one power fall under communist control, the theory argued that others would also fall, like a row of dominoes. The first explicit formulation of the theory appeared in 1954 in support of arguments for American military assistance to certain non-communist regimes in Indo-China. Both South Vietnam and Laos were seen as 'first dominoes', and their alleged strategic relationship to the rest of South-East Asia was the explanation of the importance attached by successive US administrations in preventing the forcible overthrow of their regimes by communist-supported insurgents.

Easter Rising   The major North Vietnamese offensive of March 1972 during the Vietnam War. It was ultimately repelled by South Vietnamese forces backed by US air strikes.

Eastern bloc   Term which referred to the communist states of Eastern Europe, including the Balkan states of Yugoslavia and Albania. With the dramatic changes in such Eastern European countries as Hungary and Poland in 1989, followed by the collapse of communism in the Soviet Union, the term became redundant.

Eisenhower Doctrine   In March 1957, following the collapse of Anglo-French power in the Middle East in the Suez Crisis (q.v.), President Eisenhower feared that the Soviet Union would have an opportunity to increase its influence in the region. He therefore obtained the approval of Congress to extend US military or economic aid to any state threatened with aggression by 'any nation controlled by international communism'. This policy became known as the Eisenhower Doctrine.

Enola Gay   The aircraft, named after the pilot's mother, that dropped the first atomic bomb on Hiroshima, 6 August 1945.

Enosis   From the Greek word meaning 'to unite' the term used to describe the aims of the Greek Cypriot movement for the political union of Cyprus and Greece. The Turkish minority (*c.* 20% of the population) has consistently feared and opposed such a union. The coup by EOKA supporters (q.v.) in July 1974 prompted a Turkish invasion of Cyprus, and the island is now divided, with the 40% of the island in Turkish control proclaimed as an independent Turkish federated state.

Entebbe Raid   Daring Israeli commando operation to rescue hostages. On 27 June 1976 an Air France Airbus from Tel Aviv to Paris with 12 crew and 247 passengers was hijacked by members of the Popular Front for the Liberation of Palestine (q.v.) and forced to fly to Entebbe in Uganda. Negotiations began over the hijackers demands, and non-Israeli hostages were released. During the night of 3–4 July, three Israeli Hercules C-130 transport aircraft landed at Entebbe airport, rescued the hostages and flew them back to Israel, refuelling *en route* at Nairobi, Kenya.

EOKA   The anti-British, Greek-Cypriot terrorist movement, founded and led by Colonel Grivas to force a British withdrawal from Cyprus. It was most active from 1955 to 1959, with Cyprus becoming an independent country within the Commonwealth in 1960. See also Enosis (above) and Makarios (p. 358).

ERA   The Equal Rights Amendment, a proposed amendment to the US Constitution which was passed by Congress in 1972 to provide that 'equality of rights under law shall not be denied or abridged by the United States or any state on account of sex'. It failed to receive the ratification of three-quarters of the states within the statutorily defined period.

escalation   Term for increasing the intensity or area of a conflict. It was particularly associated with the increases in the scope of the American effort in the Vietnam War. Significant stages in the process of escalation were the first bombing of North Vietnam in August 1964, after incidents in the Gulf of Tonkin, followed by the decision to begin regular bombing of the North in February 1965 and to commit ever-increasing numbers of combat troops.

ETA   Initials of the militant Basque terrorist group in Spain seeking to re-create in northern Spain the short-lived republic of Euzkadi (October 1936–June 1937). It has been responsible for numerous acts of violence. By July 1997, 773 people had died as a result of ETA violence.

ethnic cleansing   Euphemism which emerged in the break-up of the former Yugoslavia in 1992 to describe attempts to remove minority ethnic groups by persuading communities to flee through threats and near-genocidal violence. Most often used to describe Serb actions against the Muslim community in Bosnia.

Eurocommunism   The policy of individual communist parties in Western European countries to seek and pursue their own political paths, not dominated by or taking orders from Russia – as had happened under the domination of the Comintern in the inter-war period.

European Union   *See* p. 214.

Evian Agreements (March 1962)   Overwhelmingly ratified by referenda in France (April) and Algeria (July), the agreements ended the Algerian war of independence fought against France since 1954 with an immediate cease-fire and a guarantee of French withdrawal by the end of the year.

Exchange Rate Mechanism (ERM)   A system for maintaining values of European currencies at fixed rates to one another. There was originally agreement that currencies could fluctuate within a narrow (2%) or wide (6%) band on either side of a predetermined central rate, but the whole ERM was thrown into question by currency turmoil in 1993. *See* pp. 32–8.

Fair Deal   The political programme advocated by US President Truman (q.v.) in 1948, when running for his second term as President. It was a progressive set of policies which, although denying the need for a planned economy, advocated housing, health and education policies all aimed at extending social justice at home, as well as economic and military aid programmes abroad.

Falange   The only political party permitted in Franco's Spain. Founded by José Antonio Primo de Rivera in 1933 as a right-wing movement opposed to the Republic. Primo de Rivera was assassinated in November 1936, in the early months of the Spanish Civil War. The movement survived his death to be used by Franco when the Grand Council of the Falange replaced the Cortes as the legislative body in Spain between June 1939 and July 1942.

Fascism   *See* Neo-fascism, p. 411.

fedayeen   Palestinian guerrillas who raided Israel under the leadership of the Grand Mufti, following their expulsion from Palestine by the Israelis in 1948–49. The word derives from the Arabic for those who risk their lives for a cause. The fedayeen eventually came under the leadership of the PLO.

Food for Peace   An important part of America's foreign aid programme. Congress established 'Food for Peace' in 1954 in order to reduce American farm surpluses, to increase foreign consumption of American produce and to strengthen America's position with the developing nations. Vast quantities of wheat were duly sold to nations for their local currencies which were usually returned to preserve economic stability. By 1973, Congress had authorized a four-year programme involving an annual sum of $2.5 million. One of the major recipients of such American assistance has been India, a state which has not always associated itself diplomatically with the United States.

Free Officers   Radical Egyptian nationalist and republican movement of young army officers, nominally led by Mohammed Neguib but Gamal Abdel Nasser (1918–70) was its most influential figure. Egypt's military failure against Israel in 1948 encouraged growing support and the movement mounted a bloodless coup against King Farouk on 23 July 1952. Neguib became President but was deposed by Nasser in November 1954.

free world   Term used in the West to describe non-communist countries during the Cold War era.

Frente de Libertação de Mocambique (FRELIMO)   The nationalist guerrilla movement in Mozambique which, in 1964, launched an armed struggle for independence. By the early 1970s they claimed control over much of the north. The leader of FRELIMO became President of the provisional government in 1974 and President on independence in 1975.

Frente Nacional de Libertação de Angola (FNLA)   This anti-Marxist Angolan group was in control of the north of Angola at independence. Joint FNLA/UNITA troops were virtually defeated by the MPLA by February 1976. *See* p. 268.

Fretelin   The independence movement in East Timor. This former Portuguese colony was illegally seized by Indonesia. The nationalist movement has been brutally suppressed by the Suharto regime in Indonesia despite international protests.

front-line presidents   The term used to designate the black African Presidents actively involved in attempts to bring about a peace settlement in South Africa: Presidents Neto of Angola, Khama of Botswana, Chissano of Mozambique, Nyerere of Tanzania, Kaunda of Zambia and Mugabe of Zimbabwe.

Front-line States   Originally used to describe the states which faced the illegal white Rhodesian regime – Angola, Botswana, Mozambique,

Tanzania and Zambia – but, following the independence of Zimbabwe in 1980, denoting the states directly engaged against the South African apartheid government including, after 1990, Namibia.

Gang of Four   Radical Chinese Communist leaders – Wang Hongwen, Zhang Chungqiao, Yao Wenyuan and Jiang Qing – denounced by party moderates who gained power in 1976 after the death of Mao Zedong. The Gang, which argued for continuing revolutionary purity rather than economic pragmatism, was arrested and accused at a show trial of plotting to take control of the army. Jiang Qing – Mao's widow – was given a suspended death sentence in 1981.

GATT   *See* General Agreement on Tariffs and Trade.

Gaullist   A follower of General de Gaulle (q.v.), usually associated with authoritarianism and nationalist sentiment. A short-lived mass movement under the Fourth French Republic centred on the *Rassemblement du Peuple Français* (RPF), an authoritarian anti-communist party with Fascist tendencies, which enjoyed its greatest success in the late 1940s and early 1950s. The *Union de la Nouvelle République* (UNR) was formed from various Gaullist groups after establishment of the Fifth French Republic in 1958. Gaullism survived the general's retirement in 1969, and provided a basis for support for his Presidential successor, Georges Pompidou.

Gaza Strip   Disputed territory under Israeli occupation. Swollen with refugees and taken by Egyptian troops in the 1948 war, Gaza was under harsh Egyptian rule, 1948–67. Israel occupied Gaza briefly in 1956–57, and had hoped to prevent its being used to mount guerrilla attacks on Israel, but was forced to return it to Egypt. Israel conquered the area in June 1967 and put it under military administration. At first the Arab population was extremely restive and difficult to control, but the situation quietened after a time. Gazans were permitted to enter Israel to work, and were a useful source of skilled and unskilled labour. The Israeli government has established Jewish settlements in Gaza. Like the West Bank (q.v.), the Strip has been the scene of many demonstrations and riots in recent years. In 1994 it was granted limited self-rule.

General Agreement on Tariffs and Trade (GATT)   An international agreement which came into force in 1948. The countries belonging to GATT account for over 80% of world trade, and are pledged to encourage free trade. There were a series of negotiating conferences on the reduction of tariffs and the abolition of import restrictions. By 1993 over 108 countries were contracting parties and 29 others were applying GATT rules. It inaugurated the Kennedy Round (1964–67), the Tokyo Round

(1973–79) and the Uruguay Round (1986–93). Negotiations were eventually concluded in 1993 and over 120 nations signed the GATT accord in April 1994. GATT has been superceded by the World Trade Organization (q.v.).

Geneva Agreements   *See* p. 223.

Gibraltar Dispute   The British territory in southern Spain commanding the entrance to the Mediterranean, captured by Britain in 1704 and formerly a strategically important naval base, was claimed by Spain in 1939. The UN recognized the claim in 1963, with Great Britain asserting that the wish of the population, expressed overwhelmingly in a referendum, was to remain British. The Spanish Government closed the frontier in 1969, but, following discussions from 1977 to 1980, ended the blockade.

glasnost   The liberalizing 'openness' of the Soviet intellectual atmosphere encouraged by Mikhail Gorbachev, following his appointment as Communist Party Secretary in March 1985. *Glasnost* appeared to set few limits on the discussion of contemporary Soviet society and politics and of Soviet history, particularly the Stalin period.

Golkar   The political party ruling Indonesia under President Suharto (q.v.) continuously for the last thirty years.

Grand Design   Expression used to describe the early aspirations of US President Kennedy (q.v.) in international affairs. The Design envisaged a developing North Atlantic partnership, with an expanding European Economic Community becoming an equal partner with the United States. There was also to be a multilateral nuclear force in NATO.

Great Leap Forward   The Chinese Communist attempt in 1958–61 to make a rapid move towards communism. Large-scale agricultural collectivization was instituted and private consumption reduced. Bad harvests and the ending of technical assistance from the USSR following ideological disputes undermined the attempt.

'Great Society'   Expression used by US President Lyndon Johnson (1908–73) to describe what he hoped would emerge from his administration's 1963–68 progressive civil rights and welfare legislation.

Green revolution   The expansion of agricultural production in developing countries since 1945 by the increasing use of chemical fertilizers, pesticides and high-yield crop seeds. These techniques have been increasingly criticized for their environmental effects.

Greens   The West German ecology party which made a dramatic advance in state elections in 1979 and which, despite internal divisions, remains an influential force. In the late 1980s Green parties in other European countries went on to gain significant support in elections and, while winning few seats, have forced an acknowledgement of environmental issues on other political parties.

Group of Seven (G7)   The world's leading industrialized nations (Britain, Canada, France, Germany, Italy, Japan, the United States), whose heads of state meet regularly to discuss world economic problems and attempt to co-ordinate action for their solution.

Guam Doctrine   The doctrine, propounded by President Richard Nixon, of Vietnamization (i.e. handing over the conduct of the war in Vietnam to the South Vietnamese), made at a press conference on Guam on 23 July 1969. Nixon stated that after 1969 Saigon would increasingly have to rely on its own ground troops as and when US forces were withdrawn.

Guevarism   The largely ineffective guerrilla theory of Ernesto 'Che' Guevara (1928–67), set out in his book *Guerrilla Warfare*. Guevara, an Argentinian, was a leading participant in the Cuban revolution, but his attempt to repeat the success in Bolivia in 1967 led to his capture and death. His belief that a small nucleus of guerrillas could provoke a mass uprising was undermined by peasant suspicions.

guided democracy   The ideology of President Sukarno's regime in Indonesia from 1959 to 1965. Sukarno attempted to unite national, religious and communist forces under a strong executive government, but was overthrown by the army in October 1965.

Gulag Archipelago   The title of Alexander Solzhenitsyn's denunciation of the Russian communist system, based on his and other victims' experience of the Soviet labour camps. Gulag is an acronym for the Russian name of the State Administration of Correctional Labour Camps.

Guomindang   *See* Kuomintang.

Haganah   Secret force formed in 1936 by the Jews in Palestine to defend themselves against Arab attacks. Haganah fought in April and May 1948 to prevent Arabs severing links between Tel Aviv and Jerusalem, and the force became the basis of the army when Israel was created.

Halabja   Place in Iraq where Kurdish civilians were massacred by Iraqi forces using chemical weapons in March 1988.

Hamas (Arab. 'zeal')   The Islamic Resistance Movement, a radical Palestinian group active in the Israeli-occupied territories, established in February 1988 by Sheikh Ahmed Ismail Yassin. Hamas was active in the intifada (q.v.) and its armed wing, the Izz al-Din Qassam, has formed the core of opposition to the 1993 peace agreement between Israel and the Palestine Liberation Organization.

Harambee (Kikuyu. 'let us pull together')   Slogan adopted in Kenya on independence in 1963 and incorporated into the national coat of arms. *Harambee* was intended to mean national self-reliance and the avoidance of dependence on foreign aid.

Hartal   Sri Lankan general strike of 1953, organized by Marxists in protest at the rapid rise in the cost of living and particularly of the staple, rice. To end the strike the government introduced very repressive measures; in clashes with government forces 10 people were killed. Senanayake was forced to resign and his successor partially restored the subsidies. The Hartal reflected national dissatisfaction with the government. The Sri Lanka Freedom Party drew great propaganda value from it and won the 1956 election.

hawks   Term used to describe Americans who argued that intensification and escalation of US involvement in the 1965–72 Vietnam War provided the best guarantee of its most effective conclusion.

Hebron Massacre   Massacre of 50 Arabs by an extremist Jewish settler in March 1994. The massacre failed to derail the peace process, but led to retaliation by Hamas.

Helsinki Conference (30 July–1 August 1975)   European security conference attended by representatives of 35 countries. Agreement was reached on the prevention of accidental war, economic and technological co-operation, the desirability of increasing contact between citizens of East and West, together with a recognition of individual human rights.

Hezbollah   Militant Iranian-backed terrorist group active in Lebanon in the 1980s. Its name means 'Party of God'. Active since the 1980s, its rocket attacks on Israeli settlements in northern Galilee helped provoke the massive Israeli bombardment of southern Lebanon in July 1993 (Operation Accountability) which in turn created a major refugee crisis as the Lebanese fled north towards Beirut.

Historic Compromise   Term used to describe the support given by the Italian Communist Party (PCI) to the governing Christian Democrats from 1976. The support marked the end of more than a generation of Communist exclusion from the governing coalitions of modern Italy and reflected the need to form a strong base with which to deal with growing problems of inflation and terrorism. From 1978 on the Communists were virtually unofficial members of the government, largely through the mediation of Aldo Moro, the Christian Democrat Prime Minister. His death in spring 1978 at the hands of terrorists, and that of the Communist leader Enrico Berlinguer in 1984, undermined a long-term arrangement.

Ho Chi-minh Trail   Elaborate system of routes along the South Vietnam border with Laos and Cambodia used to bring North Vietnamese supplies to Viet Cong forces in the 1964–75 Vietnam War.

Hot Line   A direct telecommunications link between the White House and the Kremlin, which was set up by a memorandum of understanding signed by the United States and the Soviet Union in Geneva on 20 June 1963. The need for such a direct channel of communication for negotiations in times of crisis had been demonstrated by the Cuban Missile Crisis of October 1962. It was used, for example, during the Middle East War in June 1967. Similar links exist between London and Moscow and between Paris and Moscow.

Huk   Originally the Philippine 'People's Army against Japan' formed among communist-led peasants in March 1942, which came increasingly under Chinese communist influence. Outlawed in 1948 and 1957 for its campaign against landlords and the government, the Huk was reorganized as the 'New People's Army' in the early 1970s. The movement continued its campaign despite the fall of President Marcos in 1986.

Hundred Flowers   Chinese communist government's attempt to win intellectual support in 1956–57, based on Mao Zedong's declaration, 'Let a hundred flowers bloom and a hundred schools of criticism compete'. The policy was abandoned when it became clear how extensive the resulting criticism would be.

ILO   *See* International Labour Organization.

India, Partition of   The division of British India on independence in to India, Pakistan (and now Bangladesh), Burma (Myanmar) and Ceylon (Sri Lanka).

Indian National Congress   Party formed as an educational association in 1885 to encourage Indian political development and which grew into an opponent of British rule. Mohandas Karamchand Gandhi (1869–1948) became its leader in 1915, and Congress conducted a non-violent civil disobedience campaign through the 1920s and 1930s. Its leaders were interned by Britain between 1942 and 1945. On independence in 1947 Congress President Jawaharlal Nehru (1889–1964) became India's first Prime Minister, with a policy of industrialization and non-alignment in foreign affairs. The Congress Party, apart from a period in opposition from 1977 to 1980, formed every government from independence to the defeat of Rajiv Gandhi in 1989.

Indo-China   French South-East Asian colonies in Annam, Cambodia, Cochin-China, Laos and Tonkin. They were held by France from the 1860s until July 1954, when the Geneva Agreements recognized Cambodia, Laos and Vietnam as independent states.

Interhamwe (Kinyarwanda. 'Those who stand together')   A predominantly Hutu militia in Rwanda, organized in 1991 as the youth wing of President Juvénal Habyarimana's National Republican Movement for Democracy and Development (MRND). The Interhamwe opposed President Habyarimana's attempted constitutional settlement with rebels in 1993 and, following his assassination in 1994, formed death squads which massacred hundreds of thousands of people seen as disloyal.

International Labour Organization (ILO)   Originally established in 1919 as an independent body which would act in association with the League of Nations to improve working conditions, wage levels, industrial healthcare, etc., it is now a specialist agency of the United Nations.

International Monetary Fund (IMF)   Organization set up at the Bretton Woods Conference in 1944 which came into operation in 1947. Members contribute a quota to the fund and can negotiate a loan if they are in debt. The intention was that the IMF would help to stabilize exchange rates, but since floating exchange rates have developed, countries tended to allow their currencies to lose value rather than borrow from the IMF.

Intifada   Name given to the Arab uprising which began in 1988 in the Israeli-occupied Gaza Strip (q.v.) and West Bank (q.v.).

Iran–Contra Affair   Political scandal of the second Reagan administration (1985–89), in which it was alleged that the US government, in contravention of the law and its own stated policy, supplied arms to the government of Iran (then involved in a war with Iraq) and used the profits of these sales to fund the operations of the Contras (q.v.) in Nicaragua. The charges, which first arose in the press in November 1986, were investigated and largely substantiated by the Tower Commission in 1987 and subsequently by Congressional committees. They resulted in criminal charges being laid against certain government officials, including the National Security Adviser Vice-Admiral John Poindexter and National Security Council staff member Colonel Oliver North. However, it was not established that President Reagan had himself either sanctioned or known about the illegal activities.

Iran hostage crisis   Political crisis arising from the seizure by revolutionary students of 53 staff members at the US Embassy in Tehran in November 1979. The Americans were held hostage for 444 days in an attempt to force the US government to return the deposed Shah to Iran. The episode caused immense damage to the reputation of the then President, Jimmy Carter, and significantly weakened his re-electability in the 1980 Presidential campaign. The hostages were only released in January 1981 at the moment that President Reagan was being sworn into office. A decade later it was being alleged that the Reagan election campaign had secretly conspired with the Iranian government (in an episode known as the 'October Surprise') to manipulate the issue to the Republicans' advantage.

Iron Curtain   A symbol of the frontier between the 'communist' and the 'free' world. The term was used by Winston Churchill with reference to Eastern Europe, when he said at Fulton, Missouri, in March 1946: 'From Stettin in the Baltic to Trieste in the Adriatic an iron curtain has descended across the Continent.' The term was much in use during the Cold War. However, the advent of Gorbachev to power and the revolutionary changes in Eastern Europe in 1989, including the effective dismantling of the Berlin Wall and the symbolic opening of the Brandenburg Gate crossing, have made the term redundant.

Islamic Revolution   An outgrowth of the reassertion of Islamic values in the late 1970s, initially in Saudi Arabia, encouraged by the confidence flowing from wealth based on oil. In March 1979 Iran was declared an Islamic Republic following the overthrow of the Shah and his replacement by a Shi'ite dominated Revolutionary Council under Ayatollah Khomeini. The regime rejected Western influence and values and enforced Islamic law. Gen. Mohammed Zia ul-Haq's military government in Pakistan similarly based itself on Islamic law, and there has been pressure within other Muslim states to follow this pattern.

isolationism   Policy of avoiding alliances and having minimal involvement in international affairs. The United States remained isolationist until the early twentieth century and returned to the policy in the 1920s and 1930s following its involvement in the First World War. After 1945,

America's role as leader of the West forced an abandonment of isolationism but a return to the policy has been a recurring demand of some conservative Republicans, first in the early 1960s and again after the 1965–72 Vietnam War.

Jamahiraya Libyan expression meaning 'the state of the masses'. In March 1977 Col. Muammar Qadhafi proclaimed his country to be the Socialist People's Libyan Arab Jamahiraya.

Janata Alliance of opposition groups formed against the Indian Congress Party in 1977. Morarji Desai led Janata to victory against Mrs Gandhi in the July 1979 election but the alliance succumbed to internal divisions and went down to electoral defeat in 1980.

KANU Kenya African National Union. Led by Jomo Kenyatta (1897–1978) from 1947 onwards, the party's base was in the Kikuyu tribe and it soon became the only legal party following Kenyan independence in 1963.

Kent State On 4 May 1970 four students were shot dead by National Guardsmen on the campus of Kent State University near Cleveland, Ohio, during a violent demonstration by students against the recent movement of US troops into Cambodia (*see* Vietnam War). It was the most notorious and bloodiest episode in the widespread unrest over the war which affected American universities at that period.

Keynesianism Theory and practice derived from the economist Maynard Keynes, particularly his *General Theory* (1936). It encouraged state intervention to secure economic growth through the management of overall demand by fiscal means, and laid the basis for post-1945 welfare capitalism.

Khalistan The name of the independent homeland in the Indian subcontinent sought by militant Sikh activists.

Khalsa The Sikh Commonwealth in the Punjab, India, known as the 'brotherhood of the pure'. Derived from the Arabic for pure, sincere, free.

Khmer Rouge The communist guerrilla troops who defeated the republican forces in the Cambodian civil war (q.v.).

Knesset The 120-member single-chamber Israeli legislature. Members are elected for four years by universal suffrage under proportional representation.

Koreagate   The name given to describe a South Korean scheme to influence US legislators and top executive officials during the 1970s through cash bribes and campaign contributions totaling between $500,000 and $1 million annually. Park Tong Sun, a wealthy South Korean businessman, had entertained many Washington figures, some of whom were later indicted.

Korean War   The country of Korea was occupied by the Japanese from 1910 to 1945 when the area was partitioned, the USSR occupying the land to the north of the 38th parallel and the United States that to the south. No agreement was reached concerning the eventual reunification of the country, and in 1950 troops from North Korea invaded the south and civil war broke out. The invasion of South Korea by North Korea on 25 June 1950 led to intervention by UN forces following an emergency session of the Security Council, which was being boycotted by the USSR. The advance of UN forces into North Korea on 1 October 1950 brought the Chinese into the war on 27 July 1953. In 1972 talks took place about reunification, but little progress has been made and the country remains divided into the Democratic People's Republic of Korea and the Republic of Korea.

Kraków Declaration   Declaration made by Czechoslovakia, Hungary and Poland on 5–6 October 1991 pledging attempt to integrate their forces into NATO and to join the European Community.

Kremlin   (Russ: citadel)   Refers to the citadel in Moscow occupied by the former Imperial Palace. Now the administrative headquarters of, and synonymous with, the government of Russia.

Ku Klux Klan   A white supremacist secret society formed in the US southern states following their defeat in the American Civil War in 1865. The Klan's terrorist violence forced the imposition of martial law in some areas and it was suppressed by the 1880s. It revived in 1915 and extended its terror campaign to Catholics, Jews and the Left. A further resurgence came in response to 1960s civil rights legislation.

Kuomintang   Nationalist Chinese democratic republican party founded in 1891 by Sun Yat-sen, led from 1925 by Chiang Kai-shek. The party governed China from 1928 and led the resistance to Japanese occupation from 1937 to 1945. Under Chiang the Kuomintang degenerated into a military oligarchy, and he was overthrown by the Communists in 1949. Chiang and his followers retreated to Taiwan, with American support.

Laogai   The Chinese equivalent of the Soviet Gulag. China, as the largest abuser of human rights in the world, has an estimated 2,000 prison camps with perhaps 10 million prisoners forced to work prison farms, salt mines, etc.

Liberation election   Term used by black South Africans for the first multi-racial election of 27–28 April 1994 which paved the way for majority rule in South Africa. The election resulted in a sweeping victory for the African National Congress (ANC).

Liberation theology   The attempt by some Central and South American Roman Catholic priests to work with a 'bias to the poor' by reconciling in practice Christian theology with Marxist economic and social analysis.

Likud   An alliance of Israeli right-wing parties which won the May 1977 general election under Menachem Begin's leadership, replacing Mapai and the Labour Party for the first time. Likud went on to further success in the 1988 elections.

Little Boy   The name given to the first atomic bomb, dropped on Hiroshima by the US aircraft *Enola Gay* on 6 August 1945.

Lomé Conventions, the   Signed on 28 February 1975 between the European Community and 46 African, Caribbean and Pacific countries, of which 22 were members of the Commonwealth, 18 were formerly associated with the Six (q.v.) under the Yaoundé Convention, and 6 had no previous links with members of the European Community. The Convention included provisions to allow duty-free entry into the Community of all imports from the ACP States except about 4% of imports of agricultural products. It also set up the Stabex Scheme and the European Development Fund and concerned general industrial, technical and financial co-operation. The original Lomé Convention has been much expanded by subsequent agreements. Lomé IV, concluded in 1989, was signed by 70 countries.

McCarthyism   Unsubstantiated accusations of disloyalty and abuse of legislative investigatory power that engender fear of real or imagined threats to national security. The term derives from the behaviour of Senator Joseph R. McCarthy (1908–57) of Wisconsin who, in the early 1950s, made repeated unsubstantiated accusations of treachery against public officials (particularly in the State Department) under the protection of his Senatorial immunity. McCarthy's accusations were widely accepted and in February 1950 he claimed to know of 205 communists in the US State Department. Hundreds were imprisoned during four years of investigations but in 1954 the Senate censured McCarthy for bringing it into disrepute when he attempted to extend his criticisms to the US army.

Mahatma   Title (from the Sanskrit 'great soul') bestowed on Indian national leader Mohandas Karamchand Gandhi (1869–1948) by his Hindu followers, in recognition of his asceticism, simplicity and what they saw as saintly qualities.

Malvinas   The Argentinian name for the Falklands Islands in the South Atlantic, which both Britain and the Argentine claim. The islands were occupied by Argentina on 2 April 1982 and retaken by Britain on 14 June.

Maoism   Revision of Marxism to suit Chinese conditions undertaken by Mao Zedong (1893–1976). Mao argued that in non-industrialized countries the peasantry rather than the urban proletariat was the main force for revolutionary change. The peasantry would ally with the working class to overthrow the feudal classes, and advance to socialism without an intervening capitalist stage. Revolution had in Mao's view to be permanently renewed, as the 1966–69 Cultural Revolution demonstrated. His ideas brought China into conflict with the USSR, which claimed that it was the fount of Marxist ideology. Following Mao's death China gradually adopted economic modernisation under Deng Xiaoping.

Mapai   The Israeli Workers' Party (Miphlegeth Poalei Israel), formed in Palestine 1930. Dominated by David Ben Gurion (1886–1973) from 1930 to 1965, the party served in every coalition government from 1948 to 1977. Mapai combined with two small socialist parties in 1968 to form the Israeli Labour Party.

Marshall Plan   United States plan for the economic reconstruction of Europe, named after Secretary of State General George C. Marshall. The Organization for European Economic Co-operation was established to administer the aid in April 1948, but the Soviet rejection of the Plan meant that most of the monetary aid went to Western Europe. Between 1948 and 1952 the US provided some $17,000 million which was a crucial element in European post-war recovery.

Marxism   The ideological basis of state socialism and of communism formulated by Karl Marx (1818–83) and Friedrich Engels (1820–95), since subject to much revision and development. Marx claimed to have discovered that history moved dialectically towards socialism through a developing thesis, antithesis and synthesis. This dialectic showed itself in class struggle. The basis of any society lay in its means of production and the ownership of those means. The culture, politics and morality of any society were a superstructure built upon the economic base and reflected the interests of the ruling class. Revolution came when developing productive methods came into irreconcilable conflict with the system of ownership. Industrialism had emerged out of agricultural feud-alism and the bourgeoisie had overthrown the nobility to enable itself to carry capitalist development forward. Capitalism, which faced its own contradictions, would in turn be overthrown by the industrial working class which would create socialism. Whatever the weaknesses of Marx's claim to have discovered a scientific truth, his analysis did provide many socialists with a strong ideological self-confidence.

Marxism-Leninism   An interpretation of Marxism made by Lenin (1870–1924), whose leadership of the Bolshevik seizure of power in Russia in 1917 gave his ideas great influence. Lenin's analysis of imperialism sought to explain capitalism's continuing survival. Imperialism enabled capital-ist states to find new markets and sources of raw materials, and to wean a domestic 'labour aristocracy' from revolution with a share in the fruits of colonial exploitation. He saw the working class as incapable of realiz-ing the need for socialism unaided, and developed the concept of the Party, a professional elite which would lead the struggle against capital-ism and exercise a post-revolutionary dictatorship of the proletariat.

massive retaliation   Name given to a defence doctrine announced by John Foster Dulles (q.v.) in January 1954, which laid down that the correct way for the United States to meet local communist aggression was by responding 'vigorously at places and with means of our own choosing'. The implied threat was that the United States would no longer observe the self-imposed restraints of the Korean War (q.v.) but might use her full nuclear capability against the Soviet Union in response to acts of communist aggression anywhere in the world. The advantage of the policy was that it meant a saving on conventional forces, but there was a problem of credibility, as it would be extremely difficult to convince the Russians that the United States would really initiate nuclear war to counter all minor acts of aggression.

Mau Mau   The Mau Mau was a militant African secret society active in Kenya between 1952 and 1960. A state of emergency was declared and some 10,000 British troops sent to Kenya. About 13,500 people were killed during the troubles, and the Mau Mau emergency was a vital factor in persuading Britain to decolonize.

May events   Paris student demonstrations on 2 May 1968 over educa-tional issues developed into broader political protests. After violent riots on 10–11 May, ten million workers mounted a general strike and work-place occupations, threatening the Republic's stability. Concessions to workers and students ended *les événements*, but the position of President Charles de Gaulle was undermined.

Mercosur   South American customs union which came into force on 1 January 1995. Created originally in 1990.

Muldergate   South African political scandal in 1978 over alleged misuse of state funds by Information Minister Connie Mulder, which led ultimately to the resignation of President Vorster in June 1979. The name was a reference to the Nixon Watergate scandal.

Multilateral Nuclear Force (MNF)   An abortive American proposal of the early 1960s for the creation of a mixed-manned NATO force of 25 surface vessels. They would be armed with Polaris nuclear missiles, but there would be an American veto on their use. Despite French and British rejection of the plan, the United States and West Germany decided to go ahead in June 1964, but this decision was later reversed. An alternative British scheme, the Atlantic Nuclear Force, was also dropped.

multilateralists   Term most often used with reference to nuclear weapons, describing the position taken by those arguing that a state possessing nuclear arms should not relinquish them alone – the argument of unilateralists – but should negotiate mutual disarmament with other states.

Muslim Brethren   Founded in 1928 in Egypt by Hassan al-Banna as an Islamic revival movement. By 1939 the Brethren played a considerable role in the nationalist movement and were a powerful organization with mass support. The society often clashed with the government and was dissolved in 1948 because of its use of violence and assassination as political weapons. Following the 1948 assassination of the Prime Minister by one of the Brethren, al-Banna was himself assassinated. By 1951 the organization was permitted to reconstitute itself. Initially the society enjoyed good relations with the officers who led the 1952 revolution, but these soon deteriorated. The Brethren saw their political role evaporating and tried to undermine the government. In 1954 they made an unsuccessful attempt to assassinate Nasser. Hundreds of arrests followed. The society went underground, but was further decimated by more arrests in 1965–66. Branches were established in Syria in 1937. The Brethren there also sided with the nationalists but they never formed a paramilitary movement. In 1952 the government dissolved the society, but permitted it to reform again in 1954. Its activity was also curbed during Syria's union with Egypt.

My Lai   A Vietnamese village where US troops massacred 450 inhabitants on 16 March 1968 during an operation against the Viet Cong. The incident became public in November 1969, further undermining the already unpopular US position in Vietnam. On 29 March 1971 Lt. William

Calley was sentenced to life imprisonment for his part in the crime, but his sentence was later reduced.

NAFTA The North American Free Trade Association, established by executive agreement between the United States and Canada in 1987 and subsequently ratified by them. Also joined by Mexico. The agreement provided for the abolition of all tariffs between them by 1999.

Nassau Agreement An agreement concluded on 18 December 1962 between President Kennedy and Harold Macmillan, under which America provided Britain with Polaris nuclear missiles. This 'favoured nation' treatment proved a major factor in de Gaulle's decision to veto Britain's Common Market application shortly afterwards.

Nasserism Term used to describe the ideology propounded by President Gamal Abdel Nasser (1918–70) which was influential, but ultimately unsuccessful, in the 1950s and 1960s. Nasserism attempted to combine nationalism, socialism and moderate Islam into a coherent programme that could unite the Arab world and in 1958 Nasser established a United Arab Republic with Syria. Nasserism's effectiveness was severely undermined by Israel's victory in the 1967 Six Day War.

NATO *See* p. 216.

neo-colonialism Term coined by Kwame Nkrumah (1909–72), President of Ghana, 1960–66, to describe the ability of the Western capitalist powers to retain economic and political control over the former European colonies, despite their nominal independence.

neo-fascism Expression used to describe the fascist movements that emerged in Europe following the defeat of the German and Italian varieties in the Second World War but which attempt to preserve a democratic image. Among the most significant are the Front National in France and the Movimento Sociale Italiano in Italy. In Britain, the National Front and the British National Party have remained marginal but the collapse of Communist control in Eastern Europe saw a growth of neo-fascist groupings in the 1990s.

New Commonwealth Term used to describe the former British colonies which became members of the Commonwealth following their post-Second World War independence. The New Commonwealth, which was black and Asian, was contrasted with the 'old' white Commonwealth dominions of Australia, Canada, New Zealand and South Africa.

New Left   A term which emerged in Europe and the United States in the late 1950s to describe a strand of Marxist thought and action which followed the growing disillusion with the Soviet Union's model of socialism, particularly following the suppression of the 1956 Hungarian uprising. Rejecting the vulgar Marxism (q.v.) of economic determinism, the New Left turned its attention to such concepts as cultural hegemony and alienation. The 1968 events in France and anti-Vietnam War activism in the United States marked the peak of New Left influence.

New Right   Term embracing the conservative, Christian-based politics, an increasingly important section of the US right, in the late 1970s. Later based around the Moral Majority organization founded by the Reverend Jerry Falwell in 1979. Often fundamentalist and evangelical, it bitterly opposed such issues as abortion, pornography, gay rights, etc., and supported school prayers, anti-communism, etc.

Nine, the   Belgium, Denmark, France, Italy, Ireland, Luxembourg, the Netherlands, the United Kingdom and West Germany, that is, the nine members of the European Community after its enlargement in January 1973. Norway, which had signed the Treaty of Accession, failed to ratify it and did not join. In 1982 the Nine became Ten when Greece joined the Community, and Twelve when Spain and Portugal joined.

Nixon Doctrine   Policy of distributing the burden of collective defence more equitably as between the United States and her allies. The doctrine was first enunciated on the island of Guam in 1969, when President Nixon expressed the willingness of the United States to provide military supplies and economic assistance to friendly nations, but seemed to rule out the likelihood of providing American ground troops for local conflicts in South-East Asia. The doctrine required allies to assume 'primary responsibility' for their own defence, and was at first thought to apply exclusively to South-East Asia. Later, the concept of 'limited assistance' was developed in a series of statements and actions by members of the Nixon administration into a general principle which would guide the relations between the United States and her allies.

Non-Proliferation Treaty   Treaty intended to prevent the proliferation of nuclear weapons signed in Washington, London and Moscow on 1 July 1968. It came into force on 5 March 1970.

OAS   (1) Organization of American States (*see* p. 218). (2) *Organisation de l'Armée Secrète*, a right-wing French terrorist organization led by Gen. Raoul Salan, which threatened the 5th Republic in 1961–62. Most members were ex-Algerian colonists who opposed President Charles de Gaulle's attempts to extricate France from Algeria, and they attempted to assassinate him several times.

OAU *See* p. 217.

Oder–Neisse line This is the boundary line of the River Oder and its tributary, the Western Neisse, which was established as a frontier between Poland and Germany after the Second World War. It was accepted by the United Kingdom, the United States and the USSR at the Potsdam Conference, on the understanding that a final delimitation would take place later. An agreement made between the German Democratic Republic and Poland in 1950 described the line as a permanent frontier, and in 1955 the East German and Polish governments made a declaration to this effect. It was not accepted by the German Federal Republic, the UK and the United States. In pursuit of improved relations with Eastern Europe the Chancellor of the German Federal Government, Willy Brandt, signed a treaty with Poland in December 1970 in which both countries accepted the existing frontiers.

OECD *See* p. 217.

oil embargo In response to the October 1973 Arab–Israeli War, seven Arab states imposed an embargo on oil shipments to the United States to persuade her to press Israel to withdraw from territory occupied in the 1967 war. The embargo on the United States was lifted in January 1974.

Organization of African Unity (OAU) *See* p. 217.

Organization of American States (OAS) *See* p. 218.

Organization for Economic Co-operation and Development (OECD) *See* p. 217.

Oslo Accords *See* p. 45.

Ostpolitik Eastern policy developed in the German Federal Republic by Kurt Kiesinger to normalize relations with communist countries other than the Soviet Union who recognized the German Democratic Republic. It led to the conclusion of peace treaties with the USSR and Poland (1972), and border agreements over traffic and communications between East and West Berlin.

Palestine Liberation Organization *See* PLO.

Pan-Africanism   Expression for the movement which advocates the unity and liberation of the African continent and the solidarity of the peoples of Africa and the African diaspora. One element of Pan-Africanism in the diaspora sees the ultimate objective as the return of all people of African descent to Africa. In 1901 a Pan-African Association was established in London by Henry Sylvester Williams (1869–1911). Pan-Africanism was adopted by the Universal Negro Improvement Association (UNIA), and six Pan-African Congresses were held between 1919 and 1974. As European colonies in Africa achieved independence, Pan-Africanism on the continent appeared to become a waning force, despite the attempts of Ghanaian anti-colonialist leader Kwame Nkrumah (1909–72) to encourage African unity.

pariah state   Expression used to describe a state which is ostracized by other, usually Western democratic, states because of its actions, policies and form of leadership. South Africa under the apartheid regime (q.v.) was widely accorded pariah status. In the 1980s and 1990s, Libya and Iran have been treated as pariahs for their alleged involvement in and encouragement of international terrorism. Iraq, since President Saddam's invasion of Kuwait in 1990, Serbia (because of its alleged ethnic cleansing policies), and North Korea are more recent pariah states.

Pasdaran   The Islamic Revolutionary Guards Corps (the Sepah-e Pasdaran-e Enqelab-e Eslami) established as a people's militia in Iran following the successful Islamic Revolution of 1979. The Revolutionary Guards were zealous in the imposition of Islamic fundamentalism.

Pass Laws   The requirement that black South Africans should carry pass-books to be produced on demand, a humiliating procedure intended to restrict their movements. The laws were increasingly the source of black anger. They were abolished as apartheid collapsed.

Pathet Lao   A Laotian rebel movement led by Prince Souphanouvong (q.v.) and established in 1949. It collaborated with the Viet Minh (q.v.) in the invasion of Laos in 1953. During the civil war it fought against the Royal Lao government troops and took part in the coalition government set up in 1974. In early 1975 it effectively took over control of the country and in December its leader Prince Souphanouvong became President of the Lao People's Democratic Republic.

Patriotic Front   The unexpected grouping of Zimbabwean nationalists Mugabe (q.v.) and Nkomo (q.v.) in Geneva in 1976 led to the formation of the Patriotic Front which had the support of the OAU (q.v.). Smith refused to negotiate with them. Their military forces were divided into two separate groups: ZANU led by Mugabe from Mozambique and ZAPU led by Nkomo from Zambia.

Peace Corps   A US agency that administers the foreign aid programme adopted in 1961, under which American volunteers are sent to developing countries to teach skills and generally to assist in raising living standards. Most developing countries have taken advantage of the availability of this service, but others have been highly critical and have refused to allow the volunteers into their countries.

Peace Dividend   The reduction of government expenditure on arms – and the increase on, for example, education and social services – that was expected to follow the end of the Cold War after the collapse of the Warsaw Pact and of the Soviet and East European regimes at the end of the 1980s.

Pearce Commission   A Commission led by Lord Pearce and set up in Rhodesia following the Smith–Home agreement of November 1971. The report disclosing the result of the 'test of acceptability' was published on 23 May 1972 and showed that the people as a whole did not regard the proposals as an acceptable basis for independence.

Pentagon   The five-sided US Department of Defense building in Virginia on the outskirts of Washington, DC. Often used as a synonym for American military interests.

Pentagon Papers   Documents originating in the US Department of Defense (whose headquarters is the Pentagon building on the outskirts of Washington DC) which were leaked to the *New York Times* in 1971 by former Pentagon analyst Daniel Ellsberg. They appeared to reveal a government policy of deliberate misinformation about the Vietnam War (q.v.). The leak led President Nixon to form the Plumbers (*See* Watergate).

People power   Term used to describe the massive popular support gained in the Philippines by Corazón Aquino in her campaign of opposition to President Ferdinand Marcos. Having won a rigged election in February 1986, Marcos was faced with a demonstration by thousands of people protecting pro-Aquino forces from attack by Marcos's troops. The United States withdrew its backing from Marcos, who fled and was replaced as President by Aquino in March.

People's Republic   The name taken by states under Communist control, e.g. the People's Republics of China or, formerly, of Hungary and of Romania (until 1965, when it became a 'Socialist Republic'). There are sometimes variations on the name as in, for example, the Korean People's Democratic Republic (North Korea) or the German Democratic Republic (the former East Germany).

perestroika   From the Russian 'restructuring', an attempt led by Mikhail Gorbachev (Communist Party Secretary, 1985, President, 1988) to regenerate the stagnant Soviet economy by encouraging market forces, decentralizing industrial management, and democratizing the Party and government machinery. By mid-1990 political liberalization had taken place, soon to be overtaken by the fall of communism.

Peronismo   Political, economic and social programme, pursued by the Argentinian dictator Juan Domingo Perón between 1946 and 1955 (also called *justicialismo*). Midway between communism and capitalism and in some ways analogous to fascism, it involved a five-year economic plan; government control of the press, education and labour; nationalization of banks, railways and telecommunications; the fostering of mixed public and private enterprises and the end of British influence on the Argentinian economy. Political opposition was strictly limited. Argentinian claims to the Falkland Islands and the Antarctic were pressed and at one time an anti-US stance was adopted.

petrodollar   Following the massive increases in oil prices in 1975, OPEC members had huge balance of payment surpluses in dollars which they wished to invest. This money, known as petrodollars, was partly lent to developing countries for purchase of machinery, but much was invested in US government securities and in the money markets of London and New York.

Philadelphia Charter   Declaration issued in Philadelphia, Pennsylvania in May 1944 by the International Labour Organization (now an agency of the United Nations) expressing the right of all people to freedom, dignity, economic security, material well-being, spiritual development and equal opportunity.

Ping-pong diplomacy   Term used to describe the easing of relations between Communist China and the United States which began with an official welcome to an American table tennis team by Zhou Enlai in 1971. US Secretary of State Henry Kissinger followed this up with a mission to China in July, preparing the way for a later visit by President Nixon.

PLO Palestine Liberation Organization, formed in May 1964 in Jordan to unite Palestinian Arabs against Israel. It was dominated by the Syrian al-Fatah, led by Yasser Arafat. The PLO mounted guerrilla attacks on

Israel and Israeli-occupied territory and was involved in international terrorism. Israel for long refused to recognize the PLO, but the PLO has taken part in the recent peace process and an embryonic Palestine state is emerging.

pluralism   A pluralistic society is one in which a plurality of interests are represented by the institutions which constitute the society. Pluralism demands that independent organizations should be able to operate in the same social/political system.

Polaris   The US Navy's contribution to the United States strategic offensive forces consisted of 41 nuclear-powered submarines, each initially equipped with 16 Polaris intermediate-range ballistic missiles, which first became operational in 1961 and can be fired while the submarine is submerged.

Polish October   Period of reforming hope in Poland in 1956 following the revelation of Stalinist excesses in Khrushchev's speech to the Soviet Communist Party's 20th Congress. Workers in Poznan struck and clashed with the authorities in June, opening divisions in the Polish Communist Party which carried Wladyslaw Gomulka (1905–82) to the post of Party Leader in October. Gomulka's promotion raised hopes of wide-ranging reform and the easing of censorship, and a weakening of centralized economic control followed. However, as Warsaw Pact troops massed on Poland's borders and Khrushchev demanded loyalty, the impetus weakened.

Politburo   The Political Bureau of the Communist Party, the party's executive committee and the centre of power in communist-controlled states.

Popular Democratic Front for the Liberation of Palestine (PDFLP)   Marxist resistance movement which was formed under the leadership of Nayef Hawatmah in 1969 as a splinter group from the PFLP (q.v.). Originally it was Syrian-backed. The PDFLP, along with al-Fatah (q.v.), took a more moderate stance on the Palestinian problem since the 1973 October War. It supported participation in negotiations at Geneva and indicated a willingness to form a national authority on whatever territory can be liberated from Israel. However it has not recognized Israel's right to exist. Its members fought on the side of the Leftists in the Lebanese civil war and in November 1976 clashed with the Syrian-backed Palestinian guerrilla organization.

Popular Front for the Liberation of Palestine (PFLP)   Founded in 1967 when several smaller resistance groups merged, the organization was led by George Habash. Of Marxist-Leninist orientation, the PFLP has seen its role as that of midwife to revolutionary change in the Arab world. It has believed that only with that change could the unity necessary for a successful confrontation with Israel be achieved. It did not join the PLO (q.v.) until 1970, and after the 1973 October War has formed part of the rejectionist front – supported by Iraq and Libya – which asserted the need to continue the armed struggle with Israel and opposed a negotiated settlement. The PFLP withdrew from the PLO in September 1974 and also cut its ties with the Palestine Central Council, but remained a member of the Palestine National Council. The intervention of Syria in the Lebanese civil war brought about a limited rapprochement between the rejectionist front and the PLO, but it was short-lived. The rejectionist front has condemned the PLO's 1977 improvement in relations with Jordan and has rejected the more recent peace process.

Potsdam Conference   The last inter-allied conference of the Second World War, held at Potsdam outside Berlin (11 July–2 August 1945). The meeting between Winston Churchill (until 26 July when a general election brought Attlee and the Labour Party into power), President Truman and Marshal Stalin (with Bevin, Eden, Byrnes and Molotov attending) was to formulate future Allied policies, to lay the basis for definitive peace settlements and to reach agreed policies on the treatment of Germany. The idea of partitioning Germany into a number of states was dropped and principles governing the treatment of the whole of Germany leading to disarmament, de-Nazification and demilitarization were agreed upon. The differing views of the Russians and the Western Powers on reparations were among the most intractable problems of the conference. It was agreed that the city of Königsberg (now Kaliningrad) was to be transferred to the USSR and that the Polish–German frontier should be on the Oder–Neisse line (q.v.). The Western interpretation of the Yalta Declaration on Liberated Europe could not be realized and the question of the Turkish Straits remained unsettled.

'Prague Spring'   Name given to the period of attempted liberalization in Czechoslovakia under Dubček, who was Secretary of the Communist Party in spring 1968. The attempt was brought to an end by the intervention of Warsaw Pact troops in August 1968 and Dubček's replacement by Husak.

Pravda   Soviet newspaper. Organ of the Central Committee of the Communist Party of the Soviet Union. First Marxist daily with a mass circulation; founded in 1912.

Quai d'Orsay   The Seine embankment in Paris on which the French Foreign Office is situated: by extension, a term for the Foreign Office itself.

Quiet Revolution   The period of the 1960–66 Liberal government in Quebec led by Premier Jean Lesage. Increased government involvement in the economy, improved welfare services, and school and hospital building encouraged a sense of communal self-awareness leading to separatist demands, the Liberals seeking 'special status' within Canada and the more militant *Parti Québécois* complete independence.

Rabat Conference   The 1974 Arab summit meeting which confirmed the PLO in its role as the only legitimate representative of the Palestinians. For the first time King Hussein of Jordan agreed that the Palestinians had a right to sovereignty in all of liberated Palestine, under PLO leadership.

Rapacki Plan   Proposal in February 1958 by Polish Foreign Minister Adam Rapacki (1909–70) to create a nuclear-free zone by banning the manufacture and stationing of nuclear weapons in Czechoslovakia, Poland, East and West Germany. Rejected by Britain and the United States because the USSR would retain conventional military superiority in the area.

rapprochement   Diplomatic expression deriving from the French, signifying the re-establishment of friendly relations between hitherto hostile states.

Red Brigades   Italian left-wing urban guerrilla group which emerged in the early 1970s. As well as carrying out numerous terrorist actions, the Brigades kidnapped and murdered former Prime Minister Aldo Moro in 1978, intending to destabilize the Italian state.

Red China   The People's Republic of China, set up in Beijing on 1 October 1949 following Communist victory over Nationalist forces in the civil war.

Red Guards   Youths in the Chinese People's Liberation Army given authority to agitate through the country spreading radicalism. They became prominent for their enthusiasm as Mao Zedong's shock-troops in the 1966–69 Cultural Revolution, denouncing 'revisionism' and 'bourgeois decay'.

Republican Guard   Elite force of *c.* 150,000 troops in Iraq under Saddam Hussein (q.v.). Used to maintain his dictatorship, they were the subject of intense bombing by Allied air power in the Gulf War (q.v.).

revisionist   Term applied by orthodox Marxists to one who attempts to reassess the basic tenets of revolutionary socialism. Originating in

Germany in the 1890s and 1900s, its chief exponents were Edouard Bernstein and Karl Kautsky. Regarded as heresy in the Soviet Union, the Cuban, Chinese and Albanian communists have also used the same term to describe the Moscow line.

Rhodesian Front   White Rhodesian party led by Ian Smith (q.v.). In the 1977 elections the Rhodesian Front held all 50 white seats in the Rhodesian parliament.

Rogers Plan   A Middle East peace plan proposed in 1969 by the US Secretary of State which suggested only minor changes in Israel's pre-1967 borders with her Arab neighbours. Rogers also recommended that the Palestinians be given a choice between returning to Israel and receiving compensation for lost property. The plan was not greeted enthusiastically, but was eventually accepted by Egypt and Jordan. Israel gave a qualified acceptance. However, no progress was made and the United States abandoned the plan.

Sadat Initiative   Proposal by Egyptian President Anwar Sadat (1919–81), prompted by Egypt's inability to maintain high military expenditure, that he should visit Israel to explain the Arab position on the Middle East before the Knesset. The offer was accepted by Israeli Prime Minister Menachem Begin (1913–92) and a visit took place on 19–21 November 1977. Sadat's tacit recognition of Israel was condemned by the PLO and a number of Arab states and led to his assassination in 1981.

SALT   *See* Strategic Arms Limitation Talks.

Sandinistas   The Sandinista Liberation Front which waged a guerrilla war against Nicaraguan dictator Gen. Anastasio Somozo, driving him from power in July 1979. The Sandinistas won the sympathy of the Church, the unions and the middle classes and ruled post-revolutionary Nicaragua until their surprise election defeat in 1990.

SAVAK   Name of the Iranian Secret Police under the Shah.

SDI   Strategic Defense Initiative, also known as 'Star Wars', a plan announced by President Reagan in March 1983 to protect the United States from nuclear attack by destroying missiles with satellites outside the atmosphere. Reagan offered to share the technology to demonstrate its peaceful intent.

Sea-bed Treaty   Treaty banning the installation of weapons of mass destruction on the sea-bed and ocean floor or in the subsoil thereof beyond a 12-mile coastal zone. Signed in Washington, London and Moscow on 11 February 1971. It came into force on 18 May 1972.

Securitate   The Romanian secret police under the Ceauçescu (q.v.) dictatorship. Their brutal suppression of disturbances in Timisoara in December 1989 sparked the Romanian revolution. Their loyalty and fanaticism caused hundreds of deaths in the civil war. Disbanded by the provisional government. Many were summarily executed. *See* p. 276.

segregation   The separation of white and black races in public and private facilities. Laws requiring the segregation of the races have been on the statute books of several American states. In 1896, the Supreme Court ruled that such laws were valid under the separate but equal doctrine under which Blacks could be segregated if they were provided with equal facilities. As a result of this doctrine, segregation spread to schools, public transport, recreation and housing. By the 1940s the Supreme Court began to weaken the doctrine of 'separate but equal' by insisting on facilities being, indeed, equal. Finally, in 1954, the Court reversed the separate but equal formula, ruling that segregation based on race or colour was, in fact, incompatible with equality. Since this judgment, court-order desegregation coupled with legislation on civil rights in 1957, 1960, 1964, 1965 and 1968, has removed the edifice of government-sanctioned segregation.

Sendero Luminoso   The Communist Party of Peru, a Marxist guerrilla movement founded in 1970. The title – which means 'Shining Path' – derived from the Peruvian Marxist José Carlos Mariátegui's declaration that 'Marxism-Leninism will open the shining path to revolution'.

Sharpeville   In March 1960 South African security forces fired on Africans demonstrating against pass laws outside a police station: 67 were killed and many injured. A state of emergency was declared, African leaders arrested and the two leading African political parties, the ANC and PAC, were banned under the Suppression of Communism Act.

Shi'ites   Members of the Iranian Muslim sect Shia, which believes Muhammad's son-in-law Ali was his true successor, unlike the orthodox Sunni, who acknowledge the succession of Omar. The divergence between the two branches of Islam is now doctrinal.

Shiv Sena   Hindu nationalist party launched in Bombay in 1966 by Bal Thackeray. Began as a movement to safeguard the local Maratha culture and language against south Indians migrating to Bombay.

shuttle diplomacy   After the 1973 Arab–Israeli War, American Secretary of State, Henry Kissinger, began a series of visits to facilitate negotiations between the countries involved in the conflict. These made clear the American preference for a piecemeal approach to the issues rather than a reconvening of the Geneva Conference. Although three disengagement agreements involving small Israeli withdrawals from Syrian and Egyptian territory were achieved, this method left unresolved the central question of the Palestinians.

Sinn Féin   Gaelic for 'Ourselves alone'. Irish Nationalist party founded in 1902 by Arthur Griffiths (1872–1922) and formed into the Sinn Féin League in 1907–8 when it absorbed other nationalist groups. The group rose to prominence in the 1913–14 Home Rule crisis, when many Sinn Féiners joined the Irish Volunteers and many Dublin workers joined the organization. Sinn Féin members were involved in the Easter Rising in 1916. It is still the name of the political wing of the IRA (the Irish Republican Army). Sinn Féin has participated in the peace talks that led to the April 1998 agreement.

Six, the   The original six countries, Belgium, France, Italy, Luxembourg, the Netherlands and West Germany, which together created the European Coal and Steel Community in 1952, and the European Economic Community and Euratom in 1958.

Six Day War   The 5–10 June 1967 war between Israel and the Arab states, provoked by an Egyptian blockade of the Gulf of Aqaba. Israel bombed Egypt, Iraq, Jordan and Syria on 5 June; destroyed Egyptian armoured forces, reached the Suez Canal, and captured the West Bank of the Jordan on 7 June; then captured the strategic Syrian Golan Heights. These territories were then occupied by Israel.

Smithsonian Agreement   In December 1971, agreement was reached by the finance ministers of the Group of Ten in an attempt to restore stability to the world monetary system. The United States dropped its 10% surcharge on imports and devalued the dollar by 8.5% and some European currencies were revalued. This did not, in fact, lead to a return to fixed exchange rates.

Social Chapter   Section of the 1991 Maastricht Treaty giving power to the European Commission to impose the terms of the Social Charter on common standards in employment policy without the possibility of a national veto. The United Kingdom 'opted out' of this clause under the Conservative government. This was reversed by the 1997 Labour government.

Social Charter   The European Union (EU) Charter of Social Rights of Workers, setting a pattern for European labour law. Opposed by right-wing Conservatives, especially in the United Kingdom. It guarantees such things as freedom of movement and equal treatment for workers through-out the community, the right to strike, a guaranteed 'decent standard of living', freedom to join trade unions, the right to collective bargaining, and so on.

Solidarity   Polish trade union and reform movement formed in the 1970s in the shipyards of Gdansk to demand liberalization of the Polish com-munist regime and the formation of free trade unions. Under its leader, Lech Walesa, the movement won important concessions from the gov-ernment before the threat of Soviet invasion and the assumption of power by the Polish army led to the banning of the organization and the imprisonment of its leaders. It survived as a clandestine organization. Solidarity continued throughout the 1980s, representing the voice of the mass of the workers in Poland. In 1989, it joined in forming the first non-communist government in Poland since 1948. It declined rapidly in post-communist Poland.

South-West Africa People's Organization (SWAPO)   An independence movement founded in 1959, which in 1966 began guerrilla activity against South African forces. It was banned from Namibia and operated over the border. In 1989 its leader, Sam Numoja returned to Namibia in anticipa-tion of independence in 1990.

Soviet   Workers' councils which emerged spontaneously in the 1905 Russian Revolution and re-appeared in 1917. Intended to encourage and reflect direct working-class participation in political activity, they were effectively dominated by the Bolsheviks (later the Communists) after 1917, and became national administrative organs.

Soviet Union   *See* p. 202 under Union of Soviet Socialist Republics.

Soweto   Riots occurred here in 1976 following widespread strikes and general unrest in the South African townships. The immediate cause of trouble was opposition to the compulsory use of Afrikaans for instruc-tion in schools.

special relationship   The relationship between Britain and the United States, one allegedly based on historical links of culture and kinship running deeper than diplomatic expediency.

Stalinism   The arbitrary bureaucratic rule, personality cult and political purges underpinning Stalin's attempt to create 'Socialism in One Coun-try' through enforced agricultural collectivization and a rapid build-up of heavy industry. More recently the term has been used as a synonym for the Soviet and East European communist regimes.

state capitalism   Lenin's expression for the compromise with financial interests which, combined with increased central economic control, was an attempt to preserve Bolshevik power in 1918. Latterly, a pejorative left-wing description of Soviet society, in which a privileged bureaucratic elite allegedly exploited the working class through its own monopoly of economic and political power.

Strategic Arms Limitation Talks (SALT)   The United States and the Soviet Union embarked on SALT with the object of limiting the level of competition between them and reducing the size of their strategic nuclear armaments. Preliminary negotiations took place in Helsinki in November and December 1969, and an agreement on anti-ballistic missile systems and an interim agreement on strategic offensive arms were concluded by President Nixon (q.v.) in Moscow on 26 May 1972. The second phase of the negotiations, SALT II, opened in Geneva on 21 November 1972. In talks between President Ford (q.v.) and Chairman Brezhnev (q.v.) at Vladivostok in November 1974, an agreement was reached setting down guidelines for a pact to control the strategic arms race for the period 1977–85. However, the technical and political problems involved in framing such a pact meant that no definitive treaty was signed.

Suez Crisis   Major diplomatic crisis in 1956. Following Egyptian nationalization of the Suez Canal on 26 July 1956, Israel invaded Sinai on 29 October. When Egypt rejected a cease-fire ultimatum by France and Britain, their air forces began to attack Egyptian air bases on 31 October. On 5 November Franco–British forces invaded the Canal Zone and captured Port Said. Hostilities ended at midnight on 6–7 November following a cease-fire by the UN, and the Franco–British forces were evacuated.

summit conference   Meeting between the leaders of great powers to discuss issues of major long-term interest or to resolve specific areas of tension. The expression was used by Winston Churchill (1874–1965) when he called for a 'parley at the summit'.

Taliban   The revolutionary Islamic student movement which gained power in Afghanistan. *See* p. 272.

Tamil Tigers   The Liberation Tigers of Tamil Eelam (LTTE), a guerrilla group which emerged in 1983 to fight for an independent Tamil homeland in Sri Lanka. The Tigers were formed in response to anti-Tamil riots in the majority Sinhalese areas of the island. Despite numerous cease-fires and Indian mediation attempts from 1987 to 1990, fighting continued throughout the 1990s, with the deaths of thousands of people on both sides.

Tanker War   Attacks made on oil tankers in the Persian Gulf in the 1980–88 Iran–Iraq War. Iraq attacked shipping trading with Iran in 1984: Iran replied with attacks on tankers using the ports of Iraq's Arab supporters.

Tashkent Agreement   A declaration of truce took place between India and Pakistan after a conference convened at Tashkent in the USSR (3–10 January 1966). Alexei Kosygin, Chairman of the Council of Ministers of the USSR, acted as mediator between Lal Bahadur Shastri (q.v.), Prime Minister of India and Ayub Khan (q.v.), President of Pakistan, in a settlement which ended the war on the Kashmir border and restored Indian–Pakistani relations.

Tehran Conference   War-time meeting in Tehran, Persia (28 November–1 December 1943) between Winston Churchill, President Franklin D. Roosevelt and Marshal Stalin (with the combined chiefs of staff, Anthony Eden and Harry Hopkins attending) to plan military strategy in Europe and the Far East. It was agreed that 'Overlord', the Anglo–American invasion of northern France, would take place on 1 May 1944. Stalin promised that Russia would join in the war against Japan in the Far East after victory over Germany had been achieved. The future of Poland and Germany was also discussed.

terrorism   A tactic intended to achieve political ends or gain publicity for a cause by creating a climate of fear through assassination, bombing, kidnapping and the seizure of aircraft. Most non-communist countries have suffered from terrorism since the 1960s.

Test-Ban Treaty   Treaty signed by the United States, USSR and the United Kingdom after five years' negotiation on 5 August 1963, agreeing not to test nuclear weapons in outer space, the atmosphere or under the ocean. In the following two years over 90 other states signed, though France and China refused and have carried out atmospheric nuclear tests.

Tet   Communist Viet Cong and North Vietnamese attack on Saigon (now Ho Chi-minh City) and 140 other towns and villages during the Tet lunar new year festival. The 'Tet Offensive' ran from 20 January to 25 February 1968. The communists gained nothing materially, casualties on both sides were heavy, but the South Vietnamese government was undermined and America's commitment to the Vietnam War significantly weakened.

Third Path   Attempt by Michael Manley, Prime Minister and leader of the People's National Party (PNP) to find a democratic socialist alternative to communism and capitalism in Jamaica, 1974–80. The programme involved industrial nationalization, the formation of agricultural collectives, a minimum wage and increased medical and education expenditure. The United States, alleging that Manley was moving towards communism, provoked an economic crisis which, following the imposition of austerity measures by the International Monetary Fund, led to unrest and the PNP's election defeat in 1980.

Third World   Under-developed and poor nations in Africa, Asia and Latin America which are neither part of the capitalist industrialized West nor of the former communist Eastern bloc.

Thirty-eighth Parallel   The line of latitude 38° north dividing South Korea from communist North Korea, established at the 1945 Yalta Conference. The intention that the two states should ultimately unite was ended by the 1950–53 Korean War.

'Thousand Days'   The period in office of US President John F. Kennedy (1917–63) from his inauguration in January 1961 to his assassination in November 1963. Kennedy initiated civil rights legislation, moved towards a nuclear test ban, authorized the Bay of Pigs invasion, out-manoeuvered the USSR in the Cuban Missile Crisis, and drew the United States more deeply into the Vietnam War.

Tiananmen Square   Massacre of pro-democracy demonstrators (mainly students) in the main square of Beijing by hard-line Chinese government forces, 4 June 1989.

Tlatelolco, Treaty of   Treaty prohibiting nuclear weapons in Latin America signed in Mexico City on 14 February 1967 by 14 countries.

Tonkin resolution   Following alleged North Vietnamese attacks on American shipping in the Gulf of Tonkin, both Houses of the US Congress gave US President Lyndon Johnson (1963–69) sweeping powers to use force in the area on 7 August 1964. Immediate escalation of US involvement in the Vietnam War followed.

totalitarian capitalism   Term used to describe China's market-oriented capitalist economy within the framework of a communist one-party state.

Tripartism   Joint governments of Christian Democrats, Socialists and Communists formed in France and Italy immediately after the Second World War, reflecting their shared experience in the resistance against Germany. As the Cold War (q.v.) intensified, Communist ministers were dismissed from the French government in May 1947 and a Christian Democrat government was formed in Italy in April 1947.

Trotskyist   Follower of Leon Trotsky (1870–1940), the Soviet revolutionary leader who lost the power struggle with Stalin in 1924 and was assassinated in Mexico in 1940. Trotsky condemned Stalin's excessive Russian nationalism and the increasingly bureaucratic and dictatorial nature of his socialism. Trotskyism found support among disillusioned Western communists following the 1956 Soviet invasion of Hungary, and among student activists in the 1960s and 1970s.

Tupamaros   Marxist urban guerrilla movement in Uruguay named after Tupac Amarus who led an eighteenth-century Peruvian Indian revolt against Spain. Initially effective, the 1,000-strong movement was weakened by a police and right-wing paramilitary offensive in 1972.

U-2 Incident   On 1 May 1960 an American U-2 high-altitude reconnaissance aircraft was brought down over the Soviet Union near Sverdlovsk while on a photographic mission. As a result, the Russians cancelled the summit meeting with President Eisenhower in West Berlin on 16 May 1960. The pilot, Francis Gary Powers, was sentenced to ten years' imprisonment, but was exchanged for the Soviet spy, Colonel Abel, on 10 February 1962.

UDI   The illegal and widely condemned Unilateral Declaration of Independence made by Ian Smith's white Rhodesian Front government on 11 November 1965 in an attempt to avoid moving towards black majority rule in Southern Rhodesia.

Uniho Nacional Para a Independencia Total de Angola (UNITA) Angolan nationalist group which was in control of the south of Angola at independence. Joint UNITA and FNLA troops were defeated by the MPLA by February 1976, but UNITA continued a guerrilla struggle from its strongholds in the south of Angola. *See* p. 268.

United Nations   *See* pp. 219–20.

urban guerrillas   Groups using military methods and terrorist tactics in cities to achieve political ends. The most notable were the Red Brigades in Italy and the Red Army Faction in Germany in the 1970s, and the Provisional IRA in Northern Ireland from the early 1970s onwards.

Vatican II   Summoned by Pope John XXIII in 1962–63, proceedings began on 11 October 1962 in the presence of over 8,000 Catholic bishops and observers from Anglican and Orthodox churches. The 16 decrees that emerged encouraged greater tolerance towards non-Catholic Christian churches and provided for the use of the vernacular rather than Latin in Catholic liturgy.

Velasquismo   Expression used to describe apparently radical reforms initiated in Peru by General Juan Velasco Alvarado, President from 1968 to 1975. The programme was supported both by the Christian Democrats and by the Communist Party but proved disappointing. The term is also used to describe the populist movement in Ecuador which carried José María Velasco Ibarra to power as President five times between 1933 and 1972.

Velvet Divorce   The division on 1 January 1993 of Czechoslovakia into the separate states of the Czech Republic and Slovakia. So called because of the apparently amicable nature of the separation, but also an ironic reference to the 1989 Velvet Revolution (see below) which overthrew Communist rule.

Velvet Revolution   Title given to the popular uprisings in Prague and other Czech cities in 1989 which overthrew the Communist regime.

Viet Cong   Name meaning 'Vietnamese Communists' given by the South Vietnamese government to the supporters of the Front for the Liberation of South Vietnam (founded 1960). The government was anxious to distinguish between the Communists and the Viet Minh, the nationalist independence league which had fought against the French colonial regime and had included non-communists. The Viet Cong took an active part in the Vietnam War (q.v.) against the forces of the South Vietnamese government and the Americans. They were responsible for attacks on US bases at Pleiku and Qui Nhon in February 1965 which escalated American involvement in the war and they participated in the Tet Offensive (q.v.).

Viet Minh   A communist political group in North Vietnam founded by Ho Chi-minh (q.v.) in 1941 to work for independence. In 1945 its forces entered Hanoi and formed a provisional government under Ho Chi-minh. From 1951 it worked as part of the Deng Lao Dong Vietnam (Vietnam Workers' Party).

Vietnamization   Policy of President Nixon, pursued from 1968–69 onwards, of reducing the involvement of American ground troops in the Vietnam War and transferring most of the responsibility for the defence of South Vietnam to the army of that republic.

Wafd   The leading Egyptian nationalist party between the wars, forming a government under Nahas Pasha in 1936. He was dismissed by King Farouk in 1938 and his restoration to office by Britain in 1941 (on the grounds that he favoured the Allies) weakened Wafd's nationalist standing. Returned to power in the 1950 elections, the Wafd faced civil disorder, was sacked by Farouk in 1952 and dissolved in 1953.

War On Poverty Collective term for the series of social programmes enacted by the Johnson administration (1963–69) as part of the 'Great Society' (q.v.). These included the provision of health-care for elderly and poor Americans, the expansion of job training for the disadvantaged, increased federal assistance to the states for education, and grants to cities for the development of urban areas. However, the fiscal strain caused by US involvement in the Vietnam War (q.v.) brought the War On Poverty to an untimely end.

Warsaw Pact *See* p. 220.

Watergate General term given to a variety of illegal acts perpetrated by officials in the Nixon (q.v.) administration (1969–74), and subsequent efforts to 'cover-up' their responsibility for these acts, which led eventually to the resignation of President R.M. Nixon and the succession to the Presidency of Vice-President Gerald R. Ford (q.v.). Specifically, 'Watergate' refers to a burglary, by a group of seven men acting under the orders of the White House, of the Democratic National Party headquarters located in the Watergate building in Washington DC. Other illegal acts included within the general term 'Watergate' were: bribery, illegal use of the CIA, FBI and other government agencies for political and partisan purposes, income tax fraud, the establishment and use by the White House of an unofficial 'plumbers' group designed to discover the source of leaks to the press, the use of 'dirty tricks' during the 1972 election campaign, and illegal campaign contributions. As a result of these Watergate crimes many Cabinet officers, Presidential assistants and other administration officials were convicted of various crimes. It produced a spate of new laws concerning secrecy in government and regulation of campaign practices. It also produced a Supreme Court decision which, for the first time, limited the doctrine of 'executive privilege' by holding that the privilege cannot be used to prohibit disclosure of criminal misconduct. The most serious political scandal in American history.

West Bank The West Bank of the Jordan River was annexed by King Abdullah of Jordan after the 1948 war. It was taken by Israel in 1967 and placed under military administration. East Jerusalem was not only annexed but its boundaries were extended, in defiance of international law. To establish a firm hold on the city, Israel had evicted Arab families and replaced them with Jews. In 1970 a government plan to double the Jewish population of the city by 1980 was published. The United Nations has condemned Israel several times for its actions in East Jerusalem.

Archaeological excavations have also called forth UN protest. The Israeli government insists on maintaining secure borders in any settlement but there is conflict over how much territory this involves. Groups of religious extremists, like Gush Emunim, opposed the return of any territory and insisted on the right to settle in all of Biblical Israel. They have gone so far as to set up illegal settlements which the government has been loath to dislodge. The government itself has set up Jewish settlements on the West Bank. These, in turn, undermine its claim to be willing to return Arab territory and are an obstacle to peace. Over the past years Arabs on the West Bank have grown increasingly restive. Riots and demonstrations have culminated in the uprising known as the 'intifada' (q.v.). There is also considerable division within Israel over policy towards the West Bank. On 16 January 1997 Israeli troops began to pull out from Hebron after the Israeli parliament endorsed the Hebron agreement with the Palestinians.

White Revolution   Mounted in 1963 by the Shah of Iran to modernize and Westernize his state. Among the reforms were the granting of the vote to women.

Whitewater   Development company in Arkansas which gave its name to the 'Whitewatergate' scandal involving US President Bill Clinton and his wife Hillary Rodham Clinton in 1993. While serving as state Governor in the 1980s, Clinton – who first invested in Whitewater in 1978 – supported the company while his wife acted as the company's lawyer and allegedly filed inaccurate tax returns for herself and Mr Clinton. In 1993, White House counsel Vince Foster – Mrs Clinton's law partner – committed suicide while working on Whitewater's back taxes. There were accusations that the Clintons had attempted to mount a cover-up of the scandal and in 1994 an independent counsel was appointed to investigate the issue. Mr Clinton was, nevertheless, re-elected in 1996.

World Trade Organization   The successor organization to GATT (q.v.).

Yalta Conference   The most crucial 'Big Three' meeting of the war held at Yalta in the Crimea (4–11 February 1945). Agreements reached between Winston Churchill, President Franklin D. Roosevelt and Marshal Stalin (with the chiefs-of-staff, Molotov, Stettinus, Anthony Eden and Harry Hopkins attending) virtually determined the reconstruction of the post-war world. France was admitted as an equal partner of the Allied Control Commission for Germany but the practical details of Allied control were not worked out in Protocols III, IV, V and VI. The future of Poland, one of the most contentious issues of the conference, was referred to in the ambiguously worded Declaration on Poland in Protocol

VII, where no agreement was made as to the reconstruction of the Polish government. Being anxious to secure a firm Russian undertaking to join in the war against Japan, Roosevelt acceded to Stalin's condition that Russia should resume her old rights in China, lost as a result of the Russo–Japanese War of 1904–5, and a secret tripartite agreement was signed to this effect on 11 February 1945. Protocol I set out the agreement reached on the creation of a World Organization of the United Nations and the voting formula for the Security Council. It was agreed to call a conference in San Francisco in April 1945, to draw up a charter for the United Nations.

Year zero   The term given to the first year of the Khmer Rouge (q.v.) regime in Cambodia (Kampuchea) led by Pol Pot. After taking power in 1975, the Khmer Rouge attempted to remove all traces of modern civilization and killed over one million people in the process.

Yom Kippur   The Jewish day of atonement, a period of religious observance. During this period Egyptian and Syrian forces moved against Israel on 6 October 1973. Israel counter-attacked on 8 October, threatening Cairo and Damascus. The 'Yom Kippur War' ended with a United Nations arranged cease-fire on 24 October.

Zionism   The belief that the Jews should create a homeland in Palestine, suggested by Theodor Herzl (1860–1904) who felt the Jews were threatened by East European pogroms. Until then Palestine had been generally seen by Jews as a spiritual rather than physical homeland. An initial reluctance among many Jews who felt assimilated in Europe was overcome by the experience of the Nazi Holocaust. The state of Israel was set up in 1948.

SECTION SIX

Topic bibliography

This bibliography is arranged in broadly geographical terms to allow concentration on particular aspects of modern world history since 1945 and the sub-themes within it. Some topics such as imperial decline and decolonization are of world-wide scope, and contain works relating to more than one geographical area.

Introductory works

The later sections of J.M. Roberts, *A History of the World* (1976) and W.H. McNeill, *A World History* (1967) are excellent introductions to the modern world. Exclusively twentieth century in focus are E. Hobsbawm, *The Age of Extremes. The Short Twentieth Century, 1914–1991* (1994) and W.R. Keylor, *The Twentieth Century: an international history* (1984); see also J.M. Roberts, *The Triumph of the West* (1985) for a principal theme of world history this century. J.A.S. Grenville, *A World History of the Twentieth Century, 1900–84* (2 vols, 1980–5) and P. Calvocoressi, *World Politics since 1945* (6th edn, 1991) deal exclusively with the present century. J. Major, *The Contemporary World: a historical introduction* (1970) and G. Barraclough, *An Introduction to Contemporary History* (1967) are useful analyses of some of the major themes, while D.C Watt, F. Spencer and N. Brown, *A History of the World in the Twentieth Century* (1967) examines international relations. The development of the world beyond Europe is examined in P. Worsley, *The Third World* (1967) and C.E. Black, *The Dynamics of Modernization: a study in comparative history* (1967). Important studies of the development of the modern world are I. Wallerstein, *The Modern World System* (1974) and J.A. Hall, *Powers and Liberties: the causes and consequences of the rise of the West* (1985). On the post–1945 period, see J.P.D. Dunbabin, *International Relations Since 1945* (2 vols, 1994), G. Lundestad, *East, West, North, South: major developments in international politics, 1945–1990* (1991) and S.J. Ball, *The Cold War: an international history* (1997).

The economic history of the twentieth century is considered in W. Ashworth, *A Short History of the International Economy since 1850* (4th edn, 1987) and A.G. Kenwood and A.L. Lougheed, *The Growth of the International Economy: an introductory text* (1971). The volume in the excellent Penguin series of the history of the world economy should also be consulted: A.S. Milward, *War, Economy and Society, 1939–1945* (1977).

For the world monetary system as a whole, see D. Calleo, *The Imperious Economy* (1982); on America's role and more generally, M. Moffitt, *The World's Money* (1945); L. Tson Kalis (ed.), *The Political Economy of International Money* (1985); C.P. Kindleberger, *Power and Money: the economics of international politics and the politics of international economics* (1970);

438 TOPIC BIBLIOGRAPHY

S.E. Rolfe and J.L. Burkle, *The Great Wheel: the world monetary system: a reinterpretation* (1974); and A. Shonfield, *Modern Capitalism: the changing balance of public and private power* (1966). The specific role of the multinational companies is discussed in L. Turner, *Invisible Empires: multinational companies and the modern world* (1970) and *Multinational Companies and the Third World* (1973), E.T. Penrose, *The Large International Firm in Developing Countries: the international petroleum industry* (1968), and M. Wilkins, *The Maturing of Multinational Enterprise: American business abroad from 1914 to 1970* (1974). P. Bairoch, *The Economic Development of the Third World since 1900* (1975); H. Myint, *The Economics of Developing Countries* (4th edn, 1973) and G. Myrdal, *The Challenge of World Poverty: a world antipoverty programme in outline* (1970) specifically examine the world beyond the major industrial powers. The role of aid as part of the nexus linking the developed and less developed world is considered from various points of view in J.A. White, *The Politics of Foreign Aid* (1974), T. Hayter, *Aid as Imperialism* (1971), L.D. Black, *The Strategy of Foreign Aid* (1968) and M.I. Goldman, *Soviet Foreign Aid* (1967).

The energy question is considered in G. Foley and C. Nassim, *The Energy Question* (1976), P.R. Odell, *Oil and World Power* (4th edn, 1974), and G.C. Tugendhat and A. Hamilton, *Oil the Biggest Business* (rev. edn, 1975). The rise of OPEC is examined in M.S. Al-Otaiba, *OPEC and the Petroleum Industry* (1975), and Z. Mikdashi, *The Community of Oil Exporting Countries: a study in governmental co-operation* (1972). More recent concerns, such as the rise of Third World debt, are considered in H. Lever and C. Huhne, *Debt and Danger: the world financial crisis* (1985).

For population developments there is an excellent survey of world population from earliest times in C. McEvedy and T. Jones (eds), *Atlas of World Population History* (1978) and for more contemporary pre-occupations, see K. and A.F.K. Organski, *Population and World Power* (1961), T. McKeown, *The Modern Rise of Population* (1976), W.D. Barrie, *The Growth and Control of World Population* (1970) and R. Symonds and M. Carter, *The United Nations and the Population Question, 1945–70* (1973). For particular areas, see S. Chandrasekhar (ed.), *Asia's Population Problems: with a discussion of population and immigration in Australia* (1967), D. Chaplin (ed.), *Population Policies and Growth in Latin America* (1971), W.A. Hance, *Population, Migration, and Urbanization in Africa* (1970) and J.I. Clarke and W.B. Fisher, *Populations of the Middle East and North Africa* (1971).

Urban development is considered generally in J.H. Lowry, *World City Growth* (1975), K. Davis, *World Urbanization, 1950–1970* (2 vols, 1969–72), P.M. Houser and L.F. Schnore (eds), *The Study of Urbanization* (1965), T.H. Elkins, *The Urban Explosion* (1973), W.D.C. Wright and P.H. Steward,

The Exploding City (1972) and P. Hall, *The World Cities* (2nd edn, 1977). Urban change in Europe and North America is considered in the last section of L. Mumford, *The City in History: its origins, its transformation, and its prospects* (1961) and his *The Urban Prospect* (1968), P. Hall (ed.), *Europe 2000* (1977), J. Gottman (ed.), *Megalopolis: the urbanized northeastern seaboard of the United States* (1962), and A. Sutcliffe (ed.), *Metropolis, 1890–1940* (1984) which includes an essay on the Tokyo area. Third-world studies include D.J. Dwyer, *The City in the Third World* (1968) and *The City as a Centre of Change in Asia* (1972), T.G. McGee, *The Urbanization Process in the Third World: explorations in search of a theory* (1971), G.W. Breese, *Urbanisation in Newly-Developing Countries* (1966), W.A. Hance, *Population, Migration and Urbanization in Africa* (1970) and G.K. Payne, *Urban Housing in the Third World* (1977). P. Lloyd, *Slums of Hope? Shanty towns of the Third World* (1979) ligests an enormous amount of literature on the processes and effects of urban migration and has an excellent bibliography. Also on the social effects of urbanization, see W. Mangin (ed.), *Peasants in Cities: readings in the anthropology of urbanization* (1970), R.E. Pahl, *Patterns of Urban Life* (1970), A Southall (ed.), *Urban Anthropology: cross-cultural studies of urbanization* (1973), and B.J.L. Berry, *The Human Consequences of Urbanization: divergent paths in the urban experience of the twentieth century* (1973).

Among the ideologies affecting twentieth-century development, nationalism is of great importance. A.D. Smith, *Theories of Nationalism* (1971) looks at various approaches; see also his edited collection, *Nationalist Movements* (1976). E. Kedourie, *Nationalism* (1960) is an introduction to the ideology; see also B. Anderson, *Imagined Communities* (1985), H. Seton-Watson, *Nations and States: an enquiry into the origins of nations and the politics of nationalism* (1977) and E. Gellner, *Nations and Nationalism* (1983). Also valuable are B. Akzin, *States and Nations* (1964), K.W. Deutsch, *Nationalism and Social Communication: an inquiry into the foundations of nationality* (2nd edn, 1966) and the older F.O. Hertz, *Nationality in History and Politics* (1944). Nationalism as a phenomenon of particular regions can be studied in A. Cobban. *The Nation State and National Self-Determination* (1969) and R. Pearson, *National Minorities in Eastern Europe, 1848–1944* (1983), E. Kedourie (ed.), *Nationalism in Asia and Africa* (1971), F.R. von der Mehden, *Religion and Nationalism in Southeast Asia: Burma, Indonesia, the Philippines* (1963), G. Antonius, *The Arab Awakening: the story of the Arab national movement* (1938), S. Haim (ed.), *Arab Nationalism: an anthology* (1962), T. Hodgkin, *Nationalism in Colonial Africa* (1956), D.A. Rustow, *A World of Nations: the problems of political modernization* (1967), A.P. Whitaker and D.C. Jordan, *Nationalism in Contemporary Latin America* (1966) and R. Emerson, *From Empire to Nation: the rise to self-assertion of Asian and African peoples* (1970).

Of the other powerful ideologies, socialism and communism, there are introductory texts in D. McLellan, *Marx* (1975) and *Engels* (1975), G. Lichtheim, *Marxism, an Historical and Critical Study* (1961) and *A Short History of Socialism* (1969). Liberalism is less well served, although it had an important legacy from the nineteenth century, but see H.J. Laski, *The Rise of European Liberalism* (2nd edn, 1947) and A. Arblaster, *The Rise and Decline of Western Liberalism* (1984). The important force of social democracy can be examined in R.J. Harrison, *Pluralism and Corporation: the political evolution of modern democracies* (1980), J. Haywood, *Trade Unions and Politics in Western Europe* (1980), M. Kolinsky and W. Paterson (eds), *Social and Political Movements in Western Europe* (1976), R. Miliband, *Parliamentary Socialism* (1961), I. Campbell and W. Paterson, *Social Democracy in Post-War Europe* (1974) and W. Paterson and A. Thomas, *Social Democratic Parties in Western Europe* (1977).

Two general works which deal with the nature of regimes are Barrington Moore, *Social Origins of Dictatorship and Democracy* (1966) and R. Aron, *Democracy and Totalitarianism* (1968). See also P. Wiles, *Economic Institutions Compared* (1977) and A. Ellis and K. Kumar (eds), *Dilemmas of Liberal Democracies* (1983), T. Skocpol, *States and Social Revolutions* (1979), M. Olson, *The Rise and Decline of Nations* (1982) and J.H. Goldthorpe (ed.), *Order and Conflict in Contemporary Capitalism* (1984).

The role of revolution in the modern world is discussed in J. Dunn, *Modern Revolutions: an introduction to the analysis of a political phenomenon* (2nd edn, 1989), Chalmers Johnson, *Revolution and the Social System* (1964) and *Revolutionary Change* (1968), P. Calvert, *Revolution* (1970) and *A Study of Revolution* (1970). Third-world revolutions are specifically examined in F.J. Carrier, *The Third World Revolutions* (1967), G. Chaliand, *Revolution in the Third World: myths and prospects* (1977), J.S. Migdal, *Peasants, Politics and Revolution: pressures towards political and social change in the Third World* (1975) and E.R. Wolf, *Peasant Wars of the Twentieth Century* (1969).

Almost inseparable from the idea of revolution in the less developed world is guerrilla warfare and terrorism. For the former, Che Guevara, *Guerrilla Warfare* (1969) and G. Fairbairn, *Revolutionary Warfare: the Countryside Version* (1974) are particularly relevant. For terrorism, see G. Wardlaw, *Political Terrorism* (2nd edn, 1989), W. Laqueur, *Terrorism* (1977), P. Wilkinson, *Political Terrorism* (1974) and S. Segaller, *Invisible Armies: terrorism into the 1990s* (2nd edn, 1987). The specific phenomenon of urban guerrilla warfare is considered in R. Moss, *Urban Guerrillas* (1972), A. Burton, *Urban Terrorism* (1975), and R. Clutterbuck, *Protest and the Urban Guerrilla* (1973), while the implications for societies are discussed in P. Wilkinson, *Terrorism and the Liberal State* (1977) and R. Clutterbuck, *Living with Terrorism* (1975).

The political role of the military is discussed in S.E. Finer, *The Man on Horseback: the role of the military in politics* (2nd edn, 1976) and M.E. Howard (ed.), *Soldiers and Governments: nine studies in civil–military relations* (1957); specifically on the role of the military in the Third World, see M. Janowitz, *Military Institutions and Coercion in the Developing Nations* (1977). S. Andreski, *Military Organisation and Society* (2nd edn, 1968) is a classic exposition of the role of warfare in society, but see also A. Marwick, *War and Social Change in the Twentieth Century* (1974), M.R.D. Foot (ed.), *War and Society* (1973), B. Brodie, *War and Politics* (1973) and A. Buchan, *War in Modern Society* (1968). Much of recent discussion has been focused on the issue of 'total war', for which see Marwick (above) and N.F. Dreisziger (ed.), *Mobilisation for Total War: the Canadian, American and British Experience, 1914–1918, 1939–1945* (1981).

The influence of nuclear weapons upon the world scene is considered in J. Newhouse, *The Nuclear Age: a history of the arms race from Hiroshima to Star Wars* (1989), B. Brodie (ed.), *The Absolute Weapon: atomic power and world order* (1972), G.H. Quester, *Nuclear Diplomacy: the first twenty-five years* (1970), and L. Freedman, *The Evolution of Nuclear Strategy* (1981).

For the evolution of warfare, see J.F.C. Fuller, *The Conduct of War, 1789– 1961: a study of the impact of the French, Industrial and Russian Revolutions on War and its Conduct* (1961). C. McInnes and G.D. Sheffield (eds), *Warfare in the Twentieth Century: theory and practice* (1988) is a more recent collection of studies, while C. Cook and J. Stevenson, *The Atlas of Modern Warfare* (1978) provides an account and analysis of military history since 1945. There are excellent maps in T. Hartman (with J. Mitchell), *A World Atlas of Military History* (1984) and see also L.W. Martin, *Arms and Strategy: an international survey of modern defence* (1973). The geopolitics of military power is discussed over a long period in P. Kennedy, *The Rise and Fall of the Great Powers: economic change and military conflict, 1500–2000* (1988). There are now regular updates of world-wide armed conflicts in J. Laffin (ed.), *War Annual* (1986–   ) and in the Royal United Services and Brassey's *Defence Yearbook*. The definitive assessment of size of the world's armed forces and their composition, including nuclear armouries, can be found in the International Institute for Strategic Studies, *The Military Balance*, published annually. L.A. Sobel (ed.), *Political Terrorism* (1975) contains a narrative of terrorist activity from 1968 to 1974.

A good atlas is essential to the understanding of world affairs since 1945. G. Barraclough (ed.), *The Times Atlas of World History* (1993) and R.I. Moore (ed.), *The Newnes Historical Atlas* (1981) are two excellent examples though neither is concerned solely with the twentieth century. For reference purposes there is a wealth of statistical material in B.R. Mitchell,

European Historical Statistics, 1750–1988 (3rd edn, 1992) and *International Historical Statistics: Africa and Asia* (1986). There is a wide range of data in, *The Statesman's Yearbook*, published annually since 1864, while the United Nations' *Statistical Yearbooks* (1945–   ) provide valuable additional material. For demographic data, see the United Nations' *Demographic Yearbooks* (1945–   ). For chronological outlines of events, see S.H. Steinberg, *Historical Tables, 58BC–AD1978* (10th edn, 1979) and D. Mercer (ed.), *Chronicle of the 20th Century* (1988).

European history

There are excellent overviews in J.M. Roberts, *Europe, 1880–1945* (1967), J. Joll, *Europe since 1870* (1973), F. Gilbert, *The End of the European Era, 1890 to the Present* (3rd edn, 1984) and A. Grant and H. Temperley, *Europe in the Nineteenth and Twentieth Centuries* (7th edn, rev. A. Ramm, 2 vols, 1984). See also G. Lichtheim, *Europe in the Twentieth Century* (1972) and the two versions of the Cambridge Modern History, Vol. XII, D. Thomson (ed.), *The Era of Violence* (1960) and G.L. Monat (ed.), *The Shifting Balance of World Forces, 1898–1945* (1968). J.W. Young, *Cold War Europe 1945–1989* (1989), W. Laqueur, *Europe since Hitler* (1970) and D. Urwin, *Western Europe since 1945* (1981 edn) deal specifically with post-1945 developments, while F. Fejto, *A History of the People's Democracies* (1971) and Z. Brzezinski, *The Soviet Bloc* (1974) deal specifically with Eastern Europe. For the economic history of the continent, see the later sections of D. Landes, *The Unbound Prometheus: technological change and industrial development in Western Europe from 1750 to the present* (1972) and C. Cipolla (ed.), *The Fontana Economic History of Europe* (1973). For social change, see D. Geary, *A Social History of Western Europe, 1848–1945* (1985), P.N. Stearns, *European Society in Upheaval* (1967) and G. Mosse, *The Culture of Western Europe: the nineteenth and twentieth centuries* (1961).

On individual countries, for France see M. Larkin, *France since the Popular Front: Government and People, 1936–1996* (1997), D. Johnson, *France 1914–1983: the twentieth century* (1986), R. Gildea, *France since 1945* (1997) and J.F. McMillan, *Dreyfus to De Gaulle: politics and society in France* (1985). Also helpful is G. Dupeaux, *French Society, 1789–1970* (1976). On Spain, the standard history is R. Carr, *Spain, 1808–1975* (rev. edn, 1980), and for Italy, see D. Mack Smith, *Italy* (1959) and M. Clark, *Modern Italy 1871–1982* (1984). German history is examined in W. Carr, *A History of Germany, 1815–1985* (rev. edn, 1987), W.R. Berghahn, *Modern Germany: society, economy and politics in the twentieth century* (1982), A.J. Nicholls, *The Bonn Republic, 1945–91* (1997), L. Kettenacker, *Germany since 1945* (1997) and P. Pulzer, *German Politics, 1945–1995* (1995). For Russia see J.H.L. Keep, *Last of the Empires: A History of the Soviet Union, 1945–1991* (1996), M.

McCauley, *The Soviet Union since 1917* (1981) and G. Hosking, *A History of the Soviet Union* (1985). Eastern Europe is discussed in M. Fulbrook, *Anatomy of a Dictatorship: inside the GDR, 1949–1989* (1997), R.J. Crampton, *Eastern Europe in the Twentieth Century* (1994) and R. Pearson, *National Minorities in Eastern Europe, 1848–1945* (1983). For the British Isles, see P. Clarke, *Power and Glory* (1996), M. Pugh, *State and Society, 1870–1992* (1994), M. Beloff, *Wars and Welfare, Britain 1914–1952* (1984), R. Blake, *The Decline of Power, 1915–1970* (1985), A. Sked and C. Cook, *Post-War Britain: a political history* (1993) and D. Childs, *Britain since 1945* (1979). For Ireland, see F.S.L. Lyons, *Ireland since the Famine* (rev. edn, 1973) and R. Foster, *Modern Ireland, 1600–1972* (1988).

The Second World War

For documents, see H. Jacobsen and A. Smith (eds), *World War II* (1980) on military policy and strategy; there are also numerous collections of memoirs of which W.S. Churchill, *The Second World War* (6 vols, 1948–54) and C. de Gaulle, *War Memoirs* (3 vols, 1955–59) are perhaps the best from European statesmen, and, from the generals, D. Eisenhower, *Crusade in Europe* (1948) and Montgomery of Alamein, *Memoirs* (1958). A. Speer, *Inside the Third Reich* (1970) remains a telling account of the resilience of the German war machine. On the civilian side, O. Frank, *The Diary of Ann Frank* (1947) is a moving classic, while O. Lengyel, *Five Chimneys* (1959) is a powerful evocation of the concentration camps. The German civilian experience is recorded in C. Bielenberg, *The Past is Myself* (1985). For accounts of the war, see G. Weinberg, *A World at Arms: a global history of World War II* (1994), R.A.C. Parker, *Struggle For Survival: the history of the Second World War* (1989), J. Keegan, *The Second World War* (1989), and M. Gilbert, *The Second World War* (1989). G. Wright, *The Ordeal of Total War* (1968), B. Liddell Hart, *The Second World War* (1970), P. Calvocoressi and G. Wint, *Total War* (1974) and A.J.P. Taylor, *The Second World War: an illustrated history* (1976) are all useful, while A. Marwick, *War and Social Change in the Twentieth Century* (1974) concentrates on the social effects. D. Irving, *Hitler's War* (2 vols, 1983) gives a controversial account from the German side. On Russia, see A. Werth, *Russia at War* (1965) and on Britain, A. Calder, *The People's War* (1969). A.S. Milward, *War, Economy and Society, 1939–1945* (1977) is a brilliant synthesis of the economic ramifications of 'total war'; see also his *The German Economy at War* (1965) and *The New Order and the French Economy* (1970). On the outcome, see R.J. Overy, *Why the Allies Won* (1995).

The opening phase of the war is covered by B. Collier, *1940: The World in Flames* (1980) and *1941: Armageddon* (1982). The controversy over the effectiveness and morality of the bombing offensive against Germany is considered in N. Frankland, *The Bombing Offensive Against Germany* (1965) and M. Hastings, *Bomber Command* (1979). For the German side of the air war, see D. Irving, *The Rise and Fall of the Luftwaffe* (1973). For the war at sea, see D. Macintyre, *The Battle of the Atlantic* (1961), J. Costello and T. Hughes, *The Battle of the Atlantic* (1977), and W. Frank, *The Sea Wolves* (1955). The decisive struggle on the Eastern Front is considered in A. Clark, *Barbarossa* (1965) and J. Erickson, *The Road to Stalingrad: Stalin's war with Germany* (1975). For the final phase of the war, see E. Belfield and H. Essame, *The Battle for Normandy* (1965) and J. Erickson, *The Road to Berlin* (1983). Specifically on the new form of mobile warfare, see H. Guderian, *Panzer Leader* (1952) and F.W. von Mellenthin, *Panzer Battles* (1955). Technical developments affecting the conduct of the war are discussed in R.V. Jones, *Most Secret War* (1978) and B. Johnson, *The Secret War* (1978).

The fate of areas conquered by the Germans is considered in W. Warmbrunn, *The Dutch under German Occupation* (1963), A. Dallin, *German Rule in Russia, 1941–5* (1957) and P. Burrin, *France under the Germans* (1996), while the resistance movements are analysed in H. Michel, *The Shadow War: resistance in Europe, 1939–45* (1972) and M.R.D. Foot, *Resistance* (1976); see also O. Bartov, *Hitler's Army* (1991).

On diplomacy during the war, see H. Feis, *Churchill, Roosevelt, Stalin* (1957), W.H. McNeill, *America, Britain and Russia* (1953), G. Kolko, *The Politics of War* (1968), V. Mastny, *Russia's Road to the Cold War* (1979), R.C. Raack, *Stalin's Drive to the West, 1938–1945* (1995), and R. Dallek, *FDR and American Foreign Policy, 1932–45* (1979).

The Cold War

There is a good introduction in J. Smith, *The Cold War, 1945–65* (1989), while more detailed works are J.W. Spanier, *American Foreign Policy since the Second World War* (1980), S.E. Ambrose, *Rise to Globalism* (1983), W. Lafeber, *America, Russia and the Cold War* (1982), and L.J. Halle, *The Cold War as History* (1967). Important recent additions are J.L. Gaddis, *We Now Know: rethinking Cold War history* (1997) and D. Reynolds (ed.), *The Origins of the Cold War in Europe: international perspectives* (1995). Soviet policy is the subject of V. Mastny, *The Cold War and Soviet Insecurity: the Stalin Years* (1997), A.B. Ulam, *Expansion and Coexistence* (1968) and T.W. Wolfe, *Soviet Power and Europe, 1945–70* (1970). The early years of the Cold War have received most coverage. There are conservative accounts, such as G.F. Hudson, *The Hard and Bitter Peace* (1966) and H.L. Feis, *From Trust to Terror* (1970), and criticisms of America in G. and J. Kolko, *The Limits of Power* (1972) and D. Yergin, *Shattered Peace* (1977).

J.L. Gaddis, *The United States and the Origins of the Cold War* (1973) is good, and on the British, see V. Rothwell, *Britain and the Cold War, 1941–7* (1983). For coverage of the continental states, see G. de Carmoy, *The Foreign Policies of France* (1970) and E. Furniss, *France, Troubled Ally* (1960). See also M.J. Hogan, *The Marshall Plan: America, Britain and the Reconstruction of Western Europe, 1947–1952* (1988).

Western Europe since 1945

For general coverage of events, see J.W. Young, *Cold War Europe, 1945–89* (1991), W. Laqueur, *Europe since Hitler* (1970), D. Urwin, *Western Europe since 1945* (1981), and P. Calvocoressi, *World Politics since 1945* (1982 edn). Also good are R. Mayne, *The Recovery of Europe* (1970), M. Crouzet, *The European Renaissance since 1945* (1970), R. Morgan, *West European Politics since 1945* (1972) and S. Smith, *Politics in Western Europe* (1976). Rather narrower in interest is F.R. Willis, *France, Germany and the New Europe, 1945–67* (1969), while F. Fry and G. Raymond, *The Other Western Europe* (1980) looks at the smaller democracies. The post-war economic recovery of Europe is examined in A.S. Milward, *The Reconstruction of Western Europe, 1945–51* (1984) and M.J. Hogan (above). On France in this period, see P.M. Williams, *Crisis and Compromise: Politics in the Fourth Republic* (1964), P.M. Williams and M. Harrison, *Politics and Compromise: politics and society in de Gaulle's Republic* (1971), J. Ardagh, *The New France* (1978), and M. Anderson, *Conservative Politics in France* (1974). See also the important recent study by D.S. Bell and B. Criddle, *The French Socialist Party* (2nd edn, 1988) and M. Larkin, *France since the Popular Front: government and people, 1936–96* (1997). On de Gaulle, see D. Cook, *Charles de Gaulle* (1984). For Germany, see P. Pulzer, *German Politics, 1945–1995* (1995), T. Prittie, *The Velvet Chancellors* (1979) and *Adenauer* (1971). On Italy, see M. Clark, *Modern Italy, 1871–1982* (1984) and S. Tarrow, *Democracy and Disorder: Protest and Politics in Italy, 1965–75* (1989). For Spain, see R. Carr, *A History of Spain, 1808–1975* (rev. edn, 1982), R. Carr and J.P. Fusi, *Spain: Dictatorship to Democracy* (1979) and D. Gilmour, *The Transformation of Spain* (1985).

There are general discussions of the European unity movement in M. Dedman, *The Origins and Development of the European Union, 1945–95* (1996), W. Laqueur, *Europe since Hitler* (1970) and D. Urwin, *Western Europe since 1945* (1981). The fullest account of the early years of the unity movement can be found in W. Lipgens, *A History of European Integration, 1945–7* (1982), though this is very detailed. J.W. Young, *Britain, France and the Unity of Europe, 1945–51* (1984) is shorter and more analytical, while on the early 1950s see E. Fursden, *The European Defence Community* (1981) on the vain bid to create a 'European Army'. On the Common

Market itself, see R. Pryce, *The Politics of the European Community* (1973), J. Galtung, *The European Community – a Superpower in the Making* (1973), J. Herman and J. Lodge, *The European Parliament and the European Community* (1978), S. Holland, *Uncommon Market* (1980), L. Tsoukalis (ed.), *The European Community Past, Present and Future* (1983) and F.R. Willis, *France, Germany and the New Europe* (1968). On particular themes, see D. Swann, *Economics of the Common Market* (4th edn, 1978), R.B. Talbot, *The European Communities Regional Fund* (1977), M. Shanks, *European Social Policy* (1977) and R. Fennell, *The Common Agricultural Policy of the European Community.* American relations with the European unity movement are discussed by M. Beloff, *The United States and the Unity of Europe* (1963) and R. Manderson-Jones, *Special Relationship* (1972). British relations are discussed in M. Camps, *Britain and the European Community, 1955–63* (1964), U. Kitzinger, *Diplomacy and Persuasion* (1974), W. Wallace, *Britain and Europe* (1980) and F.E.C. Gregory, *Dilemmas of Government – Britain and the EC* (1983).

Eastern Europe since 1945

The essential background can be found in R.J. Crampton, *Eastern Europe in the Twentieth Century* (1994), G. and N. Swain, *Eastern Europe since 1945* (1993), J. Rothschild, *Return to Diversity* (1990), G. Stokes, *From Stalinism to Pluralism* (1996), O.A. Westad, S. Holfsmark and I. Neuman (eds), *The Soviet in Eastern Europe, 1945–89* (1994), F. Fejto, *A History of the People's Democracies* (1971), R. Okey, *Eastern Europe, 1740–1985* (2nd edn, 1986) and H. Seton-Watson, *The East European Revolution* (1985). On the early background to post-war eastern Europe, see M. McCauley (ed.), *Communist Power in Europe, 1944–49* (1977) and on the general decay of Soviet influence, see G. Ionescu, *The Break-up of the Soviet Empire in Eastern Europe* (1965), Z. Brzezinski, *The Soviet Bloc* (1974), L. Labedz (ed.), *Revisionism* (1962) and H. Seton-Watson, *Nationalism and Communism, Essays, 1946–63* (1964). The impact of Gorbachev is considered in K. Dawisha, *Eastern Europe, Gorbachev and Reform: the great challenge* (1988). For individual countries, see M. Fulbrook, *Anatomy of a Dictatorship. Inside the GDR, 1949–1989* (1995), D. Childs, *The GDR* (2nd edn, 1988), M. McCauley, *The German Democratic Republic* (1983), J.P. Nettl, *The Eastern Zone and Soviet Policy in Germany, 1945–50* (1951) and J. Stele, *Socialism with a German Face* (1977); on Yugoslavia, see D. Rusinow, *Yugoslav Experiment, 1948–1974* (1977), P. Auty, *Tito* (1974) and, more generally, S. Woodward, *Balkan Tragedy* (1995) and F. Singleton, *Twentieth Century Yugoslavia* (1976); on Hungary, see J.K. Hoensch, *A History of Modern Hungary, 1867–1994* (2nd edn, 1995), R. Tokes, *Hungary's Negotiated Revolution. Economic reform, social change and political succession, 1957–1990* (1996), F. Feher and A. Heller, *Hungary: 1956 Revisited* (1983), F. Vali, *Rift and Revolt in Hungary*

(1961) and M. Molnar, *Budapest 1956: a history of the Hungarian Revolution* (1971); on Czechoslovakia, see J. Valenta, *Soviet Intervention in Czechoslovakia, 1968* (1991), V.V. Kusin, *Intellectual Origins of the Prague Spring* (1971), G. Golan, *Reform Rule in Czechoslovakia* (1973), H.G. Skilling, *Czechoslovakia: the interrupted revolution* (1976); for Poland, see generally R.F. Leslie (ed.), *A History of Poland since 1863* (1983), N. Bethell, *Gomulka* (1969), N. Ascherson, *The Polish August* (1981) and T.G. Ash, *Polish Revolution: Solidarity 1980–82* (1983).

Decolonization

On decolonization, see M.E. Chamberlain, *Decolonization: the fall of the European empires* (1985), R.F. Holland, *European Decolonization, 1918–1981* (1985), H. Grimal, *Decolonization: the British, French, Dutch and the Belgian Empires, 1919–1963* (1980), J.P.D. Dunbabin, *International Relations since 1945, Vol. 2* (1994) and R. von Albertini, *Decolonization: the administration and future of the colonies, 1919–60* (1960, Eng. trans., 1971). Specifically on British decolonization, see J. Gallagher, *The Decline, Revival and Fall of the British Empire* (1982), C. Cross, *The Fall of the British Empire, 1918–1968* (1968), J. Darwin, *Britain and Decolonization: the retreat from empire in the post-war world* (1987) and *The End of the British Empire* (1991), and D. Judd and P. Slinn, *The Evolution of the Modern Commonwealth* (1982). The specific military strains upon the major colonial empire are discussed in P.M. Kennedy, *The Rise and Fall of British Naval Mastery* (1976) and *The Realities behind Diplomacy* (1981), A. Clayton, *The British Empire as a Superpower* (1986), C.J. Bartlett, *The Long Retreat: a short history of British defence policy, 1945–70* (1972) and P. Darby, *British Defence Policy East of Suez, 1947–1968* (1973). See also D. Dilks, *Retreat from Power* (2 vols, 1981), R. Douglas, *World Crisis and British Decline, 1929–56* (1986), A.N. Porter and A.J. Stockwell, *British Imperial Policy and Decolonization, 1938–64: Vol. 1* (1987) and N. Mansergh, *The Commonwealth Experience: Vol. 2. From British to multiracial Commonwealth* (2nd edn, 1982). French decolonization is discussed in R. Betts, *France and Decolonization* (1982) and A. Clayton, *The Wars of French Decolonization* (1994). The role of the League of Nations is considered in S.R. Gibbons and P. Monican, *The League of Nations and UNO* (1970) and of the UN in E. Luard, *The History of the United Nations: Vol. 2: The age of decolonization, 1955–1965* (1988). J.M. Lee, *Colonial Development and Good Government: a study of the ideas expressed by the British official class in planning decolonization* (1967) and W.H. Morris-Jones and G. Fischer, *Decolonization and After: the British and French experience* (1980) examine the attitudes of the colonial powers, while the external pressures on them are the subject of W.R. Louis, *Imperialism at Bay 1941–5: the United States and the decolonization of the British Empire* (1977); see also M. Kahler, *Decolonization in Britain and France: the domestic consequences*

of international relations (1984). For the history of colonialism and independence movements in particular countries, see the separate geographical sections below; leaders of decolonization movements can be found
in H. Tinker, *Men Who Overturned Empires* (1987).

The Middle East

For introductory reading on the Middle East, see R. Ovendale, *The
Longman Companion to the Middle East* (2nd edn, 1998), B. Lewis, *The
Shaping of the Modern Middle East* (1994), I. Asad and R. Owen, *The Middle
East* (1983), A. Hourani, *The Emergence of the Modern Middle East* (1980),
S.N. Fisher, *The Middle East. A History* (1979), G. Lenczowski, *The Middle
East in World Affairs* (4th edn, 1980), N. Bethell, *The Palestine Triangle*
(1979), A. Goldschmidt, *A Concise History of the Middle East* (1979),
P. Mansfield, *The Arabs* (1976) and W.R. Polk, *The Arab World* (1980). For
the Cold War see Y. Sayigh and A. Shlaim (eds), *The Cold War and the
Middle East* (1997). Particular themes can be explored through M.
Halpern, *The Politics of Social Change in the Middle East* (1963) and P.
Mansfield, *The Middle East: a political and economic survey* (4th edn, 1973),
B. Schwodran, *The Middle East, Oil and the Great Powers* (1973) and Y.
Porath, *In Search of Arab Unity, 1930–1945* (1986). T.G. Fraser, *The Middle
East, 1914–1979* (1980) is a helpful collection of documents.

Egypt

General accounts can be found in P.J. Vatikiotis, *The History of Egypt from
Muhammad Ali to Sadat* (2nd edn, 1980), J. Berque, *Egypt: Imperialism
and Revolution* (1972), A. Sattin, *Lifting the Veil: the British in Egypt, 1800–
1956* (1988), and J.C.B. Richmond, *Egypt, 1798–1952* (1977). For the
post-1945 period, see R. Stephens, *Nasser. A Political Biography* (1971),
R. Baker, *Egypt's Uncertain Revolution under Nasser and Sadat* (1978),
R. Ovendale, *The Origins of the Arab – Israeli Wars* (1984), R. Mabro, *The
Egyptian Economy: 1952–1972* (1974) and I. Beeson, *Sadat* (1981). On the
Suez Crisis, see W. Roger Louis and R. Owen (eds), *Suez 1956: the crisis and
its consequences* (1989). An important view of social change is contained
in J. Neinin and Z. Lockman, *Workers on the Nile: nationalism, communism,
Islam and the Egyptian working class, 1881–1954* (1988).

The creation of Israel and the Arab–Israeli conflict

J.C. Hurewitz, *The Middle East and North Africa in World Politics: Vol. II*
(1979), E. Monroe, *Britain's Moment*, W.R. Louis, *The British Empire in the
Middle East, 1945–1951* (1984) and N. Bethell, *The Palestine Triangle* (1979)

are essential works. Some useful first-hand evidence can be found in R.H.S. Crossman, *Palestine Mission: a personal record* (1947) and M. Begin, *The Revolt* (1951). The history of the Zionist movement is covered in the three volumes by D. Vital, *The Origins of Zionism* (1980), *Zionism: the formative years* (1982) and *Zionism: the crucial phase* (1987). H.W. Sachar, *History of Israel: from the rise of Zionism to our time* (1985) and *From the Aftermath of the Yom Kippur War* (1989) is a comprehensive history of Israel. R. Ovendale, *Britain, the United States, and the Transfer of Power in the Middle East, 1945–1962* (1996), W.R. Louis and R.S. Stookey (eds), *The End of the Palestine Mandate* (1986) and *Palestine and the Great Powers, 1945–1948* (1982) deal in detail with the British period. C.D. Smith, *Palestine and the Arab–Israeli Conflict* (1989) and R. Ovendale, *The Origins of the Arab–Israeli Wars* (1984) examine the growth of conflict; see also E.W. Said, *The Question of Palestine* (1980). A. Shlaim, *Collusion across the Jordan: King Abdullah, the Zionist Movement and the Partition of Palestine* (1988) and I. Pappe, *Britain and the Arab–Israeli Conflict, 1948–51* (1988) discuss the early years, while the American involvement is considered in Z. Ganin, *Truman, American Jewry and Israel, 1945–1948* (1979). A fresh study is M.J. Cohen *Palestine to Israel: from mandate to independence* (1988). On the later years of the Israeli state, see A. Sella and Y. Yishai (eds), *Israel: the peaceful belligerent, 1967–79* (1986) and B. Morris, *1948 and After* (1990). On the Palestinians, see Y. Sayigh, *Armed Struggle and the Search for State: the Palestinian National Movement, 1949–1993* (1997).

Arab nationalism and the Islamic Revolution

Y. Porath, *In Search of Arab Unity, 1930–1945* (1986) discusses the attempt to weld the Arab world into a larger whole. The important non-Arab power of great influence since the 1960s is considered in N.R. Keddie and M.K. Gasiorowski (eds) *Neither East nor West: Iran, the Soviet Union, and the United States* (1990), H. Amirsedeglu and R.W. Ferrier, *Twentieth Century Iran* (1977) and N.R. Keddie, *Roots of Revolution: an interpretative history of modern Iran* (1981), while the Islamic dimension is examined in S.A. Arjomand, *The Turban for the Crown: the Islamic Revolution in Iran* (1988). P. Marr, *The Modern History of Iraq* (1985), D. Hopwood, *Syria, 1945–1986: politics and society* (1988), and U. Dann, *King Hussein and the Challenge of Arab Radicalism: Jordan, 1955–1967* (1989) examine other states since 1945. M. Shemesh, *The Palestinian Entity, 1959–1974* (1988) and H. Cobban, *The Making of Modern Lebanon* (1985) examine two major sources of conflict. R.B. Betts, *The Druze* (1988) looks at one of the major factions in the Lebanese conflict. On the Iraq–Iran War, see D. Hiro, *The Longest War: the Iran–Iraq conflict* (1989) and on the Palestine uprising see Z. Schiff and E. Ya'ari, *Intifada* (1990).

Africa

There are useful introductions in M. Crowder (ed.), *The Cambridge History of Africa, Vol. viii: 1940–1975* (1984), J. Iliffe, *Africans: the history of a continent* (1995), P.J.M. McEwan and R.B. Sutcliffe (eds), *The Study of Africa* (1965), B. Freund, *The Making of Contemporary Africa* (1984), J. Hatch, *Africa Today and Tomorrow* (1965) and *Africa Emergent: Africa's problems since Independence* (1974), B. Davidson, *Africa in Modern History* (1978), H.S. Wilson, *The Imperial Experience in Sub-Saharan Africa since 1870* (1977) and M. Crowder, *Historical Atlas of Africa* (1985).

For the colonial period and decolonization, see J.D. Hargreaves, *Decolonization in Africa, 1945–64* (1988), L.H. Gann and P. Duignan (eds), *The History and Politics of Colonialism, 1870–1960* (4 vols, 1969–75), P. Gifford and W.R. Louis, *The Transfer of Power in Africa: decolonization, 1940–1960* (1982), P. Gifford and W.R. Louis (eds), *Decolonization and African Independence* (1988), and W.H. Morris-Jones and G. Fischer, *Decolonization and After: the British and French experience* (1980). The post-colonial period is considered broadly in D. Fieldhouse, *Black Africa, 1945–1980* (1986), J. Jackson and C. Rosberg, *Political Rule in Black Africa* (1982), S. Decalo, *Coups and Army Rule in Africa* (1976), W.F. Gutteridge, *Military Regimes in Africa* (1975), G. Hunter, *The New Societies of Tropical Africa: a selective study* (1962), R.I. Rotberg and A.A. Mazrui (eds), *Protest and Power in Black Africa* (1970), P.C. Lloyd, *Africa in Social Change* (1971), A.A. Mazrui, *Political Values and the Educated Class in Africa* (1977), C. Rosberg and T.M. Callaghy, *Socialism in Sub-Saharan Africa* (1977), T.M. Shaw and K.A. Heard, *The Politics of Africa: dependence and development* (1979), and W. Tordoff, *Government and Politics in Africa* (1984).

External influences on Africa, other than from the colonial powers, are discussed in K. Somerville, *Foreign Military Intervention in Africa* (1990), J. Darwin 'Africa in world politics', in N. Woods (ed.), *Explaining International Relations since 1945* (1996), P. Duignan and L.H. Gann, *The United States and Africa: A history* (1984) and R.D. Mahoney, *JFK: ordeal in Africa* (1984). The issue of Pan-Africanism and African Nationalism is discussed in C. Legum, *Pan-Africanism* (1962) and I. Geiss, *Pan-Africanism* (1974); see also G. Padmore (ed.), *Colonial and Coloured Unity: history of the Pan-African Congress* (2nd edn, 1963) and T.L. Hodgkin, *Nationalism in Colonial Africa* (1956). Two important sets of documents are J.A. Langley, *Ideologies of Liberation in Black Africa 1956–1970: documents on modern African political thought from colonial times to the present* (1979) and J. Minogue and J. Molloy, *African Aims and Attitudes: selected documents* (1974). Some reference data can be found in W.M. Hailey, *An African Survey* (rev. edn, 1956) and B.R. Mitchell, *International Historical Statistics: Africa and Asia* (1982).

Colonial policy

The background to African developments can be traced in R.D. Pearce, *The Turning Point in Africa: British colonial policy, 1938–1948* (1982), A. Cohen, *British Policy in Changing Africa* (1959), L.H. Gann and P. Duignan, *African Proconsuls* (1978), J.M. Lee and M. Petter, *The Colonial Office, War and Development Policy* (1982) and S. Constantine, *The Making of British Colonial Development Policy, 1914–40* (1984). The effects of the Second World War are discussed in D. Killingray and R. Rathbone (eds), *Africa and the Second World War* (1986) and for the post-war period, see Y. Baugura, *Britain and Commonwealth Africa* (1983), D. Fieldhouse, 'The Labour Governments and the Empire-Commonwealth', in R. Ovendale (ed.), *The Foreign Policy of the British Labour Governments, 1945–51* (1984), E. Mortimer, *France and the Africans, 1944–60* (1969), and G. Clarence-Smith, *The Third Portuguese Empire, 1825–1975* (1985).

North Africa

For North Africa, see J. Berque, *French North Africa: the Maghrib between two World Wars* (1967), M. Bennoune, *The Making of Contemporary Algeria, 1830–1987* (1988), D.C. Gordon, *The Passing of French Algeria* (1966), P. Bourdieu, *The Algerians* (1962), E. O'Balance, *The Algerian Insurrection, 1954–62* (1967) and A. Horne, *A Savage War of Peace* (rev. edn, 1988). The essay in J. Dunn, *Modern Revolutions* (2nd edn, 1989) has an excellent analysis of the Algerian Revolution, while F. Fanon, *Studies in a Dying Colonialism* (1955) and *The Wretched of the Earth* (1965) are two important studies of the causes of the Algerian revolt. For the post-revolutionary situation, see S. Amin, *The Maghreb in the Modern World* (1970). On other parts of North Africa, see W.D. Swearington, *Moroccan Mirages: agrarian dreams and deceptions, 1912–1986* (1988). A valuable recent study of North and West Africa is D.B.C. O'Brien and C. Coulou (eds), *Charisma and Brotherhood in African Islam* (1988).

West Africa

For West Africa, see J.F. Ajayi and M. Crowder, *A History of West Africa, Vol. 2* (1974), M. Crowder, *West Africa under Colonial Rule* (1968), J.D. Hargreaves, *The End of Colonial Rule in West Africa: essays in contemporary history* (1979) and *West Africa Partitioned: Vol. 2: The elephants and the grass* (1985), C. Harrison, *French Policy Towards Islam in West Africa, 1860–1960* (1988), S. Dunn, *West African States* (1978), and R. Schachter-Morgenthau, *Political Parties in French-Speaking West Africa* (1964); see also J. Suret-Canale, *French Colonialism in Tropical Africa, 1900–1945* (1971). Particular countries are discussed in D. Austin, *Politics in Ghana, 1946–60* (1964) and C.L.R. James, *Nkrumah and the Ghana Revolution* (1977), J. Coleman, *Nigeria: Background to Nationalism* (1958), K. Ezera, *Constitutional Developments in Nigeria* (1960), K.W.J. Post and G.D. Jenkins, *The Price of Liberty: personality and politics in colonial Nigeria* (1973), B. Dudley, *An Introduction to Nigerian Government and Politics* (1982), and S. Egite Oyovbaire, *Federation in Nigeria: a study in the development of the Nigerian state* (1983).

Tropical and Equatorial Africa

See J. Suret-Canale, *French Colonialism in Tropical Africa, 1900–1945* (1971), C. Young, *Politics in the Congo, Decolonization and Independence* (1965), H.F. Weiss, *Political Protest in the Congo* (1967), R. Slade, *The Belgian Congo* (1960), R. Anstey, *King Leopold's Legacy: the Congo under Belgian rule, 1908–60* (1966), J. Gerard-Libois, *Katanga Secession* (1966) and R. Lemarchand, *Political Awakening in the Congo* (1964). M. Njeuma (ed.), *Introduction to the History of Cameroon* (1989), R.A. Joseph, *Radical Nationalism in Cameroon* (1977) and D.A. Low, *Buganda in Modern History* (1971) examine other states.

East and Central Africa

For an introduction, see V. Harlow, E.M. Chilver and A. Smith (eds), *History of East Africa, Vol. II* (1965) and D.A. Low and A. Smith (eds), *Vol. III* (1976), J. Saul, *State and Revolution in East Africa* (1979), and K. Ingham, *A History of East Africa* (3rd edn, 1975). E.A. Brett, *Colonialism and Underdevelopment in East Africa* (1973) and P.H. Gulliver (ed.), *Tradition and Transition in East Africa* (1994) raise general issues. On the Sudan, see R.O. Collins and F.M. Deng (eds), *The British in the Sudan, 1898–1956* (1984) and D.F. Gordon, *Decolonization and the State in Kenya* (1986) on Kenya. Kenya's Mau Mau movement is discussed in C.G. Rosberg and J. Nottingham, *The Myth of Mau Mau* (1966) and in W.R. Ochieng and K.K. Janmohamed (eds), *Some Perspectives on the Mau Mau Movement* (Special edition of the *Kenya Historical Review*, Nairobi, 1977); see also on Kenya, G. Wasserman, *Politics of Decolonization: Kenya Europeans and the land issue, 1960–1965* (1976), C.J. Gertzel, *The Politics of Independent Kenya, 1963–69* (1970) and D. Goldsworthy, *Tom Mboya* (1982). J. Iliffe, *A Modern History of Tanganyika* (1979), C. Pratt, *The Critical Phase in Tanzania, 1945–1968: Nyerere and the emergence of a socialist strategy* (1976) and G. Hyden, *Beyond Ujaama in Tanzania* (1980) cover one of the other major East African states, while Uganda is examined in J.J. Jorgensen, *Uganda: a modern history* (1981) and G.A. Ginyera-Pincwa, *Apolo Milton Obote and His Times* (1977). A combined economic history of Kenya and Uganda is R.M.A. Van Zwanenberg and A. King, *An Economic History of Kenya and Uganda, 1800–1970* (1975). The Central African Federation is discussed in R. Gray, *The Two Nations* (1960) and P. Mason, *Year of Decision* (1960); see also A.J. Wills, *An Introduction to the History of Central Africa* (3rd edn, 1973), while the rise of opposition to white rule in the region is considered in R. Rotberg, *The Rise of Nationalism in Central Africa* (1965). R. Blake, *A History of Rhodesia* (1977) is a broad survey, but T.O. Ranger, *Peasant Consciousness and Guerrilla War in Zimbabwe* (1985), R. Hodder-Williams, *White Farmers in Rhodesia, 1890–1965* (1984) and R. Palmer, *Land and Racial Domination in Rhodesia* (1977) examine the rural situation, while the general economic background is discussed in I. Phimister, *An Economic and Social History of Zimbabwe, 1890–1948* (1988). For the white declaration of UDI and the subsequent war, see M. Loney, *White Racism and Imperial Response* (1974) and D. Martin and P. Johnson, *The Struggle for Zimbabwe* (1981). Two useful groups of studies are C. Stoneman (ed.), *Zimbabwe's Inheritance* (1982) and G. Peele and T.O. Ranger (eds), *Past and Present in Zimbabwe* (1983). For Zambia, see A. Roberts, *A History of Zambia* (1976), E.L. Bergen, *Labour, Race and Colonial Rule: the copperbelt from 1924 to independence* (1974), C.J. Gertzel, et al., *The Dynamics of the One-Party State in Zambia* (1984), and W. Tordoff (ed.), *Administration in Zambia* (1980).

Southern Africa

For Angola, see J. Marcum, *The Angolan Revolution, Vol. I, 1950–62* (1969), B. Davidson, *In the Eye of the Storm: Angola's people* (1974) and G.J. Bender, *Angola under the Portuguese: the myth and the reality* (1978). The other Portuguese colony, Mozambique, is discussed in A. and B. Isaacman, *Mozambique: from colonialism to revolution* (1983), E. Mondlane, *The Struggle for Mozambique* (1969), and T.W. Henriksen, *Revolution and Counter-Revolution: Mozambique's war of independence, 1964–74* (1983). For South Africa, see M. Wilson and L. Thompson (eds), *The Oxford History of South Africa, Vol. II, 1870–1966* (1971) and T.R.H. Davenport, *South Africa: a modern history* (3rd edn, 1987). G.H. Le May, *The Boers* (1995) and D. Posel, *The Making of Apartheid, 1948–61* (1991) deal with the development of the character of the South African regime, while B. Davidson, J. Slovo, and A.R. Wilkinson, *Southern Africa: the new politics of revolution* (1976) and N. Mandela, *Long Walk to Freedom* (1993) examine opposition. T.G. Karis and G. Carter (eds), *From Protest to Challenge. A Documentary History of African Politics in South Africa, 1882–1964* (4 vols, 1972–77) provides source material. L. Marquand, *The Peoples and Policies of South Africa* (4th edn, 1969), G. Carter, *The Politics of Inequality: South Africa since 1948* (1958), J. Hoagland, *South Africa, Civilisations in Conflict* (1973), T.D. Moodie, *The Rise of Afrikanerdom: power, apartheid and the Afrikaner civil religion* (1975) and M. Lipton, *Capitalism and Apartheid: South Africa, 1910–86* (1985) are all useful studies. The opposition to the dominant apartheid policy is considered in J. Robertson, *Liberalism in South Africa, 1948–1963* (1971), P. Walshe, *The Rise of African Nationalism in South Africa: the African National Congress, 1912–1952* (1970), H. Adam and H. Giliomee, *Ethnic Power Mobilized* (1979) and T. Lodge, *Black Politics in South Africa since 1945* (1983).

Asia

The Indian sub-continent

The historiography is dominated by the theme of empire and decolonization, in spite of more than 40 years of independent politics for the new states of India, Pakistan, and Sri Lanka. For imperial policy in general and decolonization, see earlier (pp. 445–6), but specifically on India, see G.M. Brown, *Modern India: the origins of an Asian democracy* (2nd edn, 1993), D.A. Low, *Eclipse of Empire* (1991), S. Wolpert, *A New History of India* (1977), P. Heehs, *India's Freedom Struggle, 1857–1947: a short history* (1988), W.T. De Bary, *The Sources of Indian Tradition* (1958), S. Sarkar, *Modern India, 1885–1947* (1988), B.R. Tomlinson, *The Political Economy of the Raj, 1914–1947* (1979) and D.A. Low, *Congress and the Raj: facets of the Indian struggle* (1977). The role of Gandhi has received short introductory treatment in A. Copley, *Gandhi* (1987), but much more substantially in J.M. Brown, *Gandhi: prisoner of hope* (1989).

Muslim nationalism and the origin of Pakistan is considered in P. Hardy, *The Muslims of British India* (1972). Their leader, Jinnah, is examined in S. Wolpert, *Jinnah of Pakistan* (1984), and A. Jalal, *The Sole Spokesman: Jinnah, the Muslim League and the demand for Pakistan* (1985); see also I. Talbot, *Provincial Politics and the Pakistan Movement, 1937–47* (1989). The run-up to Partition is considered in A. Roy, 'The high politics of India's Partition', *Modern Asian Studies* (1990), M. Hasan (ed.), *India's Partition: process, strategy, mobilization* (1994), A. Singh, *The Origins of Partition* (1987), J. Chatterji, *Beugal Divided* (1995), F.G. Hutchins, *India's Revolution. Gandhi and the Quit India Movement* (1973), B.N. Pandey, *The Break Up of British India* (1969), R.J. Moore, *Churchill, Cripps and India, 1939–1945* (1979) and *Escape from Empire. The Attlee Government and the Indian Problem* (1983), H.V. Hodson, *The Great Divide. Britain–India–Pakistan* (1969) and C.H. Philips and D. Wainwright, *Partition of India: politics and perspectives, 1935–1947* (1970). Mountbatten's role is discussed in P. Ziegler, *Mountbatten* (1987). Post-partition India is discussed in P. Brass, *The Politics of India since Independence* (2nd edn, 1994), A. Kohli (ed.), *India's Democracy* (1991) and *Democracy and Discontent* (1990), D. Butler, P. Roy and A. Lahiri, *India Decides: elections, 1952–91* (1991), C. Jaffrelot, *The Hindu Nationalist Movement and Indian Politics* (1996), K.N. Panikkar (ed.),

Communalism in India. History, Politics, Culture (1991) and D. Hardgrave and S. Kochanek, *India: Government and Politics* (5th edn, 1993). On Nehru, see S. Gopal, *Jawaharlal Nehru* (3 vols, 1975–84), M. Brecher, *Nehru: a political biography* (1959) and M. Edwardes, *Nehru: a political biography* (1971). See P.J. Nehru, *Glimpses of World History* (1989) and, on the earlier phase of the independence movement, his *An Autobiography* (1942). Indira Gandhi has been the subject of a recent biography, I. Malhotra, *Indira Gandhi: a personal and political biography* (1989). India's relations with other states after 1947 are considered in C. Heimsath and S. Mansingh, *A Diplomatic History of Modern India* (1971), W.J. Barnds, *India, Pakistan and the Great Powers* (1972) and A. Stein, *India and the Soviet Union: the Nehru era* (1969). India's agricultural development is considered in B.M. Bhatia, *Famine in India, 1860–1965* (2nd edn, 1967) and F.R. Frankel, *India's Green Revolution: economic gains and costs* (1971).

On the background to the emergence of Pakistan see the works cited above; on Jinnah, see also the essay on Jinnah in H. Tinker, *Men Who Overturned Empires: fighters, dreamers and schemers* (1987) and K.B. Sayeed, *Pakistan: the formative phase, 1857–1948* (rev. edn, 1968). Pakistan's development is considered in A. Jalal, *The State of Martial Rule* (1990), O. Norman, *The Political Economy of Pakistan, 1947–1985* (1988), L. Binder, *Religion and Politics in Pakistan* (1963) and E.I. Rosenthal, *Islam in the Modern National State* (1965); see also the essay by Halliday in F. Halliday and H. Alavi (eds), *State and Ideology in the Middle East and Pakistan* (1988). The break-up of Pakistan and the emergence of Bangladesh is considered in K. Siddiqui, *Conflict, Crisis and War in Pakistan* (1972), R. Jahan, *Pakistan: failure in national integration* (1972) and W. Wilcox, *The Emergence of Bangladesh* (1973). Pakistan's foreign policy is examined in S.M. Burke, *Pakistan's Foreign Policy: an historical analysis* (1973). The Bhutto years are considered in S.J. Burki, *Pakistan under Bhutto, 1971–1977* (2nd edn, 1988). On Sri Lanka, see S. Arasarátnam, *Ceylon* (1964) and A.J. Wilson, *Politics in Sri Lanka, 1947–1979* (2nd edn, 1979).

South-East Asia

N. Tarling (ed.), *The Cambridge History of South-East Asia, Vol. 2* (1992), D.G. Hall, *A History of South-East Asia* (4th edn, 1981) and J.F. Cady, *The History of Post-War Southeast Asia* (1974) are useful introductions; see also D.J. Steinberg, *In Search of South-East Asia: a modern history* (1971), J.M. Pluvier, *South-East Asia from Colonialism to Independence* (1974), and R. Jeffrey (ed.), *Asia. The winning of Independence* (1981).

The histories of individual South-East Asian countries are considered in S. Karnow, *Vietnam. A History* (1994), J.F. Cady, *A History of Modern Burma*

(1958) and D.E. Smith, *Religion and Politics in Burma* (1965), see also F.R. Von der Mehden, *Religion and Nationalism in Southeast Asia: Burma, Indonesia, the Philippines* (1963), and D.K. Wyatt, *The Politics of Reform in Thailand: education in the reign of King Chulalongkorn* (1969).

The Indonesian nationalist movement is considered in G.M. Kahin, *Nationalism and Revolution in Indonesia* (1953), B. Dahm, *History of Indonesia in the Twentieth Century* (1971) and *Sukarno and the Struggle for Indonesian Independence* (1969); see also J.D. Legge, *Indonesia* (1964). H.J. Benda, *The Crescent and the Rising Sun: Indonesian Islam under the Japanese Occupation, 1942–1945* (1958), L.H. Palmier, *Indonesia and the Dutch* (1962) and M. Ricklefs, *A History of Modern Indonesia* (1981) are helpful studies. The role of Sukarno is considered in the essay in H. Tinker, *Men Who Overturned Empires: fighters, dreamers and schemers* (1987) and J.D. Legge, *Sukarno: a political biography* (1972). The communist role in Indonesia is discussed in L. Palmier, *Communists in Indonesia: power pursued in vain* (1973), A. Brackman, *Indonesian Communism* (1963), and R.T. McVey (ed.), *Indonesia* (1963). The army's role is considered in H. Crouch, *The Army and Politics in Indonesia* (1978). On Malaya, see J.G. Butcher, *The British in Malaya, 1880–1941* (1979). Malayan independence receives some attention in R. Jeffrey, *Asia: the winning of independence* (1981), but see B.W. Andaya and L.Y. Andaya, *A History of Malaysia* (1982) for a more substantial account. The communist attempt at a seizure of power is considered in A. Short, *The Communist Insurrection in Malaya, 1948–1960* (1975); see also J.M. Gullick, *Malaysia* (1969), W.R. Roff, *The Origins of Malay Nationalism* (1967), M.E. Osborne, *Region of Revolt: focus on Southeast Asia* (1971) and A.C. Brackman, *South-East Asia's Second Front: the power struggle in the Malay archipelago* (1966).

For the Philippines, see T.A. Agoncillo, *A Short History of the Philippines* (1969), O.D. Corpuz, *The Philippines* (1965), the essays in F.R. Von der Mehden, *Religion and Nationalism in Southeast Asia: Burma, Indonesia, the Philippines* (1963) and M.E. Osborne, *Region of Revolt: focus on Southeast Asia* (1971). See also A. Jorgenson-Dahl, *Regional Organisation and Order in South-East Asia* (1982).

Indo-China, and especially Vietnam, has attracted great attention. For the earlier part of its history, see M. Shipway, *The Road to War: France and Vietnam, 1944–47* (1996), E.J. Hammer, *The Struggle for Indochina, 1940–55* (1966). J. Buttinger, *Vietnam: a dragon embattled: Vol. I, From Colonialism to the Vietminh; Vol. II, Vietnam at War* (1967) is a major narrative history, while R.B. Smith, *An International History of the Vietnam War: Vol. I, Revolution versus Containment, Vol. II, The Struggle for South East Asia, 1961–65* (1983–85) are the first two volumes of four placing the war in an international context; for a crucial episode, see J. Cable, *The Geneva Conference of 1954 on Indochina* (1986). A. Short, *The Origins of the Vietnam War* (1989) is a useful modern summary; see also the chapter in J. Dunn, *Modern Revolutions* (2nd edn, 1988). The dynamics of the communist insurrection are discussed in R. Smith, *Vietnam and the West* (1968), P.J. Honey, *Genesis of Tragedy: the historical background to the Vietnam War* (1968), J.M. McAlister, *Vietnam: the origins of revolution* (1969), and D.J. Duncanson, *Government and Revolution in Vietnam* (1968). The peasant origins of the war against the colonial powers are exemplified in G. Lochart, *Nation in Arms: the origins of the People's Army of Vietnam* (1989), W.J. Daiker, *The Communist Road to Power in Vietnam* (2nd edn, 1996) and J. Race, *War Comes to Long An: revolutionary conflict in a Vietnamese province* (1972). For Ho Chi-minh, see J. Lacouture, *Ho Chi-minh: a political biography* (1968) and H. Tinker, *Men Who Overturned Empires: fighters, dreamers and schemers* (1987). North Vietnam's relations with other powers are considered in P.J. Honey, *Communism in North Vietnam: its role in the Sino–Soviet Dispute* (1963) and I.V. Gaiduck, *The Soviet Union and the Vietnam War* (1996). On Cambodia, see B. Kiernan, *The Pol Pot Regime: Race, Power and Genocide in Cambodia under the Khmer Rouge* (1996).

China

J.K. Fairbank and A. Feuerwerker (eds), *The Cambridge History of China, Vols 12 and 13. Republican China* (1983, 1986; abridged and ed. L. Eastman as *The Nationalist Era in China, 1927–49*, 1991), L. Bianco, *Origins of the Chinese Revolution, 1915–49* (1972), C.P. Fitzgerald, *The Birth of Communist China* (1964), J.E. Shendan, *China in Disintegration: the republic era in Chinese History, 1912–1949* (1976) and J. Chesnaux, C. Barbier and M.C. Bergere, *China from the 1911 Revolution to Liberation* (1978) deal with the pre-Communist regime. J. Chesnaux, *Peasant Revolts in China, 1840–1949* (1973) and C.A. Johnson, *Peasant Nationalism and Communist Power: the emergence of revolutionary China, 1937–1945* (1962) look at the dynamics of peasant protests; see also R.H. Myers, *The Chinese Peasant Economy: Agricultural Development in Hopei and Shantung, 1890–1949* (1970). The standard works on Communist China are R. MacFarquar and J.K. Fairbank (eds), *The Cambridge History of China, Vol. 14: The People's Republic: the emergence of Revolutionary China, 1949–65* (1987); *Vol. 15: Revolutions within the Chinese Revolution, 1966–82* (1991; abridged and ed. R. MacFarquar as *The Politics of China: the eras of Mao and Deng*, 2nd edn, 1997) and J. Guillermaz, *The Chinese Communist Party in Power* (1976). For Mao, see S.R. Schram, *Mao Tse-tung* (1966) and *The Political Thought of Mao Tse-tung* (1969), B.J. Schwartz, *Chinese Communism and the Rise of Mao* (1967), H.H. Salisbury, *The Long March* (1985), P. Carter, *Mao* (1976), S. Uhalley, *Mao Tse-tung: a critical biography* (1975), H. Suyin, *Wind in the Tower: Mao*

Tse-tung and Chinese Revolution, 1949–1975 (1976), and L.W. Pye, *Mao Tse-tung: the man and the leader* (1976). J. Chang, *Wild Swans* (1991), W. Hinton, *Fanshen: a documentary of revolution in a Chinese village* (2nd edn, 1972), J. Chen, *A Year in Upper Felicity: life in a Chinese village during the Cultural Revolution* (1973) and Ch'ing K'un Yang, *A Chinese Village in Early Communist Transition* (1959) are good studies 'on the ground' of village life at different phases after the Revolution. A. Eckstein, *China's Economic Revolution* (1977), N.R. Chen and W. Galenson, *The Chinese Economy under Communism* (1969) and D.H. Perkins (ed.), *China's Economy in Historical Perspective* (1975) examine the economy, while the workings of the regime are considered in D.J. Waller, *The Government and Politics of Communist China* (1973) and J. Domes, *The Internal Politics of China, 1949– 72* (1973). The People's Army is considered in J. Gittings, *The Role of the Chinese Army* (1967), while J.W. Lewis, *Party Leadership and Revolutionary Power in China* (1970) and J.M.H. Lindbeck (ed.), *China: Management of a Revolutionary Society* (1971) give some insight into the dynamics of party leadership. L. White, *Policies of Chaos* (1989), W. Joseph, C. Wong and D. Zweig, *New Perspectives on the Chinese Cultural Revolution* (1991), R. MacFarquar, *The Origins of the Chinese Cultural Revolution*, 2 vols (1974 and 1984), E.J. Perry and Lu Xun, *Proletarian Power: Shanghai in the Cultural Revolution* (1997) and J. Myrdal and G. Kessle, *China: the Revolution Continued* (1971) give some insight into the Cultural Revolution. For China's foreign relations, see M.B. Jansen, *Japan and China: from war to peace, 1894–1972* (1975), W. Gungwu, *China and the World since 1949* (1977), and J. Gittings, *The World and China, 1922–1972* (1974). Russia's relationship with China is examined in O.E. Clubb, *China and Russia: the 'Great Game'* (1971), W.E. Griffith, *The Sino–Soviet Rift* (1964), D. Zagoria, *The Sino–Soviet Conflict, 1956–61* (1961) and D. Floyd, *Mao against Kruschev: a short history of the Sino–Soviet Conflict* (1964). For relations with the United States, see J.K. Fairbank, *The United States and China* (1971). The impact of the Korean involvement is discussed in A.L. George, *The Chinese Communist Army in Action: the Korean War and its aftermath* (1967) and see also P. Van Ness, *Revolution and Chinese Foreign Policy: Peking's Support for Wars of National Liberation* (1970).

Japan

There is a good modern survey in J.E. Hunter, *The Emergence of Modern Japan: an introductory history since 1853* (1989), but see also K. Pyle, *The Making of Modern Japan* (2nd edn, 1996), A. Waswo, *Modern Japanese Society, 1868–1994* (1996), G.A. Gordon (ed.), *Postwar Japan as History* (1993) and P. Duus (ed.), *The Cambridge History of Japan, Vol. 6* (1988). Specific themes are examined in M. Schaller, *The American Occupation of Japan* (1985), G. Curtis, *The Japanese Way of Politics* (1988), J.A.A. Stockwin, *Japan: Divided*

Politics in a Growth Economy (rev. edn, 1998), B. Eccleston, *State and Society in Postwar Japan* (1989), and K. Yamamura and Y. Yasuba (eds), *The Political Economy of Japan, Vol. I: The Domestic Transformation* (1987). On the economy, see G.C. Allen, *A Short Economic History of Modern Japan* (3rd edn, 1972), Supplementary chapter, T. Nakamura, *The Postwar Japanese Economy* (2nd edn, 1995), S. Tsuru, *Japan's Capitalism* (1993) and H. Patrick and H. Rosovsky (eds), *Asia's New Giant: How the Japanese economy works* (1976).

For foreign policy, see M.B. Jansen, *Japan and China: from war to peace, 1894–1972* (1975), M.E. Weinstein, *Japan's Post-war Defence Policy, 1947–1968* (1971), A. Iriye and W.I. Cohen (eds), *The United States and Japan in the Post-war World* (1989), B. Scalapino (ed.), *The Foreign Policy of Modern Japan* (1977), while K. Van Wolferen, *The Enigma of Japanese Power* (1989) poses some questions about Japan's role as an economic superpower with little military power.

Australasia

C. Hartley Grattan, *The South-West Pacific since 1900* (1963) offers a comprehensive history of the region. On the Pacific islands, see W.P. Morrell, *The Great Powers in the Pacific* (1965) and M.R. Peattie, *Nanyo: the rise and fall of the Japanese in Micronesia, 1883–1945* (1988). For Australia itself, see G. Bolton, *The Oxford History of Australia, Volume 5: 1942–1995: The Middle Way* (1996), F.K. Crowley (ed.), *A New History of Australia* (1974), F.K. Crowley, *Modern Australia in Documents, 1901–1970* (2 vols, 1973) and R. Ward, *The History of Australia: the twentieth century, 1901–1975* (1978). R. Ward, *Australia* (1965) and D. Pike, *Australia: the quiet continent* (1962) are also helpful one-volume studies.

On inter-war Australia, see J. Mackinolty (ed.), *The Wasted Years: Australia's Great Depression* (1982), while the impact of the Second World War is discussed in P. Hasluck, *The Government and the People, 1942–1945* (1970). Post-war developments are considered in D. Horner, *The Lucky Country: Australia in the sixties* (2nd edn, 1966) and J.D.B. Miller, *Australia* (1966). Australia's involvement in the region is considered in D.M. Horner, *High Command: Australia and Allied strategy, 1939–1945* (1983) and P. King (ed.), *Australia's Vietnam: Australia in the Second Indo-China War* (1983).

For New Zealand, see K. Sinclair, *A History of New Zealand* (1959) and J. Rowe and M. Rowe, *New Zealand* (1967). Also useful are W.H. Oliver, *The Story of New Zealand* (1960), W.P. Morrell and D.O.W. Hall, *A History of New Zealand Life* (1957) and H.G. Miller, *New Zealand* (1950). Particular aspects of New Zealand's history are considered in J.B. Condliffe, *New*

Zealand in the Making (2nd edn, 1959), mainly dealing with economic and social history, and his *The Welfare State in New Zealand* (1959). On the Second World War, see F.L.W. Wood, *The New Zealand People at War* (1958).

The Americas

There are numerous histories of the United States, but among the most helpful introductions are H. Brogan, *The Longman History of the United States of America* (1986) and M.A. Jones, *The Limits of Liberty: American history, 1607–1980* (1983). See also A. Nevins and H.S. Commager, *America: the story of a free people* (1976), and Carl Degler, *Out of the Past* (3rd edn, 1984). For the period after the Second World War, see W.H. Chafe, *The Unfinished Journey: America since World War II* (3rd edn, 1995), A.L. Hamby, *The Imperial Years: the United States since 1939* (1976), J. Patterson, *Great Expectations: the United States, 1945–1974* (1996), D.W. Grantham, *Recent America: the United States since 1945* (1987), W. Leuchtenberg, *In the Shadow of FDR: from Harry Truman to Ronald Reagan* (1983) and W.H. Chafe and R. Sitkoff (eds), *A History of Our Time* (1987).

On particular themes and topics in North American history, see C. Vann Woodward, *The Strange Career of Jim Crow* (3rd end, 1974) on the history of racial segregation, and on the growth of the cities, C.N. Glaab and A.T. Brown, *A History of Urban America* (1976); M.A. Jones, *American Immigration* (1960) deals with one of the major themes of the early years of twentieth-century America. H. Pelling, *American Labour* (1960) examines the organized working class, while for American social history in general, see W. Issel, *Social Change in the United States, 1945–1983* (1985). The broad sweep of America's foreign relations is discussed in R.D. Schulzinger, *American Diplomacy in the Twentieth Century* (1984), S. Ambrose, *Rise to Globalism: American foreign policy, 1938–80* (2nd edn, 1981), J. Brewer (ed.), *American Foreign Policy since 1945* (1987) and L.C. Gardner, *Covenant with Power: America and the world order from Wilson to Reagan* (1984).

For the West Indies and Caribbean region, see J.H. Parry and P.M. Sherlock, *A Short History of the West Indies* (3rd edn, 1960) and J.R. Ward, *Poverty and Progress in the Caribbean, 1800–1960* (1985). On Latin America, see, T.H. Donghi, *The Contemporary History of Latin America* (1993), E. Williamson, *The Penguin History of Latin America, Part 3* (1992), T. Skidmore and P. Smith, *Modern Latin America* (2nd edn, 1989); L. Bethell, *The Cambridge History of Latin America* (1986), and G. Pendle, *A History of Latin America* (1967) for general histories. Books which examine some of the themes dominating Latin American history are P. Calvert, *Latin America: internal conflict and international peace* (1969), S. and B. Stein, *The Colonial Heritage of Latin America: essays on economic dependence in perspective* (1970) and C. Furtado, *Economic Development of Latin America: historical background and contemporary problems* (2nd edn, 1976). The recent collection by E.P. Archetti, P. Cammack and B. Roberts (eds), *Latin America* (1987), surveys some major common elements in the history of the continent. Also useful are J. Cockcroft, et al., *Dependence and Underdevelopment: Latin America's political economy* (1972), I.L. Horowitz, *Radicalism in Latin America* (1969), and J.J. Johnson, *Latin America in Caricature* (1980). Specific issues are considered in J.J. Johnson, *The Military and Society in Latin America* (1964), A. Stepan, *The Military in Politics* (1971), W.S. Stokes, *Latin American Politics* (1959), J.L. Mecham, *Church and State in Latin America: a history of politico-ecclesiastical relations* (rev. edn, 1966), H.A. Landsberger (ed.), *The Church and Social Change in Latin America* (1970), F.C. Turner, *Catholicism and Political Development in Latin America* (1971), H.A. Landsberger (ed.), *Latin American Peasant Movements* (1969), A. Pearce, *The Latin American Peasant* (1975), L.E. Aguilar (ed.), *Marxism in Latin America* (1969) and J. Kohl and J. Litt, *Urban Guerrilla Warfare in Latin America* (1973). The relations of Latin America with its northern neighbour are the subject of S.P. Bemis, *The Latin American Policy of the United States: an historical interpretation* (1943), G. Connell-Smith, *The Inter-American System* (1966) and C. Blasier, *The Hovering Giant* (1976).

The Second World War and the Cold War

S.E. Ambrose, *Rise to Globalism: American foreign policy, 1938–1980* (rev. edn, 1980) takes the story through from the pre-war phase, while H. Feis, *Churchill, Roosevelt and Stalin* (1967) examines the Grand Alliance. D.B. Rees, *The Age of Containment: the Cold War, 1945–1965* (1967), H. Feis, *From Trust to Terror: the onset of the Cold War, 1945–1950* (1970), M. Sherwin, *A World Destroyed: the atomic bomb and the Grand Alliance* (1975), G. Alperovitz, *Atomic Diplomacy: Hiroshima and Potsdam* (2nd edn, 1985) and L.B. Davis, *The Cold War Begins: Soviet–American conflict in East Europe* (1974) deal with the early phases of the dispute between the Alliance partners. W. LaFeber, *America in the Cold War: twenty years of revolutions and response, 1947–1967* (1969) and *America, Russia and the Cold War, 1945–1971* (3rd edn, 1976), D. Horowitz, *From Yalta to Vietnam: American foreign policy in the Cold War* (rev. edn, 1969), M.P. Leffler, *A Preponderance of Power: national security, the Truman administration and the Cold War* (1992), T.G. Patterson, *Meeting the Communist Threat: Truman to Reagan* (1988) and R. Douglas, *From War to Cold War, 1942–48* (1981) are all useful. M. McCauley, *The Origins of the Cold War* (1983) and J. Smith, *The Cold War, 1945–65* (1989)

are two guides to the increasingly complex debate, also highlighted in
D. Carlton and H.M. Levine, *The Cold War Debated* (1988). The impact of
anti-communism in America is discussed in D. Caute, *The Great Fear: the
anti-communist purge under Truman and Eisenhower* (1978) and R. Divide,
Eisenhower and the Cold War (1981). America's policy towards Europe is
considered in J. Gimble, *The Origins of the Marshall Plan* (1976), M.J.
Hogan, *The Marshall Plan: America, Britain and the reconstruction of Western
Europe, 1947–1952* (1988), A. Grosser, *The Western Alliance: European–
American relations since 1945* (1980), R. Morgan, *The United States and West
Germany* (1974), R. Osgood, *NATO: the entangling Alliance* (1962), and H.
Jones, *A New Kind Of War: America's global strategy and the Truman Doctrine
in Greece* (1989). The later phase of the Cold War is considered in L.
Freedman, *The Evolution of Nuclear Strategy* (1981), F. Halliday, *The Mak-
ing of the New Cold War* (1983), and H.M. Levine and D. Carlton, *The
Nuclear Arms Race Debated* (1986).

Particular areas are considered in E.J. Hammer, *The Struggle for Indo-
China, 1940–1955* (1966), D.F. Fleming, *America's Role in Asia* (1969),
S. Klebanoft, *Middle East Oil and US Foreign Policy: with special reference to
the US energy crisis* (1974), G. Lenczowski, *Russia and the West in Iran,
1918–1948: a study in big power rivalry* (1968), W.R. Polk, The *United States
and the Arab World* (rev. edn, 1969), J. Cotler and R. Fagan, *Latin America
and the United States: the changing political realities* (1974), F. Parkinson,
*Latin America, the Cold War and the World Powers, 1945–1973: a study in
diplomatic history* (1974), R. Emerson, *Africa and United States Policy* (1967),
J. Mayall, *Africa: the Cold War and After* (1971), E.O. Reischauer, *The
United States and Japan* (3rd edn, 1965), and N. Safran, *The United States
and Israel* (1963).

On particular crises, see on Korea, C.A. MacDonald, *Korea: the war before
Vietnam* (1986), D. Rees, *Korea: the limited war* (1970), W. Stueck, *The Korean
War: an international history* (1995), B. Cummings, *The Origins of the Korean
War*, (2 vols, 1981–90), S. Goncharov, J.W. Lewis, L. Lue, *Uncertain Part-
ners: Stalin, Mao and the Korean War* (1993), V. Zubok and C. Pleshakov,
Inside the Kremlin's Cold War: from Stalin to Khrushchev (1996), K. Weathersty
Soviet Aims in Korea (1993), and P. Lowe, *The Origins of the Korean War* (2nd
edn, 1997). The American relationship with Cuba is considered in L.D.
Langley, *Cuban Policy of the United States: a brief history* (1968), R.F. Smith,
The United States and Cuba: business and diplomacy, 1917–1960 (1961), H.M.
Pachter, *Collision Course: the Cuban Missile Crisis and coexistence* (1963), E.
Abel, *The Missiles of October: the story of the Cuban Missile Crisis* (1966), and
G. Allison, *Essence of Decision: explaining the Cuban Missile Crisis* (1971).
For a recent overview of the Cuban–US relationship, see M.H. Morley,
Imperial State and Revolution: the United States and Cuba, 1952–1986 (1987).

America and the Vietnam War

R.B. Smith, *An International History of the Vietnam War: Vol. I, 1955–61, Vol. II, 1961–65* (1983–85) is a major treatment of the war in global context. See also A. Short, *The Origins of the Vietnam War* (1989). A. Buhite, *The Dynamics of World Power: a documentary history of US foreign policy, 1945–73, Vol. 4* (1973) has documents; see also D. Ellsberg, *The Pentagon Papers* (1972) and M.E. Gettleman (ed.), *Vietnam and America: a documentary history* (1985). The best general treatments are I. Bernstein, *Guns or Butter? The Presidency of Lyndon Johnson* (1995), L. Berman, *Lyndon Johnson's War: the road to stalemate in Vietnam* (1989), B. Van Den Mark, *Into the Quagmire: Lyndon Johnson and the escalation of the Vietnam War* (1991), W.S. Thurley, *The Second Indo China War* (1986), G.C. Herring, *America's Longest War* (1979) and S. Karnow, *Vietnam. A History* (1984). The history of American involvement is also viewed in Ambrose, *Rise to Globalism* (see above), J.W. Spanier, *American Foreign Policy since World War II* (10th rev. edn, 1985) and M. Berkowitz, et al., *The US Foreign Policy Process and Context: from the Marshall Plan to Vietnam* (1985), and A.F. Krepinevich, *The Army and Vietnam* (1986). F. Fitzgerald, *Fire in the Lake, the Vietnamese and the Americans in Vietnam* (1972) discusses the American role in Vietnam. G. Kahin and J.W. Lewis, *The United States in Vietnam* (2nd edn, 1975) and J.L. Horowitz, *Ideology and Utopia in the United States, 1956–76* (1977) discuss the implications of the war for America, as does A. Schlesinger, *The Bitter Heritage: Vietnam and American democracy* (1966) and G. Kolko, *Anatomy of a War: Vietnam, the US and modern historical experience* (1986). The most prominent casualty of the war is discussed in H.Y. Schandler, *The Unmaking of a President: Lyndon Johnson and Vietnam* (1977), while the repercussions on the campuses are considered in James A. Michener, *Kent State: what happened and why* (1971), J. Axelrod et al., *Search for Relevance: the campus in crisis* (1969), J. and S. Erlich (eds), *Student Power, Participation and Revolution* (1970), and J. Foster and D. Long (eds), *Protest! Student Activism in America* (1970).

American domestic politics since 1945

Some of the broad themes are considered in M. Marable, *Race, Reform and Rebellion: the second reconstruction in Black America, 1945–1982* (1984), R. Gatlin, *American Women since 1945* (1987), W. Issel, *Social Change in the United States, 1945–1983* (1985), and K. Fox, *Metropolitan America: urban life and urban policy in the United States, 1940–80* (1985).

On the Truman era, see M.J. Lacey (ed.), *The Truman Presidency* (1989), R. Donovan, *Conflict and Crisis: the Presidency of Harry S. Truman, 1945–1948* (1977) and *Tumultuous Years: the Presidency of Harry S. Truman, 1949–*

53 (1982), D.R. McCloy, *The Presidency of Harry S. Truman* (1986), and on McCarthyism, D. Caute, *The Great Fear: the anti-communist purge under Truman and Eisenhower* (1978), R.M. Freeland, *The Truman Doctrine and the Origins of McCarthyism* (2nd edn, 1985) and R.M. Freid, *Men Against McCarthy* (1976). On the Senator himself, see R. Rovere, *Senator Joe McCarthy* (1959). The Truman and Eisenhower years are considered together in W. O'Neill, *American High: the years of confidence, 1945–60* (1987). On Eisenhower, see S. Ambrose, *Eisenhower, Soldier and President* (1990), E. Richardson, *The Presidency of Dwight Eisenhower* (1979) and R.F. Burk, *Dwight D. Eisenhower: hero and politician* (1987). On civil rights, see N. Lemann, *The Promised Land* (1991), M. Marable, *Race, Reform and Rebellion: the second reconstruction of Black America, 1945–1982* (1984), D. King, *Separate and Unequal* (1996), A. Hacker, *Two Nations: black and white* (1992), T. Branch, *Parting the Waters* (1989) and D. Garrow, *Bearing the Cross* (1987).

The Kennedy period is examined in H. Parmet, *The Presidency of John F. Kennedy* (1983), J.N. Giglio, *The Presidency of John F. Kennedy* (1991), R. Reeves, *President Kennedy* (1993), T.C. Sorensen, *Kennedy* (1965) and *The Kennedy Legacy* (1969), and C.M. Brauer, *John F. Kennedy and the Second Reconstruction* (1977); see also J. Schlesinger, *Robert Kennedy and His Times* (1978).

On Lyndon Johnson, see I. Bernstein, *Guns or Butter?* (1995), V.D. Bornet, *The Presidency of Lyndon B. Johnson* (1983), R.A. Divine, *The Johnson years, 2 vols.* (1987), H.Y. Schandler, *The Unmaking of a President* (1977) and P.K. Conkin, *Big Daddy from the Pedernales, Lyndon Baines Johnson* (1987). The Ford and Nixon Presidencies are discussed in S. Ambrose, *Nixon* (3 vols, 1987–91), R. Morris, *Richard Milhouse Nixon* (1991), H. Parmet, *Richard Nixon and His America* (1990) and A.J. Reichley, *Conservatives in an Age of Change* (1987); see also R. Nixon, *The Memoirs of Richard Nixon* (1978). Two books which examine changes in American political organization and thought are A. Ware, *The Breakdown of Democratic Party Organisation, 1940–80* (1988) and G. Peele, *Revival and Reaction: the Right in contemporary America* (1984).

Canada

K. McNaught, *The Pelican History of Canada* (rev. edn, 1982) is an up-to-date introduction; but see also P.S. Li, *The Making of Post-War Canada* (1997). G.S. Graham, *A Concise History of Canada* (1968) and J.M. Bliss (ed.) *Canadian History in Documents, 1763–1966* are also useful. J.M.S. Careless and R. Craig-Brown (eds), *The Canadians, 1867–1967* (1967) is a collaborative work dealing with Canadian history decade by decade and with a series of thematic chapters, to conclude. The development of the once separate province of Newfoundland is considered in R.A. Mackay (ed.), *Newfoundland: economic, diplomatic and strategic studies* (1946) and St. J. Chadwick, *Newfoundland: Island into Province* (1967). M. Wade, *The French Canadians, 1760–1967* (rev. edn, 1968) examines the background to the tension between French Canada and the rest of the country. See also M. Rioux and Y. Martin (eds), *French Canadian Society* (1964), R. Cook, *Canada and the French-Canadian Question* (1966), E.M. Corbett, *Quebec Confronts Canada* (1967), R. Jonas, *Community in Crisis: French Canadian nationalism in perspective* (1967), T. Sloan, *Quebec: the not-so-quiet revolution* (1965), and P.E. Trudeau, *Federalism and the French Canadians* (1968).

On the economy, see R.E. Caves and R.M. Holton, *The Canadian Economy: prospect and retrospect* (1959), H.G. Johnson, *The Canadian Quandary: economic problems and policies* (1963), and H.G.J. Aitken, *American Capital and Canadian Resources* (1961). The relationship of Canada with the United States and her place in world affairs is considered in J.S. Dickey (ed.), *The United States and Canada* (1964), J.K. Gordon (ed.), *Canada's Role as a Middle Power* (1966), W.L. Gordon, *A Choice for Canada: Independence or colonial status* (1966), P.V. Lyon, *The Policy Question: a critical appraisal of Canada's role in world affairs* (1963) and L.T. Marchant, *Neighbours Taken for Granted: Canada and the United States* (1966).

The Cuban Revolution

There is a good introduction in H. Thomas, *Cuba, or the Pursuit of Freedom* (1971). For the American involvement with Cuba, see M. Beschloss, *Kennedy and Khrushchev: the crisis years* (1991), J.A. Nathan, *The Cuban Missile Crisis Revisited* (1992), M. White, *The Cuban Missile Crisis* (1996), R.J. Walton, *Cold War and Counter-Revolution* (1972), L.D. Langley, *Cuban Policy of the United States: a brief history* (1968), R.F. Smith, *The United States and Cuba: business and diplomacy, 1917–60* (1960) and M.H. Morley, *Imperial State and Revolution: the United States and Cuba, 1952–1986* (1987). On the background to the revolution, see R.F. Smith (ed.), *Background to Revolution: the development of modern Cuba* (2nd edn, 1966), R.E. Ruiz, *Cuba: the making of a revolution* (1968), and W. MacGaffey and C.R. Barnett, *Cuba: its people, its society, its culture* (1962). On the character of the Castro revolution, see A. Suarez, *Cuba: Castroism and Communism, 1959–66* (1967), K.S. Karol, *Guerrillas in Power: the course of the Cuban revolution* (1970), and H.L. Matthews, *Castro: a political biography* (1969). Also important are J. Dominguez, *Cuba: order and revolution* (1978), S. Farber, *Revolution and*

Reaction in Cuba, 1933–1960 (1976), A. MacEwan, *Revolution and Economic Development in Cuba* (1981), and C. Brundenius, *Economic Growth, Basic Needs and Income Distribution in Revolutionary Cuba* (1981). Earlier studies of the effects of the revolution are C. Mesa-Lago (ed.), *Revolutionary Change in Cuba: polity, economy, society* (1972) R. Fagen, *The Transformation of the Political Culture in Cuba* (1969), D. Seers (ed.), *Cuba: the economic and social revolution* (1964) and M. Zeitlin, *Cuban Working Class* (1967). On Cuba's effects more widely, see B. Levine (ed.), *The New Cuban Presence in the Caribbean* (1983) and C. Blasier and C. Mesa-Lago (eds), *Cuba in the World* (1979).

The Caribbean, Central and Latin America

On the Caribbean, J.H. Parry and P.M. Sherlock, *A Short History of the West Indies* (3rd edn, 1960), J.R. Ward, *Poverty and Progress in the Caribbean, 1800–1960* (1985) and M. Cross and G. Henman (eds), *Labour in the Caribbean: from emancipation to independence* (1988) are all useful. For individual countries, see, on Brazil, F. Bradford Burns, *A History of Brazil* (2nd edn, 1980), W. Baer, *The Brazilian Economy: growth and development* (2nd edn, 1983), W. Dean, *The Industrialisation of São Paulo, 1880–1945* (1969), and C. Furtado, *The Economic Growth of Brazil* (1963). The general political history is considered in J.D. Wirth, *The Politics of Brazilian Development, 1930–1954* (1970) and T.E. Skidmore, *Politics in Brazil, 1930–44: an experiment in democracy* (1967). The role of the military is considered in A. Stepan, *The Military in Politics: changing patterns in Brazil* (1971) and in P. Flynn, *Brazil: a political analysis* (1978). The role of labour is examined in K.P. Erickson, *The Brazilian Corporative State and Working-Class Politics* (1977) and J. Humphrey, *Capitalist Control and Worker's Struggle in the Brazilian Auto Industry* (1982), while racial issues are discussed in C.N. Degler, *Neither Black Nor White: slavery and race relations in Brazil and the United States* (1971); see also J.H. Rodrigues, *Brazil and Africa* (1965), T.E. Skidmore, *Black into White: race and nationality in Brazilian thought* (1974) and D.T. Heberly, *Three Sad Races: racial identity and national consciousness in Brazilian literature* (1983). Some general interpretations are A. Stepan (ed.), *Authoritarian Brazil: origins, policies and future* (1973), T.C. Bruneau and P. Fancher (eds), *Authoritarian Capitalism: Brazil's contemporary economic and political development* (1981), S.A. Hewlett, *The Cruel Dilemmas of Development: twentieth-century Brazil* (1980) and P. Evans, *Dependent Development: the alliance of multinational, state and local capital in Brazil* (1979).

For Argentina, see in general, Y.F. Rennie, *The Argentine Republic* (1945), J.R. Scobie, *Argentina, a City and a Nation* (2nd edn, 1971), D. Rock, *Argentina, 1516–1982* (1986) and *Argentina in the Twentieth Century* (1975),

G. Pendle, *Argentina* (3rd edn, 1963) and H.S. Ferns, *Argentina* (1969). The early history of the country in this century is dealt with in P.H. Smith, *Politics and Beef in Argentina: patterns of conflict and change* (1969), while the role of the military is considered in R.A. Potash, *The Army and Politics in Argentina, 1928–1945* (1969), continued in *The Army and Politics in Argentina, 1945–1962* (1980); see also P.H. Smith, *Argentina and the Failure of Democracy, 1904–55* (1974). The economic background is examined in C.F. Diaz Alejandro, *Essays on the Economic History of the Argentine Republic* (1970), while the experience of Argentina's economy in the depression is considered in M. Falcoff and R.H. Dolkart, *Prologue to Peron: Argentina in depression and war, 1930–1943* (1975). The link with the rise of Peronism is also considered in J.R. Barager (ed.), *Why Peron Came to Power: the background to Peronism in Argentina* (1968). The Peronist phenomenon is examined in F.C. Turner and J.E. Miguens, *Juan Peron and the Reshaping of Argentina* (1983) and there is a good biography by J.A. Page, *Peron: a biography* (1983), while on Eva, see N. Fraser and M. Navarro, *Eva Peron* (1980) and J.M. Taylor, *Evita Peron: the Myths of a Woman* (1979). The labour policies pursued by Peron are the subject of S.L. Bailey, *Labour, Nationalism and Politics in Argentina* (1967). For the post-war history, see R.A. Potash, *The Army and Politics, 1945–1962* (above) and P.H. Smith, *Argentina and the Failure of Democracy* (above); see also G.W. Wynia, *Argentina in the Postwar Era: politics and economic policy making in a divided society* (1978) and C.H. Waisman, *Reversal of Development in Argentina: postwar counter revolutionary policies and their structural consequences* (1987).

For a general history of Chile, see B. Loveman, *Chile: the legacy of Hispanic capitalism* (1979). Also useful are M.J. Mamalakis, *The Growth and Structure of the Chilean Economy: from independence to Allende* (1976), and B. Loveman, *Struggle in the Countryside: politics and rural labour in Chile, 1919–1973* (1976). The armed forces are considered in F.M. Nunn, *The Military in Chilean History: essays on civil–military relations, 1810–1973* (1976). The labour movement is examined in A. Angell, *Politics and the Labour Movement in Chile* (1972) and P.W. Drake, *Socialism and Populism in Chile, 1932–52* (1978). The controversial events leading to the overthrow of Allende are the subject of P. Sigmund, *The Overthrow of Allende and the Politics of Chile, 1964–1976* (1977), B. Stallings, *Class Conflict and Economic Development in Chile, 1958–1973* (1978), A. Valenzuela, *The Breakdown of Democratic Regimes: Chile* (1978) and F.C. Gill, R. Lagos and H.A. Lansberger (eds), *Chile at the Turning Point: lessons of the socialist years, 1970–1973* (1979). Big business is discussed in T.H. Moran, *Multinational Corporations and the Politics of Dependence: copper in Chile* (1974), and on the Church, see B.A. Smith, *The Church and Politics in Chile: challenges to modern Catholicism* (1982).

There is a single-volume history of Uruguay in R.H. FitzGibbon, *Uruguay: portrait of a democracy* (1986) and on Paraguay, see G. Pendle, *Paraguay: a riverside nation* (1967) and P.H. Lewis, *Paraguay under Stroessner* (1980).

The Andean states are discussed in J.M. Malloy, *Bolivia, the Uncompleted Revolution* (1970) and H.S. Klein, *Parties and Political Change in Bolivia, 1880–1952* (1969) while for Peru, see F. Pike, *The Modern History of Peru* (1967), V. Alba, *Peru* (1977), and R. Thorp and G. Bertram, *Peru, 1890– 1977: growth and policy in an open economy* (1978); the agrarian unrest in Peru is considered in F.E. Mallon, *The Defense of Community in Peru's Central Highlands: peasant struggle and capitalist transition, 1860–1940* (1983), P.F. Klaren, *Modernization, Dislocation and Aprismo: origins of the Peruvian Aprista Party, 1870–1932* (1973) and S. Stein, *Populism in Peru: the emergence of the masses and politics of social control* (1980). The role of military rule is examined in G.D.E. Philip, *The Rise and Fall of the Peruvian Military Radicals, 1968–1976* (1978), F. Lowenthal, *The Peruvian Experiment: continuity and change under military rule* (1975), D. Booth and B. Sorj (eds), *Military Reformism and Social Classes: the Peruvian Experience, 1968–80* (1983), F. Bourricand, *Power and Society in Contemporary Peru* (1970), and F. Lowenthal and C. McClintock (eds), *The Peruvian Experiment Reconsidered* (1983); see also E.V.K. Fitzgerald, *The State of Economic Development: Peru since 1968* (1976). The continuing social upheaval on the land and in the slums is examined in H. Handelman, *Struggle in the Andes: peasant mobilization in Peru* (1975), C. McClintock, *Peasant Cooperatives and Political Change in Peru* (1981), and D. Collier, *Squatters and Oligarchs: authoritarian rule and policy change in Peru* (1976); see also H. Blanco, *Land or Death: the peasant struggle in Peru* (1972). For Venezuela, see E. Leiuwen, *Venezuela* (1965) and J. Ewell, *Venezuela: a century of change* (1984) and, for Surinam, H.E. Chin and H. Buddingh, *Surinam: politics, economics and society* (1987).

The history of the Amazon region is considered in J. Hemming, *Amazon Frontier: the defeat of the Brazilian Indians* (1988) and *Red Gold: the conquest of the Brazilian Indians* (1988).

For Central America, see R. Lee Woodward, *Central America: a nation divided* (1976), D.E. Schulz and D.H. Graham, *Revolution and Counter Revolution in Central America and the Caribbean* (1984), and T.L. Karnes, *The Failure of Union: Central America, 1824–1960* (1961). On individual countries, see R.N. Adams, *Crucifixion by Power: essays on the Guatemalan national social structure, 1944–1966* (1970), W.J. Griffith, *Empires in the Wilderness: foreign colonization and development in Guatemala, 1834–1944* (1965), S. Kinzer, *Bitter Fruit: the untold story of the American coup in Guatemala* (1981), and R.H. Immerman, *The CIA in Guatemala: the foreign policy of intervention* (1982). Nicaragua is discussed in R. Millett, *Guardians of the Dynasty* (1977), T.W. Walker, *Nicaragua: the land of Sandino* (1981), and for the post-1979 period, H. Weber, *Nicaragua: the Sandinista Revolution* (trans, edn, 1981). On El Salvador, see T.P. Anderson, *Metanza: El Salvador's communist revolt of 1932* (1971), E. Layoyra, *El Salvador in Transition* (1982), S. Webre, *José Napoleon Duarte and the Christian Democrat Party in Salvadorian Politics: 1960–1974* (1975); and on the recent civil war, M.E. Gettleman et al., *El Salvador: Central America in the new Cold War* (1981).

MAPS

MAP   471

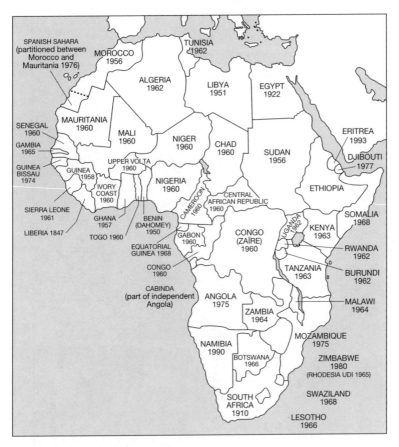

1   Chronology of African independence

2   South-East Asia in the 1960s

MAP   473

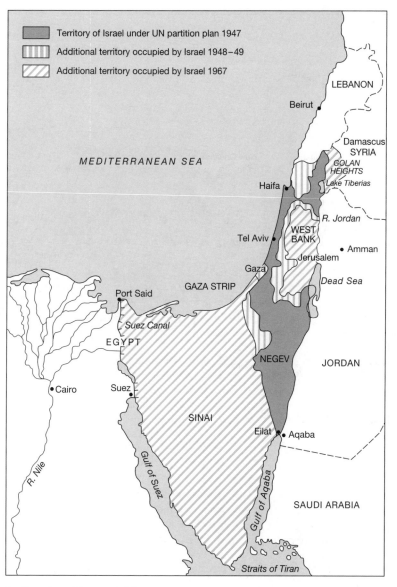

3 Israel and her neighbours

4   The Caribbean and Central America

MAP   475

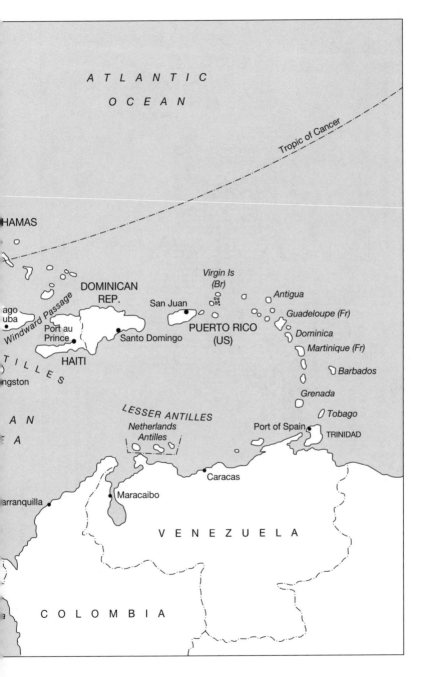

ATLANTIC

OCEAN

Tropic of Cancer

BAHAMAS

Windward Passage

DOMINICAN
REP.

Virgin Is
(Br)

San Juan

Antigua

Guadeloupe (Fr)

PUERTO RICO
(US)

Dominica

Port au
Prince

Santo Domingo

Martinique (Fr)

HAITI

Barbados

ANTILLES

ngston

Grenada

Tobago

LESSER ANTILLES

Port of Spain

Netherlands
Antilles

TRINIDAD

Caracas

arranquilla

Maracaibo

V E N E Z U E L A

C O L O M B I A

ago
uba

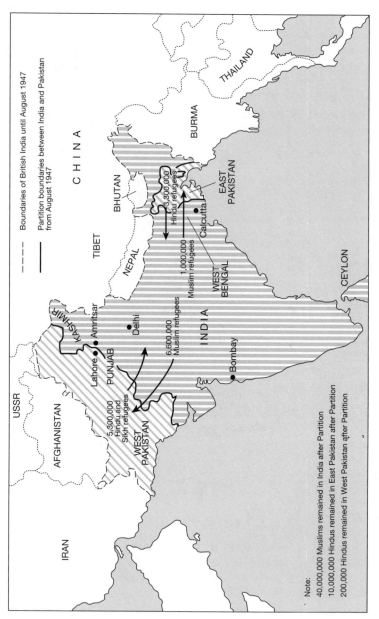

CHINA

USSR

IRAN

AFGHANISTAN

TIBET

NEPAL

BHUTAN

BURMA

THAILAND

KASHMIR

Lahore ● ● Amritsar

PUNJAB

● Delhi

WEST PAKISTAN

5,300,000 Hindu and Sikh refugees

6,600,000 Muslim refugees

INDIA

Bombay ●

3,300,000 Hindu refugees

1,000,000 Muslim refugees

EAST PAKISTAN

Calcutta ●

WEST BENGAL

CEYLON

Note:
40,000,000 Muslims remained in India after Partition
10,000,000 Hindus remained in East Pakistan after Partition
200,000 Hindus remained in West Pakistan after Partition

5   India and Pakistan after Partition, 1947

Index

Honduras 123, 125, 127, 128, 132, 253
  natural disasters 323
  'Soccer' War with El Salvador (1969)
    131, 263
Honecker, Erich 14, 28, 172
Hong Kong 27, 75, 77, 226, 304, 320
Hoover, J. Edgar 351
Horn, G. 176
Hosokawa, M. 79, 182
'Hot-line' agreement 149, 224, 226, 284,
  402
Houphouet-Boigny, F. 50
Howard, John 101, 161
Howe, Sir Geoffrey 243
Hoxha, E. 7, 159, 351
Hrawi, E. 183
Hu Yaobang 75, 166
Hua Guofeng 74, 75, 166, 351
Huang Hua 241
Huggins, Sir G. 207
Huh Chung 182
Huk 402
human rights 11, 151, 225, 229, 232, 401
Humphrey, Hubert 138
Hun Sen 93, 95, 96, 164
Hungary 4, 7, 8, 12, 13, 14, 19, 175–6,
  221, 236
  border opening with Austria (1989) 29
  Communists 7
  and European Union 37, 38, 406
  GNP 320
  and NATO 21, 406
  population 304
  uprising and Soviet invasion (1956) 9,
    252, 389
  and Warsaw Pact 220, 252
Hunter, William 110
Hurd, Douglas 243
Hurtado, M. del la Madrid 186
Husak, Gustav 10, 13, 167, 418
Hussain, Z. 176
Hussein, Abdullah Ibn 39, 182
Hussein bin Onn 186
Hussein, Ibn Talal 45, 182, 265, 351,
  384, 419
Hussein, Saddam 40, 41, 42, 178, 255,
  277, 351–2
Huysmans, C. 161

Ibáñez, Carlos 104–5
Ibáñez del Campo, C. 165
Ibarra, José María 428

Iceland 6, 22, 25, 213, 216, 222, 388
Idris al-Senussi, Mohammed 39, 40, 54,
  184
Ifni incident (1957) 253
Ikeda, H. 78, 181
Iliescu, Ion 15, 18, 193
Illia, Arturo 119, 120, 159
Inche Yusuf bin Ishak 195
India 76, 79–85, 176–7, 222, 223, 236,
  274, 336
  Atomic Energy Commission 81
  coal and lignite 312
  electricity output 315
  GNP 320
  Janata 405
  motor vehicle production 314
  natural disasters 322, 323, 324
  nuclear weapons 285
  oil 316, 318
  partition of 80, 327, 402
  population 297, 304, 327
  rice 311
  steel 313
  wheat output 310
  see also Indo-Chinese War; Indo-
    Pakistan Wars
Indian National Congress 402–3
Indo-China 85–9, 403
  see also Cambodia; Laos; Vietnam
Indo-China War (1946–54) 85–6, 90,
  223, 246, 393
Indo-Chinese Treaty (1954) 81
Indo-Chinese War ('Himalayan War')
  (1962) 74, 81, 257
Indo-Pakistan Wars
  (1947–49) 229, 246
  (1965) 81, 259–60, 425
  (1971) 224, 265
Indonesia 91, 93, 95, 96–7, 177, 212,
  221, 236, 280, 329, 399
  war of independence (1945–49) 245
  independence granted 90, 222, 229
  civil war (1950–62) 249
  'confrontation' with Malaysia
    (1963–66) 91, 224, 257, 390
  attempted communist rising
    (1965–66) 91, 260
  and East Timor 95, 268–9
  GNP 320
  'guided democracy' ideology 400
  and the Netherlands 90, 221, 229, 245
  oil 316, 319